Mercer Commentary on the Bible

Volume 2

History of Israel

Mercer University Press

Mercer Dictionary of the Bible
July 1990; 5th and corrected printing August 1997

Mercer Dictionary of the Bible Course Syllabi
July 1990

Mercer Commentary on the Bible
November 1994

Mercer Commentary on the Bible

Volume 2

History of Israel

GENERAL EDITORS
Watson E. Mills, Richard F. Wilson

ASSOCIATE EDITORS
Roger A. Bullard, Walter Harrelson, Edgar V. McKnight

MERCER UNIVERSITY PRESS EDITOR
Edmon L. Rowell, Jr.

WITH MEMBERS OF THE
National Association of Baptist Professors of Religion

MERCER UNIVERSITY PRESS
December 1998

ISBN 0-86554-507-3   MUP/P134

Mercer Commentary on the Bible: History of Israel
Volume 2 of an 8-volume perfect-bound reissue of
the *Mercer Commentary on the Bible* (©1995).
Copyright ©1999
Mercer University Press, Macon GA 31210-3960
Printed in the United States of America
First printing, December 1998

The paper used in this publication meets the minimum requirements
of the American National Standard for Information Sciences—
Permanence of Paper for Printed Library Materials, ANSI Z39.48-1984.

Library of Congress Cataloging-in-Publication Data

Mercer commentary on the Bible.
Volume 2. History of Israel /
general editors, Watson E. Mills and Richard F. Wilson;
associate editors, Walter Harrelson . . . [et al.].
xxxviii+272pp. 6x9" (15x23cm.).
1. Bible—commentaries. I. Mills, Watson Early. II. Mercer University Press.
III. National Association of Baptist Professors of Religion.

CIP data available from the Library of Congress.

Contents

Preface

This volume comprises commentaries on the books of Joshua–Esther (according to the order of the Greek Old Testament or "Septuagint") from the *Mercer Commentary on the Bible* (MCB) and with certain appropriate articles from the *Mercer Dictionary of the Bible* (MDB).

The designation of the books of Joshua–Esther as "History of Israel" is arbitrary and somewhat misleading. But this is no more arbitrary than the order in the Hebrew Bible where Joshua, Judges, Samuel, and Kings are among the so-called "Former Prophets" and the rest are among the "Writings." Also, Ruth and Esther are more specifically categorized among the so-called "Festal Scrolls" (or simply "Five Scrolls": Song of Songs, Ruth, Lamentations, Ecclesiastes, and Esther). The present grouping, however, seems appropriate for classroom use, with the understanding that this categorization is provisional only.

This volume is for use in the classroom and for any other setting where study focuses on the "historical books" and where a convenient introduction text is desired. This is number 2 in the series of MCB/MDB portions or fascicles.

All of these divisions—and their titles—are rather arbitrary. These divisions originate in the classroom as convenient and appropriate blocks of text for focused study during a semester- or quarter-long course of study. Other divisions are possible, perhaps even desirable (designating Ruth and Esther among the "Writings," for example, rather than as "History"), but the present divisions seem appropriate for most users.

Regarding the use of this and other MCB/MDB portions, please note the following.

A bracketed, flush-right entry at the head of each MDB article and MCB commentary indicates the page number(s) in the original: for example, "Chronicles, First and Second [MDB 146-47]" and "First and Second Chronicles [MCB 323-72]." The text of both MDB and MCB is essentially that of the original, for the most part differing only in format, that is, redesigned to fit a 6x9-inch page (MDB and MCB are on 7x10, two-column pages). (Some corrections—of typographical and other errors—have been made.)

In the text of the MCB commentaries and MDB articles included here, references to other MDB articles are indicated by small caps. For example, NAOMI and BOAZ in the first paragraph of the MDB article on "Ruth, Book of" refer to the articles on "Naomi" and "Boaz" in MDB; ZADOK and ZEDEKIAH in the fifth from the last paragraph of the MCB commentary on Nehemiah refer to the MDB articles on "Zadok" and "Zedekiah." In addition, the *See also* sections at the end of the MDB articles indicate other articles appropriate for further study.

(Notice, however, that small caps are used also for B.C.E. and C.E., for certain texts and versions [LXX, KJV, NRSV], for the tetragrammaton YHWH, and for LORD when citing certain English translations.)

In addition to MDB and MCB, there is available a booklet of sample course syllabi that includes actual outlines of courses in which a Bible version and MDB are the required texts. (Regarding this booklet, please contact the Mercer University Press marketing department.)

For abbreviations, see the lists in MDB or MCB (xxvii-xxx and xvii-xxii, respectively). Regarding the editors and contributors, see MDB (xv-xxv) and MCB (xi-xvi). The *Course Syllabi* handbook has a complete listing of MDB articles (pp. 73-80), and MDB includes a complete listing of articles arranged by contributor (pp. 989-93).

We intend that these texts be available, appropriate, and helpful for Bible students both in and out of the classroom and indeed for anyone seeking guidance in uncovering the abundant wealth of the Scriptures. Your critical response to these and other texts from Mercer University Press is most welcome and encouraged.

December 1998   *Edmon L. Rowell, Jr.*, senior editor
Macon, Georgia   Mercer University Press

Introduction

•**Chronology.** The goal of chronology is to determine the correct order of events and, if possible, their absolute date. Given the conflicting historical data in the Bible and the disagreement between the Bible and other ancient Near Eastern and Greco-Roman sources, this goal is not easily achieved. In some cases an *absolute* chronology is possible, i.e., the events can be dated by some external CALENDAR and can be computed to either the exact date or to within a few years. On the other hand, one must often be content with a *relative* chronology in which events can be dated and arranged in reference to each other, but whose precise historical reckoning can only be approximated.

The canonical text of the Bible begins with an account of creation and the pre-Abrahamic ancestors, which includes elaborate genealogical records. From data, Bishop James Ussher (1581–1656) calculated that the world was created in 4004 BCE Though few today would consider this an historical datum, we are beginning to understand, at least in part, the elaborate chronological system worked out by those who compiled the biblical tradition.Theirs was a theological agenda, not an historical one in the modern sense.

The chronological information about ABRAHAM, ISAAC, and JACOB in Genesis was arranged according to a mathematical scheme, which may be illustrated in terms of their respective ages at death.

	Age at Death	Sum of Digits
Abraham	$175 = 7 \times 5^2$	$[7+5+5 = 17]$
Isaac	$180 = 5 \times 6^2$	$[5+6+6 = 17]$
Jacob	$147 = 3 \times 7^2$	$[3+7+7 = 17]$

This rather simple scheme is in turn part of what appears to be an elaborate mathematical system worked out by ancient chronologers, which runs through the Hebrew Bible.

Particular numbers are associated with specific eras as one moves through the Pentateuch and beyond. The larger scheme seems to be oriented toward the manner in which ancient scribes thought about the future. In the modern period we face the future; people in the ancient Near East faced the past. To determine the future, they simply read the events of the past and projected them, as it were, behind themselves into the future, which then became a "rerun" of the past in reverse. The picture may be diagrammed as follows.

JOSHUA/JOSEPH ▸ NEW ISRAEL ▸ FATHERS ▸ NEW CREATION

Both JOSHUA and JOSEPH in this scheme are allotted 110 years, and together serve as a narrative frame to bracket the appearance of a new MOSES—perhaps originally understood in terms of the promulgation of the Torah as canonical scripture in ancient Israel, the historical moment in which the scheme was worked out. Since Israel consisted of twelve tribes, those ancient chronologers apparently chose the sum of the squares of the digits one through twelve, namely 650. The number associated with the Fathers is 140, the sum of the squares of the digits one through seven. Abraham was 140 years of age when Isaac married REBEKAH, a marriage which lasted 140 years. Rebekah was barren for twenty years before she gave birth to the twins Jacob and ESAU, who are identified before their birth as two nations (i.e., Israel and Edom). Since Isaac was sixty years old at the birth of Jacob and Esau (Gen 25:26), the twins were 120 when Jacob fled to Aram shortly before the death of Isaac at age 180. After serving LABAN for twenty years (Gen 31:38), Jacob returned following his wrestling match with the mysterious night visitor at the JABBOK. Jacob/Israel was thus 140 years old when he reentered the land of Canaan to encounter his brother Esau who, of course, was also 140. The 140 years allotted JOB (42:16) after his time of testing place him within this same scheme among the Fathers of Genesis.

Within the narrative tradition in Genesis, Abraham was 160 years old at the birth of his grandson Jacob/Israel. Isaac was sixty when Jacob was born; and Jacob lived with Isaac for sixty-three years and with Laban for twenty. At the time of Joseph's descent into Egypt at age seventeen, Isaac was thus 160 years old (60+63+20+17). Moreover, the number of years between the birth of Shem and Terah in Gen 11 is 320, which is twice 160. Since the sum of the numbers 110 (Joshua/Joseph) + 650 (Israel) + 140 (the Fathers) is 900, it is interesting to note that 900 × 160 = 144,000. This curious number, which becomes the community of the elect within apocalyptic speculation (see Rev 14:1), apparently began in ancient Israel as simply the symbolic lapse of time in a chronological scheme from the promulgation of the Torah of Moses to the *eschaton,* conceived in terms of a grand reversal of past events in ancient Israel according to the formula

JOSEPH ▸ NEW ISRAEL ▸ FATHERS ▸ NEW CREATION
$$(110 + 650 + 140) \times 160 = 144,000$$

It is not possible to construct an absolute chronology so far as the PATRIARCHS of Genesis are concerned, since none of the people or events of the narrative can be correlated to external events of their era. While it is true that these narratives reflect certain customs that can be documented in Amorite and Hurrian cultures of the early second millennium BCE) dating the Fathers remains problematic. In recent years the *Patriarchs* have been dated as early as the twenty-second century BCE, and their literary creation as late as the sixth century BCE The majority of scholars, however, still prefer a relative chronology of ca. 2000–1850 for Abraham, ca. 1900–1750 for Isaac, and Jacob around 1800–1700. Joseph and the entrance into Egypt are dated around 1750–1650 BCE.

Kings of Israel & Judah	Thiele	Albright
[*=Judah]		
*Rehoboam	931/30–913	922–915
Jeroboam	931/30–910/9	922–901
*Abijah	913–911/10	915–913
*Asa	911/10–870/69	913–873
Nadab	910/9–909/8	901–900
Baasha	909/8–886/85	900–877
Elah	886/85–885/84	877–876
Zimri	885/84	876
Omri	885/84–874/73	876–869
*Jehoshaphat	874/73–848	873–849
Ahab	874/73–853	869–850
Ahaziah	853–852	850–849
*Jehoram	853–841	849–842
Jehoram	852–841	849–842
*Ahaziah	841	842
Jehu	841–814/13	842–815
*Athaliah	841–835	842–837
*Jehoash	835–796	837–800
Johoahaz	814/13–798	815–801
Joash	798–872/1	801–786
*Amaziah	796–767	800–783
Jeroboam II	793/2–753	786–746
*Azariah/Uzziah	792/1–740/39	783–742
Zechariah	753–752	746–745
Shallum	752	745
Menahem	752–742/1	745–738
*Jotham	750–732/1	750–735
Pekahiah	742/1–740/39	738–737
Pekah	752–732/31	737–732
*Jehoahaz [=Ahaz] I	735–716/15	735–715
Hoshea	732/1–723/22	732–724
*Hezekiah	716/15–687/6	715–687
*Manasseh	687/6–643/2	687–642
*Amon	643/2–641/40	642–640
*Josiah	641/40–609	640–609
*Jehoahaz II	609	609
*Jehoikim	609–598	609–598
*Jehoiachin	598–597	598
*Zedekiah	597–586	598–587

The date of the EXODUS is also uncertain. The scholarly consensus for a thirteenth century date has been challenged recently by those who would place it two centuries earlier. From 1 Kgs 6:1 we learn that the Exodus was established by ancient chronologers as having occurred 480 years before the founding of the Temple in King SOLOMON's fourth year. The Bible thus dates the Exodus to sometime in the fifteenth century, during the reign of Thutmose III (1490). J. Bimson has defended this traditional view on the basis that whereas there is no archaeological evidence for the destruction of such cities as JERICHO, AI, GIBEON, HEBRON, Hormah, ARAD, DEBIR, LACHISH, and HAZOR during the Late Bronze Age, when the thirteenth century option would necessitate the Conquest, there is evidence for this shortly before 1400 BCE Thus Bimson dates the Exodus to ca. 1450 and the conquest to ca. 1410 BCE This solution, however, creates as many problems as it solves, since the period of the Judges in Israel would then last 600 years. Moreover, Exod 1:11 states that the Hebrews were building the cities of Pithom and Ramses, which were largely built by RAMSES II (1290–1224). Furthermore, if the conquest had occurred in 1410 BCE, then why does the book of Judges make no reference to the Asiatic campaigns of Seti I (1319–1301) and Ramses II (1301–1234)? From the Merneptah Stele (ca. 1220 BCE) we learn that Israel was among the peoples in Palestine that Merneptah (ca. 1224–1214) defeated. The archaeological evidence for the destruction of a number of biblical sites in the thirteenth century suggests that this is the setting of the Conquest. Most scholars still date the Exodus to ca. 1290–1260 BCE and the Conquest to about a half century later.

With the rise of the monarchy in ancient Israel historians have their first opportunity to establish an absolute chronology, but even here there are problems. The biblical data in the books of Kings can be cross referenced with known Assyrian and Babylonian king lists, which have been precisely dated by means of calculating the exact dates of solar and lunar eclipses to which these lists (called *limmu* or eponym lists) refer. Two dates in the biblical text have consequently been established beyond reasonable doubt: the date for the battle of Qarqar in which King Ahab fought (853 BCE) and Jehu's giving of tribute to the Assyrian king Shalmaneser III (841 BCE). From these two fixed dates, the rest of the dates of the kings of Israel and Judah can be obtained by careful reckoning.

It must be noted, however, that the figures for the reigns of individual kings in Israel and Judah are not as clear as one would hope. There are numerous problems in matters of detail, which E. Thiele has resolved, though not to the satisfaction of all historians. Prior to Thiele, the two sets of figures given in the regnal summaries for the kings of Israel and Judah could not be made to agree without textual emendation. Thiele has demonstrated that the system of cross-referencing is in agreement, once one understands three complex factors. First, there are several implied coregencies in the text, which would explain some of the excess years in these lists. Second, there were two systems for counting regnal years in the ancient Near East: the accession-year system, in which the rule of the kings was counted to have begun only with the beginning of the first new year; and the nonaccession-year system, which counted the year in which the coronation took place as a full year. A year in which there was a royal transfer of power was counted twice by this latter method, which accounts for some of the problems in the biblical data, since both systems were used at different points in time. Finally, there were two different calendars in use in the ancient Near East. One began in the spring with the month of Nisan (Israel), while the other began in the fall with the month of Tishri (Judah). Complicating matters still further, Thiele argues that each of the kingdoms switched their methods of dating, and then switched back after a time. None of these factors, however, is explicitly cited by the text, and can only be deduced by careful reasoning and cross-checking with other ancient Near Eastern sources.

The positing of unmentioned coregencies remains a problem to some historians, who see Thiele's method as overly subjective. While most current scholars side with Thiele, others hold to the older Albright chronology. Since there is still room for debate, both chronologies are given.

The fall of JERUSALEM and the Babylonian exile can be precisely dated by Babylonian documents. According to these texts, the fall of Jerusalem occurred on the second of Adar, i.e., 16/15 March of either 598 or 597 BCE The ultimate destruction of Jerusalem and a second deportation occurred in the fall of 587 BCE The third deportation recorded in Jer 52 is usually dated to 582/1 BCE The Exile came to an end with the fall of Babylon under the Persian general Cyrus, who issued a decree allowing the exiles to return home in 539 BCE

The events of the return of the Jews to Palestine and the restoration in Jerusalem are harder to date with absolute precision. While the work on the restoration of the Second Temple began in the second year of the return (Ezra 3:8), this work was suspended until the second year of Darius I in 520 (Ezra 4:24) and completed in 515 BCE (Ezra 6:15).

If one correlates the traditional dates of EZRA and NEHEMIAH with Persian king lists, the respective dates for these two men would be 458 and 445 BCE Because of inconsistencies in the biblical text, however, many scholars are convinced that the work of Ezra presupposes that of Nehemiah. Some who hold this view argue that Ezra returned in the seventh year of Artaxerxes II in 398 BCE, rather than Artaxerxes I. Others suggest that a mistake has slipped into the biblical record, and that Ezra 7:7 originally read the *thirty-seventh* year of Artaxerxes I, namely, 428 BCE

Any chronology of the NT must take into account the Roman hegemony over the Jewish people established on 10 Tishri in 63 BCE under the Roman general Pompey. Though much is known about the subsequent history of Roman rule in Palestine, the data do not match up well with what is given in the NT.

The birth of JESUS is particularly difficult to ascertain with certainty. In Matt 2:1 we learn that he was born during the reign of Herod the Great, and Luke 2:2 speaks of a census at the time Quirinius was governor of Syria. It has been argued that the census mentioned here is to be associated with one that Augustus initiated in either 9 CE or 6 CE, which would place the birth of Jesus in 8/7 or 5/4 CE Another possibility is that the star was connected with Halley's comet in 12 BCE Others argue for an otherwise undocumented census in 4 BCE, to which Luke refers, or simply posit an error on Luke's part.

Dates according to Luedemann	Jewett	Event
27 (30)	Oct 34	Paul's conversion
33 (36)	Oct 37	First Jerusalem visit
34 (37)	40–45	In Syria/Cilicia
36 (39)ff.		Mission in Europe: Philippi, Thessalonica
	43–45	First missionary journey: Cyprus, Pamphylia, Galatia
	46–51	Second missionary journey: Galatia, Philippi, Thessalonica, Corinth
41	49	Claudius expelled Jews
41	50	Paul in Corinth
47 (50)	Aug-Oct 51	Second Jerusalem visit (Jerusalem Conference)
Summer 48 (51)	47	Paul in Galatia
	52–57	Third missionary journey
50 (53)	53–55	Paul in Ephesus
Winter 49/50	Winter 54/5	Ephesian imprisonment?
Spring 50 (53)		Journey to Macedonia
Summer 50 (53)		Corinthian correspondence
Winter 50/1 (53/4)		Paul in Macedonia
Spr/Sum 51 (54)		Journey to Corinth
Winter 51/2 (54/5)		Paul in Corinth (Romans)
Spring 52 (55)	April 57	Departure for Jerusalem
	June 57	Arrival in Jerusalem
	June 57–59	Imprisonment in Caesarea
	July 59	Paul before Festus
	Oct 59	Departure from Fair Havens
	Nov 59–Feb 60	Paul in Malta
	March 60	Arrival at Rome
	March 62	Paul's execution

An equally difficult chronological problem lies in trying to ascertain the precise dates for the ministry of Jesus. Not only do we not know exactly when he began his public ministry; we do not know exactly how many years it lasted. Scholars have debated whether it lasted one year, in connection with the order of events connected with Jesus' trip to Jerusalem as presented in the synoptics, or three years based on the three trips to Jerusalem recorded in the Gospel of John. Some have also argued that a two-year ministry is possible. The usual solution is to give the nod to John, and posit a three-year ministry, with the possibility of a two-year ministry based on the fact that some of the trips to Jerusalem recorded in John actually occurred in the same year. Luke 3:1-2 dates the baptism of Jesus to the precise date of the fifteenth year of TIBERIAS, whose rule can be interpreted to have begun in three different manners. In short, the majority of scholars date the beginning of Jesus' ministry to the years 27, 28 or 29 CE The crucifixion would then have occurred either one, two, or three years afterwards, depending on the length of his ministry. Thus Jesus died somewhere between 27 and 32 CE

The basic problem with establishing a Pauline chronology lies in the discrepancies that exist between Paul's own account of things, as portrayed in his letters, and the account of his life offered in Acts. PAUL mentions two trips to Jerusalem in Gal 1–2 whereas the record in Acts records five. Such discrepancies make it difficult to reconstruct the life of Paul with absolute confidence. Nonetheless, some dates can be given with certainty thanks to the Gallio inscription, which enables the historian to establish the events of Acts 18:12 to the year 51 CE From this fixed point the biblical historian can work backward and forward. The two most recent treatments of this problem are those of P. Jewett and G. Luedemann, which may be summarized as in the table below. It should be noted that these two studies depart from traditional reconstructions of Paul's life in several ways. The JERUSALEM COUNCIL is generally placed around 48–49 CE, between the first and second missionary journeys. Many scholars posit a Roman imprisonment in 62–64 CE, and others, a trip to Spain after this, based on the information in the pastoral epistles.

Though NT chronology ends with Paul in Rome, some books such as the Revelation probably came from the time of Domitian's persecution of the Christians in 95 CE Beyond 100 CE the era of the apostolic fathers begins.

See also CALENDAR; NUMBERS/NUMEROLOGY.

Bibliography. W. F. Albright, "The Chronology of the Divided Monarchy of Israel," *BASOR* 100 (Dec 1945): 16-22; W. Armstrong and J. Finegan, "Chronology of the NT," *ISBE*; J. Barr, "Why the World was Created in 4004 B.C.: Archbishop Ussher and Biblical Chronology," *BJRL* 67 (1985): 575-605; J. J. Bimson, *Redating the Exodus and Conquest* and "Redating the Exodus," *BAR* 8/5 (Sep-Oct 1982): 40-68; G. Caird, "Chronology of the NT," *IDB*; D. L. Christensen, "Biblical Genealogies and Eschatological Speculation," *PRS* 14 (1987): 59-65; "Job and the Age of the Patriarchs," *PRS* 13 (1986): 225-28; S. J. De Vries, "Chronology of the OT," *IDB* and *IDBSupp*; J. Finegan, *Handbook of Biblical Chronology*; A. R. Green, "The Chronology of the Last Days of Judah: Two Apparent Discrepancies," *JBL* 101 (1982): 57-73; J. Hayes and P. Hooker, *A New Chronology For the Kings of Israel and Judah*; J. Hayes and J. Miller, eds., *Israelite and Judean History*: 678-83; D. Henige, "Comparative Chronology and the Ancient Near East: A Case for Symbiosis," *BASOR* 261 (1986): 57-68; S. H. Horn, "From Bishop Ussher to Edwin R. Thiele," *AUSS* 18 (1980): 37-49; R. Jewett, *A Chronology of Paul's Life*; M. Johnson, *The Purpose of Biblical Genealogies*; G. Luedemann, *Paul, Apostle to the Gentiles; Studies in Chronology*, vol. 1; J. Oswalt, "Chronology of the OT," *ISBE*; J. Shenkel, *Chronology and Recensional Development in the*

Greek Text of Kings; E. Shulman, *The Sequence of Events in the Old Testament*; H. Tadmor, "The Chronology of the First Temple Period," *The World History of the Jewish People*; E. J. Thiele, *The Mysterious Numbers of the Hebrew Kings,* 3rd ed.; *A Chronology of the Hebrew Kings.*

—DUANE L. CHRISTENSEN

Conquest of Canaan   [MDB 166-68]

•**Conquest of Canaan.** Three distinct blocks of tradition recount the conquest and settlement of Israel in Canaan: (1) Num 13–14 and 20–21; (2) Josh 1–12; and (3) Judg 1:1–2:5. In addition, the accounts in Gen 34; 49; Deut 2:26-37; 3:1-20, 33; and Judg 3–21 play a significant part in the scholarly discussion.

After the EXODUS from Egypt, the people of Israel arrived at Kadesh (Num 13–14). From there spies were sent into the land of the Canaanites. The conquest was postponed because of the negative report of these spies; and that entire generation of Israelites was judged and sentenced to die in the wilderness, except for CALEB and JOSHUA. To circumvent this decree, the people attempted a frontal attack from the south, resulting in a resounding defeat by the Amalekites and the Canaanites (Num 14:44-45). Some forty years later the Israelites passed around Edom and Moab in eastern Transjordan, seeking passage through Amorite territory. This resulted in conflict with OG and SIHON (Num 21), in which Israel defeated these two Amorite kings and took possession of their lands. At this time they established their camp in the plains of Moab across from Jericho (Num 22) and proceeded to give tribal allotments to Reuben, Gad, and half the tribe of Manasseh. After Moses' death, Joshua mobilized the Israelite tribes to conquer the central territory west of the Jordan. JERICHO was taken (Josh 2–6) from a base camp established at GILGAL. Soon afterwards they advanced westward into the central hill country, taking AI (Josh 7–8) and GIBEON (Josh 9–10). Next the Israelites turned their energies toward the south, which resulted in the conquests of Libnah, LACHISH, EGLON, HEBRON, and DEBIR. With southern Palestine under Israelite hegemony (Josh 10), Joshua then led an expedition against a coalition of five kings led by Jabin of HAZOR (Josh 11), resulting in the destruction of Hazor and the possession of northern Palestine. At this time Joshua divided the land among the remaining nine and one-half tribes (Josh 13–19; PLATE 10).

A rather different picture appears in Judg 1:1–2:5, where the Israelites are described as merely gaining a foothold in Canaan. The text lists scattered military operations by single tribes and presents what appears to be a peaceful settlement with the indigenous population of Canaan, including a list of twenty cities which Israel is said not to have conquered (cf. Deut 7:22 for a rationale for this). A number of tensions with the narrative in the book of Joshua are evident. In Josh 10, Hebron and Debir are said to have been conquered by Joshua, but in Judg 1:9-19 (and Josh 15:13-19) this is attributed to Caleb and OTHNIEL. Similarly, Num 32:39-41 attributes certain conquests in Transjordan to individual tribal groups like the Machirites, Jairites, and Nobahites, whereas Num 21:21-35 has the whole region (except for Edom, Moab, and Ammon) conquered as a result of a unified effort by all Israel. It should be noted that some scholars see a "pre-Exodus" conquest tradition in Gen 34. Thus it seems that the basic conquest story as related in Josh 1–12 is oversimplified.

The internal evidence for a more complex historical interpretation of events is compounded by conflicting archaeological data. A number of cities suffered violent destructions at the end of the Late Bronze Age (thirteenth and twelfth centuries BCE) including MEGIDDO, BETH-SHAN, Hazor, Tell Abu Hawam, APHEK, BETHEL, GEZER, BETH-SHEMESH, Tell Beit Mirsim, Ashdod, etc. (PLATE 3). Following these destructions, numerous villages sprang up in the central hill country, the lower Galilee, the northern Negeb, and in central and southern Transjordan. Although at first sight this evidence seems to support the presentation of Josh 1–12, a close look reveals considerable tension with the biblical account. The archaeological evidence suggests that the cities of Hormah, Arad, HESHBON, Jericho, Ai, Gibeon, and Jarmuth were not occupied in the thirteeth century BCE Most of these sites suffered either destruction or abandonment in the Middle Bronze Age or earlier. The major destruction of Ai took place hundreds of years before Joshua came on the scene. On the other hand, there are cities like Megiddo, Beth-shan, Gezer, and Bethel which did suffer destruction during the thirteenth century BCE; but the biblical record states that the Israelites could not drive out the inhabitants of these cities (Judg 1). The historian is thus forced to reckon with more than one invading force at this time, perhaps the SEA PEOPLES, who also entered Palestine about the time of Israel's conquest. To complicate matters further, the Bible lists only five places which are said to have been destroyed: Hormah, Jericho, Ai, Lachish, and Hazor. Of these, only Hazor and Lachish are supported by archaeological evidence. In short, archaeological evidence points to far wider destruction at the end of the Late Bronze Age than is attributed to Joshua and his troops. The combination of internal tensions within the biblical text and the poor fit with the archaeological evidence has produced three different theories for the conquest and settlement of Israel.

The first school of thought is that of the conquest or forced entry model, in which the biblical picture as depicted in Josh 1–12 is taken as essentially historical and accurate. Those representing this point of view include G. Ernest Wright, J. Bright, P. Lapp, Y. Yadin, and A. Malamat. It was W. F. Albright who first adduced the evidence of the extensive destruction throughout Palestine during the Late Bronze Age as confirmation of the biblical account. In addition to the archaeological evidence already cited, the Merneptah stele (ca. BCE 1224–1211) is taken as evidence for "Israel" being among the nations of Palestine at this time.

The poor fit of archaeological evidence with the biblical account in such instances as Jericho, Ai, and Bethel has caused some to abandon or revise the conquest model. D. Ussishkin has argued that Hazor and Lachish were destroyed nearly a century apart (end of thirteeth and twelfth centuries respectively). Thus, he concludes that the conquest was a much more drawn out affair than that described in

Josh 1–12. A more radical solution to this archaeological problem is set forth by J. Bimson who notes that, whereas there is no archaeological evidence for the destruction of such cities as Jericho, Ai, Gibeon, Hebron, Hormah, Arad, Debir, Lachish, and Hazor during the Late Bronze Age, there is evidence for this shortly before 1400 BCE Thus, Bimson redates the conquest and Exodus to a period 200 years earlier than the normal dating (as based on the references to Pithom and Ramses in Exod 1:1. This further entails a lowering of the end of the Middle Bronze Age from 1550 BCE to shortly before 1400 BCE It should be noted that Bimson does not cite sufficient evidence for lowering the date of the Middle Bronze Age. Moreover, his solution creates as many chronological problems as it solves (i.e., the period of the judges in Israel would now be nearly 600 years long).

A second model for interpreting the evidence was advanced by A. Alt and M. Noth, and more recently by M. Weippert, the so-called infiltration or peaceful settlement theory. Here the Genesis narratives are taken as the starting point, with Israel as nomadic or seminomadic tribes. Each year, in search of new pastures, they would enter the land, gradually becoming a sedentary people. At first their relationships with the urban population in Canaan was peaceful. It was only in the second stage, at the end of the Period of the Judges, that there would have been military conquests. The principle datum that Alt relied on was the fact that the Israelite tribes settled in the thinly populated mountainous regions which would have best enabled this process of gradual assimilation to Canaanite culture. Recently, this theory has been defended by Y. Aharoni, who argued that the biblical traditions associated with the Negeb battles are not to be associated with Moses and Joshua, but rather predate this period by almost three hundred years. A similar thesis has been offered by V. Fritz, who presents what he calls a "symbiosis model," developed from an anthropological perspective. Recent studies have shown that Alt was wrong in positing that nomads from the desert would invade the urban centers. Rather, the reverse is true. Studies have shown that pastoralists migrate from the urban center to the desert, not vice versa, and are sent out by the village in order to increase economic productivity during the nonproductive months of the agricultural year. Furthermore, archaeology has shown a dependence of Iron Age culture on that of the Late Bronze Age. Since the Iron Age settlements are not an offshoot of the Canaanite cities, this continuity is explained by Fritz as due to prolonged contact with Canaanite culture. Thus, there was no conquest as such, but rather a steady stream of independent migrations by separate tribal groups. The weakness of this theory is that it does not account for all of the archaeological data, and it too quickly dismisses the biblical stories as etiological in nature.

An interesting synthesis of the different proposals of these two schools of thought was offered by R. de Vaux, who proposed that there were four different regions each with a distinctive type of settlement. The southern region was characterized by a peaceful settlement by various tribes, as was the case in the central hill country. On the other hand, in Transjordan and the northern region there was more of a military operation as such.

A third alternative, the internal revolt model, has been proposed by G. Mendenhall and N. Gottwald, which proposes that Israel was the result of a social reorganization among the indigenous Canaanite population of the Late Bronze Age. This reorganization was the result of a social revolt within Canaanite society. Mendenhall drew attention to the social conditions reflected in the AMARNA letters, where the 'apiru class of people appear as uprooted individuals of varied origins. They stood outside the societal structures. These 'apiru are identified by Mendenhall as forerunners of the Hebrews. In this view, the ideological and religious structures had broken down in the Late Bronze Age, resulting in the withdrawal of the peasant class from urban society. Thus the Israelite conquest is a misnomer, having nothing to do with the massive destructions of the mid-thirteeth century, but rather with certain transitions within the Iron Age itself (1200–1175 BCE).

Gottwald has defined the peasants' revolt along political and social lines rather than religious ones. He posits that there was conflict, not between pastoral and agricultural groups, but between urban and rural life. Israelite Yahwism is identified with rural life, which consciously rejected Canaanite centralization of power. The result of this conflict was a peasants' revolt which resulted in the formation of Israel. M. Chaney has advocated that the catalyst to this peasant revolt was the infusion via the Exodus group into an already unsettled Canaanite population.

The major weakness of this theory is threefold: (1) the identification of 'apiru elements with Hebrews is tenuous at best; (2) the peasant revolt model seems to be a modern Marxist construct superimposed on biblical traditions; and (3) the biblical tradition insists that Israel's ancestors came from Mesopotamia and not Canaan. This view, however, does promise greater control of the biblical traditions through the use of sociological categories. Its growing popularity is suggested by the third edition of J. Bright's *A History of Israel,* which states that the conquest must "to some degree" be an inside job.

In summary, the biblical picture of the conquest, as presented in Josh 1–12, has come under considerable scrutiny. The biblical and extra-biblical evidence gives rise to three different models: conquest, infiltration, and internal revolt. Given the variety of statements within the Bible itself, and the conflicting archaeological results, it may not be too much to say that the truth of the conquest probably lies somewhere in the synthesis of these three models. Such a synthesis must also be cognizant of the fact that memory of the conquest was transmitted within a worshipping community in ancient Israel, in which the Exodus-conquest was a celebrated ritual event in the current life of the people, as well as a memory of actual experiences in the more distant past.

See also EXODUS; CANAAN; CANAAN, INHABITANTS OF; ISRAEL; TRIBES.

Bibliography. Y. Aharoni, *The Land of the Bible,* and "The Israelite Occupation of Canaan," *BARead* (May/June 1982): 14-23; A. Alt, "The Settlement of the Israelites in Palestine," in *Essays on Old Testament History and Religion*; J. Bimson, *Redating the Exodus and Conquest, JSOTSupp* 5, "Redating the Exodus," *BARead* (Sep/Oct 1987): 40-68; J. Bright, *A History of Israel,* 3rd ed.; M. Chaney, "Ancient Palestinian Peasant Movements and the Formation of Premonarchic Israel," *Palestine in Transition*; F.M. Cross, Jr., "The Ritual Conquest," *Canaanite Myth and Hebrew Epic;* F. Frick, *The Formation of the State in Ancient Israel;* N. Gottwald, *The Tribes of Yahweh;* B. Halpern, *The Emergence of Israel in Canaan;* A. Malamat, "How Inferior Israelite Forces Conquered Fortified Canaanite Cities," *BARead* (Mar/Apr 1982): 24-35; G. Mendenhall, "The Hebrew Conquest of Palestine," *BA* 25 (1962): 66-87; J. Miller, "The Israelite Occupation of Canaan," *Israelite and Judean History;* D. Ussishkin, "Lachish: Key to the Israelite Conquest of Canaan?" *BARead* (Jan/Feb 1987): 18-39; R. de Vaux, *The Early History of Israel;* M. Weippert, *The Settlement of the Israelite Tribes in Palestine;* Y. Yadin, "Is the Biblical Account of the Israelite Conquest of Canaan Historically Reliable?" *BARead* (Mar/Apr 1982): 16-23; Z. Zevit, "The Problem of Ai," *BARead* (Mar/Apr 1985): 58-69.

—DUANE L. CHRISTENSEN

Deuteronomist/Deuteronomistic Historian[MDB 210-11]

•**Deuteronomist/Deuteronomistic Historian.** [dy*oo*'tuh-ron"uh-mist / dy*oo*'tuh-ron"uh-mis"tik] In 2 Kgs 22:3–23:25, there is an account of the finding of a "book of the law" (22:8) in the Jerusalem Temple during renovations authorized in 621 BCE by the young king JOSIAH. In a dramatically told narrative, the king hears and obeys the provisions of this law (confirmed by a word from the prophetess HULDAH), and reverses the religious policies of his grandfather Manasseh. Since the time of Jerome, it has been suggested that Deuteronomy (or at least the legal section of the book) was the law book that justified Josiah's transformation of the cultus of the Jerusalem TEMPLE and his abolition of all cultic activity outside this Temple (23:4-24; cf. Deut 12:1-28).

The legal sections of Deuteronomy (chaps. 12–25), in contrast to their sources in earlier Israelite legal collections (Exod 20–23; Lev 17–26, and the priestly strata of the Pentateuch), seem to reflect an effort to provide a comprehensive law code, formulated from a coherent theological point of view. The opening section is primarily sacral law: sacrifice at the chosen sanctuary (12), apostasy (13), kosher, tithe (14), debt, the firstborn (15), festivals (16), high officials (17), and priests (18). Dominantly civil laws follow, beginning with provisions for accidental homicide (19) and warfare (20), and passing to more complex collections, one dominated by marriage law (21–22), and one alternating purity rules and civil regulations (23–25). These have been discussed in relation to Near Eastern legal codes, such as those of the HAMMURABI dynasty in Babylon.

These sections of Deuteronomy reflect significant legal developments. A comparison of the law limiting the term of slavery for Israelites (Deut 15:12-18) with the older law preserved in the Covenant Code (Exod 21:1-11) is a popular example. The third person form of traditional law ("he shall go out free," Exod 21:2) has been replaced by direct address ("you shall let him go free" Deut 15:12). This direct address adds a rhetorical dimension to law, which accounts for the effect of "your brother" (12) and for the art of persuasion reflected in "for you were a slave" (15), "he has served you six years" (18), "God will bless you" (18), and even the transfer of the "love" that leads to the acceptance of the mark of permanent slavery to the owner (16; cf. Exod 21:5). A tendency toward humaneness has been seen in the requirement that the manumitted slave be compensated for his service (13–14), in the equivalent treatment of male and female slaves ("or a Hebrew woman" displaces the provisions of Exod 21:7-11 [cf. Deut 21:10-14] where prisoners of war are given the rights of a concubine), and in the absence of the provision that a slave-wife and her offspring belong to the "master" (Exod 21:4; see Weinfeld).

The basis for current discussion of Deuteronomy is the hypothesis of Gerhard von Rad that the book is organized upon elements of an ancient tribal "covenant ceremony": a historical recitation of the Sinai story, with instruction and admonition (Deut 1:11); the account of the reading of the law (12:1–26:15); the sealing of the COVENANT (26:16-19); and an enumeration of blessings and curses (chaps. 27–28). American biblical scholars have placed particularly strong emphasis upon this "covenant theology," echoing the structure of Near Eastern treaty/covenant forms in which a powerful king recites the benefits he has provided, binds his vassals to particular obligations, and specifies blessings for those who carry out these obligations and curses for those who fail to carry them out.

The influential study by Martin Noth has seen this work by "the Deuteronomist" (Dtn) as the ideological basis for the "Deuteronomistic history" (Dtr) of Israel from the entry into the land to the Babylonian Exile. This history, held together by speeches and historical reflections (speeches: Josh 1; 23; 1 Sam 12; 1 Kgs 8:14-53; reflections: Josh 12; Judg 2:11-19; 2 Kgs 17:7-41), offers a clear interpretation of history as an expression of God's response to human obedience or disobedience (to deuteronomic principles expressed by authoritative speakers; cf. Deut 29–30). Later, von Rad described a pattern of prophetic word followed by its fulfillment.

Written soon after the beginning of the Babylonian Exile of 587/6 (the reference to the release of Jehoiachin from prison in 2 Kgs 25:27-30 is later), this history interprets the fall of JERUSALEM in relation to the persistence of God's covenant with ISRAEL, and holds out the obligation to obedience in the present situation. Despite recent critical reservations about the magisterial simplicity of Noth's hypothesis, the idea of divine justice as a principal force in the shaping of the course of history is clearly present in this history. As if expressing the criterion in the speech of SAMUEL—"if you will not hearken to the voice of the Lord, . . . the hand of the Lord will be against you and your king" (1 Sam 12:15)—the history passes judgment upon each king within the formula that opens and closes each account. With the exception of Hezekiah and Josiah, each king of Judah uniformly "walked in all the sins which his father did before him; and his heart was not wholly true to the Lord his God, as the heart of David his father" (1 Kgs 15:1-8), and every king of Israel "did what was evil in the sight of the Lord, and walked in the way of Jeroboam and in his sin which he made Israel to sin" (1 Kgs 15:33-34; 16:5-6).

Frank Moore Cross has qualified Noth's bleak characterization of the deuteronomistic historian as one who imagines no concrete future beyond the destruction and exile brought about by persistent disobedience, failure to worship only Yahweh, and failure to worship him at the one sanctuary where he dwells. In the refrain, "for the sake of my servant David," Cross sees the historian's affirmation of the persistence of the dynastic promises to Israel, which are not present in Deuteronomy, as the basis of hope for the future.

See also DEUTERONOMY, BOOK OF; PRIESTLY WRITERS; SOURCES OF THE PENTATEUCH.

Bibliography. F. M. Cross, *Canaanite Myth and Hebrew Epic*; A. D. H. Mayes, *Deuteronomy, NCB*; M. Noth, *The Deuteronomistic History, JSOTSupp* 15; G. von Rad, *The Problem of the Hexateuch and Other Essays*; M. Weinfeld, *Deuteronomy and the Deuteronomic School*.

—ROY D. WELLS

Israel   [MDB 417-20]

•**Israel.** [iz'ray-uhl] The precise original meaning of this name remains uncertain. The folk etymology of the term in Gen 32:22-32 leaves uncertain whether the root *śrh* is to be understood as "strive, struggle" ("he struggles with God ['el]" or "God struggles") or "to have dominion over" ("he has dominion over God [or a divine being]" or "God has dominion"). The association of the name with *śrh* or *śwr* (a by-form of *śrr*), suggesting the idea of dominion, is indicated by Hos 12:5 (cf. Hos 8:4 and Judg 9:22). *Miśrah,* from *śrh,* in Isa 9:5-6 clearly indicates "dominion, authority." Thus, it would appear that the name should be connected with the idea of dominion/rule, rather than with the idea of struggle or striving. Less likely is the association of the name with the verb *yšr* "to be upright" found in the name Jeshurun, used as a synonym for Israel in Deut 32:15; 33:15, 26; and Isa 44:2 (so Nahmanides and other medieval Jewish interpreters). Such an association understands Israel ("he who is upright with God") as an antonym to Jacob ("deceitful, crafty"). Even less probable is Philo's view that the name is an abbreviation for *'iš-ra'ah-'el,* "the one who saw god."

The terms Israel and Israelites (children of Israel) were used with a number of different but related referents in the Bible and in biblical times. Among these are (1) a secondary name for the patriarch JACOB, (2) the "descendants" of the patriarch Israel/Jacob, (3) a tribal grouping in central Palestine in premonarchical times, (4) a kingdom composed primarily of northern tribal groups ruled by SAUL, (5) the monarchical state and its citizens ruled by DAVID and SOLOMON, (6) the northern state that separated from Davidic authority at the death of Solomon, (7) the cooperative union between the Kingdom of Israel, with its capital in SAMARIA, and Judah, with its capital at JERUSALEM, during the ninth and eighth centuries, (8)

Judah and Judeans as the remnant of the old union of north and south after the Assyrian capture of Samaria in 722/1 BCE, and (9) adherents of various forms of Hebrew and OT religion (including its use as an early Christian self-designation).

Interestingly, the term "Israel" is practically never used as a geographical or territorial designation, indicating that the term was not geographical but religious and political in origin. Biblical references to the land of Israel are infrequent and late (cf. 2 Kgs 5:2; 2 Chr 30:25; 34:7; Ezek 27:17; 40:2). Only one ancient near eastern text refers to the "land" of Israel. In describing his battle at Qarqar (in 853) with a coalition of western powers, the Assyrian king Shalmaneser III (858-824) refers to King Ahab of the land of Israel (*Sir-'i-la-a-a*).

(1) Two biblical narratives report the change of Jacob's name to Israel, one associated with PENUEL in Transjordan (Gen 32:28) and the other with BETHEL in the central hill country, west of the Jordan (Gen 35:10). The renaming of Jacob to Israel may indicate the combining of two patriarchal figures (a Transjordanian Jacob and a west Jordan Israel?) revered by two originally separate peoples or else a nationalizing of the ancestral figure of Jacob by "identifying" him with the political entity Israel.

(2) Israelites or the children of Israel refer to the people who were members of the tribal and political entity bearing the name "Israel." They are idealistically depicted in the scriptures as one genealogically related group, namely, as the descendants of the twelve sons of the patriarch Israel/Jacob (cf. Gen 30:1-24; 35:16-20; 48:1-20). The description of these descendants as the offspring of four different women (LEAH, RACHEL, Zilpah, and Bilhah) and the diversity in the lists of the sons/tribes (Gen 49; Num 1:20-2:31; 26:1-65; Deut 33; Judg 5) suggest a diverse background for the people and a fluidity in the groups understood as belonging to Israel at any particular time.

(3) Reference to a people called Israel appears in a hymnic inscription set up in Egypt by Pharaoh Merneptah in the last decade of the thirteenth century, or shortly before the year 1200 (cf. *ANET* 378). This "Israel" was located in the northern hill country of Palestine, and is probably to be identified with the Ephraim/Manasseh/Benjamin tribes that occupy center stage in the Book of Judges. These tribes were settled in the central hill country of Palestine, primarily north of Jerusalem and south of the Esdraelon Plain, with some spillover into Gilead, east of the Jordan. More loosely associated with this group were the Galilee-Jezreel tribes of Asher, Naphtali, Issachar, and Zebulun and the Transjordanian tribes of Reuben and Gad.

The leaders of this Israel appear to have been tribal elders and occasional savior figures such as DEBORAH, BARAK, GIDEON, and JEPHTHAH. These savior figures were of diverse background with diverse patterns of leadership. The name Israel used of this tribal affiliation, containing a reference to the deity EL, suggests that at least some of the elements that made up early Israel originally venerated the god El in a special way (cf. Gen 33:20; 35:7; 31:13) and that Yahweh, a militant deity under whose banner they fought (Exod 15:3; Num 10:35-36; Judg 7:20), only secondarily became the dominant tribal deity.

Recent sociological approaches to early Israelite history have concluded that the earliest Israel was a conglomerate of peoples, composed of indigenous local villagers, displaced persons, and social refugees as well as migrant groups entering Canaan from the outside. The social upheavals and disruption of trade throughout the eastern Mediterranean seaboard ca. 1250–1100 BCE created the conditions in which the tribal-based entity Israel arose in the Palestinian hill country. Archaeological evidence supports this hypothetical view and suggests no major invasion of the central hill country of Canaan and no massive destruction of biblical proportions at the time but only continuity of the previous culture with degeneration in material artisanship.

The individual tribe in the Israelite affiliation was distinguished by geography, common lifestyles, real and conjectured kinship, and the shared need of physical protection. As the Book of Judges indicates, the cooperation of two or more tribes was generally the consequence of confronting a common enemy.

(4) The appearance of greater external threats and gradual internal political evolution toward more centralized and perduring leadership eventually led to the establishment of kingship and the founding of Israel as a monarchical state. The external threats were posed by peoples from Transjordan, such as the Moabites, Ammonites, and Midianites, and by the Philistines from southwest Palestine. Early stages in this process and the gradual evolution of tribal life toward more stable and continuing leadership can be seen in the role of the family of Gideon (Judg 6–9) and the figure of Jephthah (Judg 11:1–12:10).

Like Abimelech and Jephthah (cf. Judg 9:4; 11:3), SAUL rose to prominence at the head of a small personal army capable of rallying tribal support, defending Israelite territory, and protecting the people from external plunder and attack (cf. 1 Sam 11; 13:1–14:46). Under Saul's leadership, monarchy became and continued to be the fundamental pattern of Israelite government.

The general territorial extent of Israel at the time of Saul is reflected in the description of the kingdom inherited by his son (or grandson?) ISH-BOSHETH (2 Sam 2:8-9). "All Israel" at the time consisted of Gilead (territory around Mahanaim in Transjordan), the Asherites (probably an enclave of the tribe of Asher in southwest Ephraim; cf. 1 Chr 7:35-45), Jezreel (the hill country abutting the Jezreel Valley), Ephraim, and Benjamin. Either before or at the time of Saul's death, DAVID had established an independent kingdom in Judah although Saul certainly seems earlier to have enjoyed the support of Judeans (cf. 1 Sam 23:7, 19; 24:1; cf. 1 Sam 15:1-12). Thus Saul's Israel was limited to the central Palestinian hill country south of the Valley of Jezreel, limited terrain in central Transjordan, and portions of the Judean hill country.

(5) Under David and Solomon, the state of Israel expanded to incorporate extensive territory in Transjordan, the region of Galilee, and all of "greater" Judah.

Although the editorial glorification of the Solomonic state claimed that Solomon "ruled over all the kingdoms from the Euphrates to the land of the Philistines and to the border of Egypt" (2 Kgs 4:21) and that "he had dominion over all the region west of the Euphrates from Tiphsah to Gaza, over all the kings west of the Euphrates" (2 Kgs 4:24), other and more realistic texts suggest a much more limited territory. The traditional expression "from Dan to Beersheba" (2 Sam 17:11; 1 Kgs 4:25) is probably more descriptive of the extent of the Israelite state.

Two texts, perhaps based on authentic records, indicate something of the territorial dominion claimed by David and Solomon. Even these texts, however, cannot be taken as reflective of firm boundaries of a kingdom totally ruled by these two monarchs since boundaries in ancient times were often idealized phenomena, realistic only when a king could collect taxes and muster troops from the citizenry of an area. (a) 2 Sam 24:1-10 reports on David's census, which began at the River Arnon (the traditional northern border of Moab), extended to north of Dan, and reached westward to the territories of Tyre and Sidon. Whether any or how much of the Mediterranean coastal region belonged to Israel at the time remains uncertain. (b) 1 Kgs 4:7-19 preserves a list of Solomonic officers appointed to serve over twelve Israelite districts (in its present form, the text does not include Judah as one of the twelve districts) to supply provisions for Solomon's table and fodder for his horses (1 Kgs 4:27-28). The territory of these districts conforms with what can be known about the territory included in David's census and the list provides greater specificity about cities and regions. Obviously between Saul's time and the reign of Solomon, vast areas of Palestine had been brought under Israelite control.

Israel's economic well-being during the reigns of David and Solomon was in no small measure the product of Phoenician largess. Numerous texts speak of Israel as beneficiary of Phoenician expertise (2 Sam 5:11; 2 Kgs 5:1-12; 9:26-28; 10:11, 22) and even of Solomon's balance of trade deficits and concession of territory to Hiram of Tyre (1 Kgs 9:10-14). With its lack of natural resources, limited population, and restricted access to world markets, Israel's periods of reasonable prosperity were dependent upon cooperative participation with outside, more resourceful powers.

(6) Following the death of Solomon (probably in 927), the northern tribes broke away from the Davidic state protesting against the oppressive policies of the Jerusalemite monarchy (1 Kgs 12:1-20). This northern group assumed the name Israel which, as already noted, had earlier designated a political entity in the central highlands (see no. 3 above) even though the Judeans could continue to be called children of Israel (cf. 1 Kgs 12:17). The northern tribal elders meeting at SHECHEM selected JEROBOAM I (927–906), a former Solomonic official, as their new king (1 Kgs 11:26-28; 12:20). As part of his royal program, Jeroboam established two major cult centers, at Bethel and Dan, and thus at important points near the two extremities of his kingdom (1 Kgs 12:28-33).

Warfare between Israel and Judah developed after the split (1 Kgs 15:6) but was probably limited to skirmishes fought to establish the boundary between the two states, a boundary that lay within the old territory of the tribe of Benjamin and only a few miles north of Jerusalem. The Egyptian invasion of Palestine by pharaoh SHISHAK (1 Kgs 14:25-28) no doubt diverted attention from local hostilities for a time.

In comparsion with Judah, the northern kingdom of Israel possessed greater territory, a large population, the largest cities, and a location more open and accessible to international trade and political relationships. Probably all territory east of the Jordan passed out of Israelite control early in the rule of Jeroboam, climaxing a process of attrition already begun under Solomon (1 Kgs 11:1-25).

The reign of the family of Jeroboam came to an end in its second generation when Baasha assassinated King NADAB and exterminated all the royal house (1 Kgs 15:27-30). Border warfare between Israel and Judah flared anew. When Baasha sought to fortify the town of Ramah, the Judean king Asa bribed the Aramean king of Damascus to attack Israel from the northeast. This counterattack diverted Israelite forces and allowed Asa to fortify the towns of Geba and Mizpah as permanent border points (1 Kgs 15:17-22).

(7) In the second quarter of the ninth century, Israel and Judah entered a period of cooperative alliance which lasted, with only intermittent interruptions, until PEKAH's takeover in Samaria in 734. After OMRI's coup and his success in a four year civil war (1 Kgs 16:8-23), JEHOSHAPHAT, his southern counterpart, "made peace with" (or "submitted to") the king of Israel (1 Kgs 22:44). "Israel" now became a bipartite state with two monarchs, but with clear dominance belonging to the northern king.

The following factors indicate the close union of the two kingdoms. (a) The royal houses intermarried. Athaliah, an Omride princess but whose parents remain uncertain (2 Kgs 8:18, 26), was married to JEHORAM son of Jehoshaphat. (b) Although Assyrian texts make references to practically all the kingdoms in Aram-Palestine, no Assyrian text mentions Judah until 734 indicating that Judah was subsumed under "Israel" (cf. ANET 279, 281, 282). (c) For a time, both Israel and Jusah were ruled simultaneously (about 851-840) by a king named Jehoram. Rather than two kings with the same name, this was probably the same person, namely the Davidic Jehoram son of Jehoshaphat. (d) When King AMAZIAH of Judah challenged the Israelite king at Beth-shemesh, a traditional Judean site, he was severly defeated (2 Kgs 14:8-14). Amaziah's effort was probably an attempt to assert Judean independence from Israel. (e) Two contemporary prophets refer to the bipartite kingdom of Israel: Mic 1:14 speaks of the "kings of Israel" (probably Jotham of Judah and Jeroboam II of Israel) and Isa 8:14 refers to "both houses of Israel."

Under Omri and AHAB, Israel reached a level of territorial expansion and wealth equal to the time of Solomon, as archaeological remains have indicated. Portions of Transjordan and Galilee were retaken from Aram (cf. 2 Kgs 14:25 and the Mesha

Inscription, *ANET* 320-21) and the port of Elath was restored to Judean control (2 Kgs 14:21-22). As in the days of Solomon, Israel's prosperity was a by-product of good relations with outside powers. Israel became a cooperative partner in a Aramean-Palestinian alliance of powers that joined to protect eastern Mediterranean interests against Assyrian dominance (cf. *ANET* 278-79 for the alliance that halted the Assyrian king Shalmaneser III at Qarqar in 853). With such ecumenical economic arrangements, ecumenism in religion also prevailed, as indicated by an inscription set up in Aramean territory by an Aramean monarch but dedicated to Baal Melqart, a Phoenician deity (cf. *ANET* 501). With Omride intermarriage with and economic ties to the royal house of Tyre, some acknowledgment of the Phoenician Baal occurred in Israel as well (1 Kgs 16:31-32) but to the chagrin and consternation of the prophet Elijah and his supporters.

Following its defeat by Shalmaneser III in 845–844 and the usurpation of the Aramean throne by HAZAEL (cf. *ANET* 280-81), the Aramean-Palestinian alliance disintegrated. Hazael attacked Israel probably to regain territory in the northern Transjordan previously lost to the Omrides (2 Kgs 8:28-29; 9:14b-15a). When Shalmaneser III was again in the region, in 841–840, JEHU, the commander of the Israelite army, led a coup against the wounded King Jehoram and, paying tribute, placed Israel under the custody and protection of the Assyrians (*ANET* 281). Jehu moved to gain control of the country and stabilize his rule. The Israelite and Judean monarchs along with other members of the royal house were killed, Samaria taken, and much of the national leadership killed (2 Kgs 9:1–10:17) in what must have taken considerable time and great civil strife although the scriptures describe these events as if they occurred in a matter of days.

Jehu's submission to the Assyrians established an international policy for Israel that lasted for over a century. Throughout the reign of Jehu and the four successors from his house (JOHOAHAZ, Jehoash (or JOASH), JEROBOAM II, and ZECHARIAH) as well as during the rule of MENAHEM and his son PEKAHIAH, the offical stance of the government in Samaria was pro-Assyrian. None of these seven monarchs ever adopted an anti-Assyrian posture or joined the western alliance against Assyria. Two consequences followed from this policy. (a) When Assyria was strong and active in the west, Israel enjoyed prosperity and territorial expansion (again through the help and intervention of an outside power) and was weak and economically distressed during Assyrian decline. (b) Israel—and Judah, which shared a common foreign policy—was militarily and economically isolated and became the object of local harassment when anti-Assyrian sentiment was strong in the west.

Throughout much of the reign of Hazael (ca. 844–806), Israel and Judah were subject to Aram (the Elisha narratives in 2 Kgs 3-8; 13:14-19 and the battle narratives in 1 Kgs 20 and 22 probably describe conditions during the reign of Jehu and his two immediate successors). From 838 until 806, Assyrian power was basically absent from the west and Israel and Judah were dominated by "Greater Aram" ruled by Hazael (2 Kgs 11:32-33; 12:17-18; 13:3, 7, 22). In the fifth year of his reign (806–805), the Assyrian king Adad-Nirari III (810–783) began to reassert Assyrian authority in the west (*ANET* 281-82) and Israel's fate took a turn for the better (2 Kgs 13:24-25). Under Jeroboam II (788–748), Israel and Judah recovered economically and territorially for a time, retaking all of Galilee, parts of Transjordan, and reacquiring control of the seaport of Elath (2 Kgs 14:21-25; 2 Chr 5:11-22). The Hebrew text of 2 Kgs 14:28 speaks of how Jeroboam II "returned Damascus and Hamath to Judah in Israel" but this text is corrupt and probably should be understood as referring to the fact that Jeroboam II reconquered territory in Galilee and Transjordan held by Hamath and Damascus during the days of Jehu, Jehoahaz, and Jehoash. For a time, the house of Israel was again, in cooperation with Assyria, a power in the eastern Mediterranean world.

In the late 760s and throughout the 750s, Assyrian power waned and Israel too entered a phase of decline. A revitalized anti-Assyrian coalition in the west led by Rezin of Damascus pressured Israel-Judah (Amos 1:3-15; Isa 9:12). PEKAH, killed in 731–730 (2 Kgs 16:29-30) after a rule of twenty years (2 Kgs 16:27), apparently led a portion of Israel to break away from Jeroboam's kingdom in 751–750 and threw in their lot with Rezin and the anti-Assyrian coalition (2 Kgs 15:37). From the 750s until the final fall of Samaria in 722/1, civil strife and civil war plagued Israel constantly.

The Jehu dynasty in Samaria ended with the assassination of Zechariah (2 Kgs 15:8-10). The assassin, Shallum, perhaps anti-Assyrian politically, was quickly attacked and killed by Menahem who secured his hold on the throne with the assistance of Assyria, now ruled by Tiglath-pileser III (744–727), an aggressive and successful monarch (2 Kgs 15:17-20). Menahem ruled over only the old tribal territory of Ephraim and Samaria, the capital city. Major portions of Israelite territory, including Galilee and Transjordan, were now under the control of Aram and Pekah (Isa 9:1; 2 Kgs 15:29) and much of Judah was sympathetic to the anti-Assyrian cause (Mic 1:10-16; Isa 8:6). In 734, the anti-Assyrian Pekah assassinated Menahem's successor, PEKAHIAH, seized the throne in Samaria, and brought the entire north into the anti-Assyrian coalition (2 Kgs 15:23-25). King AHAZ was expected to follow the lead of the north since the Jerusalemite king was an inferior power to the Samarian monarch. When Ahaz refused to take up arms against Assyria, Pekah and Rezin moved against Jerusalem to depose Ahaz and exterminate the Davidic house and to place a cooperative Tyrian prince, the son of Tabeel, on the throne of Judah (2 Kgs 16:5; Isa 7:6). The siege of Jerusalem failed and the dynasty of David survived, as Isaiah promised (Isa 7:3-17), for Tiglath-pileser moved into Aram-Palestine late in 734 or early in 733 and the siege was lifted.

The Assyrians fought the western coalition for three years and defeated its leading powers—Aram, Phoenicia, Philistia, and the Arabs. In his third campaign (732–731), Tiglath-pileser killed Rezin and incorporated the sixteen districts ruled by him into the Assyrian empire (*ANET* 282-84). HOSHEA was recognized as ruler over Israel and the Assyrians left the task of defeating Pekah and the anti-Assyrian

Israelites to Hoshea and his supporters, probably including Ahaz (2 Kgs 15:30; Hos 1:11).

Hoshea (730–722/1) presided over the last days of Israel's existence as a nation although he was apparently unable to control the anti-Assyrian fervor in the north. He joined a revolt against the Assyrians, probably before the death of Tiglath-pileser III, which was suppressed by Shalmaneser V, probably in his accession year (before Nisan 726). Later, Israel rebelled again and sent to Egypt for help (in 726). Hoshea was subsequently arrested (725) but rebellion continued in Samaria. The city was placed under siege (in 724–723) and fell to Shalmaneser in late 722 or early in 721 (2 Kgs 17:1-6; 18:9-10). Shalmaneser V died before the final disposition of Samaria. Rebellion flared anew and Sargon II took Samaria again, in his second year (720–719), and presided over the rebuilding of the city and its incorporation into the Assyrian empire (*ANET* 285). Israel ceased to exist as a political entity.

(8) After the demise of the Northern Kingdom and its incorporation into the Assyrian empire as the province of Samerina, Judeans continued to use the name Israel as a self-designation. This was only natural since they had been part of the house of Israel not only during the times of David and Solomon but also throughout much of the ninth and eighth centuries and now survived as the remnant of Israel. Jeremiah, for example, uses the name Israel both for the old Northern Kingdom and for his contemporaries in Judah. The name, when applied to Judeans was used primarily in a spiritual or religious sense since the political entity of the Davidic kingdom was clearly known as Judah (cf. *ANET* 287, 291, 294). In the Jerusalem cult, as reflected in the psalms, Yahweh was worshiped as the God of Israel; the expression "Yahweh of Judah" never appears.

(9) The terms Israel and Israelite was used in postexilic and later times to refer to Yahweh worshipers and adherents to Jewish religion in various forms. Even Samaritans in the diaspora, as indicated in a Delos inscription, could refer to themselves as Israelites. Adherents to apocalyptic communities such as the early church could speak of themselves as the true or new Israel (cf. Gal 6:16; Jas 1:1; 1 Pet 1:1).

See also JUDAH, KINGDOM OF; KINGSHIP.

Bibliography. G. W. Ahlström, *Who Were the Israelites?*; R. B. Coote and K. W. Whitelam, *The Emergence of Israel in Historical Perspective*; G. A. Danell, *Studies in the Name Israel in the Old Testament*; J. H. Hayes and P. K. Hooker, *A New Chronology for the Kings of Israel and Judah*; J. M. Miller and J. H. Hayes, *A History of Ancient Israel and Judah*; W. T. Pitard, *Ancient Damascus*; S. Sandmel, *The Several Israels*; L. M. White, "The Delos Synagogue Revisited: Recent Fieldwork in the Graeco-Roman Diaspora," *HTR* 80 (1987): 133-60.

—JOHN H. HAYES

Kingdom of Judah   [MDB 474-77]

•**Judah, Kingdom of.** [joo'duh] Judah proper consisted of the southern part of the central Palestinian hill country (Mount Judah) between JERUSALEM and HEBRON from which the tribe living there received its name. The kingdom of "Greater Judah," created by DAVID, was more extensive geographically, including territory southward to BEERSHEBA and westward to include the shephelah, and more extensive ethnographically, incorporating the Calebites, Korahites, Kenizzites, Jerahmeelites, Kenites, and Simeonites. After a stint of service to the PHILISTINES (1 Sam 27), David and his private army moved into Hebron where he was anointed as king over "the house of Judah" (2 Sam 2:1-4a). Although the biblical narrative places this event after the death of SAUL, the chronological references in 2 Sam 2:8-11 suggest that David may have established himself in Hebron while Saul was still alive. "Greater Judah" was no doubt created during David's seven-and-one-half-year rule in Hebron.

When David became king over Saulide territory, Judah became part of greater Israel (2 Sam 5:1-5). With the death of SOLOMON and the secession of the North from the United Kingdom, the Davidic Kingdom again consisted of the state of Judah.

From Rehoboam to Jehoshaphat (ca. 926–878). REHOBOAM not only had to bear the brunt of Solomon's economic and public labor policies but also to suffer the consequences of his own and his advisers' ineptitude in handling the succession to the throne (1 Kgs 12:1-20). After the North rebelled against the policies and ideology of the Davidic family, Rehoboam was able to retain control of only Judah and apparently a portion of southern BENJAMIN. According to 2 Chronicles, Rehoboam heavily fortified his kingdom (11:5-12) and settled members of the royal family throughout the land (11:23). The location of his fortified cities, scattered throughout his kingdom rather than just at its borders, indicates that they were intended to provide as much for internal security against his own subjects as for external security against invaders. In the fifth year of his reign, the Egyptian pharaoh SHISHAK (Sheshonq) campaigned in Palestine, probably to buttress his authority at home and to insure Egyptian influence in regional trade (1 Kgs 14:25-26). At this time, or perhaps at the death of Solomon, Judah lost control of the seaport at Elath.

Military conflict between Israel and Judah, probably limited border strife, was characteristic of the period from Rehoboam to JEHOSHAPHAT (1 Kgs 14:30; 15:6, 16, 32) and constitutes a major topic of the narrative about Asa (1 Kgs 15:16-22). The latter resorted to paying the Arameans to intervene in the struggle on his behalf.

From Jehoshaphat to Athaliah (ca. 877–840). During the early part of this period, Judah was dominated by Israel ruled at the time by the Omrides who participated in the western anti-Assyrian coalition and shared in the economic well-being this internationalism produced. Jehoshaphat inaugurated a policy of Judean submission to the north (1 Kgs 22:44). Second Chr 17–20 provides an account of Jehoshaphat's activities, which stresses the prosperity of his reign, his military strength and triumphs, and his religious and administrative reforms; no doubt the consequences of cooperation with the Omrides.

JEHORAM, the son of Jehoshaphat, succeeded his father (probably in 852) at a time when an injured Omride, Ahaziah, was ruling in Samaria (2 Kgs 1:2, 17). With the latter's death (probably in 851), Jehoram of Judah apparently ascended the throne in SAMARIA as well. Although the later biblical editors assumed Jehoram to be a brother to Ahaziah, it seems more probable that one and the same Jehoram ruled over both kingdoms (contrast 2 Kgs 3:1; 8:16, 25 with the Hebrew of 1:17). If this was the case, then for a time a Davidic king again ruled over both Israel and Judah. Under Jehoram, Judah lost control over Edom, and even one Judean town (Libnah), for reasons unknown, asserted its independence from Jerusalem (2 Kgs 8:20-22). Jehoram had serious conflict with Aram, now ruled by the aggressive HAZAEL. When Jehoram was wounded in battle against Aram, his son Ahaziah apparently assumed the kingship in Jerusalem (2 Kgs 8:25-29). Both Jehoram and Ahaziah, along with other members of the royal family, were killed in JEHU's coup that brought him to the throne in Samaria (2 Kgs 9:24, 27; 10:12-14).

Judah during the Reign of the House of Jehu. As the new ruler of Israel, Jehu placed his kingdom under the protection of the Assyrians (*ANET* 281), a move that characterized the international policies of Samaria for over a century or until PEKAH seized the Samarian throne in 734. With the deaths of Jehoram and Ahaziah, Athaliah (839–833) seized the throne in Jerusalem (2 Kgs 11:1), perhaps saving it from Israelite usurpation, and reigned for seven years until she was toppled in a coup led by the high priest JEHOIADA (2 Kgs 11:2-20). Jehoash or JOAHS (832–803), a youngster seven years old, was placed on the throne (2 Kgs 11:21). During much of Jehoash's reign, Judah was a vassal to Aram.

Following SHALMANESER III's last western campaign in 838, in his twenty-first year (*ANET* 280), the Assyrians were not directly involved in Aramean-Palestinian politics for over three decades. During this time, Hazael dominated practically all Aram-Palestine in his "Greater Aram" including Israel and Judah (2 Kgs 10:32-33; 12:17-18; 13:3-7, 22).

Beginning in the fifth year of Adad-Nirari III (810–783), Assyria again became active in the west (*ANET* 281-82) and the fortunes of Israel and Judah took a turn for the better (2 Kgs 13:4-5, 14-19, 24-25). AMAZIAH (802–786) of Judah won a victory over the Edomites (2 Kgs 14:7) but his efforts to assert independence from Israel led to Judah's defeat by Jehoash of Israel, the seizure and plunder of Jerusalem, the destruction of part of Jerusalem's fortifications, and the capture of Amaziah and probably his being held as a hostage for a time in Samaria (2 Kgs 14:8-14).

Judah under UZZIAH/AZARIAH (785–760) shared in the renewed prosperity characteristic of the early reign of JEROBOAM II, a prosperity consequent upon

Assyria's presence in the west (2 Kgs 14:21-28; 2 Chr 26:1-15). After Uzziah was smitten with leprosy, he was replaced on the throne by JOTHAM (759–744) although Uzziah probably lived until late in 734 (cf. Isa 6:1).

The latter part of Jotham's reign witnessed a radical weakening of Judah and the kingdom was placed on the defensive (2 Chr 27). The following factors contributed to this condition. (1) Assyria was torn by internal trouble, plagues and civil strife, and its authority became inconsequential in the west. (2) A strong anti-Assyrian coalition developed in Aram-Palestine and placed increasing pressure on pro-Assyrian Israel and Judah (Hos 1:4-5; Amos 1:3-15). (3) Jeroboam II was confronted with an anti-Assyrian rival to the throne in the person of Pekah who apparently under Aramean influence led a group in defection from Samaria beginning in 751–750, twenty years prior to his death in 731–730 (note the reference to his twenty-year rule in 2 Kgs 15:27b). Pekah and REZIN not only harassed Israel but Judah as well (2 Kgs 15:37). (4) Many Judean towns threw their support to the anti-Assyrian coalition and thus against Jerusalem (Isa 3:16-4:1; 8:6; Mic 1:8-16).

Judah and the Assyrian Empire. Jotham and his successor AHAZ (743–728) continued to support the pro-Assyrian policies of Samaria during the reigns of MANAHEM (746–737) and PEKAHIAH (736–735). When Pekah seized the throne in Samaria in 734, Ahaz refused to follow the new Israelite monarch in supporting the anti-Assyrian coalition. Ahaz asserted Judean independence from Israel (Isa 9:2) and Rezin and Pekah moved to depose Ahaz, exterminate the Davidic family (2 Kgs 16:5; Isa 7:3-6), and bring Judah completely into the anti-Assyrian coalition, a policy favored by most Judeans (Isa 8:6). The appearance of TIGLATH-PILESER and the Assyrian army in the west late in 734 or early in 733 rescued Ahaz and Jerusalem.

The kingdom of Judah remained pro-Assyrian and avoided any involvement in the rebellions against Assyria in the 720s during which Samaria was captured, part of its population deported, and the region incorporated into the Assyrian empire (2 Kgs 17:1-6; 18:1-12). At the beginning of his reign, the new Assyrian king SARGON II (721–705) instituted a policy of cooperation with the Egyptian Delta princes in opposition to the Ethiopians in Upper Egypt. HEZEKIAH (727–699), as a cooperative pro-Assyrian, seems to have profited from this arrangement (cf. 1 Chr 4:39-43; Isa 19:16-25).

During the Ashdod revolt (ca. 714–711), Judah became involved in anti-Assyrian activity (*ANET* 289) much to the chagrin and opposition of Isaiah (Isa 20; 22). Apparently, Hezekiah's illness in his fourteenth year (2 Kgs 18:13; 20:6) coincided with this revolt and leadership fell to the monarch's subordinates, Shebna and Eliakim (Isa 22:15-25).

In 705, following Sargon's violent death on the battlefield in Anatolia, Hezekiah, supported by Isaiah (Isa 24–27), helped lead a revolt against Assyria. This revolt was planned in advance with the cooperation of the Ethiopian (twenty-fifth) Dynasty which had gained dominance over the Delta in about 712. Hezekiah's religious reform and efforts to centralize Yahwistic religion in Jerusalem (2 Kgs 18:4;

19:22; Isa 27:9) were probably carried out to avoid the defection of Judean cities which had plagued Ahaz. The reform policies of Hezekiah were probably embodied in the earliest form of the book of DEUTERONOMY, which either served as the basis of his reform or was written down as a summation of his program. The anti-Assyrian revolt, however, was a failure. The western powers were defeated, Hezekiah had to pay special tribute, and Judean territory was reduced (*ANET* 287-88; 2 Kgs 18:13-16), although Jerusalem was not taken nor Hezekiah forced to abdicate.

Hezekiah was succeeded by his young son MANASSEH who reigned for fifty-five years (698–644). Judean policy returned to one of submission to Assyria and the Deuteronomic policy of religious centralization in Jerusalem was reversed. The editors of the Kings material on Manasseh (2 Kgs 21:1-18) depict him as one of the worst of Judah's monarchs because of his reversal of Hezekiah's policies and his religious programs contrary to Deuteronomy. Assyrian texts (*ANET* 291, 294) indicate Manasseh's participation in projects carried out by ESARHADDON (680–669) and his support of, if not presence on, an invasion of Egypt by ASHURBANIPAL (668–627) to expel the Ethiopians (664–663). With the expulsion of the Ethiopians from Lower Egypt and the establishment of the Twenty-sixth Dynasty in Egypt, renewed cooperation between Assyria and the Delta Egyptians ensued.

Manasseh's successor, AMON (643–642), was assassinated by some of his officials after only a two-year rule (2 Kgs 21:19-26). His assassination was probably motivated by an anti-Assyrian movement in Judah at a time when several Transjordanian kingdoms and Tyre were in revolt (*ANET* 297-98). The coup was suppressed by the people of the land who placed the eight-year old JOSIAH on the throne.

Judah as an Egyptian Vassal. Josiah (640–610) was able to carry out a major reform of Judean/Jerusalemite religion in his eighteenth year, and thus became a great hero to the editors of Kings (2 Kgs 23:4-14, 21-23). It is doubtful whether he was able to exercise much political freedom and territorial expansion except to incorporate the territory around BETHEL into his kingdom (2 Kgs 23:15-18). During his reign, Egypt and Assyria shared control over Palestine and the lower eastern Mediterranean seaboard (cf. Jer 2:16-18, 36-37). Egypt had become more dominant in the eastern Mediterranean seaboard as Ashurbanipal had become more involved elsewhere. The Babylonian Chronicles indicate that the Egyptians were fighting against the Babylonians in Mesopotamia itself in support of their Assyrian allies (at least by 616 BCE when the extant chronicles resume after a break). This suggests Egyptian dominance throughout Palestine and Aram and the vassalage of the Judean monarch to the Egyptian pharaoh.

Josiah was killed at MEGIDDO in 610 by Pharaoh NECHO II (610–595) who had only recently assumed the throne (2 Kgs 23:28-31). What precipitated this killing remains unknown (compare 2 Chr 35:20-27). The expression "went to meet him" (2 Kgs 23:29), which describes Josiah's movement to Megiddo, would not normally indicate hostile intent.

The Judeans enthroned JEHOAHAZ II as Josiah's replacement without Egyptian approval. Egypt imposed a stiff penalty on its vassal, deposed Jehoahaz, and replaced him with JEHOIAKIM, his brother (2 Kgs 23:3135). The latter appears to have been a fairly oppressive monarch or at least one with whom the prophet JEREMIAH had serious differences (cf. Jer 22:15-23; 36:20-32).

In the years that followed the enthronement of Jehoiakim (608–598), the Kingdom of Judah was caught up in the international struggles between Egypt and Babylonia. The external pressures on the kingdom were paralleled by internal party factions—pro-Babylonian and pro-Egyptian—that further unraveled the fabric of Judean society. These factors were also exacerbated by religious and nationalistic sentiments that accelerated the nation's plunge into tragedy.

Judah as a Babylonian Vassal. At the battle of CARCHEMISH in the summer of 605, the Babylonian crown prince, NEBUCHADREZZAR (604–562), routed the Egyptian army (cf. Jer 46:2). After Nebuchadrezzar sacked Ashkelon in Chislev (Nov/Dec) 604, Jehoiakim submitted to Babylonian vassalage (see Jer 36:9-10). After three years (604–603, 603–602, 602–601), he rebelled against Babylon (2 Kgs 24:1) when Nebuchadrezzar's invasion of Egypt in Chislev 601 suffered defeat (*ANET* 564). Over three years passed before the Babylonians attacked Jerusalem in force (sometime after Chislev 598; *ANET* 564). Jehoiakim died, apparently shortly after the city was put under siege, and was replaced by JEHOIACHIN who surrendered to Nebuchadrezzar when the latter put in an appearance at the siege (2 Kgs 24:8-12). A Babylonian text notes that the city was "taken" on what corresponds to 16 March 597 (2 Adar in Nebuchadrezzar's seventh year).

Nebuchadrezzar returned home with some Judean exiles (Jer 52:28b) for the new year festival, but apparently decided not to leave Jehoiachin on the throne and subsequently had him and other deportees brought to Babylon (2 Kgs 24:12b-16; 2 Chr 36:9-10). A new "king of his liking" (*ANET* 564), ZEDEKIAH, was placed on the throne in Jerusalem.

Under Zedekiah (596–586), pronationalist and pro-Egyptian factions began pushing for rebellion against Babylonia in the king's first year (Jer 27–28). Revolt was eventually precipitated following a triumphal visit to Palestine-Phoenicia by the Egyptian pharaoh Psammetichus II (595–589) in his fourth year (592–591). Zedekiah was eventually captured and Jerusalem fell to Nebuchadrezzar's forces in July 586 after a siege begun about January 587 (2 Kgs 25:1-7). The Temple and much of the city were burned about a month later (2 Kgs 25:8-12). The Davidic Kingdom of Judah ceased to exist.

The nature of the Judean political situation under Babylonia immediately after 586 remains uncertain. Biblical texts report that GEDALIAH and the pro-Babylonian faction, of which the prophet Jeremiah was a primary spokesperson, were placed in charge of affairs (2 Kgs 25:22; Jer 40:7). No text stipulates the office to which Gedaliah was appointed. Possibly, the Babylonians experimented for a time with a non-Davidic Judean monarch with Mizpah as the royal seat (cf. Jer 41:8-10).

See also DAVID; ISRAEL.

Bibliography. J. Bright, *A History of Israel*; J. H. Hayes and P. K. Hooker, *A New Chronology for the Kings of Israel and Judah*; J. M. Miller and J. H. Hayes, *A History of Ancient Israel and Judah*; M. Noth, *The History of Israel*; J. A. Soggin, *A History of Israel*.
                                                                          —JOHN H. HAYES

Kingship   [MDB 490-91]

•**Kingship.** The concepts of God and humanity, and the relationship between them, are affected by the biblical view of kingship. In the OT this takes the form of praising Yahweh as king and defining his relationship with the human king of Israel. The idealized human king eventually led to the messianic hope. In the NT, the OT categories of kingship are understood in terms of Jesus' messiahship and in the concept of the Kingdom of God.

God is described as king in several ways in the OT. He is most commonly seen as king of Israel. There is some disagreement over how early in its history Israel came to think of God as king, but it is generally agreed that its formulation was very old, going to a time when Israel did not claim that there were no other gods but Yahweh, but only that there were no others for Israel (Exod 20:1-3). In time this view expanded until Yahweh was considered also to be the king of the whole world (Jer 10:7; Zech 14:9). In the Psalms we find God presented as king over the gods (95:3; 103:19-22); this may reflect the old henotheistic view in which Yahweh was one god among many. His original kingship over Israel was rooted in his special relationship with her, grounded in his saving acts in the liberation from slavery in Egypt and in the establishment of the covenant on Mount Sinai (Exod 19:6; Deut 33:5).

Because God was the original king of Israel, the introduction of human kings was not easy. Judges presents a picture of a disorganized people unable to make any real headway against the enemies who populated their land, largely because there was no king (19:1; 21:55). Israel was united not by any sort of political organization but by acceptance of a COVENANT with Yahweh. The tribes were guided by village elders in day-to-day affairs (Judg 11:5) and by leaders especially empowered by the spirit of God during military crises (Judg 3:10). No king was needed because Yahweh reigned over Israel (Judg 8:22-23). Charismatic deliverers provided leadership during emergencies, which was a sufficient arrangement for sporadic fighting against the Canaanites and other groups but was inadequate to meet the threat from the powerful PHILISTINES. This led to the introduction of a human king over Israel (ca. 1000 BCE).

The Books of Samuel present two views of the development of the kingship. One sees the establishment of the monarchy as a gift of God (1 Sam 9:16). According to this interpretation the king will rule "the people of Yahweh" and save them from their enemies (1 Sam 10:1). The other view, however, treats the monarchy as developing out of the desire of the people to be like the other nations

(1 Sam 7:13-14; 8:19-20). According to this view, the monarchy was a blasphemous rejection of God's kingship (1 Sam 8:7) and a source of hardship for the nation (1 Sam 7:11-18). This bipolar evaluation of kingship continued throughout Israel's history: on the one hand the monarchy provided the glories of David (2 Sam 7:8–9), while on the other the abominable apostasy of Manasseh was also its product (2 Kgs 21). The successes were more than matched by the failures. Every king of the Northern Kingdom was found wanting, in the judgment of the OT accounts.

Kings provided security by giving dependable leadership and conducting a consistent foreign policy. They led the armies when military action was necessary. The monarch was responsible for maintaining domestic justice and occasionally for adjudicating difficult legal cases (2 Sam 14:47; Ps 101). He had cultic responsibilities as well, officiating at sacrifices, supplications and blessings on important occasions (2 Kgs 3:4; 19:14-19; 2 Sam 6:18). The king could discipline the priests (1 Kgs 2:26-27) and even reform the cult when necessary (2 Kgs 18:1-8): the TEMPLE itself was built through royal sponsorship (1 Kgs 5:1-6). The health and welfare of the nation was considered to be bound up with the reign of the monarch (Ps 72). The loss of the monarchy in the Exile was a devastating blow (Lam 4:20).

Saul, the first king, was more like the charismatic deliverers than like the later kings (1 Sam 11:6-8; 22:6-8). His successor David set the standard for kingship. His personality and actions left a permanent mark on the way Israel viewed its kings. He was the unifier, the poet, the conqueror of Jerusalem. God made a covenant with him to establish his throne and his seed forever (2 Sam 7:8-16). He and the kings after him were to be sons of God (2 Sam 7:14). Passages celebrating the king as the firstborn (Ps 89:27) begotten son of God (Ps 2:7), who sits at his right hand (Ps 110:1), may be misinterpreted as evidence of divine kingship in Israel. Divine kingship was accepted in some of the ancient Near East. The Egyptian Pharaoh was worshipped as the incarnation of a god. In Babylon the king became divine through adoption, but he was not worshiped, although his divine mediation with the gods of the pantheon was crucial to the well-being of both people and land. Certainly Israel's king enjoyed a special relationship with God as the divine instrument in governing Israel; the Lord's anointed should not be killed (1 Sam 26:9) or cursed (Prov 24:21-22). He was nonetheless a man, under God's judgment (Deut 17:14-20), and whatever blessings his reign brought were from God (Ps 132:11-18). Although not a god, he was the vehicle for God's ruling of his people. This high view of kingship under God inevitably led to disappointment in the reigning kings. None was perfect, and so the ideal king always remained as a hope for the future. Aided by the fall of the monarchy, the inherent hope related to kingship became messianic hope, the belief that an ideal son of David would come to lead his people into a time of peace and justice (Isa 11:1-9; Ezek 34:24; Hos 3:5).

The OT view of kingship is understood in the NT: God is the true king whose kingdom is in the hands of his Son (John 1:49). Jesus Christ is both the charismatic, spirit-filled leader and the anointed king, proclaiming the kingdom of God to all who will hear and accept it. The justice and peace of the idealized kingdom in the OT (Isa 11:6-9; Mic 4:1-4) is actualized in the KINGDOM OF GOD (Luke 4:18-20). Like the ideal kingdom of the OT, the sovereignty of God is both present in the power of Christ (Matt 12:28) and in those who have faith (Rom 4:1-5) and at the same time future in its fulfillment on earth (Matt 24:14).

See also KINGSOM OF GOD; JOTHAM'S FABLE; MESSIAH/MESSIANISM.

Bibliography. W. Eichrodt, Theology of the Old Testament; H. Frankfort, Kingship and the Gods; J. D. Levenson, Sinai and Zion; S. Mowinckel, He That Cometh; G. von Rad, Old Testament Theology.

—CAROL STUART GRIZZARD and MARVIN E. TATE

Succession Narrative   [MDB 859]

•Succession Narrative (aka the "Court History of David"). The portion of the so-called "Former Prophets" included in 2 Sam 9–20 and 1 Kgs 1–2 is now generally identified as the "Succession Narrative." Its separate existence was first suggested and worked out in detail by Leonhard Rost in 1926. The material contained in it deals with the struggles in Israel for the right to succeed David upon the throne of the Hebrew Kingdom. This section appears to be quite distinctive from the rest of 1 and 2 Samuel, lacking the dual accounts which appeared so regularly there. Further, instead of the occasional disconnections and the jumpiness of the earlier material, this unit appears to be unified by a common theme, as well as character-ized by a common style and vocabulary. It also has quite consistent characteriza-tions of the major personalities involved in its narrative.

Inserted right in the midst of this material is a miscellaneous collection dealing with a number of various subjects (2 Sam 21–24). The explanation offered for this arrangement is quite simple. Most commenatators agree that the original books of 1 and 2 Samuel and 1 and 2 Kings were all one work. They were apparently separated from each other for the very practical reason that a scroll containing such a lengthy work was simply too large to handle. The divisions were made to keep the scrolls to manageable lengths. At the time of the division of Samuel from Kings, the Succession Narrative was simply separated. According to this theory, sometime later the miscellaneous stories of 2 Sam 21–24 were added to the end of Samuel, due to the fact that they dealt with the last days of David.

The Succession Narrative itself deals with the events involved in the struggle among those who wished to succeed David upon the throne of Israel. The author appears to have been an eyewitness to those events. His work is considered to be the greatest history writing Israel ever produced. It is also among the earliest history writing found anywhere in the world. If this evaluation is correct, this work becomes even more significant simply in terms of its achievement. However, in modern terms, the narrative is not pure history, for it has a great deal of theological insight and evaluation. The author is a master storyteller and a good preacher. His narrative has entranced readers from his time until ours.

In the Succession Narrative, all of the major and most memorable events of DAVID's reign are found. Both David's greatness and his humanity are portrayed with vividness. No excuse is made for his weakness and his sin. Neither is any attempt made to gloss over the failings and the frailties of the king. Within the narrative are described David's kindness to MEPHIBOSHETH, JONATHAN's son (9), his conflicts with the Ammonites (10), and his sin with Bathsheba and its consequences (11–12). Following this, the struggle among David's children begins. Here is AMNON's rape of TAMAR, ABSALOM's murder of Amnon, and Absalom's subsequent flight and exile (13). This is followed by the intrigue of JOAB leading to David's reluctant permission to allow Absalom's return to Jerusalem. Sadly, this led ultimately to Absalom's rebellion and finally to his death (14–18). In the aftermath, David was faced by other struggles among those around him who sought to take the throne from him (19–20).

The Succession Narrative concludes with the final struggle between David's two sons, Solomon and ADONIJAH (1 Kgs 1–2). The end result of this was the succession of Solomon to the throne, the execution of Adonijah and Joab, and the banishment of ABIATHAR the priest from Jerusalem to ANATHOTH. By the conclusion of the narrative, the throne was firmly established in the hands of Solomon, with all major rivals having been eliminated.

Bibliography. Walter Harrelson, *Interpreting the Old Testament*.

—ROBERT L. CATE

Joshua [MCB 227-41]

John C. H. Laughlin

Introduction

Some years ago the late G. Ernest Wright observed: "The gap between a popular understanding of the Book of Joshua and a [critical] understanding is so wide that one may well wonder whether it can ever be eliminated or even narrowed" (n.d.). In the years since he wrote this, the gap has only widened.

On the surface the Book of Joshua seems to recount in a straightforward manner how ISRAEL, under the leadership of JOSHUA, entered the land of CANAAN from the TRANSJORDAN, opposite JERICHO, and within a short period of time conquered the entire country, eliminating all of its inhabitants. Following this initial success, Joshua divided the land among the twelve tribes, and following a ceremony at SHECHEM, where "Israel" pledged its fealty to Yahweh, the tribes dispersed to occupy their respective allotments. Beneath this simple story line, however, lies an array of literary, historical, theological, and archaeological complexities.

Authorship

The question of the authorship of Joshua is complex and involves more than just this book. Following the pioneering work of Martin Noth, it is now commonplace among most OT scholars to assign Joshua to a larger complex of writings known collectively as the Deuteronomic or Deuteronomistic History of Israel (DH). These books, in addition to Joshua, include Judges, most of 1 and 2 Samuel, and 1 and 2 Kings. This collection is called "Deuteronomic" because the theological norm presupposed by their author(s) is thought primarily to have come from the traditions now contained in the Book of Deuteronomy. It is thus incumbent upon anyone wishing to understand Joshua to the fullest extent possible to become informed about Deuteronomic methodology (see esp. Polzin 1980; Weinfeld 1972). It should also be noted that some scholars identify two Deuteronomic editions of the book: the first completed during the time of JOSIAH (late seventh century BCE), and the second following the beginning of the EXILE (598 BCE).

In the following commentary, I will refer to the final author of Joshua simply as the Deuteronomic Redactor (DtR). Whether or not this term is thought to refer to a single individual or a school of thought representing more than one person is immaterial to this study.

Life Setting and Date

If Joshua stands at the beginning of a theological history that ends with the last king of JUDAH in captivity (2 Kgs 25:29-30), then the situation that called forth this work, as well as the other books in the "history," is the Babylonian Exile (598–539 BCE). However, a distinction must be made between the final form of the book as we now have it and the original traditions, whether written or oral, from which the book is composed. Many of these traditions may be quite old and belong to Israel's historical memory. However, whatever might have been the original intent of these older traditions has now been completely superseded by the theological concerns of the DtR. In fact, it is questionable whether or not these traditions had any theological meaning before their adaptation by the final author. Thus, it will be assumed throughout this brief commentary that the original audience for whom Joshua was written was the remnant of the Israelite community in exile who had lost land and most likely hope. Ultimately, Joshua is for people in EXILE (cf. Butler 1983, xxiii–xxvii).

Literary Forms and Major Themes

The literary forms making up this book are very complex and varied. They include such things as speeches, etiologies (i.e., stories or sayings that explain and account for some custom, name, or idea), historicized cultic celebrations or liturgical stories, tribal boundary descriptions, and city lists.

One of the most innovative approaches to the literary form of this book in recent years has been the structuralist analysis of Robert Polzin (1980). He has highlighted one of the major literary features of the book, the use of speeches by various characters, particularly those by God and Joshua ("reported speeches"), and has attempted to show their relationship to the direct narration of the DtR himself ("reporting speech"). By so doing Polzin demonstrates how various "voices" can be heard on the playing surface of the book. Beneath this surface, however, he hears the two major voices of the book: the voice of "authoritarian dogmatism" that claims that all of God's promises to MOSES were fulfilled by the "conquest" of Canaan by Joshua; and the voice of "critical traditionalism" (the DtR himself) that insists that this fulfillment was very ambiguous and that Mosaic laws required constant reinterpretation, modification, and application.

Since it will be seen that little in the Book of Joshua can be called "historical reality" as moderns understand that expression, Polzin's analysis has been found particularly fruitful for dealing with the theological value of Joshua. In what follows, an attempt will be made to combine some of Polzin's insights with recent historical and archaeological data to demonstrate, it is hoped, that ultimately the Book of Joshua ia a kind of "novella." It is a short story written to impress upon its intended readers or listeners that, contrary to whatever they might have believed up to their present moment, Israel's existence in the land of Canaan had always been ambiguous and tenuous—made possible only by God's undeserved acts of grace and a creative and dynamic application of the laws of Moses. Only under such circumstances has God's people ever existed, then or now.

It is customary to divide the book into three major, but unequal, sections: chaps. 1–12, which treat the theme of conquest; chaps. 13–19, which describe the division of the land among the tribes; chaps. 20–24, which include several stories with which the book closes.

A Note on the Text

There are many textual variations in this book raising numerous questions concerning the history of the text. A comparison of the Hebrew (MT) with the Greek (LXX) traditions will quickly bear this out. This brief treatment will be based primarily on the MT as published in *Biblia Hebraica Stuttgartensia*. For major textual questions, the reader must refer to full-length commentaries.

For Further Study

In the *Mercer Dictionary of the Bible*: AMPHICTYONY/CONFEDERACY; ARCHAEOLOGY; CIRCUMCISION; CONQUEST OF CANAAN; COVENANT; DEUTERONOMIST/DEUTERONOMISTIC HISTORY; HOLY WAR; JOSHUA; JOSHUA, BOOK OF; LEVI/LEVITES; MOSES; PALESTINE, GEOGRAPHY OF; RED SEA/REED SEA; TENT OF MEETING; WOMEN IN THE OT.

In other sources: R. G. Boling, *Joshua*, AncB; J. Bright, "Joshua," IB; T. C. Butler, *Joshua*, WBC; E. M. Good, "Joshua," IDB; L. J. Greenspoon, *Textual Studies in the Book of Joshua*; M. Noth, *Das Buch Josua*; R. Polzin, *Moses and the Deuteronomist*; J. A. Soggin, *Joshua*, OTL; M. Weinfeld, *Deuteronomy and the Deuteronomic School*.

Commentary

An Outline

Introduction to the Conquest of Canaan, 1:1-18

The Commissioning of Joshua by Yahweh, 1:1-9

As mentioned in the Introduction, Polzin has shown that one of the major characteristics of the Book of Joshua is its usage of speeches, both reported and reporting (1980, 73ff.). Thus the book begins by use of a reported speech of God by which the leadership of the nation is passed from MOSES to JOSHUA (cf. Deut 31:7-8). While a royal background (Porter 1970, 102–32) has been suggested for the formula used here, these opening verses are thoroughly Deuteronomic.

1:3-4. The limits of the land. The geographical boundaries described in v. 4 include the desert to the south and east (*wilderness*), most of what was, and is, Syria to the northeast, and the Mediterranean (*the Great Sea*) to the west (*this Lebanon* is lacking in LXX). Historically, the only time Israel controlled such a large piece of real estate was during the time of David and Solomon (cf. 2 Sam 8:3-12). Whether the DtR has specifically the ancient extent of David's empire in mind or some ideal frontier, as suggested by some, is unclear. What is clear is the redactor's belief that the divine promise made to Moses (Deut 11:24) cannot be thwarted, not even by exile.

1:7-8. The thematic program of the DtR. The basic theme of the entire DH is expressed in these two verses. Israel was able to occupy the land and enjoy Yahweh's blessings when the people lived *in accordance with all the law that my servant Moses commanded you* (v. 7). The reference to *the book of the law* (v. 8) is believed by most to refer to the legal material in the Book of Deuteronomy, especially chaps. 12–26 (cf. Deut 31:9). However, as the DtR will make clear in the story he is about to tell, living "according to all the law" is no simple task but requires constant reinterpretation and adaptation.

The Commissioning of the People by Joshua, 1:10-18

Just as Joshua was prepared in a speech by Yahweh to possess the land, now the people are prepared in a speech by Joshua.

1:12-15. The Transjordanian tribes. At first reading, it seems curious that the only tribes mentioned by name here are those who historically had lived in the TRANSJORDAN and who had played an insignificant role in Israel's history. However, by referring to them directly, the DtR anticipates a problem that will require further treatment in the story (chap. 22), namely, the status of those tribes who were *of* Israel but not *in* Israel (Polzin, 134ff.).

1:16-18. Joshua's authority legitimated. The transfer of Moses' authority to Joshua is completed when the people respond. His authority will be valid only if *the LORD your God [is] with you* (v. 17). With the authority of the Davidic king destroyed by exile, the DtR reverts to a charismatic model of kingly authority (cf. Deut 17:14-17).

Preparation for the Conquest of Canaan, 2:1–5:15

Rahab and the Jericho Spies, 2:1-24

With this story of the spies sent out by Joshua the DtR begins his account of how Israel came to occupy the land of CANAAN. The literary and historical questions raised by this story are legion. Recent archaeological discoveries have seriously undermined the historicity of Israel's exploits described here (see below). What impact this undermining should or should not have on how one hears and responds to the DtR's theological themes must be left up to the individual.

Originally the story in chap. 2 may have had little to do with the city of JERICHO (cf. Boling 1982, 144). In v. 1 the spies are commanded to *Go, view the land*; and only *the land* is mentioned when they return (v. 24). The phrase *especially Jericho* (v. 1) may have been added to tie this story to that in chap. 6.

None of these historical-critical conclusions, however, explains why the DtR told this story in the first place. The answer, according to Polzin, is in the narrator's concern to show how Mosaic law was interpreted and applied in Israel's life, specifically in this case, the rules of HOLY WAR (Polzin 1980, 86ff.).

2:1-24. Rahab and the rules of holy war. According to the rules governing holy war, Israel was to "save alive nothing that breathes" (Deut 20:16 RSV). In the story of RAHAB, however, the spies, *not* God, agreed to spare her and her family for the help she gave them, ostensibly violating the ban. In chap. 7, on the other hand, ACHAN and his family are put to death for committing the same offense, i.e., violating the ban. How is one to understand what is going on here? According to Polzin, this story

> raises two hermeneutic questions for the Israelites concerning the word of God. First, how does one interpret and apply God's command to put complete trust in him while taking over the land? . . . Second, how does one interpret the Mosaic rules for holy war? (1980, 86–87)

Polzin argues that what we see here, then, is the DtR's concern "to counter an authoritarian dogmatism" by telling stories that illustrate both the conditional (Rahab) and the unconditional (Achan) aspects of the Sinai/Horeb COVENANT (1980, 87). Thus, in the immediate story, Israel is allowed to occupy a land that it does not deserve (Deut 9:4-5), while Rahab and her family are spared a death that they do deserve (at least according to the narrator's perspective!). The story of Rahab can be interpreted as a variation of the DtR's larger themes of the "justice and mercy of God vis-a-vis Israel" (1980, 88).

That a HARLOT was chosen to be the heroine of this story seems no accident. Contrary to Soggin's conclusion (1970, 39), Rahab's profession is central to the story for several reasons. First, she is said to live in the city wall (v. 15), which reflects her status as a prostitute, that is, she is portrayed as living literally on the fringes of her own society (Fewell 1992, 66). Secondly, as is commonly pointed out, by virtue of her profession, neighbors would not be made unduly suspicious by the presence of men in her house, and, of course, the location of her house made it easy to dispatch the spies. But most importantly, as a prostitute, Rahab throws into bold relief the issue of "insider" vs. "outsider" that dominates the DtR's concern. In this regard, Polzin makes an interesting suggestion when he concludes that the story of Rahab is "really the story of Israel told from the point of view of a non-Israelite" (1980, 88).

The Jordan and Gilgal Traditions, 3:1–5:15

The traditions recounted here of the crossing of the JORDAN RIVER and the activity associated with GILGAL are filled with textual and literary difficulties that have led to various proposed historical reconstructions (cf. Soggin 1970, 47–67; Boling 1982, 156–58; de Vaux 1978, 598–603).). Many years ago H.-J. Kraus suggested that this complex of traditions make up a "cultic legend" (1951, 152–65). Others have called these stories a "liturgical narrative (Polzin 1980, 92) and a "sacred drama" (Soggin, 54). Whatever term one chooses to categorize this section in Joshua, it seems highly likely that as it now stands it represents a historicizing of ritual acts involving the themes of Passover and conquest. Originally this ritual reenactment may have involved only the tribe of BENJAMIN, in whose territory Gilgal was located.

By juxtaposing the themes of the crossing of the Jordan with PASSOVER (4:10) the tradition of the Exodus from Egypt has been connected with that of the entry into the land. Whether historically there was such a connection is a moot point among scholars (cf. Halpern 1983, 81–94; 1992, 89–113). This connection with Passover is strengthened by the use of the verb '*br* (to pass, passover) eight times in chap. 3 alone (vv. 1, 4, 6, 11, 14, 16).

In a very detailed literary analysis, Polzin (1980, 91–110) argues that this ritual drama is used by the biblical narrator to illustrate once again the fulfillment of God's word. Nevertheless, the story told here seems more ideal than real.

3:1-17. Crossing the Jordan. The analogies here of Moses to Joshua (v. 7), and the Reed Sea to the Jordan River (vv. 14-16) are obvious. Just as God was with Moses at the Reed Sea, now he is with Joshua, and the Jordan becomes dry land just as the sea had done (Exod 14:21c). When the literary structure of this story is appreciated, questions of its historicity become superfluous. One of the major differences, however, between the story told here and that in Exodus is the presence of the Ark of the Covenant in the former. The ARK (always a different word in Hebrew from the ark of Noah) seems originally to have been associated with war (cf. Num 10:35). Its fortunes in Israel prior to the monarchy are not clear but it was the symbol par excellence of Yahweh's presence among his people (see Boling 1982, 159; Soggin 1970, 55–56; Bailey 1990, 63).

4:1-5:1. Gilgal and the circle of stones. The importance of GILGAL in premonarchic Israel has long been noted (Miller 1990, 332), but the traditions preserved about this site in Joshua have proven to be extremely difficult to interpret. Soggin believes that the textual confusion here over the two traditions of the twelve stones makes a "more thorough study impossible" (1970, 64). Polzin's literary solution, namely that the tradition of Joshua's setting *up the twelve stones in the middle of the Jordan* (v. 9) is a DtR device to enhance the "interpretive role of Joshua" with regard to God's word seems forced (1980, 109). Furthermore, how stones set up in the middle of a river could still be seen *to this day* (v. 9) is not clear. Whatever the historical or literary solutions to these questions may be, the message to the exiles seems obvious: these stones were to be a memorial to the people of Israel forever (v. 4). Thus God's promises could not be destroyed by time nor by exile.

This episode ends with the DtR reporting the response of the inhabitants of Canaan (5:1). Polzin reminds us that as an "omniscient observer," the DtR frequently penetrates "the psychological consciousness of all his characters" (1980, 102).

5:2-15. Circumcision and a commander from Yahweh's army. The origin and meaning of CIRCUMCISION in Israel cannot be discussed here. However, the reason given in 5:4-7 why the circumcision of those born in the wilderness could not have been done prior to the present context seems contrived at best. Perhaps it was intended to link the rite of circumcision with that of Passover, which immediately follows in this story (cf. Exod 12:48). Note that there is no hint here that the rite included infants as it ultimately would (the Priestly tradition in Gen 17 is dated by many scholars to the EXILE or later). The etymological ETIOLOGY in v. 9 for *Gilgal* is forced. But the practice of circumcision and its symbolic meaning of belonging to the family of Abraham and thus heirs to the promises God had made him, would have found receptive ears among the exiles.

The reference to rolling away the *disgrace of Egypt* (v. 9) has also elicited a variety of responses. Perhaps the most helpful is Polzin's suggestion that Josh 5:9 is the DtR's response to Deut 9:20 (1980, 111).

5:13-15. A visit from a commander of Yahweh's army. The ambiguous nature of this pericope has given rise to many interpretations. The most common suggestion is that something has fallen out of the text, because the passage seems to anticipate some sort of a command to Joshua after v. 15 (cf. Exod 3:5ff.). However, seen in the over-all context of the DtR's purpose, the ambiguity of this passage may be deliberate. God's relationship to Israel is not automatic. Just as there is a struggle to occupy the land in the Book of Joshua, there is also a struggle to understand and apply God's word (cf. Polzin 1980, 111–13).

The Conquest of Canaan, 6:1–12:24

Archaeology and the Conquest Traditions

A literal reading of the traditions contained in these chapters would force the conclusion that roughly forty years after the people left Egypt with Moses, their descendants, under the command of Joshua, marched into the land of Canaan from the desert and annihilated all of its inhabitants, beginning with the miraculous destruction of JERICHO.

This literal reading of the story was rejected many years ago for historical-critical reasons (cf. Alt 1967, 173–221). Now recent archaeological discoveries have confirmed this judgment. The issues involved here were succinctly focused by the late P. de Vaux several years ago: "The problem raised by the settlement of the Israelites in Canaan and the growth of the system of the twelve tribes is the most difficult problem in the whole history of Israel" (1978, 475; cf. Mazar 1990, 281).

There are too many issues with which to deal adequately here. The interested reader is encouraged to pursue these questions through the references given here and in the bibliographies contained in them.

Beginning in the 1920s and 1930s, two totally opposed scholarly theories were suggested to explain Israel's settlement in the land of Canaan. The most popular—and most influential in America—was the view advocated by William Foxwell Albright, who for many years taught at The Johns Hopkins University. Using the archaeological discoveries that were being made at such great Late Bronze Age Canaanite tells (a TELL is an earthen mound that frequently contains the remains of early settlements) as Tell Beit Mirsim—Albright identified it, probably erroneously, with Debir—Lachish and Bethel, Albright accepted the basic historical reliability of the opening chapters of Joshua, and created the so-called "military" model for the way in which Israel acquired the land of Canaan (1939, 11–23). Of the three basic theories discussed here, Albright's is the least satisfactory and is simply no longer viable in light of present literary, historical and archaeological knowledge.

While Albright and his students were supporting the military model, Albrecht Alt, in Germany, was approaching the problem from a different perspective altogether. Using the tools of form and traditio-historical criticism, he and his students concluded that the stories of the conquest in Joshua were for the most part etiological legends with little or no historical value (see esp. Alt 1967, 173ff.; Noth, 1958). They concluded that "Israel" emerged on the land of Canaan through the "peaceful infiltration" of pastoral groups over a long period of time. One of the major strengths of this theory is its recognition that the Israelite settlement was a long, complicated and multifaceted process. But Alt's insistence on the "nomadic" origin of these peoples has brought the theory a great deal of criticism, especially from the advocates of the third model or theory.

In 1962, George Mendenhall argued that the origin of Israel was due neither to a pan-Israelite invasion under Joshua nor to a peaceful migration of pastoral NO-MADs, but to an internal revolt of indigenous Canaanites against their overlords (1962, 66–87). This theory has been expanded by Norman Gottwald (1970, 191–233) and has gained some acceptance, in part at least, by others. Based upon sophisticated social theories, this "sociological" model has raised many pertinent issues relevant to ancient Israel's emergence. However, it too has been severely criticized both for its perceived methodological flaws and its failure to explain adequately the material culture now known to have existed in Canaan during the period under investigation (for descriptions and critiques of all of the above theories see: Dever 1990, 37–56; 1992, 27–85; Finkelstein 1988, 295–314; Halpern 1983, 47–63).

The issue at point here is the most adequate explanation for the material culture dating to Iron Age I (roughly 1200–1000 BCE) that has recently come to light through archaeological discoveries in the HILL COUNTRY of Palestine (for the most up-to-date synthesis of the archaeological data see esp. Finkelstein 1988). The data include pottery forms, architectural remains (esp. the so-called "pillared buildings" and "four-room" houses), layout of sites (i.e., site plans), silos and water cisterns; they also include hundreds of Iron I sites now known through surveys to have existed during this period but that have not yet been excavated (Finkelstein 1988, 15–234). Archaeologists are not all agreed on where the people came from who built and lived in these towns and villages. Some believe they were displaced Canaanites who settled in the sparsely inhabited regions of the central hills during and following the breakup of the Late Bronze Age (Dever 1990, 37–84; 1992, 27–56; Fritz 1987, 84–100), while others have argued that the newcomers were pastoralists who were in the process of being "resedentarized" (Finkelstein 1988, 336–51; see also Finkelstein's response to Dever and Dever's response to Finkelstein in Dever 1992, 63–69; 79–82).

Many questions still remain and all conclusions are tentative and mostly likely will need modification, if not total revision, as more information is forthcoming. Nevertheless, taking into consideration all of the evidence that is currently available, especially the archaeological data, the following conclusions by Dever seem reasonable:

> The literal biblical story of an Exodus from Egypt, and a subsequent pan-Israelite conquest of Canaan, can no longer be salvaged, for all the wishful thinking in the world (1992, 84);

and:

> the inescapable conclusion . . . is that the Israelite settlement in Canaan was part of the larger transition from the Late Bronze to the Iron Age. It was a gradual, exceedingly complex process, involving social, economic, and political—as well as religious—change, with many regional variations (1990, 79).

The full implications of this emerging new synthesis for understanding the origin of the Israelite religion and its worship of the God, Yahweh, has yet to be clarified (for one effort, see McCarter, Jr. 1992, 119–36). Closer to home are the implications of this "archaeological detour" for the story told in Joshua 6:1–12:24.

Jericho and Ai, 6:1–8:29

In light of the preceding archaeological discussion, the historical problem raised by the conquest stories of JERICHO and AI can be summed up very succinctly: neither of these sites was occupied at the end of the Late Bronze Age. In fact, Ai was not occupied for over a thousand years, from its destruction in the Early Bronze Age until a small village was founded on the site in Iron Age I (Callaway 1976, 18–30). Whatever may have been the original nucleus and purpose of these stories in Joshua, the form in which we now have them appears to be a literary construct created by the DtR to serve his own theological agenda. That agenda seems to be the meaning and application of the rule of *h̠erem* or the ban within the context of HOLY WAR (Deut 20:16; see Polzin 1980, 113ff.).

6:1-21. The march around Jericho. The secondary literature on this well-known story is vast, but suffice it to say that while the archaeological evidence for this ancient city is ambiguous (see Kenyon, 1957), it is abundantly clear that no Late Bronze Age city of any size existed during the time most scholars would date the first appearance of the "Israelites." All rationalizations to explain this absence (e.g., rain or wind erosion, the questioning of the identification of Tel es-Sultan as Jericho, placing the event during the Middle Bronze Age) are examples of Dever's "wishful thinking." Furthermore, close literary analysis reveals that the story as we have it seems to be composed of twodifferent traditions altogether. One version, using the popular motif of a ruse (Rahab), implies that the city was taken by normal military siege procedures. This story is picked up in 6:2, 17, 22-25 (see Coogan 1990, 19ff.) After capturing the city, Rahab and her family were spared, as agreed to, while all the other citizens, along with the city itself, were burned (6:24). It should also be noted that the mention of Jericho in Joshua 24:11 presupposes that the city was taken by military means.

The story of the miraculous fall of the city's walls would then have been added at some point in the usage of this tradition by later Israelites celebrating the "conquest." Coogan points out that there is no biblical reference to this tumbling wall story outside its present location, indicating that the story was "a local tradition incorporated only at a fairly late date into the biblical recital" (1990, 21).

6:24. The house of the Lord. This reference to *the house of the LORD* (i.e., the Temple) is obviously anachronistic and refers to the practice of bringing the booty of holy war for dedication to the God. What became a later practice in Israel is simply assumed here.

6:25-27. Joshua's curse on Jericho. This curse by *Joshua* seems to be a prophecy after the fact ("prophecy *ex eventu*") based upon the story in 1 Kgs 16:34. Curiously, in the Kings story we are told that someone ("Hiel of Bethel") other than the king built Jericho. Jericho lay in ruins from the fourteenth to the tenth-ninth centuries BCE. The story in Kings takes place during the reign of AHAB, an Israelite king during the ninth century. The practice of burying one's children beneath the foundation of a city was obviously viewed as an abomination by the DtR.

7:1-8:29. The story of Ai (et-Tell). Just as the story of Jericho illustrates how the rules of holy war could be ignored to spare those under the ban (Rahab and her family), the story of Ai illustrates just how complex and dynamic the interpretation and application of these rules could be. First, we are told that ACHAN and his family were destroyed for breaking the rules (7:1, 16-26). Then we are told (8:2, 27) that the rest of the Israelites were granted permission by God to do the exact same thing Achan had done! Polzin's observation is worth quoting:

> There seems to be no doubt at all that the narrative (the Ai episode) is intent upon outlining some of the possible hermeneutic situations that could arise in the continued understanding, interpretation, and application of divine commands (1980, 114–15).

8:28. A heap of ruins. The reference to *a heap of ruins* (i.e., "tell") is probably the source of the story told here, whatever the real etymology of the name "Ai" may be.

The Altar on Mount Ebal, 8:30-35

This story follows 9:2 in LXX and seems to interrupt the flow of the narrative, which continues in 9:3 in MT. Furthermore, the base of operations at this point in the story is GILGAL, not SHECHEM (cf. 9:6;10:15,43). The argument that has erupted over the claim that the remains of this altar have actually been found only serves to illustrate the extreme difficulty of identifying excavated data with biblical texts (see Zertal 1985, 26–43; Kempinski 1986, 42–49; Rainey 1986, 66; Dever 1992, 32–34, 76–78, 84–85). The "most important feature of this narrative" (Polzin 1980, 115) is the way Joshua interprets and applies the law of Moses in his new situation (cf. Deut 11:29; 27:1-26).

The Ruse of the Gibeonites, 9:1-27

Again the DtR's preoccupation with the interpretation of the Mosaic law is clearly in view here. According to Deut 20:10-18, Israel could offer peace to a city *not* in Canaan, but all the inhabitants of Canaanite cities were to be put to death. The fact that Israel was deceived by a ruse (just as they had deceived Jericho [the Rahab episode] and Ai [8:3-8!]) does not allow them to violate their oath to spare the Gibeonites (v. 19). The situation under which GIBEON is allowed to live is analogous to Israel's: Gibeon should have been devoted to the ban, but was spared by a "covenant" made with Joshua (v. 15). ISRAEL should also have been destroyed for its unrighteousness and stubborn heart, but was spared because of a COVENANT made by God with its ancestors (Deut 9:1-29). Gibeon and Israel, then, both exist, not because they deserve to but because of sworn covenants. To people in exile the meaning of this story would be very clear: because of God's promises to their ancestors they, undeserving as they might be, once more had the possibility of becoming his people in the reoccupation of the land.

The long identification of Gibeon with the site of el-Jib, located a few miles southwest of Ai, need not be disputed. However, that Gibeon does not seem to have existed in the Late Bronze Age is another indication of the literary construct of the Book of Joshua.

The Southern Campaign, 10:1-43

There are really three episodes or stories in this chapter that have been combined: the attack against Gibeon and its miraculous deliverance (vv. 1-15); the *five kings* in the *cave of Makkedah* (vv. 16-27); and the attacks against certain cities in the southern part of CANAAN (vv. 28-43). The chapter is also filled with textual difficulties, the MT being often at variance with LXX and other versions.

10:1-15. The attack against Gibeon. This story has some connection to chap. 9, especially the first three verses. There we are told that the kings of Canaan began to unite, having heard of Israel's initial military success. Now, with Gibeon in Israel's hand (either by ruse, MT, or simply by going over to Israel's side, LXX), and because it was a *large city* (v. 2), the kings unite at the initiative of *Adoni-zedek of Jerusalem* (v. 1; in the LXX this king is called "Adoni-bezek," as he is in Judg 1:5; are they the same person?). However, originally there must have been six kings, not five (cf. Soggin 1970, 130). *Debir*, in v. 3 is the name of a city (cf. vv. 38-39), not a person, and is not mentioned again in the accounts of the five unnamed kings (vv. 5, 16, 17, 23). Making Debir a city in v. 3 may represent a later attempt to harmonize the story with the tradition of five kings.

Whatever the solution to the ambiguities in this story, it was told by the DtR to emphasize his belief that Israel's victories were due less to its own military prowess than to God's merciful intervention (v. 11). The quotation from the Book of Jashar (vv. 12-13; cf. 2 Sam 1:18) has evoked numerous and, for the most part, meaning-less attempts at rational explanation. In the first place, in context, Joshua's admonition to the sun and moon comes *after* the battle had already been won (v. 11). Thus it was a gross literalizing of this poetic verse by the biblical author (v. 13d), interpreting it to mean that the amount of daylight available for fighting was extended. In the second place, the quotation may originally have had to do with an entirely different event then the one recorded here (Soggin 1970, 122). Whatever the case may be, the story now serves the theology of the DtR: Israel succeeded only because of an act of HOLY WAR; it was God's victory, not Israel's.

10:16-27. The cave of Makkedah. The fleeing kings, no longer named, are captured in the cave, humiliated (v. 24), and killed. This story may have originated to explain a pile of stones *which remain to this very day* (v. 27; cf. v. 18). The precise location of this site in question is unknown, although Khirbet el-Qôm has been suggested (see Dever 1990, 57).

10:28-43. The southern campaign. Whether or not the traditions recorded here preserve any real historical memory is questionable. Older attempts (e.g., Albright) to identify Late Bronze Age destruction layers discovered at some of these sites with the story recorded here are untenable. Furthermore, *Eglon* (if it is Tell el-Hesi) and *Hebron* have revealed no evidence of any such destruction as described here, at least not during the Late Bronze–Iron I periods. The location of *Libnah* is still uncertain, thus its fate during this time is still unknown. The DtR's summary in vv. 40-42 again reflects the holy war construct within which Israel's conquering of the south has been placed. It may be no coincidence that the territory taken in this account closely corresponds to the reinhabited area of the returning exiles in the sixth century BCE.

Hazor and the Northern Campaign, 11:1-15

The excavations of the imposing site of *Hazor*, the largest Canaanite city tell in Israel, have long been used to suggest the historical credibility of the story told here in Joshua. But not only does the archaeological evidence not do this (see Finkelstein 1988, 301), the story in Judg 4–5 contradicts the version reported here. This does not detract from the use of this story by the DtR, however, which is to affirm that Joshua did all that Moses commanded him to do (v. 15). Still, as Polzin observes: "There are ways and there are ways to fulfill Moses' commands" (1980, 123). Thus, applying the ban to Hazor and to the cities of those people who joined Hazor in fighting Israel, apparently every living thing was killed (v. 11). But in the other cities, those on mounds (i.e., tells, v. 13), booty was allowed!

Conclusion of the Conquest and a List of Conquered Kings, 11:16–12:24

11:16-20. A summary of the conquest. These verses provide a DtR summary to the completion of the conquest, although v. 18 strikes a note of reality in suggesting that the process was much longer than the preceding stories might imply. That Yahweh acted to *harden their hearts* that they *might receive no mercy* (v. 20; cf. Exod 9:12; 10:1, etc.) is the capstone of a holy war mentality. This summary makes no sense, of course, in light of the current critical synthesis of modern scholarship. The implications of this conclusion for the usage of this tradition to support modern wars by some religious groups cannot be detailed here. But obviously such usage is misguided at best.

11:21-23. The Anakim and another summary statement. The story of the *Anakim* preserves an independent tradition of this legendary race of giants (cf. Num 13:32-33; Deut 1:28; 9:2). It has only a tenuous connection to the preceding stories and contradicts what has already been narrated (according to 10:36-39, Joshua had already destroyed Hebron and Debir). The date of this tradition is uncertain (Soggin thinks it is "ancient," 1970, 141), but in its present form it can date no earlier then the late tenth century since it presupposes the split of the monarchy into Judah and Israel (v. 21). The three cities mentioned where the Anakim could not be destroyed—Gaza, Gath, and Ashdod—were all major Philistine strongholds.

This chapter concludes with another sweeping summary of the totality of Joshua's victories and prepares for the story of the distribution of the land detailed in chaps. 13–19. In its present context this summary reinforces the DtR's purpose to portray Joshua as having done *all that the LORD had spoken to Moses* (v. 23).

12:1-24. The list of conquered kings. This chapter is of unknown origin (see Boling 1982, 322) and consists of a kind of statistical summary of the preceding victories, although some of the cities listed here have not previously been mentioned. The first part (vv. 1-6) summarizes Moses' activities in the Transjordan (cf. Num 21:21-35; Deut 2:24–3:11). *The Sea of Chinneroth* and the Salt Sea (MT) mentioned in v. 3, are references to the Sea of Galilee and the DEAD SEA respectively.

The second part (vv. 8-24) recounts Joshua's victories west of the Jordan. The main importance of this list is that it mentions places conquered not included in any other version. Actually, many of these cities were not occupied and controlled by Israel until the time of David or later. There are also important textual differences in this chapter between the MT and LXX (see full-length commentaries).

The Distribution of the Land, 13:1–19:51

The boundary descriptions and city lists in these chapters have a long, complicated history. Their origin and dates are not clear, and they represent a different version of the conquest from that told in chaps. 1–12. In fact, in the past, many scholars have denied Deuteronomic authorship to these chapters. On the other hand, Polzin sees this section as being used by the DtR as an ironical exposé of the sweeping claims made by the voice of "authoritarian dogmatism" such as is found in 21:43 (Polzin 1980, 126–34). We will refer to the final author of this section simply as the "narrator" without presupposing the author's identity. None of these considerations answers questions concerning the date and function of the lists, which originally were independent of their present context. Zvi Gal, on the basis of his recent archaeological surveys of Lower Galilee, has concluded that the border descriptions and city lists for ZEBULUN, ASHER, NAPHTALI and ISSACHAR could not be any earlier than the tenth century BCE (1992, 98–106). Others would date the entire list no earlier than the time of JOSIAH (late seventh century).

Furthermore, the personage of Joshua may be a secondary addition to these traditions. Not only is he introduced as the *son of Nun* (cf. 1:1), but 13:5 clearly implies that the people allotted the land themselves.

At what stage in the production of the Book of Joshua this material was added is unknown, but all indicators point to a late date. Also, whatever theology is to be found here is almost certainly the work of the final author or compiler (in addition to Polzin's comments, see Butler 1983, 144–208).

Introduction, 13:1-7

In a reported speech of Yahweh, we are told that Joshua is old, and much *land still remains to be possessed* (v. 1). This observation contrasts sharply with the summary of Joshua's efforts in 11:16-20. The speech highlights the major concern of this part of the Book of Joshua: the allotment of land to the nine and one half tribes who lived west of the Jordan. The major point of the author here seems to be that the land was given by God to the *people*, not to kings or the wealthy and powerful. Thus God's will would not be accomplished until he had given Israel *all the land that he swore to give to their ancestors* (21:43). The successful occupation of the land, based upon this reading, was conditional on the peoples' obedience to God's laws (cf. Butler 1983, 207–208).

The territories described here are more ideal then real and in most cases presuppose the kingdom of DAVID and SOLOMON. Soggin believes that vv. 2-6 are an "interpolation on the part of a redactor" (1970, 152).

The Transjordanian Tribes, 13:8-33

The actual history of the tribes who lived east of the Jordan River is complicated. Furthermore, these tribes never played a major role in Israel's history. The literary description given here reflects the sources at the disposal of the narrator, and is filled with difficulties. For details the reader should consult some full-length commentaries.

13:8-14. Introduction to the Transjordanian allotment. In a reporting speech, the narrator introduces the theological rationale guiding his usage of all the allotment traditions. REUBEN, GAD and the *half tribe of Manasseh* (v. 8), all received their land because *Moses, the servant of the LORD* gave it to them (cf. Deut 3:12-22). Only *the tribe of Levi* (v. 14) is excluded since from its ranks came priests who were scattered throughout Israel. The reference to *offerings by fire* probably refers to the proper sacrificial functions performed by these priests (cf. Lev 10:1-3).

13:15-33. The division of the land. The historical value of the description given here is very questionable. In any event, what few sites on the list have been located and excavated (such as HESHBON and DIBON) do not seem to have been occupied and controlled by Israel before the time of David.

The Cisjordanian Tribes: Introduction, 14:1-5

In order to bring the ancient traditions of tribal allotment on line with the "official" story, this general introduction claims that the allotments were made by *the priest Eleazar, and Joshua the son of Nun* (v. 1). However, the fact that Eleazar is listed before Joshua; that Joshua is identified as the *son of Nun* again; and the fact that v. 5 claims the people allotted the land, all raise questions concerning the connection between Joshua and this tradition. But just as the Transjordanian allotments had fulfilled God's commands to Moses, the division of the land of Canaan also fulfilled divine intentions.

Caleb and Judah, 14:6–15:63

14:7-15. Caleb given Hebron. This story of CALEB's receiving HEBRON as a reward for faithfully following Yahweh during the wilderness experience (cf. Num 13:30; 14:24) is strange, given the role of Hebron during the history of Judah. Elsewhere (Judg 1:10) Judah is said to have taken Hebron. Furthermore the chronology of this tradition is also strange. Josh 13:1 implies that a long time had passed since the people of Israel accomplished their initial conquest of the land, but 14:10 suggests it had only been five years. All of this leads to the suspicion that this tradition of Caleb and Hebron was originally independent of the context in which it is now found. In any event, it is Judah, not Caleb who controlled Hebron throughout the history of the monarchy.

15:1-12. The geographical boundary of Judah. The boundaries of Judah given
here are as follows: the southern border (vv. 2-4) ran roughly from the southern end
of the Dead Sea westward to the Mediterranean; the eastern border was *the Dead
Sea* itself (v. 5a); the northern border ran from the northern end of the Dead Sea to
the Mediterranean (vv. 5b-11); and the western boundary *was the Mediterranean* (v.
12). Only in the days of the monarchy did Judah ever come close to controlling the
geographical limits described here, and even then the extreme desert regions and
coastal plains were not a fundamental part of the tribe's territory.

15:13-19. Another tradition about Caleb. We are told again that Caleb was
given Hebron (v. 13) and that it was OTHNIEL, not Joshua (cf. 10:38-39), who took
Debir. But the most interesting part of this tradition is the role of Caleb's daughter,
Achsah (vv. 16-19). Few women figure prominently in the Book of Joshua: *Rahab*
(chaps. 2, 6); the daughters of *Zelophehad* (17:3-6; see below); and *Achsah* (for an
interesting perspective on all of these stories, see Fewell 1992, 63–66). Here the
woman and not her husband seems to realize that in addition to land (the NEGEB is
basically desert) they must have water in order to live. This story is repeated in
Judg 1:12-15, though there it occurs after the death of Joshua (Judg 1:1).

15:20-63. Judah's towns and cities. Some scholars believe that the list preserved
here may have come from "official archives" kept in Jerusalem. This may explain
why Judah is given more attention then any of the other tribes in this listing. The
reminder (v. 63) that the people of Judah did not *drive out the Jebusites* who lived
in Jerusalem is one of several scattered about in this part of the Book of Joshua that
again indicates the conquest was not nearly as complete as the first twelve chapters
claim (cf. 13:13; 16:10; 17:12,16).

Ephraim and Manasseh, 16:1–17:18

16:1-4. General introduction. EPHRAIM and MANASSEH occupied the central HILL
COUNTRY north of the tribe of BENJAMIN. Actually, for all intents and purposes,
Ephraim came to dominate the northern part of the country and would become
synonymous with "Israel" during the period of the Divided Monarchy (ca. 926–722
BCE). The descriptions given here are sketchy and there are no extensive lists of
cities and towns as in the case of Judah.

16:5-10. The territory of Ephraim. The note about the Canaanites still occupying
Gezer (v. 10) reflects historical reality. GEZER did not become an Israelite city until
the time of Solomon (cf. 1 Kgs 9:15-17).

17:1-18. Manasseh. The tradition concerning Manasseh is longer then the one
about Ephraim due to the fact that two narratives have been added to the material.
The first is the story of the daughters of *Zelophehad* (vv. 3-6), which interrupts the
description of the allotment to Manasseh. This story is based in part on the tradition
in Num 27:1-11, which arose to deal with cases where the normal male heir did not
exist. In the male dominated society of ancient Israel, women did not normally
inherit family property. However, in situations where this did occur, apparently they
were expected to marry within their own tribe to ensure that the property would stay

within tribal bounds (cf. Num 36:1-12). Not only does this story serve to show once more how Joshua did everything *according to the commandment of the LORD* (v. 4), but also that women, not usually paid much attention to in the OT, were included in God's commands to Moses as well as the men.

17:7-13. The territory of Manasseh. The description includes those cities in the Jezreel Valley such as Megiddo and Taanach that the Canaanites controlled long after Israel settled the land (v. 12). That the Canaanites were made slaves (v. 13; cf. 9:23; 16:10) may be more literary creation than historical memory.

17:14-18. The tribe of Joseph. There seem to be two parallel traditions here (vv. 14-15; 16-18; cf. the full-length commentaries), both assuming the time when JOSEPH was one tribe, hence the editorial expansion in v. 17 (i.e., *to Ephraim and Manasseh*). The solution to this problem had already been given by the narrator by the previous allotments to these two tribes. This story also explains why Israel was unable to take the well-defended Canaanite cities located in the fertile valleys of Bethshean and Jezreel. The reference to the Canaanites's *chariots of iron* is to the metal protective plates that were attached to the chariots. That this tradition remembers the *forest* of the hill country (vv. 15, 18) may be indicative of its age, since significant deforestation rapidly occurred during the Iron Age.

The Shiloh Tradition, 18:1–19:51

18:1-10. Introduction. The location for the distribution of land to the remaining seven tribes takes place at SHILOH, not GILGAL (cf. 14:6). Shiloh was an important cult center early in Israel's history (cf. 1 Sam 2:22). Some think its appearance here is an "interpolation" (so Soggin 1970, 189; on Shiloh, see Boling 1982, 422–23). The account told here seems logically to follow 14:2, especially since this latter passage states that the tribes were to receive their inheritance by lot (cf. 14:2). Here representatives from the remaining tribes are sent out to reconnoiter the land, dividing it into seven parts. Upon returning, Joshua is said to have *cast lots* (v. 6) before Yahweh. Casting lots was supposedly an impartial way of determining God's will (cf. 1 Sam 10:19-24). The actual process by which these tribes settled this part of Canaan was far more complex then this tradition indicates.

18:11-28. Benjamin. The first lot fell to Benjamin and included the territory squeezed in between Judah and Ephraim (Joseph). Benjamin's historical importance is that it was the tribe from which SAUL came. The description of its territory given here is thought to come from a much later period.

19:1-9. Simeon. Simeon's portion is said to be within the tribe of Judah. There are few details in the Bible concerning this tribe; apparently it was quickly absorbed by Judah. According to the tradition preserved in Gen 49:5-7, Simeon, as well as Levi, were scattered throughout Israel as a result of their violent nature.

19:10-16. Zebulun. This short description of the inheritance of Zebulun is filled with textual difficulties as well as a difficult history of composition. Historically, the tribe occupied territory in central lower Galilee and is praised in the Song of Deborah (Judg 5:18a). The city of *Bethlehem* (v. 15) is not, of course, the Bethlehem in Judah, but in Galilee.

19:17-23. Issachar. Zebulun's neighbor to the southeast was the territory of Issachar. Recent archaeological surveys have shown that after the Bronze Age, this area was not occupied before the time of the Monarchy (Gal 1992, 87, 90–91; for the most recent attempt to locate the boundaries of Zebulun, Issachar, Asher and Naphtali, see Gal, 98–106). Once more, the archaeological data indicate that the settlement process was long and complicated.

19:24-31. Asher. Asher's territory is described as stretching along the Mediterranean coast from Mount Carmel in the south to the Phoenician city of Tyre in the north. According to 1 Kgs 9:10-14, Solomon gave some of this territory to Hiram, king of Tyre.

19:32-39. Naphtali. Most of the territory assigned to this tribe is in Upper Galilee but its southern border reached as far south as Issachar. The reference to *Judah on the east at the Jordan* (v. 34) is unclear.

19:40-48. Dan. The tribal history of Dan is complex; the place names listed here do not form recognizable borders. The tradition preserved here recalls the time when the Danites occupied territory west of the tribe of Benjamin. This area is the geographical context of the stories of SAMSON, a Danite (Judg 13–15). But Dan was ultimately unable to hold this area and migrated north (v. 47; cf. Judg 18:1-31). Elsewhere, the biblical evaluation of this tribe is not very positive (cf. Gen 49:17; Deut 33:22; Judg. 5:17b).

19:49-51. Joshua's personal reward and the conclusion to allotments. Unlike the preceding allotments, all of which went to tribes, an allotment is now given to Joshua *by command of the LORD.* Thus, individuals as well as nations could be blessed for faithful service. This tradition is also important because it connects Joshua with *the hill country of Ephraim* (v. 50). This chapter ends with a reference to the door of the TENT OF MEETING, even as it began (cf. 18:1).

To all of this, one might very well ask: "So what?" In what way, if any, can a modern reader of what appears to be a totally confused and confusing list of ancient borders and town lists hear "God" speaking? This question becomes more difficult when the artificiality of these traditions is appreciated. What took approximately 200 years to accomplish has been telescoped into what seems a very short period. There may be many ways to read these stories theologically (see Butler 1983, 207–208). Some would say that this material shows how Israel, when it obeyed God, was given the land.

However, the voice of "critical traditionalism" seems to be saying that despite Israel's origins, which at best were obscure; and despite its own unworthiness (see Deut 9:1-24), and despite the ambiguity in applying the laws of Moses, Yahweh had triumphed over the gods of Canaan and established his people on the land. We may never know all of the historical facts that actually occurred in this process. But for faith we know enough. For the ultimate message of the DtR seems to be that Israel was nothing less than God's miracle. For those who claim to be Israel's spiritual heirs, it is a message worth pondering.

Closing Stories, 20:1–24:33

With 19:51, the second of the two major themes running through Joshua is brought to a close. Even though the traditions making up these themes were found to be complex and varied, they were used by the biblical narrator to express his own theological concerns. In the remaining five chapters, however, no such embracing theme is discernible. These stories appear to be independent of one another (see Butler 1983, 209).

Cities of Refuge, 20:1-9

To deal with the issue of involuntary manslaughter, cities of refuge were established; three in Cisjordan and three in the Transjordan (cf. Num 35:1-15; Deut 4:41-43; 19:1-10). While the idea of sanctuary was widespread in the ancient world, setting aside entire cities for this purpose appears to be unique to Israel. However, the date of the tradition preserved here is uncertain and there is no clear example in the OT of the practice described here (but see 1 Kgs 2). Furthermore, the reference to the *high priest* (v. 6) could only have come from the postexilic period.

Cities for the Levites, 21:1-42

The history of the Levitical priesthood cannot be traced here. The Levites appear to have been country preachers scattered throughout the tribal territory of Israel. Not having any territory of their own (cf. 13: 14, 33), they are said to have been given forty-eight cities, thus fulfilling God's command to Moses (Num 35:1-8). Included in this list are the six cities of refuge listed in the previous chapter.

Agreement over the origin, date and nature of the list given here among authorities has been in short supply. What does seem clear is that these cities would not have been in Israelite control *at the same time* prior to the eighth century BCE (Boling 1982, 492–94). Note should also be made of the fact that v. 42 in LXX is much longer than it is in MT.

Editorial Conclusion, 21:43-45

The dogmatic, absolutist claim made in these verses are incomprehensible in light of the actual process by which Israel came to occupy the land of Canaan. Not only have archaeological discoveries laid to rest any notion of such a complete conquest as idealized here; other voices within the Book of Joshua itself sing a different tune, recognizing that the process was neither swift nor total (13:13; 15:63; 16:10; 17:12-13). Perhaps the most helpful suggestion has been from Polzin who interprets these verses as "irony" (1980, 130–34). The question of how God fulfilled his promises to Israel in the ambiguities that characterize the real world is as complex as it is important. But the simplistic answer of authoritative dogmatism only serves to cloud the issue, both then and in any age.

The "Show and Tell" Altar of the Transjordanian Tribes, 22:1-34

In an almost comical story about the Transjordanian tribes, we are told of an altar that was built only for show, not sacrifice. As most commentaries point out, the story is made up of three different segments: vv. 1-6, which form the conclusion to the story begun in 1:12-18; vv. 7-8, an editorial transition to what follows; vv. 9-34, the story of the altar.

What actual episode lay behind this story is unclear. Apparently in its original version it did not include Manasseh, who is absent from vv. 25, 32, 33, and 34. Basic Deuteronomic theology allowed for the erection of an altar of sacrifice only where God's name dwelt (cf. Deut 12:11, etc.), always JERUSALEM during the time of the Davidic Monarchy. This may explain the emphasis here on the fact that the altar in this story was built only for show (vv. 23, 26, 28). It may also explain why the location of *the altar of the LORD* in v. 19 is not specified (Shiloh, Gilgal, and Shechem are options).

Beyond this, the story deals with the larger question of who constitutes the people of Israel. The term "Israel" is used in this story to the exclusion of the Transjordanian tribes (vv. 11, 12, 13, etc.). Can one be a part of "Israel" but live outside *the LORD's land*? (v. 19). This question of the connection between geographical space and religious correctness would have been of paramount concern to the exiles who were very far from *the LORD's land*.

Joshua's Farewell Address, 23:1-16

This chapter has evoked a great deal of discussion among scholars with regard to its date, authorship, and its relationship to the rest of the Book of Joshua, especially to chap. 24. It almost certainly comes late in Judah's history, if not from the EXILE itself (cf. Soggin 1970, 218–19). At one time it may have formed the conclusion to the book, though it ends on an especially pessimistic note (v. 16). Also, notably absent from this chapter is any indication as to where this speech was thought to have taken place. As Boling has pointed out (1982, 526), by giving Joshua a "farewell speech," the narrator has placed him in a select group of people within the larger DH: MOSES (Deuteronomy as a whole); SAMUEL (1 Sam 12:1-24); and DAVID (1 Kgs 2:1-9).

While Joshua admits that, while not all the nations have been subdued (v. 4), Israel will still possess the land if it is *steadfast to keep and do all that is written in the book of the law of Moses* (v. 6). The warning against mixed marriages (cf. Ezra 9:1-15), and the threat of loss of the land for transgressions against God's covenant demands, stand in stark contrast to the utopian claim already encountered (21:43-45).

Shechem and Covenant Renewal, 24:1-28

The original setting of this chapter is not clear. The LXX reads "Shiloh" both in v. 1 and v. 25 (cf. 18:1 and see Boling 1982, 533; Soggin 1972, 223). Both

SHECHEM and SHILOH were important cultic centers in Israel's history. The tradition of the former was traced back to patriarchal times (Gen 12:6; 33:18-19; 35:4). Also some scholars believe that there is some connection between this chapter and Josh 8:30-35, but that assumes a basic historicity for these stories that seems most doubtful in light of the actual settlement process. More probable is the suggestion of some sort of cultic festival that was carried out here, perhaps on an annual basis that was concerned with the theme of COVENANT renewal. Thus the contents of this chapter may have been independent of its present context.

24:1-13. Introduction and the speech of Yahweh. The chapter begins much like the preceding one with the stereotyped formula of address. This is followed by a reported speech of Yahweh who recites a series of divine acts, beginning with the ancestors, performed on Israel's behalf. Notably absent from this recital is any mention of Moses and the stipulations of the Sinai covenant. According to this speech, the people of Israel were able to occupy the land of Canaan for one reason only: God's gracious acts (vv. 12-13).

24:14-28. Joshua and the people respond. It becomes obvious that Israel's becoming the people of God was not as automatic as the preceding speech by Yahweh implies when we are told that Joshua, not God, reminds them that they must choose *whom [they] will serve* (v. 15). When they respond that they will serve Yahweh because of divine acts, they are told by Joshua that they cannot serve God because of God's holiness and righteous demands (v. 19). This addition to God's words by Joshua illustrates again how, for the DtR, the history of Israel was an exercise in the interpretation, modification and application of the divine will (cf. Polzin 1980).

As has been noted more than once, the theological overlay of the Book of Joshua by the DtR is complex and easily distorted. But perhaps this much can be said. That Israel existed at all was due to God's gracious acts on Israel's behalf. But God's grace is always paradoxical: free, but not cheap. The cost to Israel was understood to be its willingness to live in covenant fidelity to the will of Yahweh. That Israel had not done so was the testimony of both the prophets and the DtR. The consequences of this failure were disastrous: exile! But hope did not die with Israel's faithlessness. Perhaps now, confronted with this failure Israel would once more face the challenge of Joshua of old and choose to serve Yahweh.

Burial Traditions, 24:29-33

The Book of Joshua closes with the three burial traditions of Joshua, Joseph and Eleazar the priest. Originally, the DtR's work probably stopped with 24:28, because he continues his story in what is now Judg 2:6. In fact it is not until Judg 2:8 that he reports the death of Joshua (cf. Judg 1:1). But at some point in the final editing of these two books, the material in Judg 1:1–2:5 was added. Since the traditions recorded in Judges already assumed the death of Joshua, the announcement of his death was appended to the book bearing his name.

Works Cited

Albright, W. F. 1939. "The Israelite Conquest of Canaan in the Light of Archaeology," *BASOR* 74:11–23.

Alt, Albrecht. 1966. *Essays on Old Testament History and Religion.*

Bailey, Lloyd. 1990. "Ark," MDB.

Boling, Robert G. 1982. *Joshua.* AncB.

Butler, Trent C. 1983. *Joshua.* WBC.

Callaway, Joseph. 1976. "Excavations at Ai (Et-Tell), 1964–1972, *BA*:18–30.

Coogan, Michael D. 1990. "Archaeology and Biblical Studies: the Book of Joshua," in *The Hebrew Bible and Its Interpreters.* Ed. W. H. Propp, B. Halpern, David Noel Freedman.

Dever, William G. 1990. *Recent Archaeological Discoveries and Biblical Research.* 1992. "How to Tell a Canaanite from an Israelite," in *The Rise of Ancient Israel.*

Fewell, Danna N. 1992. "Joshua." TWBC. Ed. Carol A. Newsom and Sharon H. Ringe.

Finkelstein, Israel. 1988. *The Archaeology of the Israelite Settlement.*

Fritz, Volkmar. 1987. "Conquest or Settlement? The Early Iron Age in Palestine," *BA*:84–100.

Gal, Zvi. 1992. *Lower Galilee during the Iron Age.*

Gottwald, Norman K. 1979. *The Tribes of Yahweh: A Sociology of the Religion of Liberated Israel, 1250–1050 BCE.*

Halpern, Baruch. 1983. *The Emergence of Israel in Canaan.* 1992. "The Exodus From Egypt: Myth or Reality?" in *The Rise of Ancient Israel.*

Kempinski, Aharon. 1986. "Joshua's Altar—An Iron Age I Watchtower," *BAR* (Jan/Feb): 42–49.

Kenyon, Kathleen M. 1957. *Digging up Jericho.*

Kraus, H.-J. 1965. *Worship in Israel.*

Mendenhall, George E. 1962. "The Hebrew Conquest of Palestine," *BA* 25:66–87.

McCarter, P. Kyle, Jr. et al. 1992. "The Origins of Israelite Religion," in *The Rise of Ancient Israel.*

Miller, J. Maxwell. 1990. "Gilgal," MDB.

Noth, Martin. 1960. *The History of Israel.*

Polzin, Robert. 1980. *Moses and the Deuteronomist: A Literary Study of the Deuteronomic History.*

Porter, J. Roy. 1970. "The Succession of Joshua," in *Proclamation and Presence: Old Testament Essays in Honor of Gwynne Henton Davies.* Ed. John I Durham and J. R. Porter.

Rainey, Anson F. 1986. "Zertal's Altar—A Blatant Phony," *BAR* (July/August): 66.

Soggin, J. Alberto. 1970. *Joshua.* OTL.

de Vaux, Roland. 1978. *The Early History of Israel.*

Weinfeld, Moshe. 1972. *Deuteronomy and the Deuteronomic School.*

Wright, G. Ernest. n.d. "The Conquest Theme in the Bible," unpublished paper.

Zertal, Adam. 1985. "Has Joshua's Altar Been Found on Mt. Ebal?" *BAR* (Jan/Feb): 26–43.

Judges

Robert C. Dunston

Introduction

The Book of Judges is the seventh book of the OT and tells the story of the tribes of Israel from the death of Joshua to the birth of Samuel. The book receives its name from the individuals who are called by God to judge Israel, specifically by saving one or more Israelite tribes from enemies. In the Hebrew canon the book appears as the second book of the Former Prophets, which indicates that the book is primarily a theological history of the period rather than an exhaustive history of the times.

The Nature of the Judge

Typically in Israel a judge was primarily charged with administering justice based on the laws of Israel (Exod 18:21-22, 1 Sam 7:15-17, 2 Chr 19:6). Yet in the Book of Judges only Deborah functions in this capacity (4:4-5).

The judges in the Book of Judges are warrior heroes who are called by God to deliver their people from oppression by enemies. Several judges are specifically referred to as deliverers (3:9, 15; 10:1; 13:5) indicating that their chief function was not legal but military. Although most of the judges are said to have "judged Israel" after their military victories, this function may indicate that they are respected figures rather than legal functionaries.

The judges came from varying backgrounds and were not connected to tribal or local government. They were understood to have been called by God in time of emergency to defeat the enemies of their people. The judges exercised authority over only a few tribes, never over all of Israel. When the enemy had been defeated they seem to have returned to normal life. The only two judges who demand lifetime appointments as authoritative leaders—Abimelech and Jephthah—are portrayed as unsavory characters (9:56-57; 11:1). The loose confederation of tribes led by tribal leaders simply did not tolerate a centralization of power.

The judges are often divided into the categories of major and minor judges based not on their stature but on the length of the material we have concerning them. Some scholars identify the major judges as military deliverers and the minor judges as legal authorities. While there may be some truth to this claim, at least one minor judge (Shamgar) was a military rather than a legal figure (3:31). The information in the text is too meager to provide a precise distinction between the function of the major and minor judges.

Authorship

Ancient Jewish tradition stated that Samuel was the author of the Book of Judges but scholars today doubt that claim. Most scholars see the book reaching its final form after centuries of collecting, editing, and revising.

The bulk of the book (3:7–16:31) probably rests on stories of tribal heroes passed down orally from generation to generation. Some aspects of these tales are quite old and may well be contemporaneous with the events (e.g., the Song of Deborah—5:1-31, Jotham's fable—9:7-15). These stories would have been collected between the tenth and seventh centuries BCE.

Sometime in the late seventh century BCE Deuteronomic editors supplied the original collection of stories with an introduction (2:6–3:6) that recounted the death of Joshua and subsequent apostasy of the people and a story (17:1–18:31) that discussed the forced migration of the tribe of Dan. In the sixth century BCE Deuteronomic editors added a prologue (1:1–2:5) detailing the tribes' failure to conquer Canaan and an epilogue recounting the near destruction of Benjamin by the other eleven tribes (19:1–21:25). The book then became an explanation and retelling of Israel's dark period between Joshua and Samuel when there was no national leader and anarchy ruled the day (cf. 21:25).

Date of Composition

The events of the time occurred before Israel had a king (18:1, 19:1, 21:25). The book further refers to the fall of Shiloh (18:31), which occurred during the time of Eli and Samuel (1 Sam 4:12-18). Thus the book cannot be any earlier than the late eleventh century BCE, the time of Saul. The mention of the captivity of Israel (18:30) dates the final editing of the book to the seventh or sixth century BCE.

Literary Structure

The final form of the book is beautifully structured. Following an explanatory introduction, the stories of three minor judges are recounted followed by the stories of two good major judges, Deborah and Gideon. The story of Gideon, who seems to be the model judge, leads into the story of Abimelech, a son of Gideon who attempts to become king by force.

Abimelech's story is the central narrative of the book and begins the account of Israel's steady decline. The mention of two minor judges is followed by a second introduction and then the story of Jephthah, who sacrifices his daughter. The stories of three final minor judges lead to the story of Samson, who selfishly squanders his ability. The two final stories of the Levite for hire and the near destruction of the tribe of Benjamin complete the tale of Israel's spiritual and moral decline.

The book thus begins in difficult times with little hope for the future. Two good judges raise the possibility that Israel might survive and prosper, but that possibility is quickly dashed by Abimelech, Jephthah, and Samson. By the end of the book one wonders if Israel will survive at all.

Much has been written concerning the cyclical pattern of disobedience-punishment-pleading-deliverance-disobedience that occurs in the book. Since Israel viewed history in linear terms rather than cyclical terms, this pattern has caused some consternation. Rather than a cyclical pattern, the book's structure indicates more of a spiral pattern. The same pattern is repeated, but each repetition moves history to a different point. Israel is never back where it started; it is typically in worse condition.

Value of the Book

Historical. The Book of Judges presents a chronological problem. If the years of service of each judge is added to the length of oppressions by enemies, the total is 410 years. According to the OT only 480 years passed from the exodus from Egypt to the laying of the foundation of Solomon's Temple (1 Kgs 6:1). Thus the sum of the years of the judges is far too long. It must be the case that some of the judges were active simultaneously. Since the judges served in differing areas and led only a few tribes, the assumption that some judges had simultaneous periods of influence is highly probable.

Still the Book of Judges provides the best information available on this period of Israel's existence (ca. 1220–1040 BCE). The difficulties created by a loose confederation of tribes (sometimes referred to by the Greek term "amphictyony") feuding with one another and still attempting to conquer their portion of the land and defeat their enemies are painfully recounted. Without a strong leader like Moses or Joshua Israel certainly must have been reduced to such a state.

Cultural. The Book of Judges also supplies information regarding Israel's early culture. The Song of Deborah (5:1-31) provides an excellent example of early Israelite poetry. The individual stories provide interesting insights concerning wedding customs (14:5-18), differences in local dialects (12:6), and other aspects of Palestinian culture.

Theological. Certainly the book's greatest contribution rests in its theological teachings. Religion was simple during the period. There were many sacred spots and no strong central cultic organization or practices. Within such a religious environment people were left to their own devices and moral behavior sank to abysmal depths.

At the same time, the community of Israel was confronting Canaanite religion head-on and was being changed, both for good and ill, in the process. The notion of God's control over the universe, and especially over the processes of life and fertility, was greatly expanded, bringing both danger and promise to Israel's faith. The danger lay in the attraction presented by religious practices in which the community understood itself to be sharing the creative powers of the deity. Such practices easily became corrupt, leading to efforts to control the power and purposes of the deity and make these conform to the community's own desires. But the positive side of this confrontation was a great advance in the recognition of the range and depth and subtlety of God's control and direction of the universe and of the life and destinies of the people of the covenant. Virtually every one of the classical Yahwist's theological affirmations of early Israel was deepened and broadened through contact with Canaanite culture and religion.

During most of the period of the judges, however, this confrontation with Canaanite culture was in its early stages. And as we see, the editors of the Book of Judges severely condemned the religious practices of those who inhabit the land with Israel.

The absence of a strong faith and practice led to some of the bloodiest and most abhorrent stories in the OT. Israelite society was turned upside down. The stories show women, who were not usually viewed as the stronger individuals, triumphing in both faith and military prowess. We also see women degraded, treated as property, and terribly abused. Religion often became a crutch used in times of emergency and then abandoned. By the end of the book it is clear that a strong form of central government led by a strong and faithful leader is desperately needed. At least this is the view of the editors of the book.

For Further Study

In the *Mercer Dictionary of the Bible*: DEUTERONOMIST/DEUTERONOMISTIC HISTORIAN; JUDGES, BOOK OF; NAZIRITES.

In other sources: R. G. Boling, *Judges*, AncB, and "Judges, Book of," AncBD; J. Gray, *Joshua, Judges, and Ruth*, rev. ed., NCB; E. J. Hamlin, *Judges*, ITC; C. F. Kraft, "Judges, Book of," IDB; G. F. Moore, *A Critical and Exegetical Commentary on Judges*, ICC; J. A. Soggin, *Judges*, OTL; P. Trible, *Texts of Terror*.

Commentary

An Outline

I. Introduction, 1:1–3:6
   A. Efforts to Occupy Canaan, 1:1–2:5
   B. Life after Joshua, 2:6–3:6
II. First Series of Judges, 3:7–8:32
   A. Othniel, 3:7-11
   B. Ehud, 3:12-30
   C. Shamgar, 3:31
   D. Deborah, 4:1–5:31
   E. Gideon, 6:1–8:32
III. Abimelech, 8:33–9:57
IV. Second Series of Judges, 10:1–16:31
   A. Tola, 10:1-2

   B. Jair, 10:3-5
   C. A Second Introduction, 10:6-16
   D. Jephthah, 10:17–12:7
   E. Ibzan, 12:8-10
   F. Elon, 12:11-12
   G. Abdah, 12:13-15
   H. Samson, 13:1–16:31
V. Epilogue, 17:1–21:25
   A. Migration of Dan, 17:1–18:31
   B. Destruction of Benjamin, 19:1–21:24
   C. Conclusion, 21:25

Introduction, 1:1–3:6

Efforts to Occupy Canaan, 1:1–2:5

With the death of Joshua Israel lost its charismatic, faithful leader and a new chapter of Israel's history began. Scholars have viewed Judg 1:1-36 as an alternate and contradictory account to the conquest of Canaan recorded in Josh 1–12. Others have assumed this passage simply tells the story of life after Joshua. Joshua's efforts may have broken the back of Canaanite power but there would have been many pockets of strong resistance that would have continued to be a threat to Israel's existence. With Joshua gone the tribes are left to decide which one of them will first dare to attack the remaining Canaanites.

1:1-21. Struggles by Judah. The Israelites inquire of God concerning which tribe should first attack the Canaanites, and Judah is selected. God reminds Israel that the land is his but he will give it to Judah. With the help of Simeon, Judah defeats Adoni-bezek at Bezek, a city probably near Jerusalem. Adoni-bezek, who has treated his victims as mutilated dogs, is repaid in kind. His thumbs and big toes are cut off, making him unfit to rule or fight. He is then brought to Jerusalem as an example of Judah's power and resolve.

Judah then destroys Jerusalem as well as cities further south. A brief story (1:11-15) recounts how Othniel became the son-in-law of Caleb, one of the last links to Israel's faithful past. The story has a parallel in Josh 15:13-19. The Kenite relations of Moses' father-in-law move toward the south and settle with the Amalekites. Caleb takes the city of Hebron and drives out the three sons of Anak, perhaps a reference to the remnants of the legendary GIANT race of antiquity. The section ends with the failure of Judah to take the cities of the plain and the failure of Benjamin to take, or perhaps inhabit, Jerusalem.

The southern tribes led by Judah manage to take the hill country but not the coastal plain of Philistia. Although the coastal cities are listed as conquered (1:18) the next verse mentions that they were not. The choice land has been denied the southern tribes but at least they along with Caleb and the relatives of Moses can begin to enjoy the fulfillment of their promise of land.

1:22-36. Struggles by the central and northern tribes. The Joseph tribes manage to take Bethel after an inhabitant of the city agrees to help them. As a reward for his help he and his family are spared, much as Rahab and her family had been spared by Joshua (Josh 6:25).

The remainder of the section lists cities that the central and northern tribes could not take. Here there is no concerted action by tribes to attack the Canaanites; this undoubtedly caused their failure. The coastal plain and fertile valleys are denied these tribes and they are forced to coexist with the Canaanite inhabitants of the cities. Some Canaanites are pressed into slave labor; others live alongside of Israel, providing a source of continuous temptation to Israel through intermarriage and religion. This relationship also brings cultural and religious enrichment to Israel, along with the dangers.

2:1-5. An angelic message. An ANGEL speaks to Israel at Bochim where the Israelites had apparently gathered to worship. After briefly recounting God's mighty deeds and promise, the angel accused Israel of breaking the covenant by making covenants with the inhabitants of the land and failing to destroy their worship centers. God decides to allow these non-Israelite peoples to remain in the land to fight against Israel and to tempt Israel to serve their gods. Israel responds by weeping, which explains the name of the site Bochim (Heb. "weepers"). Israel there sacrifices to God, probably in an effort to persuade him to change his mind. Apparently Israel already views religion as an emergency measure, available to reverse painful, present situations.

Life after Joshua, 2:6–3:6

The first verses (2:6-10) of the section parallel Josh 24:29-31. At the age of 110 Joshua dies and is buried in the land for which he valiantly fought. As the others of Joshua's generation die off, Israel continues to serve God, but when there are no more witnesses to God's great acts of deliverance Israel forgets God. The statement that Israel *did not know the LORD* (2:10) is painfully reminiscent of Pharaoh's remark (Exod 5:2).

The pattern of history that spirals through the book now begins. Israel abandons God and embraces the gods of the Canaanites, especially BAAL and the Astartes. In anger God abandons them leaving them powerless before their enemies. Yet God never completely abandons them. In his love he raises up judges to deliver his people from their enemies. Although the judges' military success is admirable, God's deliverance has little effect on Israel's religious life. When a judge dies, the people become more disobedient to God than before. Their disobedience provokes more punishment.

Three reasons are given to explain God's refusal to drive out the nations in Canaan. The first is as punishment for Israel's breaking of the covenant (2:2-3). The second is to test Israel to see whether or not the people will obey God, especially when circumstances are difficult (2:21-23). The final reason is to test and teach Israelites who had never experienced war (3:1-2). An earlier explanation suggests that the land would be desolate and wild beasts would multiply, if all the Canaanites were destroyed at once (Exod 23:29-30 and Deut 7:22). The common element is always obedience to God, which Israel pursues only in times of difficulty and then only in a superficial manner. Typically Israel engages in intermarriage with its neighbors and joins in the worship of their gods.

First Series of Judges, 3:7–8:32

The first series of narratives concerning judges indicates that the judges are good, faithful individuals who make a positive impact on Israel. Deborah and Gideon especially demonstrate the best in charismatic leadership.

Othniel, 3:7-11

The spiral of disobedience-punishment-pleading-deliverance-disobedience begins. Othniel serves as a prime example of what the judges will do. Israel disobeys, and God allows Cushan-rishathaim of Aram Naharaim (perhaps in Syria near the Euphrates or, more likely, in the hill country) to dominate Israel for eight years. When the people cry out to God for help, God raises up Othniel, the son-in-law of Caleb, to deliver the people. Interestingly enough, the first judge is from Judah, the tribe God called to go up against the Canaanites first (1:2). Empowered by God, Othniel removes the threat and the people enjoy forty years, one generation, of peace.

Ehud, 3:12-30

Israel again disobeys God and is tormented by King Eglon of Moab. In league with the Ammonites and Amalekites, he takes Jericho and subdues Israel for eighteen years. God raises up Ehud to overcome Moab. Although he comes from the tribe of Benjamin (Heb. "son of the right hand," cf. Gen 35:18), Ehud is left-handed, a characteristic of some of Benjamin's best warriors (cf. 20:16; 1 Chr 12:2). Left-handedness was unusual and gave the individual a distinct advantage in ancient hand-to-hand combat.

Ehud is sent with a tribute payment to Eglon. Ehud requests and receives a private audience with Eglon after delivering the tribute. When they are alone Ehud draws his double-edged sword from his right side, an unexpected location but perfect for a left-handed person, and stabs Eglon. Eglon is so fat that the entire sword including the hilt enters his stomach. His gruesome death is only the first of many in the book.

After escaping, Ehud sends out the call for assistance in Ephraim. He and his compatriots secure the fords of the Jordan River and there kill 10,000 Moabite warriors. Following this victory Israel enjoyed 80 years, two generations, of peace. Here we see that the tribe nearest to Benjamin comes to the aid of Ehud. Probably Ephraim had most to gain from the defeat of the Moabites.

Shamgar, 3:31

Shamgar is referred to as *the son of Anath*. Some scholars suggest this indicates he was from Beth-Anath in Galilee but others suggest that he was a mercenary soldier under the service or auspices of the fertility/war goddess Anat. The latter interpretation would certainly explain his prowess as a warrior using only an oxgoad.

Two problems surface with Shamgar. Although he is mentioned twice in the book (3:31; 5:6), 4:1 indicates that there was no judge between Ehud and Deborah. Some Greek manuscripts moved the mention of Shamgar after 16:31, the end of the story of Samson. Moving the mention of Shamgar to that location also alleviates the problem caused by the mention of the Philistines. Many scholars agree that the

Philistines were not troublesome to Israel early in the period of the judges. If Shamgar is correctly listed, the mention of Philistines might refer to an infiltration of Israel by earlier SEA PEOPLES.

Deborah, 4:1–5:31

Deborah is one of the more fascinating judges of Israel. She is the only woman judge and was recognized by Israel as having both legal and prophetic authority and responsibility. The story of Deborah has been passed down in two forms, a prose narrative (4:1-24; 5:31b) and a poetic victory song (5:1-31a), both of which celebrate the power of God and the role of women.

4:1-24, 5:31b. Deborah and Jael. Following the death of Ehud Israel again turns from God and God again hands his people over to be oppressed. In this instance the oppressor is King Jabin of Hazor whose general is Sisera. Sisera's name is Indo-European which may indicate that he is from the Sea Peoples; it is likely, therefore, that Jabin led a coalition of kings from among the Canaanites and the Sea Peoples (5:19). Sisera commands a large and highly mobile force of 900 chariots with which he is able to oppress Israel cruelly for twenty years.

Israel's savior in this time of need is Deborah, who functions as a prophet and a legal arbitrator. Like other prophets, she calls for a holy war and herself designates the leader of the Israelite forces, Barak. Barak is willing to lead the Israelite troops only if Deborah will accompany him. Although his request may be seen as a sign of weakness, he may desire to have the continuing directions from God that a prophet could provide. Deborah agrees to come but states that her presence is unnecessary. God has promised victory whether Deborah is physically with Barak or not. Deborah states that she will accompany Barak, but a woman will receive credit for the victory.

Barak musters 10,000 troops from the tribes of Naphtali and Zebulun and leads them to Mt. Tabor. Mt. Tabor dominates the east of the plain of Esdraelon and is an excellent strategic location for Israel's troops. Sisera draws up his forces to attack from the southeast. The battle is joined when Barak and his soldiers sweep down from Mt. Tabor. God throws the forces of Sisera into utter panic. Sisera flees for his life while his troops are pursued and completely destroyed.

Sisera has a particular safe haven in mind as he flees for his life. Heber, the Kenite had moved into the northern region of Canaan, separating his clan from the other Kenite clans that were related to Moses. Heber and Jabin were allies, a situation far more beneficial to Heber than to Jabin since nomads would have depended on friendly relations with the more settled population. Sisera trusts that with Heber he can find hospitality and protection. Jael, the wife of Heber, meets him and shows him the hospitality he was expecting. The warmth of the rug covering, the satisfaction of the milk, and the assumed protection combine to lull Sisera to sleep. While he sleeps, Jael picks up a hammer and drives a tent peg into his temple, through his head, and into the ground. When Barak arrives, Jael welcomes him and shows him the dead general. Deborah's prophecy that a woman would prevail may have been understood by her to refer to her winning the victory, but now that interpretation expands to include Jael's deed.

The action of Jael is difficult to understand. When she saw a defeated Sisera staggering into her camp she may have felt that the alliance between her husband and Jabin would no longer be of value. Perhaps she and her husband would do better to throw their lot in with whoever had won the victory. Since Heber was an ally of Jabin, perhaps he had been drafted into the fight as well and Jael now realized he was dead. The murder of Sisera would have avenged her husband's death. Another rationale for her action might have been the appeasement of the Israelite forces who would soon arrive. By killing Sisera she would prove herself to be sympathetic to Israel and spare the lives of herself and her clan. Or perhaps she was simply reverting to an earlier alliance more in harmony with her own views of faith and family. The Kenites, or some of them at least, are thought to have been worshipers of Israel's God (see Exod 18:10-12). Certainly her actions were based on a complex reaction to a complex series of events. Her bloody deed nevertheless remains sinister.

The victory of Deborah and Jael begins a series of attacks on Jabin that ends with his complete destruction. Israel then enjoys security and peace for forty years, one generation.

5:1-31a. The Song of Deborah. The victory song sung by Deborah and Barak is considered to be the oldest text in the OT. Scholars agree that the song is most likely contemporaneous with the victory of Deborah and Jael over Jabin's coalition.

The song celebrates the victory not as evidence of Israel's power but as evidence of the power of God. According to the song Israel was in difficult straits. Travel and trade were disrupted (v. 6) and Israel's armed might was almost non-existent (v. 8). Israel could not have won the victory by itself. God alone delivered the people.

It is interesting that according to the song more tribes were involved in the battle than Naphtali and Zebulun. Ephraim, Benjamin, and Manasseh (represented by Machir) also participate. Reuben, Gilead (representing the tribe of Gad), Dan, Asher, and an unknown group, Meroz, fail to answer the call to arms. Judah, which has played such an important role in earlier stories, is not even mentioned. The tribes that participate in the battle are those that are most threatened. The other tribes that are not threatened apparently see no reason to join in the battle. This was probably the situation throughout the time of the judges.

More information is also provided concerning how the victory was won. God destroys the forces of Sisera by using weather as a weapon. A torrential rain soaks the ground and swells the Kishon into a raging river. The heavily armored chariots are bogged down and useless. The battle plan of Sisera is worthless and the troops are easily routed.

As is to be expected, Jael is praised for her actions. The picture of the death of Sisera is somewhat different from that in the prose narrative. Here Sisera sinks and dies at Jael's feet. Perhaps Jael struck the first blow while Sisera was still standing, or perhaps he sank in exhaustion. In either case his death is still bloody.

A brief poignant moment now occurs in the song (vv. 28-30). Sisera's mother is portrayed gazing out the window wondering why her son is so late returning from battle. Those with her try to relieve her anxieties, but one gets the distinct impression that she knows that her son will not return. Sisera's mother is one in the long line of those who do not see their loved ones return from war.

The poignant moment does not last long. The song concludes with a wish that God might always be as victorious as on that day. If God will continue to act like this, his enemies will be destroyed and his friends will be blessed and preserved. The concluding statement is certainly a call to be friends with God, a call that Israel typically ignored, according to the testimony of the book.

Gideon, 6:1–8:32

The story of Gideon is the longest narrative concerning a judge who functioned as a military leader. Gideon received a variety of special revelations from God and exhibited unusual power and influence among the people. Many scholars have suggested that this man to whom the people offered kingship was the ideal judge.

6:1-10. The problem. A new round of disobedience by Israel brings a new threat. The Midianites, with assistance from the Amalekites and other groups from the east, begin a series of annual raids into Israel, destroying the produce of the fields and leaving nothing for the Israelites and their livestock to subsist upon for the next year. Even though Midian was related to Israel (Gen 25:1-6; Exod 18:1) this was not the first instance of Midianite opposition to Israel (Num 22:4-7; 25:6-18). As a nation of camel nomads, Midian was primarily involved in trade rather than agriculture and their destruction of Israelite crops implies that they did not need the provisions for themselves primarily. Their actions appear more designed to keep Israel weak and unable to participate in caravan trade. The statement that the Midianites appeared *as thick as locusts* (v. 5) when they converged upon Israel is reminiscent of one of the divine plagues against Egypt (Exod 10:4-6) and indicates that the Midianite threat is also a divine judgment.

When the people cry out to God for deliverance, they are answered by an unknown prophet. He explains the reason for the people's misfortune by briefly reciting God's gracious acts toward Israel and by stating that God expected the complete loyalty of his people. The Canaanite gods might be tolerant of the worship of other deities but Israel's God is not. The people's disobedience has caused their suffering. The prophet promises no deliverance, leaving the people to suspect that they have been abandoned by the God whom they have abandoned.

6:11-32. The selection of Gideon. Two call experiences seem to be reflected in the present narrative. The first is in vv. 11-24 and the second is in vv. 25-32. Both calls are confirmed by signs.

In vv. 11-24 an angel appears under the oak at Ophrah, apparently a site at which Gideon's father Joash inquired of Baal. Gideon is threshing the wheat in a wine press to avoid detection by the Midianites and thus save some grain for his family. The angel greets Gideon as a mighty warrior who is blessed with the presence of God. Gideon doubts God's presence with either himself or his people. The angel commissions Gideon to deliver his people from the Midianites. Gideon's protestations are reminiscent of those of Moses (Exod 4:1-17) and Jeremiah (Jer 1:6-8) and they are likewise dismissed by the angel.

Gideon requests a sign that will validate the messenger and his words and receives one. Gideon prepares a large meal of a kid and unleavened bread, which is consumed by fire when the angel touches it with his staff. The angel disappears and Gideon fears for his life because he has looked upon the face of God. God, perhaps through the angel again, reassures him and offers peace. Gideon constructs an altar to commemorate his experience and, perhaps to indicate his new allegiance to God, calls the altar *The LORD is peace* (v. 24).

The second call in vv. 25-32 begins with a feat of strength and faith by Gideon and ten of his servants and ends with the bestowing of a new name upon Gideon (cf. Gen 32:28). Acting on the instructions of God, Gideon destroys the altar of his father, constructs an altar to God, and sacrifices a bull upon it as a whole burnt offering. The next day when the townspeople discover the deed and its perpetrator, they sentence Gideon to death. Joash saves his son by cleverly arguing that if Baal is the powerful god that his worshipers claim him to be, he can defend himself. Apparently Joash has also undergone some kind of conversion to faith in God or at least has decided to step out from behind the protection of the local religion, since it seems unlikely, according to the narrative, that Joash expects Baal to retaliate by killing his son. Gideon receives the new name Jerubbaal meaning *Let Baal contend* (v. 32).

6:33–7:18. Preparation for battle. Gideon calls out to Manasseh, Asher, Zebulun, and Naphtali for troops to fight against the Midianites, and each tribe responds positively. Gideon inquires of God again, asking for a sign that success will indeed be the result of his venture. Divination before battle was typical in the ancient Near East. He asks that in the morning the dew might be on a fleece of wool but not on the hardened threshing floor. As a gift from heaven the dew is a particularly appropriate element for this heavenly sign from God. In the morning it is just as Gideon has asked which is to be expected. The fleece would naturally retain moisture as opposed to the hardened earth floor. Now Gideon asks for the reverse to occur, which would seem unlikely if not impossible. When the sign is provided, it is a convincing good omen for Gideon.

Having provided Gideon with signs of victory, God now tests Gideon and his troops. The number of Israelite troops is so great that if they win the victory they will be strongly inclined to attribute it to their own strength. To eliminate this understanding, God tells Gideon to reduce his army. Those who are afraid are allowed to return home. According to Deut 20:8, this is because fear is contagious and will dishearten all in the army, a belief that is confirmed by the fear instilled by a Midianite soldier's dream (vv. 13-14).

Still the number is too great. God commands Gideon to take the remaining men to water and let them drink. Gideon is to watch the men and divide them into two groups: those who lap like dogs and those who kneel and with cupped hands bring the water to their mouths. Those who lap number 300 and are kept as Gideon's fighting force. No reason is given to explain why those who lap are selected but the assumption is that they are simply the smallest group. Some suggest they are selected because they have such trust in God they will let God protect them while they drink in a completely vulnerable manner. Yet if the other group had been selected it could be rationalized that they were selected based on their alertness and ability to respond instantaneously to fight for God. It is futile to seek some underlying motive for selection. The point is that God can deliver Israel with either many troops or a few. Now it is up to Israel to believe.

God grants Gideon one final sign so that his courage and confidence will be strong for battle. As Gideon and his servant spy outside the Midianite camp, they hear a soldier telling a friend a dream he had. A barley cake (representing agricultural Israel) rolled into camp and knocked down the tent (representing nomadic Midian). His friend fearfully interprets this dream to mean that the small Israelite forces will unexpectedly decimate Midian. The dream and its fearful interpretation apparently spread through the Midianite camp and the Midianites are beaten before the battle begins.

A brief word must be said at this point regarding signs. In the NT signs are typically discounted (Matt 12:39; 16:1; Mark 8:11-12; Luke 11:16; John 20:29), although John records several signs performed by Jesus (cf. John 2:11; 4:54). The OT is not so antagonistic toward signs and, in fact, some are requested to ask for a sign (cf. Isa 7:10-25). It is unfair to assume that the signs Gideon receives indicate that his faith is weak. His practice of inquiring of the deity before battle is typical of his time—and God offers more signs than Gideon seeks.

7:19–8:21. The defeat of Midian. Gideon's battle plan is unusual. His 300 men are to divide into three companies and place themselves around the Midianite camp. Each soldier would carry a lighted torch covered by a pottery jar, and a horn. At Gideon's signal each man is to break his jar thus exposing the light of the torch, blow his horn, and give a battle cry. Certainly a person could not do all of this simultaneously, but the effect of these actions on a demoralized enemy camp would be and is devastating. Believing themselves to be surrounded, the Midianites are thrown into a panic and begin killing one another.

Gideon and his small force pursue the escaping Midianites and call for Ephraim to block the fords of the Jordan River so that the Midianites would be trapped. The Ephraimites do so and in the process capture and execute the two Midianite captains, Oreb and Zeb, bringing their heads to Gideon. The Ephraimites are incensed that they were not summoned earlier, but Gideon manages to soothe their hurt feelings with flattery.

The remaining narrative of the fight against the Midianites concerns personal vengeance. When the people of Succoth and Penuel refuse to provide Gideon and his exhausted force with food, he vows to return after his victory and punish them. Gideon fulfills his threat after he captures Zebah and Zalmunna, the two kings of Midian. Gideon's desperate search for Zebah and Zalmunna is explained as his desire to avenge the deaths at their hands of his brothers, the sons of Joash and Gideon's mother. Gideon orders his firstborn son Jether to kill these two, but he is afraid and refuses. The two kings state that they should die by Gideon's hand, so he kills them and takes the ornaments from their camels.

8:22-28. An invitation to be king. The people are highly impressed with Gideon's leadership and ask him to be king but he refuses. God is to be the king of Israel and not a human being (cf. 1 Sam 8:7). This is the theologically correct answer and sets the stage for Abimelech's attempt at kingship in the next chapter.

Gideon does agree to accept a gift; he asks that the golden earrings worn by the dead Midianite soldiers be given to him. From these he makes an ephod, a priestly garment worn or displayed when consulting the deity. It is interesting that although Gideon refuses the office of king he does not refuse the trappings of power and authority that indicate his special relationship with God as a recipient of divine revelation. The ephod proves to be a snare to Israel when it is used as an idol.

8:29-32. Conclusion. Following the victory of Gideon, Israel enjoys a forty year, one generation, respite. Gideon returns to his home and fathers seventy sons (a perfect number, not necessarily the actual count of his children) from various wives. One son in particular, Abimelech, is singled out and serves to point to the following narrative. Gideon dies after enjoying a long life and is buried in the tomb of his father, a fitting reward for this man of faith.

Abimelech, 8:33–9:57

According to most scholars, the Abimelech story is the central narrative of the book. The story explores and soundly rejects kingship as a possible alternative to leadership by charismatic judges.

The name Abimelech is translated by most as "my father is *melech*" with *melech* being the name of a deity. The name can also be translated "my father is (or was) king," a name that provides a link between the Gideon and Abimelech narratives. Although Gideon did not accept kingship over his people, he certainly received high regard and respect from the people and to them may have seemed to be a king. The story of Abimelech records Abimelech's desire to retain this recognition and respect and expand upon it.

8:33-9:6. Abimelech seizes power. Upon the death of Gideon, Israel again strays from God and embraces *Baal-berith* (v. 33, Heb. "Baal of the covenant"). The remembrance of the saving deeds of God and Gideon are buried with Gideon and the people quickly embrace a new deity with a new covenant. Abimelech may be reaffirming some Israelite connection with SHECHEM, since the site was important religiously for Abraham and especially for Jacob, according to the Genesis traditions (Gen 12:1-7; 33:18–35:4; see also Josh 24). In any event, when punishment comes this time, it will not come from outside but from within.

Abimelech journeys to Shechem and offers himself, as a kinsman, to be king of Shechem rather than one of the other of Gideon's seventy sons. Apparently the people of Shechem assume that one of Gideon's sons is to rule over them and they embrace Abimelech. The lords (probably landowners) of Shechem provide Abimelech with money from the temple treasury, which Abimelech uses to hire scoundrels to help him in his bloodthirsty plan. Abimelech and his hired thugs kill seventy of his brothers (cf. 2 Kgs 10:1-7) on a single stone. The reference to the slaughter occurring on a single stone most likely suggests that the slaughter has a ritual purpose. Perhaps Abimelech intends to drain off the blood, the life (Deut 12:16, 24), of his brothers in proper cultic fashion and prevent any further trouble from them. If that is his plan, it does not succeed. Nevertheless the lords of Shechem proclaim him king.

9:7-21. Jotham's fable. Jotham, the youngest son of Gideon, escaped the slaughter of his brothers but now comes forward to address the lords of Shechem. He begins his address with a fable. Animal and plant fables are typical in WISDOM LITERATURE and Jotham may well have borrowed his fable from wisdom circles. The parable states that those things that serve a good and useful purpose (olive tree, fig tree, vine) refuse to serve as king because they do not have the time or inclination to cease their beneficial work in order to rule. It is only the useless bramble that agrees to serve as king. Good Gideon had refused to become king but now useless Abimelech has seized kingship. JOTHAM'S FABLE finds echoes in the last words of David (2 Sam 23:1-7).

After having spoken his fable to the lords of Shechem, Jotham decries their abandonment of his father's memory and their embrace of Abimelech. If they want to be ruled by a bramble, then let them enjoy it. The lords should be warned that Abimelech will be a curse to them and them to him. Jotham then flees from the scene and the story, although his words correctly predict Abimelech's end.

9:22-57. The fall of Abimelech. Abimelech rules in Israel for three years. Certainly he does not rule all of Israel but his campaigns indicate that he rules some Canaanite and Israelite cities in central Palestine. His rule is shortened by the vengeance of God who sends an evil spirit (cf. 1 Sam 16:14; 18:10; 1 Kgs 22:21-23) to set in motion the avenging of the deaths of Gideon's seventy sons. The lords of Shechem begin to move against Abimelech, perhaps because of his failure to raise the city to glorious new heights or his involvement with his troops in matters not directly beneficial to the city. In any case, the lords of Shechem begin robbing travelers who pass through the mountain pass, thus depriving Abimelech of trade revenue.

When Gaal and his clan move in to Shechem, the lords of Shechem side with him. Zebul, the ruler of the city, warns Abimelech of the treason and Abimelech moves against the city. Gaal's boastful threats against Abimelech give way to fear when the time for battle approaches; Gaal is quickly driven out of town by Abimelech.

The next day Abimelech destroys Shechem, killing the people inside, and sowing the city with salt, a symbol of the city's perpetual desolation, a place where nothing would ever thrive again. The lords of Shechem retreat to the stronghold of the temple of *El-berith* (v. 46, Heb. "God of the covenant"), which despite its name is not a place where the God of Israel is worshiped. Abimelech sets the stronghold on fire and burns alive the 1,000 people inside.

Abimelech then moves against Thebez and takes all but the tower. He plans to burn this tower down too but as he approaches the tower a woman drops an upper millstone on his head. An upper millstone was typically a hard stone, a foot or more in diameter, and two inches thick. The stone crushes his skull. Mortally wounded, Abimelech asks his armor bearer to kill him so that he will not be remembered as one who died at the hands of a woman (cf. 1 Sam 31:4).

When Abimelech dies the battle ceases and the people return home. Abimelech's slaughter of his seventy brothers has been avenged. Even had Abimelech lived he would have had very little of a kingdom left. His attempt at kingship meets a bloody end and prefigures the kingship of Saul.

Second Series of Judges, 10:1–16:31

The second series of narratives concerning judges does not present a single example of a good, faithful judge. The minor judges who are mentioned are distinguished only by their wealth. The two major judges, Jephthah and Samson, are distinguished by their personal failings. It becomes evident from these stories that judges are not the answer to Israel's difficulties.

Tola, 10:1-2

Tola was from the tribe of Issachar but resided in Shamir within the territory of Ephraim. He delivered Israel from some unknown enemy and then judged Israel for twenty-three years. Many scholars believe that, since the years of his influence are not rounded off, the number might reflect his precise length of service.

Jair, 10:3-5

Jair was from Gilead and judged Israel for twenty-two years. Although no information is given concerning what deeds he might have accomplished, he exerted a good deal of influence through his family. Each of his thirty sons rode a donkey, indicating wealth and prestige, and ruled over a city. The thirty cities carried on Jair's legacy even to the editor's day.

A Second Introduction, 10:6-16

The present passage likely serves as an introduction to the second half of the book. The passage picks up themes from 2:11-23 and sets the stage for Israel's descent into chaos.

The people cry out to God for help after eighteen years of oppression. God answers them by reminding them of past acts of salvation toward Israel and then stating that he will no longer save them. The people's reported response is indicative of the author's concept of their covenant with God. Trying to catch God in a loophole, the author reports, they acknowledge God's decision not to save them and ask if he will not deliver them. The words are different but the results would be the same. To the people the covenant is a legally binding document, the language of which can be manipulated to secure their self-interests. The people's subsequent repentance is probably superficial but the story concludes with God acting out of love on their behalf.

Jephthah, 10:17–12:7

The Jephthah narrative continues the trend of violence and tragedy begun with Abimelech. By the time of his death after just six years of service to Gilead, Jephthah had experienced early rejection by his half-brothers, the death of his only child, and had led in a punitive attack upon a fellow Israelite tribe. Although he is portrayed in somewhat sympathetic terms, it is difficult to applaud his actions, especially the rash and deadly dangerous vow he made that results in the death of his daughter.

10:17–11:11. The selection of Jephthah. Israel's most recent apostasy leads to persecution by the Philistines and Ammonites. Jephthah will destroy the Ammonite threat while Samson will fight the Philistines.

Jephthah the Gileadite is a son of Gilead by a prostitute. His half-brothers, the sons of Gilead's wife, later drive Jephthah away from the family because they have no intention of sharing their father's inheritance with him. Jephthah becomes head of a band of outlaws, developing quite a reputation for himself as a mighty warrior.

When the Ammonites prepare to attack Israel, Israel seeks a leader for the troops. The tribal elders of Gilead are sent to Jephthah to ask him to become the commander of the army. Jephthah reminds the elders of their previous rejection of him and then offers to lead the troops if the elders will appoint him head of Gilead. The elders have no choice but to grant him this highest tribal office.

11:12-28. An attempt at diplomacy. Rather than attack Ammon, Jephthah first tries to negotiate with them. The Ammonites demand the return of the land east of the Jordan River between the Arnon and Jabbok rivers, land that Israel had taken from them. Jephthah recounts the history of how Israel got the land (cf. Num 20:14–24:25) stressing that God had conquered both Ammon and its god Chemosh and thus by divine conquest Israel was entitled to the land. Since Chemosh could not defend his land, the Ammonites have no right to ask for it back. The Ammonites reject this argument and war becomes inevitable.

11:29-40. Jephthah's vow. As Jephthah prepares to fight against Ammon he is empowered by the spirit of God. This may indicate that, according to the tradition, Jephthah was not necessarily God's choice for deliverer but that God chose to work through the selection of the Gileadites.

Jephthah's vow is probably the most well-known feature of the narrative. If God will give him success in battle, Jephthah vows to sacrifice as a whole burnt offering whoever comes out the door of his house to meet him when he returns. While some suggest that Jephthah is thinking only of an animal sacrifice, the language indicates that the sacrifice will be human. The sacrifice will be someone who greets him, not something that ambles out the front door. The offer of a human sacrifice may be the result of a perceived state of emergency (cf. 2 Kgs 3:26-27 when a Moabite king sacrifices his firstborn) since human sacrifice is prohibited in Israel (Lev 18:21; Deut 18:10). As a nominal Israelite Jephthah may be following a Canaanite practice. In any event he is taking a calculated risk, one that ends in bitter tragedy.

When Jephthah returns home victorious, he is met by his daughter, his only child, who like other women come out to greet the victorious warrior with singing and dancing (Exod 15:20-21; 1 Sam 18:6-7). Her joyous welcome brings unbearable grief to her father. The story presents both father and daughter as persons of integrity who will not retreat from the fulfillment of the vow. The daughter asks for and is granted two months to bewail the fact that she will die childless. When she returns, her father sacrifices her.

This example of human sacrifice is one of the rare cases in the OT in which the sacrifice is not censured by God. A concluding note states that the sacrifice of Jephthah's daughter is commemorated by an annual four-day period of lamentation. Perhaps the commemoration is meant to serve as a vivid reminder to Israel that human sacrifice brings nothing but personal tragedy. It is also a testimony to this unnamed daughter of a leader who was ready to sacrifice a child for the prize of victory in battle.

12:1-7. Conflict with Ephraim. Once again (see 8:1-3) the Ephraimites are furious that they were not summoned earlier to participate in the battle. Jephthah again tries to settle the matter through diplomacy but fails. His attack on Ephraim is successful and he sends them fleeing back toward the Jordan River. The Gileadites guard the fords and test each person who desires to cross by asking them to pronounce a word that will betray their accent. Those who pronounce the word with the Ephraimite accent are killed. In all, the tradition reports that 42,000 Ephraimites die at the hands of Jephthah's troops. Following this battle Jephthah judges Israel for six years and then dies.

Ibzan, 12:8-10

Ibzan judged Israel for seven years and lived in Bethlehem of Judah. Ibzan used his large family to cement ties with other clans and thus expand his influence. Nothing else is known of him.

Elon, 12:11-12

Elon was of the tribe of Zebulun and judged Israel for ten years. Beyond this brief note there is no information regarding his activity in Israel.

Abdon, 12:13-15

Abdon was a member of the tribe of Ephraim. He is distinguished as having forty sons and thirty grandsons, all of whom rode donkeys, indicating their wealth and position (cf. 10:3-5). He judged Israel for eight years.

Samson, 13:1–16:31

The stories of Samson's exploits have been favorites for centuries, and undoubtedly also were to the early Israelites. Imbued by God with prodigious strength (14:6, 19; 15:14; 16:28) and possessing a prodigious sexual appetite, Samson lived as a solitary hero engaged in his own selfish and vengeful ventures rather than as a military leader dedicated to freeing Israel from oppression. His enormous potential is never fully realized and he dies as a result of succumbing to his greatest weakness, women.

13:1-25. Samson's birth. Israelite apostasy leads to Philistine domination for forty years. Samson's tribe of Dan, which was bounded by Ephraim on the north, Benjamin on the east, Judah on the south, and Philistia on the west, would have borne the brunt of Philistine oppression.

The narrative begins with an angel announcing to the wife of Manoah, a Danite, that after years of infertility she will have a son. Typically sons born to women childless for a long time are recognized as special gifts of God and are destined to great things (Gen 17:15-16; 30:22-24; 1 Sam 1:19-20; Luke 1:13-17). The child of this nameless woman is to be no exception. He will begin the deliverance of Israel from the Philistines. The angel's words imply that Samson will not complete this deliverance, thereby hinting at the tragedy to come.

The child is to be set apart from his conception. Manoah's wife is to raise the boy as a nazirite and must immediately embrace the rules of the nazirite herself. The typical vows of the NAZIRITES are refraining from drinking alcohol, cutting the hair, and touching corpses (Num 6:1-8). To these vows the angel adds avoiding unclean foods, a strange addition, since an Israelite should avoid unclean foods anyway. The additional command may indicate significant lapses in Israel's faith and practice.

When Manoah, who was not privy to the angel's visit and words, prays for confirmation, he also receives an angelic visit and miraculous confirmation. The child is born and given the name Samson. From an early age the spirit of God begins to empower him.

14:1–15:8. Samson's doomed marriage. Samson's search for a wife leads him to a Philistine woman from Timnah. He asks his father to arrange the marriage, a typical responsibility of the father of the groom. Both his father and mother protest, wondering why he would want to marry an enemy of Israel. His request is made particularly abhorrent since he is specially dedicated to God and should refrain from contact with pagans. The marriage is divinely sanctioned, for God intends to use the events that follow to begin the divine deliverance of Israel from the Philistines.

Samson and his parents travel separately to Timnah to arrange the marriage. On the way Samson encounters a young lion and rips it apart with his bare hands, much as a person might pull cooked meat from a bone. He does not tell his parents of his action, but on his return trip to marry the woman he stops to see the carcass. A swarm of bees has invaded the carcass and produced honey. Samson scrapes the honey into his hands, eating some on the way home and giving the rest to his parents. With this action he has broken two of the vows his mother had kept for him. He has touched a corpse and eaten unclean food. The vows his mother had kept so faithfully mean little to him.

At his seven-day wedding feast Samson probably breaks the vow to abstain from alcohol; thus, only the vow not to cut his hair is left. At the feast he propounds a RIDDLE to the guests along with a wager. Some have suggested that it was a custom for the groom to offer a riddle for the bride's family to solve. The riddle functioned not only as a game but as an indication of the groom's worthiness as a husband. Samson's riddle is impossible to solve without knowledge of his encounter with the lion and the subsequent cache of honey. The Philistine men therefore soon turn to Samson's wife to help them discover the solution to the riddle. Her constant imploring wrests the solution from Samson; in turn she tells it to the men. Samson is furious; his response to the men implies improper behavior, perhaps sexual, by the men toward his wife. Samson pays the wager by traveling to the Philistine city of Ashkelon, killing thirty men, and bringing their festal garments back. He then leaves in anger, and his wife is then given to his best man.

Many scholars suggest that Samson's marriage was a *sadiqa* marriage. This type of marriage was arranged by the groom rather than his father, which might have been necessitated by Manoah's displeasure with Samson's choice. In a *sadiqa* marriage the wife remains with her family and the husband visits her on a regular basis. Later, Samson does return to see his wife, only to be told that she has been given to another.

In his anger he captures 300 foxes (or more likely jackals), ties them together in pairs by the tails, attaches a burning torch between each pair, and sets them in the Philistine grain fields to burn the crop. The Philistines respond by burning his wife and her father. Samson then responds by killing the men who have committed the deed and then hiding out. Such bloody, personal vendettas mark the Samson narrative.

15:9–16:3. More mighty deeds. The Philistines attack Judah in an effort to find and destroy Samson. The Judeans ask Samson to allow himself to be turned over to the Philistines so that Judah might be saved. Samson agrees, is bound by two new ropes, and is brought to the Philistines. When the Philistines rush to meet him, Samson breaks the ropes as if they had been burned through. He picks up a fresh—thus not brittle—jawbone of a donkey and uses it as an effective weapon to kill 1,000 men (cf. 3:31).

The following brief poem (v. 16) is filled with wordplays. The same Hebrew word means "donkey" and "heap," thus his statement *With the jawbone of a donkey, heaps upon heaps* results in a piling up of one Hebrew word much like the bodies must have piled up. The word for "jawbone" (*lehi*) also serves as the name for the location of the event, *Ramath-lehi*.

After the fight Samson is thirsty and God refreshes him with a miraculous gift of water. The notation that Samson judged Israel for *twenty years* (15:20) may indicate the original conclusion of the Samson story. The tragic finale of Samson's life may well have been a later addition.

Again driven by his sexual appetite, Samson travels to the Philistine city of Gaza to be with a prostitute. The men of the city lie in wait for him. Believing that they have their nemesis trapped within the city walls, the men sleep. During the night Samson arises, pulls the city gate from its sockets, and—bars and all— carries it forty miles to a hill outside Hebron. Again Samson's great strength has helped him elude capture and death.

16:4–31. Samson's death. Samson's downfall comes at the hands of a woman, Delilah. The Philistine lords offer her an exorbitant reward if she can discover the secret of Samson's phenomenal strength. Samson toys with her as he gives his first two answers to her question. Fresh bowstrings and new ropes (cf. 15:13-14) are easily broken. He comes closer to the truth with his third response, since his strength is related to his hair, but weaving his hair tightly into a loom that is secured to the ground is still not enough to subdue him. Finally Delilah's coaxing forces Samson to divulge his secret. While he sleeps in Delilah's lap a man is summoned to cut off his hair. The final vow is broken, and Samson awakens with his strength completely gone. The Philistines bind him, blind him, and force him to turn the grinding mill.

While in forced labor Samson's hair grows back. When he is brought in to entertain the Philistine lords, he asks to stand between the two main pillars that support the roof. The building was filled with people, with 3,000 more sitting on the roof watching the spectacle of the defeated hero. Calling upon God for strength one last time, Samson pushes against the two pillars and the building comes crashing down. All in it and on it die.

The tragedy of Samson's life is summarized by the note that he killed more in his death than in his entire life. Samson's incredible strength made him the ultimate warrior but he squandered his abilities. His death accomplishes more than does his life. The story may be intended to underscore the need both for God's spirit, which Samson has in abundance, and God's guiding word, which Samson consistently fails even to ask for. Therein lies Samson's great failing.

Epilogue, 17:1–21:25

The two narratives of the epilogue have no introduction to tie them to the preceding sections of the book. Yet, the epilogue itself is linked together by the repetition of the observation *In those days there was no king in Israel; all the people did what was right in their own eyes* (17:6; 25:21; a similar saying occurs in 18:1 and 19:1). The two narratives are also joined by having as a main character a Levite who lives in Ephraim. In general the narratives illustrate the tragic results of Israelite faith and morals under its weak, disorganized tribal system. These two narratives complete the descent of Israel into anarchy.

Migration of Dan, 17:1–18:31

These two chapters explain how Dan moved from its assigned southern territory to its northern territory (cf. Josh 19:40-48). The narrative is difficult to place chronologically because 5:17 already seems to assume that Dan is in the north close to Asher. The narrative does logically follow the Samson story, which indicated that Dan was being hard-pressed by the Philistines.

17:1-13. Micah creates a shrine. The narrative opens with the introduction of Micah, an Ephraimite, who confesses to his mother that he had stolen 1,100 pieces of silver from her. The curse his mother had placed on the thief and the silver likely had tormented him and forced his confession. His grateful mother blesses him, which serves to neutralize the curse. She then consecrates the silver to God for the purpose of making an idol. She gives 200 pieces of the silver to a silversmith who casts an idol for her. Micah then makes an ephod and teraphim and installs his son as priest in his shrine.

Already two theological problems surface. Although all of the silver was consecrated to God, only 200 pieces are used to make an idol. Apparently the rest of the money was simply kept by the mother for her own use. In addition, the making of an idol is hardly a way to honor God (Exod 20:4-6).

Later a wandering Levite from Judah arrives and Micah employs him to serve as priest at his shrine. Micah believes that having a shrine will bring blessing to him, but having a shrine supervised by a trained religious functionary who knows the prayers and psalms and who can consult and interpret oracles will surely make him prosper.

One interesting aspect of the text is the mention that the Levite is from Judah. Although 18:30 identifies the Levite as Jonathan, a grandson of Moses, his ancestry seems unimportant. Even as Samuel from Ephraim served as a priest for Israel, so this one who claims Judah as his home can also serve as a priest. Apparently in early Israel, religious knowledge and ability were more important criteria for selecting a priest than was ancestry.

18:1-31. Dan finds a new home. Five spies from Dan are sent north to find a new territory. On their way they stay with Micah for the night and recognize the voice of the Levite—perhaps because of his accent, or his use of prayers, or because they have met him before. The spies ask the Levite to inquire of God concerning the success of their mission. The Levite does, and the spies receive a favorable oracle.

After having spied out Laish in the north, the spies return and present a good report concerning the place to the tribe. The spies describe Laish as an unsuspecting and wealthy city, a description that agrees well with Phoenician culture. The Phoenicians were more interested in commerce and agriculture than war, so Laish would present a tempting target. The Danites send 600 soldiers with their families (18:21) to conquer the city.

On the way the Danite force stops at the home of Micah and asks the Levite to become the priest of not one family but an entire tribe. The Levite accepts the offer and accompanies the Danites, who also take the idol, ephod, and teraphim. Micah discovers his shrine and priest are gone and gives chase. In a pitiful scene he asks for the return of his homemade gods and employed priest. When the stronger Danite force threatens Micah, he returns home.

The Danites continue their journey, destroy Laish, and rebuild it as Dan. The Levite sets up the shrine, and he and his descendants serve as priests until the deportation by Assyria, probably under Tiglath-pileser III in 733 BCE

Although the narrative describes how Dan settled in the north, another purpose seems to be to mock the temple constructed in Dan (1 Kgs 12:28-30). As ancestry became more important for the priesthood, it was noted that the Levite had good credentials (18:30) but he was a priest for hire, serving his own selfish interests. Furthermore, the shrine itself was the result of thievery, a curse, greed, and death. Such a shrine could not help but produce a faithless people. In 1 Kgs 12, the shrine set up by Rehoboam at Bethel also is criticized for being under the care of unsuitable priests.

Destruction of Benjamin, 19:1–21:24

The final narrative of the book recounts the worst tale by far. The lack of hospitality shown to a Levite by the town of Gibeah in Benjamin leads to a civil war in which Benjamin is almost lost as one of the twelve tribes. The story is filled with horrible crimes and bloodthirsty vengeance. In addition to the horror of the events, interpreters have difficulty accounting for the tremendous, probably inflated, numbers of soldiers, the united action of the Israelite tribes, and Israel's action, considered not politically but theologically.

19:1-30. The rape of the Levite's concubine. The narrative begins with marital difficulty. A Levite who lives in Ephraim journeys to Bethlehem to retrieve his concubine who had left him out of anger. Apparently the Levite suitably apologizes because the reconciliation of the Levite with his concubine and her father is complete and joyful. After five days of feasting the Levite sets out late in the afternoon with his concubine, a servant, and two donkeys. As night comes the servant encourages him to spend the night in Jebus (Jerusalem). The Levite refuses because Jebus is not an Israelite city. They journey on to Gibeah in Benjamin.

Gibeah gives them a cold reception. No one shows hospitality to them until an old man from Ephraim offers to take them in. The fact that the only hospitable person in Gibeah has turned out to be a resident alien himself is not a good omen. During the night the men of the city come to the old man's house demanding to rape the Levite. The host offers his virgin daughter and the concubine instead but his offer is not accepted. The Levite pushes his concubine out the door to the men and she is raped to death. The story is reminiscent of Lot's experience in Sodom (Gen 19:1-8).

The next morning the Levite exits the house and coldly calls to his concubine to get up. When he sees that she is dead, he puts her body on one of the donkeys and takes her back to his home. He then divides her body into twelve pieces, sending one piece to the head of each tribe. Although symbolic divisions are common in the OT (cf. 1 Sam 11:7; 1 Kgs 11:29-31), the physical division of the concubine is not necessary to summon the tribes and is used primarily to arouse the horror of the other Israelites. Such an act might be tolerated among the Canaanite nations but never should have occurred or been tolerated in Israel. The Levite seems to be acting the part of a judge in inspiring Israel to defeat its enemy, but that is all he will do. He seems bent on personal vengeance and will not lead the troops.

20:1-48. The war against Benjamin. For the first time in the book all of the Israelite tribes assemble for a common cause. The Levite recounts his story and the tribes resolve to deal with Gibeah. When Benjamin is asked to turn over the guilty ones from Gibeah, the tribe refuses, probably out of a sense of tribal solidarity. Their refusal prompts the war against Benjamin.

The eleven tribes muster 400,000 soldiers while Benjamin fields 26,000. Both numbers are extremely large and are most likely exaggerated. Of the Benjaminite forces 700 are left-handed slingers who are incredibly accurate. Benjamin was known for its left-handed warriors (3:15; 1 Chr 12:2) and their accuracy explains the heavy losses the Israelites experience on the first two days of fighting.

At Bethel, Israel inquires as to which tribe should lead the attack on Benjamin and Judah is selected (cf. 1:1-2). The first two days of the battle are victories for Benjamin with Benjamin killing 40,000 from Israel. Prayer, fasting, and sacrifices on the afternoon of the second day of battle bring a favorable oracle from God promising victory to Israel. On the third day of battle a new strategy is employed (cf. Josh 8:3-23) and Benjamin is defeated. Of the Benjaminite forces only 600 escape to hide out in the rocky wilderness. The remaining inhabitants of Benjamin, their cities, their animals, and their possessions are all destroyed. Through this destruction the evil is removed from Israel (cf. Num 16:31-33; Josh 7:24-26).

21:1-24. The restoration of Benjamin. Now that Benjamin is almost destroyed, the eleven tribes grieve that this one tribe may soon cease to exist. They have vowed not to give their daughters in marriage to any Benjaminite but to sustain the tribe, wives must be found for the 600 men who escaped.

Discussion reveals that Jabesh-gilead did not send any troops to join in the attack of Benjamin. Apparently Jabesh-gilead was as strong an ally of Benjamin at this time, as it was later (1 Sam 11:1-11; 31:11-13). Israel sends a force of 12,000 to destroy Jabesh-gilead and all of its inhabitants, excluding the virgin girls. The 400 virgin girls found in Jabesh-gilead are brought back to become wives for 400 of the Benjaminites.

Still 200 of the Benjaminites do not have wives. Israel instructs them to lie in wait in the vineyards outside Shiloh. The annual festival to God is being celebrated in Shiloh, and during the festival the virgin girls dance in the vineyards. The 200 men are each to carry off a girl for a wife. Any complaint from Shiloh will be settled by the tribes. When this is accomplished, the men of Benjamin and their new wives return home to rebuild.

The narrative of the destruction of Benjamin is perhaps the most offensive in the Bible. It is a story in which people abuse others, overreact, and think only after they have acted. It is a dreadful conclusion to the tragic period of the judges, underscoring the author's view of this lawless period.

Conclusion, 21:25

The book ends in suspense with the observations that *there was no king in Israel* and *all the people did what was right in their own eyes*. From the book as a whole it is obvious that this state of affairs cannot continue. Religion will have to be reformed and somehow standardized. A national leader will have to be appointed who has more than simple charismatic authority. The loose system could have worked, the author implies, if the people had followed God, but they did not. If the horrors are to cease, another stronger, centralized system will have to be set in place.

Ruth [MCB 259-67]

Mona West

Introduction

Ruth is one of two books in the Hebrew Bible named after a woman. It is unique in the CANON of Hebrew scriptures and Israelite patriarchal society because it celebrates human friendship found in the love and devotion of one woman for another.

The Book of Ruth tells the story of two women in a man's world. One woman is an Israelite named NAOMI. The other is a Moabite named Ruth. They are women in tension with patriarchal culture. Both exist within the complex web of laws and customs of ancient Near Eastern society that define and limit their existence (see WOMEN IN THE OT). Both work out their salvation as agents of the divine, moving in and out of these laws, choosing for themselves and each other.

Not only are the women in tension with a patriarchal culture, but the story itself is in tension with the redactors and interpreters of the Hebrew Bible. The narrative exhibits a struggle between the women's story and the story of patriarchal Israel. At the end of the book readers may well wonder who will have the last say. Will it be the townswomen who pronounce a blessing on Ruth's love for Naomi? Or will it be the narrator and the final redactor who emphasize that the child *born to Naomi* is the grandfather of King David?

Ultimately, it is the interpreters of the Hebrew Bible who have the last say. Ruth has been romanticized by traditional biblical scholarship as a meek maiden in distress who is rescued by Boaz. Her only virtue is that she is the great-grandmother of King David. This predominantly white-male interpretive tradition has found itself in tension with feminist interpretations of Ruth that seek to reclaim Ruth, the woman from Moab who struggled against the odds to make a way for herself and Naomi in a foreign land.

Ruth's story is also in tension with Israel's story. Its heroine is a Moabite and the Moabites were a people who had a long history of strife with the Israelites. This story exists within the Hebrew canon as witness to the fact that even though the Hebrew Bible is the story of Israel, scripture is not monolithic in its presentation of faith. Ruth's story, embedded in the story of Israel, reminds us that God does not always play by the rules of the status quo. God comes to us in the midst of life, life that is sometimes difficult and does not follow a neat story line.

Date and Literary Form

There are two dates possible for the composition of the Book of Ruth: the period of the EXILE and during the UNITED MONARCHY. Arguments for an exilic date include: the need to explain earlier customs (4:7); emphasis on the marriage of BOAZ to a foreigner, which would be a polemic against the strict marriage laws of Ezra and Nehemiah after the exile; and the appearance in the book of certain archaic Hebrew terminology that is prominently used during the exilic period.

Those who claim an earlier date for the book counter these exilic arguments by exposing the weakness inherent in establishing a chronology for narratives based on the laws they reflect or need to explain; by claiming that there is nothing polemical about the tone of the book; and by using the same Hebrew archaisms in support of a date of composition during the united monarchy.

The literary form of the book adds to the debate. Scholars are agreed that Ruth is a Hebrew short story, but there are differences of opinion concerning the origins and development of that literary GENRE. For some, the short story developed in the postexilic period and includes examples such as Esther, Jonah, and the apocryphal Book of Judith. For others, the short story (or novelle) can be found as early as the time of Solomon (961–922 BCE), with examples such as the Joseph narrative (Gen 37–50) and the Court History of David (2 Sam 9–20; 1 Kgs 1–2).

The Book of Ruth shares more stylistic and theological features with the earlier material. Like the Joseph Novelle and the Court History, Ruth foregrounds human action, while actions of the deity are backgrounded or nonexistent. The theological emphasis of these stories is that courageous and kind actions of individuals mirror the deity and provide life for the community. In contrast, selfish and violent actions do not mirror the deity and do not benefit the larger community. These comparisons, coupled with the fact that the book is set during the period of the judges (ca. 1200–1020 BCE) and ends with the mention of King David (1000–961 BCE), provide adequate arguments for the composition of the book during the reign of Solomon.

Place in Canon, Setting, and Purpose

Place in Canon. The Book of Ruth is found in the third division of the Hebrew CANON called the Writings. According to the most reliable Hebrew manuscripts, it is placed after Proverbs and before the Song of Solomon. Ruth is an example of the "worthy woman" described in the closing acrostic poem of Proverbs (Prov 31:10-31; cf. Ruth 3:11 where Boaz calls Ruth a *worthy woman*). Ruth's relevance to Song of Solomon is demonstrated by her example of freedom and expressiveness in human relationships, two attributes emphasized in the love poetry of the Song.

Ruth is also grouped among the Megilloth, or five festival scrolls, which are read during important Jewish religious celebrations. Ruth is read during the feast of Weeks. This festival commemorates the giving of the law on Sinai and celebrates the end of the grain harvest. The Book of Ruth is a fitting text for this Jewish observance because of its references to legal customs and its themes of harvest and famine.

Setting. Because of its setting Ruth is placed among the historical books, between Judges and 1 Samuel, in Christian Bibles. Ruth provides a balance to the lawlessness and violence exhibited in the Book of Judges, while looking toward monarchy. The editorial comment at the end of Judges—"In those days there was no king in Israel; all the people did what was right in their own eyes"—establishes a context for the beginnings of the monarchy, which will be described in 1 and 2 Samuel. Ruth provides a bridge from judges to monarchy with genealogical references to David at the end of the book.

While Ruth provides a canonical bridge from judges to monarchs, it may also provide a sociohistorical bridge. Recent sociological analyses indicate that the formative years of premonarchical Israel reflect a time when men and women enjoyed near-equal status. They would have participated "equally" in the areas of procreation, protection from enemies, and production of food as they strived to make the ideal of the COVENANT community of Yahweh a reality. Once the monarchy is established there is a certain loss of the covenant ideal and the imposition of a hierarchical/hereditary leadership structure that precludes women from equal participation in society, thereby resulting in their lowered status (see Meyers 1978 and 1983).

Purpose. Canonical placement and setting indicate that the characters of Ruth are examples of how human beings are to live responsibly toward one another in the context of covenant. Ruth, Naomi, and Boaz are exemplary characters in Israel's history. However, Ruth's actions as a foreigner and a childless widow (see WIDOW IN THE OT) stand out above the other characters. She establishes a place for herself in Israel's history and canon by making responsible choices out of love and devotion to Naomi. The book also redeems women's loss of status during the period of the monarchy by presenting the "equal participation" of Ruth in the areas of procreation, protection, and production.

Law and Narrative

There has been much debate concerning the legal material in the Book of Ruth and its relationship to the narrative. Two laws seem to be most prominent. The Levirate, which required a living brother to marry his deceased brother's widow and have a son by her (Deut 25:5-10), is alluded to by Naomi in 1:12-13 and by Boaz in 4:7-10 (see MARRIAGE IN THE OT). The *goēl* law requiring a kinsman to buy back (redeem, Heb. גאל) a relative or his land (Lev 25) is mentioned throughout the Book of Ruth, once Boaz has been introduced to the narrative. (cf. 2:20; 3:9, 12-13; 4:1, 3, 4, 6, 7). Both the Levirate and *goēl* legislations are placed in a unique context when applied to the situations of Ruth, Naomi, and Boaz.

Other laws that affect the narrative are gleaning and "spreading the skirt or cloak." In chap. 2 Ruth "happens" into the field of Boaz when she decides to take advantage of the Israelite gleaning law that provides for the poor, the orphaned, the widow, and the foreigner (Lev 19:9-10; 23:22; Deut 24:19-22). At the threshing floor in chap. 3, Ruth proposes to Boaz by using the phrase *spread your cloak over your servant* (3:9). This phrase is symbolic of marriage in Israelite tradition (Deut 22:30; 27:20; cf. Ezek 16:8).

It is important to realize that the artistry and message of Ruth are dependent on the interplay of law and narrative within the book. This artistry is lost if the book is approached as a legal treatise or test case for the laws it contains. Instead, the legal material should be viewed as a creative matrix for plot movement and character development. The laws are intentionally ambiguous in order to provide possibilities for the characters to act above and beyond what society requires of them. Laws define their identity and challenge their existence. As each character makes choices that go beyond the letter of the law, that character moves toward a more authentic existence within the narrative and Israel's society.

Ruth's choices are more astounding because she makes her way in this society and legal system as a foreigner. Not only are her actions more astounding, but they provide an example for Naomi and Boaz. Ruth inspires these Israelites to act responsibly toward her and toward each other. Without her example Naomi would have remained an empty, bitter old woman and Boaz would not have been part of the lineage of King David.

In this interplay another tension is exhibited: the creative tension between law and narrative. Law embodies the strictures of patriarchal culture that define and limit authentic existence. Narrative represents the ways in which risks must be taken and decisions made that move one toward authentic existence.

Major Themes

Themes in the Book of Ruth function in much the same way as the laws: they promote plot movement and characterization. Many themes parallel the laws found in the book; several occur in pairs. For example, the theme of redemption (see REDEMPTION IN THE OT) that dominates chaps. 2–4 is related to the duty of the *goēl*. This theme combined with its legal background provides a context for Naomi, Ruth, and Boaz to make choices concerning the letter of the law. It also provides suspense as the readers of the story wonder who will emerge as the one with the right to re-deem Ruth and Naomi, Boaz, or the nearer redeemer?

Covenant kindness or *chesed* (LOVING-KINDNESS) is also related to the laws of redemption. Naomi mentions the kindness of her daughters-in-law in 1:8 as she tries to convince them to return to their homeland, Moab. More importantly, Boaz recog-nizes the kindness of Ruth toward Naomi when he states, *"you left your father and mother and your native land and came to a people that you did not know before"*

(2:11). Boaz also identifies a second kindness of Ruth toward Naomi that is greater than the first: *"you have not gone after young men, whether poor or rich"* (3:10).

Foreignness and familiality intertwine with the laws of gleaning, levirate, and goel as Ruth moves from a foreigner in the fields of Boaz to wife and mother in Israel. Ruth's names at different stages in the narrative reflect this movement. In chap. 1 the narrator emphasizes she is *the Moabite . . . who came back . . . from the country of Moab* (1:22). She is ambiguously referred to as *daughter* and *servant* in relation to Boaz throughout chaps. 2 and 3. She is proclaimed a *worthy woman* by Boaz in 3:11 (the same phrase used to describe Boaz in 2:1). At the end of the story she is called *wife* (4:10, 13).

The themes of emptiness/fullness and harvest/famine function on parallel levels. Emptiness/fullness describe the human realm, while harvest/famine describe the agricultural realm. Naomi goes to Moab because there is a famine in Bethlehem. Yet she leaves Bethlehem *full* because she has a husband and two sons. Once there is food in Bethlehem she returns. However, she returns *empty* because her husband and sons have died in Moab (1:21).

The emptiness/fullness of Naomi and Ruth will be worked out against the backdrop of harvest in Bethlehem. The narrator mentions in 1:22 that while Naomi and Ruth have returned from Moab empty, they have returned at the beginning of the barley harvest. This sounds a note of hope for the women's situation. Likewise, a word of caution is given at the end of chap. 2 when the narrator states that the wheat and barley harvests have ended.

Literary Structure

Each chapter in the Book of Ruth exhibits a three-part structure. The first part of each chapter introduces the choices of a particular character, which will set the stage for the choices of other characters in the middle part of that chapter. The final section of the chapter presents doubt about the outcome of the choices that have been made.

This same structure can be seen in the overall pattern of the book. Chapter 1 presents the choice of Ruth to return with Naomi. This choice sets the stage for Ruth's encounters with Boaz in the field in chap. 2 and at the threshing floor in chap. 3. Chapters 2 and 3 constitute the middle of the book in which Ruth, Boaz, and Naomi make choices that go beyond the letter of the law. Chapter 4 deals with the consequences of their choices, with its scene at the city gate, the blessing of the elders, and the pronouncement of the townswomen.

For Further Study

In the *Mercer Dictionary of the Bible*: MARRIAGE IN THE OT; MOAB/MOABITES; NAOMI; RUTH, BOOK OF; WEEKS, FESTIVAL OF; WOMEN IN THE OT.

In other sources: J. W. H. Bos, *Ruth, Esther, Jonah*, Knox Preaching Guides; E. F. Campbell, *Ruth*, AncB; P. Trible, *God and the Rhetoric of Sexuality*.

Commentary

An Outline

Choosing Between Moab and Bethlehem, 1:1-22

Trouble in Moab: Elimelech Decides to Leave the Homeland, 1:1-5

Because of famine, a man from Bethlehem decides to move his family to the foreign land of Moab. This choice of life soon becomes a choice of death as the man, Elimelech, and his two sons Mahlon and Chilion eventually die in this foreign land. Elimelech's choice not only leads to the loss of physical life, but it leaves his wife NAOMI with a loss of security and identity. Naomi left Bethlehem full, now after ten years in Moab she is empty. In a patriarchal culture a woman's worth is measured by her husband and sons. Not only has Naomi lost her own worth, but her two Moabite daughters-in-law, Orpah and Ruth, have been widowed as well.

In these few verses all the major characters of the story have been introduced with the exception of Boaz. The choice of Elimelech has set the stage for the choices of Naomi, Orpah, and Ruth in the verses that follow.

Between Moab and Bethlehem: Decisions about Returning, 1:6-18

These verses highlight the struggle of the women as they seek to survive in a patriarchal culture. They join together, dependent on one another for support, and begin the long journey back to Naomi's homeland, Bethlehem. On the way, Naomi, being the older, wiser woman, realizes that even in their solidarity they are three widows in a man's world. Her daughters-in-law have a better chance for survival and acceptance if they remain in their homeland and remarry.

Naomi is a woman conditioned by the laws of patriarchal Israel. Through her mention of the Levirate law (1:11-13) she claims she has nothing to offer Orpah and Ruth: no husband, no sons. She fails to recognize that she has herself to offer as a mother-in-law to these two *daughters* (v. 11) who have chosen to return with her.

Each woman is faced with a decision about returning. These decisions are made between Moab and Bethlehem, between what seems to be the security of homeland and the risk of foreign land. Moab is homeland for Orpah and Ruth. It is a symbol of patriarchy, echoed in the words of Naomi to her daughters-in-law: the only way to find security is in the house of a husband (1:9).

Moab is foreign land to Naomi. It has been a place of death and, by patriarchal standards, a place where the security and identity of all the women have been lost. One wonders what the possibilities of life may have been had Naomi decided to stay in Moab, against the odds, joined to her two daughters-in-law.

Bethlehem is homeland for Naomi. For all of the security the homeland is supposed to offer, it is a place where Naomi returns to live out her bitterness and emptiness. As foreign land for Orpah and Ruth, Bethlehem is a place to risk life with Naomi. The risk is too great for Orpah. She is persuaded by Naomi to return to her homeland of Moab. Though her choice seems the most sensible one by patriarchal standards, it is a choice that causes her to disappear from the story.

Ruth chooses Bethlehem and Naomi. Out of love and devotion she willing changes places with her mother-in-law. In Moab Naomi is the foreign woman with no husband, no sons, no identity. In Bethlehem Ruth will be the foreign woman with no husband, no sons, no identity. It is within this context that the force of Ruth's words of commitment to Naomi are heard:

> *Do not press me to leave you*
> *or to turn back from following you!*
> *Where you go, I will go;*
> *where you lodge, I will lodge;*
> *your people shall be my people,*
> *and your God my God.*
> *Where you die, I will die—*
> *there will I be buried.*
> *May the Lord do thus and so to me,*
> *and more as well,*
> *if even death parts me from you!* (vv. 16-17)

Ruth refused to accept the status quo of a male-centered society that said women were nothing without men. Instead she chose, against the odds, to commit herself totally to another woman. Truly Ruth, Naomi, and Orpah demonstrate by their choices what it means to be women in patriarchal culture, against patriarchal culture, and transforming patriarchal culture (Trible 1978, 196).

Arriving in Bethlehem: What Will Become of the Two Women?, 1:19-22

This scene echoes the first with its themes of emptiness and fullness. After their arrival in Bethlehem Naomi makes clear her sense of loss and bitterness by her response to the townswomen, *"Call me no longer Naomi* [pleasant], *call me Mara* [bitter]" (v. 20). She is still a woman who sees her own worth in terms of patriarchal society. She claims she is empty, no husband, no sons. She does not acknowledge that Ruth has returned with her. Naomi is not totally empty: there is her daughter-in-law who has taken an oath to be with her until death.

The narrator sounds a note of hope mixed with doubt in v. 22. Ruth and Naomi arrive in Bethlehem during the beginning of the barley harvest. What started as the story of a family of six has narrowed to the plight of two. What would become of these two women—the one who had chosen homeland and by implication patriarchy and the status quo, and the other who had risked the foreign land, Ruth the Moabite, who had chosen for herself and for her mother-in-law?

Choices in the Field, 2:1-23

Introduction of Boaz: Ruth Decides to Glean, 2:1-7

BOAZ is introduced for the first time in the narrative in v. 1. The narrator emphasizes Boaz's patriarchal potential for Ruth and Naomi by stating that he is a *kinsman, a prominent rich man,* and *of the family of Elimelech.* In v. 2 Ruth decides to take advantage of the Israelite gleaning law that provided for widows and foreigners. In these two verses there is a tension between patriarchy and the women. How will Ruth and Naomi survive in Bethlehem? Patriarchy's answer is Boaz. Ruth's answer is to glean.

This tension is further displayed in Ruth's statement to Naomi and in Boaz's conversation with his foreman. Ruth claims she is going into the field to glean *behind someone in whose sight I may find favor* (v. 2). She "happens" to glean in the field of Boaz (v. 3b). Upon noticing her, Boaz asks a question only a man of his culture could: *"To whom does this young woman belong"* (v. 5)? It is a question of ownership, to which the name of a husband or father would have been a normal response. The foreman's response implies that Ruth belongs to no man. Instead, she belongs to Naomi: *"She is the Moabite who came back with Naomi from the country of Moab"* (v. 6).

Was it by chance or by design that Ruth "happened" to glean in Boaz's field? Did she have previous knowledge of Boaz? She had been married to a kinsman of his for as long as ten years in Moab (1:4). If she was not aware of Boaz as a kinsman, she at least knew (along with everyone else in town) that Boaz was a prominent rich man. She deliberately went to Boaz's field to glean, to *find favor,* to take fullest advantage of the Israelite gleaning law. Would not it make sense to glean in the field of one of the wealthiest men in town?

Ruth's choice to glean in Boaz's field is in keeping with the deliberate choice she made to return with Naomi in chap. 1, and the deliberate choices she will make throughout the book. Her choice puts her in contact with Boaz. There is some ambiguity about his relationship to Naomi and Ruth. The word used to describe him as a kinsman in v. 1 can mean "intimate friend" or "blood relative."

First Encounter: Boaz Decides to Protect; Ruth Continues to Glean, 2:8-16

As a male in Israelite society and owner of the field, Boaz offers Ruth protection from molestation as she gleans (vv. 8-9). These are the first words he speaks directly to Ruth, to which she responds, *"Why have I found favor in your sight, that you should take notice of me, when I am a foreigner?"* (v. 10) These words seem out of place given the fact that Ruth intended to find favor. She is concerned about her foreign status and wants to know *Boaz's intentions*. Ruth had hoped to find favor from an economic standpoint. She wants to know if Boaz intends anything else by his offer of protection.

Boaz makes his intentions clear. His offer of protection is out of kindness and respect. He knows of her devotion to Naomi and blesses her (vv. 11-12). Once Ruth is sure of his intentions she replies, *"May I continue to find favor in your sight, my lord, for you have comforted me and spoken kindly to your servant, even though I am not one of your servants"* (v. 13). The word Ruth uses for *servant* is from the same root as the word used to describe Boaz as *kinsman* in 2:1. Once again the language used to depict the relationship between Ruth and Boaz is multilayered and ambiguous. Ruth's words indicate that Boaz is not attempting to take advantage of her as a foreigner and a widow. Instead, he has treated her as a family member or close friend even though at this point in the story she is not. The ambiguity suggests that there is the potential for Ruth to become a family member of Boaz.

Gleaning provides the backdrop for Ruth and Boaz to make decisions that go beyond what is minimally required by the law. Ruth decides to continue gleaning in the best field in town so that she can provide food for herself and Naomi. Boaz decides to offer protection and provide special gleaning privilege to Ruth (vv. 14-16) out of kindness and respect for Ruth's devotion to Naomi.

Report to Naomi: How Long Will This Arrangement Last?, 2:17-23

When Naomi sees how much Ruth has gleaned, she asks, *"Where have you worked?"* Before Ruth can answer, Naomi proclaims, *"Blessed be the man who took notice of you"* (v. 19). Naomi's words continue to reflect her patriarchal conditioning. She assumes Ruth could not have gleaned all that she had without the help of a man. When Ruth tells her that the name of the man is Boaz, Naomi clears up any ambiguity concerning him that Ruth, or the reader, may have had. She states that the man is "near to us, one of our redeemers" (v. 20). By introducing the goel or law of redemption Naomi implies that Boaz does have a certain legal relationship to her and Ruth.

At the end of the chapter it looks as if these two women will make it in a man's world after all. Ruth had found a way to live out her commitment to Naomi: she gleaned in Boaz's field and lived with her mother-in-law (v. 23). However, the barley and wheat harvests have ended, implying that there are limits to what Ruth can do. She does not own the field. She has worked out the best arrangement she could under the circumstances, but now some other arrangement must be made.

Choices at the Threshing Floor, 3:1-18

Preparation for the Threshing Floor: Naomi Decides to Help, 3:1-5

With words reminiscent of 1:9, Naomi decides to seek security for Ruth. As a woman defined by patriarchal culture Naomi reciprocates Ruth's devotion in the only way she knows how: she instructs Ruth to make herself available to Boaz. What is Naomi's intent? Is it seduction? A romantic encounter? An attempt to jolt Boaz to action? Her intentions are ambiguous, just as the encounter itself will be. This ambiguity is echoed at the beginning of Naomi's instructions in the word she uses to relate Boaz to herself and Ruth (3:2). It is the same word from 2:1, which can mean kinsman or close friend.

Naomi's decision to act on Ruth's behalf will set the stage for the second encounter between Ruth and Boaz. On the threshing floor these two characters will make choices that place them in tension with the goel law.

Second Encounter: Ruth Decides to Marry; Boaz Decides to Redeem, 3:6-15

The encounter between Ruth and Boaz at the threshing floor is similar to their first meeting in chap. 2. In what could have been a sexual rendezvous in which Boaz has the advantage, Ruth clarifies the situation and states her intent. Like gleaning in the fields, Ruth takes advantage of the *goēl* law and proposes to Boaz by instructing him to "spread his skirt or cloak" over her because he is *next-of-kin* or *goēl*" (v. 9). Ruth repeats the words Boaz spoke to her in the field in chap. 2. The same word for *wing* in 2:12 is the word used for *cloak* in 3:9. Ruth claims that Boaz will be the means by which she and Naomi will find refuge under the wing of *the God of Israel* (cf 2:12).

Ruth's decision to marry Boaz should be seen as a business proposition in an effort to continue to take care of Naomi. The wheat and barley harvest have ended. Marriage is the alternative arrangement she suggests to Boaz. Boaz's response in v. 10 confirms the nature of the arrangement: *"This last instance of your loyalty is better than the first* [the first being choosing Naomi over Moab, cf. 2:11]*; you have not gone after young men, whether poor or rich."*

In v. 11 Boaz agrees to the marriage and decides to perform the duty of the *goēl*. He does this because Ruth is a "woman of *worth*" (RSV). This is the same word the narrator used in 2:1 (NRSV, *rich*) to describe Boaz. Could this be a turning point in the story? Has the tension between the women and patriarchy been resolved? In chap. 1 Ruth had no worth by the standards of patriarchal society. In v. 11 Ruth's worth is pronounced by Boaz (and recognized by all the people of Bethlehem) on the basis of her devotion to Naomi. The choices of Ruth have been an example for all of Bethlehem. They have spurred Naomi and Boaz to action.

Just as the narrative possibility of each character begins to come to life in this chapter, the tension of the patriarchy is reintroduced in the person of the nearer REDEEMER and the strictures of the *goēl* law. This tension is represented by the haunting repetition of the word *goēl* or *kinsman* and *next-of-kin* in vv. 12-13. Boaz states:

> "Though it is true that I am a near **kinsman**, there is another **kinsman** more closely related than I. . . . if he will act as **next-of-kin** for you, good. . . . If he is not willing to act as **next-of-kin** for you, then . . . I will act as **next-of-kin** for you."

At the end of v. 13 Boaz tells Ruth to "*Lie down until the morning.*" This phrase has been repeated throughout the encounter between Ruth and Boaz at the threshing floor. It is indicative of the sexual tension in this chapter. Naomi was the first to introduce the possibility of a sexual encounter with her instructions in 3:1-5. She told Ruth in v. 4, "*When he lies down, observe the place where he lies; then, go and uncover his feet and lie down; and he will tell you what to do.*" The narrator reiterates the possibility of sexual encounter by repeating the phrase *lie down* twice in v. 7. Then, after the marriage agreement has been made between Ruth and Boaz and Boaz instructs Ruth to "*Lie down until the morning*" (v. 13), the narrator repeats this in v. 14.

The repetition of this phrase signifies that Ruth and Boaz make their choices not only as human beings in the context of the *goēl* law, but as man and woman in the privacy of the night. While the possibility of sexual encounter exists, the reality of their previous choices would indicate that no intercourse took place at the threshing floor.

Report to Naomi: What about the Nearer Redeemer?, 3:16-18

As in chap. 2, Ruth reports the results of her encounter with Boaz to Naomi. Naomi's instructions are to wait. These instructions contrast the aggressive ones she had given Ruth at the beginning of the chapter. Ruth and Naomi wait to see what will become of the choices made on the threshing floor. They wait for Boaz to settle the matter of the nearer redeemer.

Choices at the City Gate, 4:1-22

Business as Usual: Deciding Not to Redeem, 4:1-6

What had been decided in private at the threshing floor in chap. 3 gets worked out in public at the city gate in chap. 4. In Israelite society, the city gate is the place where legal matters are settled. In contrast to the sexual overtones of the phrase *lie down*, the phrase *sit down* is repeated in 4:1-4. Boaz himself sits down at the city gate, calls to the nearer redeemer to *sit down*, then beckons to the elders to *sit down* (see vv. 1, 2, 4). The business of patriarchy takes over as the two women left waiting at the end of chap. 3 fade into the background, while decisions about their futures are worked out within the confines of the laws of Israelite society.

Boaz sets up the nearer redeemer by telling him about a parcel of land that Naomi is selling. There has been no mention of the field in the story until this point, and readers are left wondering how Boaz knows about it and why Naomi has not mentioned it. Boaz does not refer to Ruth when the field is discussed, and the tension/suspense of the *goēl* from the end of chap. 3 continues with the repetition of the verb *redeem* throughout this section: *"If you will redeem it, redeem it; but if you will not, tell me, . . . for there is no one prior to you to redeem it. . . . "* So he said, *"I will redeem it"* (v. 4).

When the next-of-kin chooses to redeem the land (v. 4), Boaz mentions Ruth and combines the Levirate law with the duty of the *goēl* (v. 5). With Ruth in the picture, the *next-of-kin* decides not to redeem the land and passes the option to Boaz. Like Orpah's choice in chap. 1, the nearer redeemer's choice represents the practical. It is indicative of the status quo, defined by the law. While neither Orpah nor the nearer redeemer is condemned for the choice made, they die to the story because they do not choose beyond what is minimally required by the law. The act of taking risks that go beyond the status quo brings life—life to the story, life to the individuals who take the risks, and life to the community.

Finalizing the Deal: Boaz Announces His Marriage to Ruth, 4:7-12

In this section the business of the men at the city gate is extended by an explanation from the narrator concerning a legal custom of drawing off the sandal. It is associated with redemption and may be related more to sealing a business transaction than to the Levirate law (cf. Deut 25:8-10). In the context of this transaction, Boaz makes public his private arrangement with Ruth at the threshing floor (vv. 9-10). In contrast to the nearer redeemer, Boaz does more than the law requires.

The entire exchange between Boaz and the nearer redeemer has taken place in the presence of the elders (vv. 2, 4, 9). In v. 11 they speak as symbols of this society and its laws. They give voice to the tension between law and narrative in this part of the story. Will patriarchy have the last say? Will the story of these two women working out their salvation against the odds of this culture be subsumed under the legal proceedings of acquiring and exchanging fields and women? What will happen to the worth Ruth has acquired for herself, not through legal means but through her love and devotion for Naomi?

The elders speak a blessing to Boaz, *"May the LORD make the woman who is coming into your house like Rachel and Leah. . . . like . . . Tamar"* (vv. 11-12).

Ruth is not mentioned by name. She is simply the woman—the woman who is valued in this society by the children she produces for the men she belongs to. The only way the elders see the worth of Boaz's woman is in light of the stories of Rachel and Leah and Tamar, women who had gone before Ruth, who struggled within this culture for identity and worth.

Rachel and Leah could not envision their worth beyond the offspring they provided for Jacob/Israel. Their situation was carried to the extreme, to the absurd, as they bargained for nights spent with the patriarch (Gen 31). Tamar, a foreigner like Ruth, worked out her own place in this society through trickery and deception (Gen 38). How will Ruth's worth measure up to these who have gone before her?

The Birth of a Son: Who Will Have the Last Say?, 4:13-22

The struggle between patriarchy and the women's story continues as the narrator states that Boaz took Ruth as his wife, Yahweh *made her conceive, and she bore a son* (v. 13). Where is the Ruth of chaps. 1–3? The Ruth who proclaimed her devotion to Naomi, who forsook the security of homeland for foreign land, who took advantage of gleaning laws, who called Boaz to the task of redeemer, who jolted Naomi out of her complacency? Is the deal at the city gate complete?

Just when it seems the structures of patriarchal culture will win, the townswomen speak (vv. 14-17). They interrupt the narrator's words with their own pronouncement of blessing. Their blessing resolves Naomi's troubles presented in chap. 1. They identify the son who is born as a *goēl*. He will restore life and happiness to Naomi who had returned from Moab empty and bitter.

Upon a first hearing, their blessing sounds no different than that of the elders. Naomi's happiness (worth) is established by a son, whom society values more than its daughters. But the townswomen go on to proclaim, *"Your daughter-in-law who loves you, who is* [worth] *more to you than seven sons, has borne him"* (v. 15). In these words the townswomen pronounce a counterblessing that reclaims the worth of Ruth in the face of patriarchy. Yes, by patriarchal standards a son will restore Naomi. But by the standards of the story, Ruth is more than seven sons. The townswomen dare to proclaim what has been obvious since the beginning of the book: Ruth *loves* Naomi. This is the only time the verb "to love" occurs in the story. It does not describe the relationship between Ruth and Boaz, nor does it describe the relationship between Boaz and Naomi. Ruth is the subject of this verb and Naomi is its direct object (Bos 1984, 58).

The townswomen continue their celebration of Ruth's love for Naomi by claiming, *"A son has been born to Naomi"* (v. 17). This counterblessing undermines the patriarchal intent of the elder's blessing to Boaz. Ruth will not be like Rachel and Leah, nor like Tamar, all of whose sons were children of patriarchy. Ruth has given Naomi a son, and it is the townswomen of Bethlehem, not Boaz, who name him

Obed (v. 17). Indeed, this is a cultural transformation brought about by one woman joining herself to another woman in a culture that defines women through men.

As soon as the townswomen name the son, the narrator quickly adds, *He became the father of Jesse, the father of David* (v. 17). In a story that has presented the struggle of two women in culture, against culture, and transforming culture, it seems that the narrator and later redactors of the book will have the last say. In the mind of the narrator, a son has not been born to Naomi; he has been born to Boaz.

Verses 18-22 expand this notion with a later genealogical addition. The genealogy picks up where the blessing of the elders had left off: the elders' *"May your house be like the house of Perez, whom Tamar bore to Judah"* (v. 12b) leads to *Now these are the descendants of Perez . . .* (v. 18).

With this genealogy, the struggle between the women's story and patriarchy is presented to the very end of the book. Phyllis Trible has called the Book of Ruth a comedy—all's well that ends well (1978, 195)—but the closing words of the narrator and the redactor sound a note of tragedy. Who really does have the last say? The words of the narrator and the redactor serve as a reminder that throughout Israelite culture and the cultures of today women continue to work out their own salvation with courage and creativity, with their choices of love and devotion toward themselves and one another.

Works Cited

Bos, Johanna. 1984. "Out of the Shadows: Genesis 38; Judges 4:17-22; Ruth 3." *Semeia* 42:37–67.

Meyers, Carol. 1978. "The Roots of Restriction: Women in Early Israel." *BA* 41:91–103. 1983. "Procreation, Production, and Protection: Male-Female Balance in Early Israel." *JAAR* 51:569–93.

Trible, Phyllis. 1978. *God and the Rhetoric of Sexuality*.

First and Second Samuel

Carol Stuart Grizzard [MCB 269-301]

Introduction

First and Second Samuel cover the beginning of Israel's experiment with the monarchy and go on to detail the lives of Saul and David, the first two kings. Manuscript evidence indicates that the book was divided into two parts in 1477 CE. First Samuel begins with Samuel's birth in the 1070s BCE and 2 Samuel ends shortly before David's death in 961 BCE In the Hebrew Bible 1–2 Samuel is part of the Former Prophets (Joshua–2 Kings). This account of the nations of Israel and Judah from founding to fall is often called "the Deuteronomistic History" in recognition of its having undergone at least one editing by an individual or school taking its basic theological understanding from Deuteronomy: if the nation is faithful to God it will be blessed, but lack of faithfulness will lead to disaster (cf. Deut 6:10-15, 8:11-20).

Sources and Date

Scholars have long enjoyed dissecting 1–2 Samuel in search of sources lying behind the present text. These two books—originally one—certainly invite such explorations. Some of the most important events in 1 Samuel are told two or three times: the rejection of Eli's house (2:27-34; 3:11-14 [cf. 4:12-22]), the selection of Saul as king (9:1–10:16; 10:17-27), Saul's subsequent rejection (13:5-14; 15:1-35), the meeting between Saul and David (16:14-23; 17:31-58), the killing of Goliath (17:4-54; cf. 2 Sam 21:18-19), Saul's attempt to kill David with a spear (18:10-12; 19:9-10), David's sparing of Saul's life in the wilderness (24:1-15; 26:1-16), and Saul's death (31:1-7; cf. 2 Sam 1:1-16).

The repetition at times creates awkwardness, for example, when David enters Saul's service (1 Sam 16:14-23) and then is unknown by his master in a following story (17:55-58). Furthermore, sometimes the stories display markedly different attitudes towards the characters and the situations in which they find themselves. A comparison of 1 Sam 8:7-9 and 9:15-17 provides a clear example of different attitudes. The first story claims that God views the people's request for a king as rebellion; the second story claims that God calls Saul the ruler who will *save my people from the hand of the Philistines* (9:16).

A reasonable and popular explanation of the repetition and resulting awkwardness has been that 1–2 Samuel (esp. 1 Samuel) is an interweaving of two or more sources, each with unique theological perspectives and characterizations. The additional evidence that the Hebrew text is corrupt, containing more differences with the LXX than most OT books, makes it easier to view the books as having a long and complex history of transmission.

Julius Wellhausen, the German scholar widely recognized as a pioneer of SOURCE CRITICISM, was not the first to engage in the source-hunting enterprise. In 1878, however, he put together what was at the time the most meticulously argued statement on the subject. He found two sources in 1 Samuel, distinguishing between them based on whether they were pro- or antimonarchical. Wellhausen assigned the first source to the period before the EXILE, while he saw the other source as exilic or postexilic. Other notable scholars such as Noth, Eissfeldt, and Gressmann followed; while many disagreed on the dates he assigned to his sources or the designation of individual verses, like Wellhausen they tended to find sources differentiated by attitude toward the monarchy. Material clustered around particular characters or specific sites and objects are also often considered to be sources (cf. Eslinger 1985, 11-37).

The search for the sources behind 1–2 Samuel may be drawing to a close; the ground has been worked and reworked to exhaustion. The source-critical enterprise nonetheless has helped readers understand the complex process through which biblical books were developed and preserved. As a method of study source criticism has also helped readers understand the many and conflicting reactions that Israel expressed at various times to its forms of government.

Some problems with the emphasis on possible sources in the books of Samuel, however, are apparent. (1) Distinguishing sources based on their attitude towards the monarchy gives the impression that the books are only about the monarchy. Noting the vast amount of material given to the kings' personal lives— rather than their reigns—indicates that the narrator is at least as much concerned with the relationships of the characters as with the political change itself.

(2) The search for sources may betray a subconciously patronizing attitude towards the original composers and audience, suggesting that they were not capable of careful editing or of noticing gaps and contradictions between sources. The assumption that modern literary skills enable us to unravel this pastiche that earlier, less sophisticated communities considered to be unified could be evidence of arrogance. A more appropriate attitude towards 1–2 Samuel would be to recognize its coherent structure, its characters that are consistent in their well-roundedness, and its use of conflicting viewpoints to achieve a subtle presentation of the issues.

(3) Most importantly, the intensive analysis 1–2 Samuel has received in the last 100 years has resulted in a literary work so fragmented that its essential coherence may be (and, indeed, has been) overlooked. By now it has become a given that the twice-told stories and apparent contradictions represent the viewpoints of multiple

authors and editors spanning a period of more than 400 years. This presupposition means that readers do not have to inquire into any other reason for the repetitions and ambiguity, making it more difficult for readers to notice the depth and emphasis given to the text by its complex characterization and never-quite-identical repetitions.

Certainly a work like 1–2 Samuel was not composed overnight; research into the different traditions surrounding the pivotal characters of Samuel, Saul, and David went into its presentation. Earlier collections of stories dealing with Samuel, the ARK, the transition from the tribal confederacy to the kingship, Saul, David, and David's family may well have existed (either in oral or written form). Such stories probably circulated orally in and after the eleventh and tenth centuries BCE in which they are set. Some of them may have been written as early as the late tenth century.

The books of Samuel did not assume their final form, however, until their deuteronomistic editing during or immediately after the Babylonian Exile in the sixth century. But the editors did not simply string together hitherto unrelated stories with no thought given to the effect they produced in their new context. Rather, the older traditions were assembled in such a way that they both modify and enhance each other, giving a balanced view of one of the most complicated times in the biblical period. Therefore, instead of focusing on the shadowy sources that may lie behind the text, this commentary will approach 1–2 Samuel as a finished product, dealing with it as a carefully and intentionally constructed literary work.

Primary Themes

Whatever else it may be, 1–2 Samuel is an exciting story, full of action, love, betrayal, flawed heroes, and understandable villains. This does not mean that we cannot look for historical truth or theological meaning. We find traditions describing Israel's rise to power and stability in Canaan, as well as material about both divine and human nature and the relationship between them. Nonetheless, the themes of the book are expressed through the action of a crowded plot and the interactions of complex and powerful characters. The book focuses on SAMUEL, SAUL, and DAVID, who in their own ways rise and fall in the course of this work. The relationships among these main figures and the parallels and differences in their lives reveal the narrator's agenda.

The narrator seldom intrudes on the scene, preferring to let the characters speak for themselves without necessarily endorsing what they say. This technique has the effect of quickly engaging the readers in the story, as we are called upon to decide when the characters are being honest, what their motivations are, and whether or not their decisions are wise ones. The narrator will not always make this easy for us.

The emotional impact of 1–2 Samuel is due largely to the narrator's skill in drawing the reader into the action and creating even minor characters who are vivid and complex. We are far removed from the overt issues that these stories deal with: correct procedure in sacrifice and holy warfare, the establishment of theocratic monarchy, the peculiar perils of polygamy, and so forth. This carefully woven story continues to resonate with us not because of these issues but because of the underlying themes.

Some of the main themes are the subtlety with which God works in the lives of nations (electing and speaking, but staying undramatically behind the scenes); the necessity of good leaders who will take God seriously and the difficulty in finding them; the rivalries within families and especially the tensions between fathers and sons; the difficulty of maintaining trustworthy relationships when society is changing and political and religious power are available for the taking; and perhaps most of all, the incredible potential for good and evil that is found in every human being.

Ultimately, this is a book about relationships: those between God and a nation or individuals, and those among people. None of these themes is limited to any one time or culture; it is as the characters grapple with these themes that they transcend the eleventh and tenth centuries BCE and become not merely ancient Hebrews but understandable human beings. It is this universal quality that is the mark of great literature.

For Further Study

In the *Mercer Dictionary of the Bible*: ARK; DAVID; DEATH; DEUTERONOMIST/DEUTERO-NOMISTIC HISTORIAN; KINGSHIP; HOLINESS IN THE OT; HOLY WAR; JOTHAM'S FABLE; JUDGES, BOOK OF; LITERATURE, BIBLE AS; LOT/LOTS (CASTING OF) IN THE BIBLE; PHILISTINES; SAMUEL; SAMUEL, BOOKS OF FIRST AND SECOND; SAUL; SOURCES, LITERARY; TRIBES; UNITED MONARCHY.

In other sources: A. F. Campbell, *Of Prophets and Kings: A Late 9th-Century Document (1 Samuel 1–2 Kings 10)*; L. M. Eslinger, *Kingship of God in Crisis: A Close Reading of 1 Samuel 1–12*; B. Peckham, "The Deuteronomistic History of Saul and David," *ZAW* 97 (1985): 190–209.

Commentary

An Outline

Prologue, 1:1–2:11

Samuel Is Born, 1:1-20

As is the case with many other important biblical figures (ISAAC, JACOB, SAMSON, JOHN THE BAPTIST, JESUS), we meet Samuel's family before his birth, showing that God was involved in this life from its conception. Samuel is the leading human actor in chaps. 3 and 7–12; after that he is an authoritative but often absent figure in Saul's reign. Samuel sets David on his path to power and gives him aid at a low point in the younger man's career, but in 1 Sam 25:1 he dies (although one of Samuel's unique characteristics among OT figures is that he is granted a post-mortem appearance). The fact that 1–2 Samuel is named for him rather than for David, who is center-stage far more than anyone else, emphasizes the importance of what Samuel represents: totally God-guided leadership.

This opening section has an oddly timeless quality. Except for the fact that the shrine at Shiloh is functioning, there are no clues about the chronological setting of the story. No mention is made of the national situation, the military leaders, or the Philistines (and other enemies) who were so prominent in the Book of Judges, and will be so again in the rest of 1 Samuel.

Most of this book is about the nation, but it begins with an intimate story about a family. For this reason the first chapters appear to be a prologue, introducing many of the issues dealt with later in the book.

1:1-8. Peninnah attacks Hannah. The news that Elkanah has two wives places his family in the context of the ancestral families in Genesis in which the men had more than one woman. Remembering those stories prepares us for what follows: only one wife can bear children; the other is infertile. The Genesis pattern tells us that, like Sarai and Hagar, or Leah and Rachel, the wives will compete, but that finally the barren wife will bear.

Verse 3 introduces another family. HOPHNI and PHINEHAS are referred to as *the two sons of Eli*, but Eli himself seems to need no introduction. The annual pilgrimage and miserable family banquet establish the family of Elkanah as both pious and threatened by rivalry among its members. Like Abraham and Jacob, Elkanah seems unable to make peace in his family, but he is loving if not redemptive to the weeping Hannah.

1:9-20. God helps Hannah, whom Eli misunderstands. Hannah speaks for the first time, not to Elkanah but directly to the Lord. Rachel demanded children from Jacob (Gen 30:1), but Hannah goes to God. In her heartfelt prayer she not only asks for help but also promises to God that which she most desires. If the Lord will give her a son, she will return that son to the giver, making the child a gift to both of them.

The piety of Hannah is contrasted to that of Shiloh's patriarch, who cannot even recognize prayer when he sees it. Like the onlookers in Acts 2, Eli mistakes deep communion with God for drunkenness. Eli's warmth to Hannah in v. 17 marks him as a kindly yet still oddly insensitive priest.

The Lord's act of remembering Hannah emphasizes more than power over infertility. It shows the divine initiative in vindicating and empowering one of the least valued members of a patriarchal society (cf. Elizabeth in Luke 1:24-25) without necessarily endorsing the values of that society. Just as Hannah acted independently in asking for the child and promising him to God, she and not her husband names him Samuel. There is no formal divine visitation in the story of Samuel's birth. Pronouncements were given to Hagar (Gen 16:7-14), Abraham and Sarah (Gen 18:9-15), Rebekah (Gen 25:21-23), and Samson's mother (Judg 13:25). The lack of one here gives the experience an element of ambiguity for Hannah. The narrator explicitly tells us that God answered Hannah's prayer, but no one at all tells Hannah. The requirements for the fulfillment of her private vow are simply met. Will she regard prayer and pregnancy as unrelated events rather than cause and effect?

Hannah Responds in Gratitude, 1:21–2:11

1:21-28. Samuel journeys to Eli. Our question is raised again when we find Elkanah returning to Shiloh *to pay his vow* (v. 21). The vow, of course, is Hannah's. A husband can nullify any vow made by his wife (Num 30:8-15). Elkanah allows hers to stand and accepts it as requiring a response from him, but the blessed Hannah has not yet responded to the miraculous event. Even her statement at Samuel's birth simply repeats that she *asked him of the LORD* (v. 20), not that God responded.

Verse 24 resolves any doubts the reader may have had about Hannah: she is faithful. While Elkanah accompanies Hannah and her son to Eli's shrine, the husband is not mentioned until the very end of the scene (v. 11). As was the case with the vow and the naming, Hannah takes the initiative.

2:1-11. Hannah exults. Although this trip to Shiloh could have been a mournful affair, Hannah makes it a time of remembering God's grace and exalting the LORD who has redeemed her from trouble. Her first prayer was brief and desperate, but her second is luxuriously triumphant. Like Mary in Luke 1:46-55 (a speech modeled on this one), Hannah understands that both nations and individuals—the powerful and the barren—equally need and can know the strength of God's intervention. Her prayer emphasizes God's reversal of status: the mighty, the full, and the fertile find loss, but the feeble, hungry, and barren find help. The same situation will be encountered by many other characters later in this book. Her prayer ends with the promise that God will be with the king (v. 10). There is no king in Israel yet, but in this verse, as in so many ways, Hannah's prayer foreshadows later events of the book.

In this prologue a troubled Hannah finds solace from God, becoming more assertive and responsible as a result. In many ways she is the prototype of Israel. She appears to be of no account, but through God she is vindicated. We have observed in her an optimum relationship with God: bringing misery before the LORD in trust and responding with faithfulness and gratitude when her prayer is answered, even though there might be room to doubt that the improved conditions have been anything but fortuitous. She takes initiative and acts faithfully in this relationship. Her experience also raises the issue of qualified leadership: the priests of Shiloh are the sons of a priest with little spiritual sensitivity, which suggests trouble ahead.

Eli and Samuel: the Old Leadership of Israel, 2:12–7:17

Shiloh under Elide Leadership, 2:12–4:1a

2:12-21. The ministry of the sons of Eli and Hannah. Our doubts about Eli are immediately justified: we are told that "the sons of Eli are sons of worthlessness" (author trans.), a striking judgment equating the incompetent, but not evil, Eli with nothingness. Leviticus 7:30-36 establishes what the priests' proper portion of the sacrifice can be, but Eli's sons take whatever they can get, not caring whether their portion is one of the prescribed parts so long as it is large.

When the sincere sacrificers try to stop them, at least to the extent of allowing the fat to be burned off first (Lev 7:3-4, 31), the priests' representative threatens them with violence. Although Eli's sons are the subject of this passage, they are not referred to by name but only as *the sons of Eli* (v. 12), emphasizing his culpability for their behavior. Eli himself is present in name but absent in fact, showing him to be negligent as both father and priest.

In contrast to Eli's sons, Hannah's is ministering before the LORD. Eli, absent but needed in the first scene, is present but not needed in the next (as was also true in his first encounter with Hannah, cf. 1:9-18), blessing the family that already has been blessed by God. Our last glimpse of Hannah shows her basking in God's continuing grace (v. 21).

2:22–4:1a. God chooses between the sons of Eli and Hannah. Eli confronts his sons feebly when forced, not reminding them of their duty to God or people but only of the danger they are courting for themselves. He is not successful because *it was the will of the LORD to kill them* (2:25). Like the frequently repeated motif of God's hardening Pharaoh's heart (Exod 4:21, 9:12, etc.) and Isaiah's calling to stop the ears, shut the eyes and dull the minds of the people (6:10), this statement is not intended to relieve anyone of the responsibility for their own actions. Eli's sons, like Pharaoh and the Judeans of Isaiah's day, commit their crimes on their own. Rather, this passage underscores both the difficulty of repentance once evil has been chosen over and over again and the inevitability of punishment for unfaithfulness. Samuel, however, grows in human and divine favor (a phrase applied to Jesus in Luke 2:52).

First Samuel 2:27-36 recounts the oracle delivered to Eli by *a man of God*. Why the priest cannot receive this oracle from God himself is by now clear. An ORACLE is an explicit foreshadowing of events, serving on one level to emphasize God's knowledge and control and on another to bind the multifaceted action of 1–2 Samuel together. We will see this pattern of oracles and signs being fulfilled again. This oracle expands on the statement of 2:25, referring to events in the near future as well as some occurring in the reigns of Saul and David (for 2:33 cf. 22:20-23; for 2:34 cf. 4:11; for 2:35 cf. 2 Sam. 8:17, 1 Kgs 2:35).

The statement in 3:2 that the uninsightful Eli is losing his sight reminds us why there is a dearth of visions: few in this time are faithful enough to have them. It is Samuel and not Eli who guards the lamp and ARK of God by night. God speaks now for the first time in the book; his first word is Samuel's name. The boy does not know the voice of the LORD, but Eli, who is not favored with direct divine discourse, is at least able to discern it when it comes to another.

We have now the third warning of destruction for the Elides. Each performs a necessary function. The first informed us (2:12-17), the second informed Eli (2:22-25), and the last informs Samuel (3:10-14). Although he is but a child, as the next leader of Israel and especially as a prophet he must know what God is doing (cf. Amos 3:7).

Israel versus the Philistines under Elide Leadership, 4:1b–7:2

Hans Hertzberg claims that this section "has no direct connection" with what has come before (1965, 46), but it is here that we see the effect on the nation of Shiloh's leadership crisis, and it is here that the judgment on the Elides begins.

4:1b-22. Israel suffers under the Philistines. The PHILISTINES threatened Israel in the Book of Judges. They were the enemy Samson harried but did not defeat (Judg 13–16). The conflict between them and the more loosely organized Israelites provides the context for much of the action in 1 Samuel. After the loss of the first battle at Aphek, the people send to Shiloh for the Ark of the covenant. When it arrives in the custody of Hophni and Phinehas, we know from 2:27-36 that in spite of its powerful history it will not help the people now. The point is that faithfulness to God is more powerful than supernatural objects.

While many of the people of Israel have been faithful, their leaders have not; as always, the people pay for bad government. God does not fight against them but is simply absent, and they cannot defeat the enemy without divine help. The devastation of the day is shown poignantly by the fulfillment of the doom on Eli's sons and its effect on the rest of his family (cf. 2:34).

5:1–7:2. The Philistines suffer under the LORD. The Philistines could stand against Israel, but not against Israel's God. The narrator even links later Philistine priestly practice to their recognition of Dagon's subjugation to the God of Israel—a foray into the ontology of ritual that probably found more agreement in Israel than in Philistia.

The chapter ends with a comic picture of the once victorious but now panicking Philistines spreading the plague by sending the Ark rapidly through three of their five cities.

Their priests provide careful instructions on how to pacify Israel's God without forcing their own people to come close to either Ark or Israelites. Undirected cows with nursing calves left at home will naturally return to them, but these cows, protesting as articulately as cows can, head in the opposite direction to take the Ark back to Israel.

The Philistine's return of the Ark signals their awareness of God's power but not any desire to align themselves with it. According to the Hebrew text of 6:19–7:2, the Israelites of Bethshemesh look into the Ark. They do not seem to fear it as much as the Philistines do; the latter took more care not to offend the Ark's god—a god who is not even their own.

This section ends like chap. 5 with the dangerously powerful Ark being circulated in fear from city to city, but now the fearful ones are God's own people.

Israel versus the Philistines under Samuel's Leadership, 7:3-17

Samuel could not appear in the previous section describing Israel's massive loss because that is seen as the result of the flaws of the Elides. Now that they are gone, the God-called Samuel appears to provide leadership. As so often in the Book of Judges, the defeated people cry out to the LORD, who raises up a judge to lead them in repenting of their syncretism and in destroying their enemies. The use of this pattern establishes Samuel as the last and greatest of the judges.

Israel's repentance has led to the restoration of right relationship with God: exclusive worship. Now the people will be restored to what they, at least, consider to be right relationship with the Philistines: victory. They immediately look to Samuel to be their help, and like Moses in Exod 17:8-13 he intercedes for them with God during the battle.

Because of Samuel, the LORD is not absent as was the case at Aphek and so the Philistines are routed. In the first battle Israel encamped at Ebenezer, literally "stone of help," but there was no help (4:2). Now Samuel establishes a new Ebenezer in recognition of the returned help of the LORD.

This section ends with a survey of Samuel's tenure as judge of Israel (although like Eli, Samuel will serve priestly functions as well). This is not a completely happy ending, however; Samuel only achieves a stalemate with the Philistines, leaving them a strong power base from which they can again emerge to threaten God's people.

The difference in Israel's battle experience is due to the change of leadership. The old and new leaders are carefully compared, and Samuel emerges as superior in every way. Unlike the Elides, Samuel performs the sacrifices correctly, intercedes with God on the people's behalf, enables them to achieve victory, and takes pains to be aware of what happens on his watch. The stable period Israel enjoys under Samuel is scarcely summarized, however. We are not given time to see Israel at peace before the narrator catapults us into another crisis.

Samuel and Saul: the Last Judge and the First King, 8:1–12:25

This is easily the most complex section of 1 Samuel. Different understandings of the word "king," and different reactions to the possibility of having one in Israel, compete for attention while the actual individual in whom all the arguments will coalesce seems unaware of the great change his presence represents.

Israel considered the kingship twice in the Book of Judges (8:22-23; 9:1-57), but its rejection is seen positively. Even so, Judges shows that there are problems with the tribal confederacy; not all the tribes respond to Deborah's cry to fight the Canaanites in chap. 4 and 5, and the last chapters of the book show Israel degenerating into a lawless place because "there was no king in Israel" (Judg 21:25). Therefore the request for a king in 1 Samuel comes in a context of confusion.

As Gideon feared (Judg 8:22-23), a king may take God's prerogatives for his own, but it is also true that lack of strong centralized authority may result in anarchy and injustice. In a similar way, the Bible as a whole is ambiguous about government.

In the OT, many psalms extol the special relationship between God and the Davidic king, but the prophets often find those kings oppressive and unresponsive to the LORD. In the NT the evil potential of government is seen in the crucifixion of Jesus and the persecution of the church, and yet Rom 13:1 says to be "subject to the governing authorities; for there is no authority except from God."

This ambiguity is well reflected in the chapters in 1 Samuel that deal with the inauguration of the monarchy. Like most people of any nation or time, Israel had both positive and negative feelings about government—and both those reactions were grounded in realistic perceptions of it.

Samuel Disapproves of the Request for a King, 8:1-22

It is ironic that Samuel, who came to power because Eli's sons were corrupt, has equally corrupt offspring. His unorthodox attempt to establish his sons in the nonhereditary judgeship leads to the intervention of Israel's elders. In one sense they are not trying to start over with a new system; they ask Samuel, whom they have long recognized as God's chosen leader over them, to establish a different form of government. But in another sense they are making a complete break with the past. The phrase *like other nations* (v. 5), denies Israel's role as "God's treasured possession out of all the peoples . . . a priestly kingdom and a holy nation" (Exod 19:5-6) because holiness means above all being separate, distinct, and other. By requesting a king like the nations, Israel is refusing its status as God's chosen instrument in blessing the nations (cf. Gen 12:1-3).

As a God-directed leader, Samuel's initial reaction is to seek God's guidance. God is angry but will not impose the divine will on the people, a motif that permeates the Bible all the way back to Gen 3 (where human freedom is so great that all of creation is marred by it, but that freedom is nonetheless permitted). At that point God continued to deal with humanity, but not in the same way as before human decision changed the relationship.

The same thing will happen here. Samuel's warning, like that of Eli to his sons, appeals to self-interest. He does his best to dissuade the people, detailing the great financial cost of the kingship and describing an absolute monarchy similar to those of the Canaanites. The last two verses warn the people that they risk reversing their own history: they were slaves in Egypt when God heard their cry and rescued them (Exod 2:23-25), but a king will make them slaves in their own land and God will not hear their cries.

In response the people only make their request more specific. Their idea of a king is one who will *go out before us and fight our battles* (v. 20). Samuel dismisses the assembly with the political and theological issues unresolved.

God Chooses Saul Both Privately and Publicly, 9:1–10:27a

We move from the acrimonious debate of chap. 8 to a story that introduces one of the favorite themes of literature. While Saul is not in rags when we meet him, and never exactly finds riches, his story still concerns a lowly innocent who becomes great—a motif foreshadowed in Hannah's song. His rise will take place in three connected stages: the LORD will choose him in 9:26–10:27a, the people will accept him in 10:24, 27b–11:13, and finally Samuel will acquiesce in 11:14–12:25.

9:1-17. Saul journeys to Samuel, who expects him. Most biblical characters are not physically described. Saul, however, is presented as an imposing figure, one we are surprised to find searching for donkeys. He is soon discouraged; it is the servant who has the resources of knowledge and purse to enable them to continue their mission. This boy is not aware of the true status of *the man of God* (v. 7; but vv. 14 and 19 will identify him as Samuel), but Saul does not know of him at all, and so they seek out the greatest man in Israel to help them find some donkeys.

The scene shifts to the previous day, and now we find at least partial resolution of the issues left hanging at the end of chap. 8. God has chosen Saul as *ruler* (v. 17) or "designate" (the word *nagid* literally means "the one in front"), reminding us of the people's demand of 8:20. "King" (Heb. *melek*) will not be used of Saul until the people support God's choice and acclaim him so in 10:24, but this does not mean that God does not intend Saul to be king; *nagid* is used of David and other kings (cf., e.g., 2 Sam 6:21; 1 Kgs 1:35; 1 Kgs 14:7).

That this king will be anointed by God's spokesperson shows he will not be an autocratic king like the one described in chap. 8, but a theocratic one, a king under God. Like the people in 8:20, God envisions the king as being primarily a military leader. Verses 15-17 echo Exod 2:23-25 again, but unlike 8:18 that echo is positive. In Exodus, however, God responded to the people's plea by calling Moses. Because the people now make a demand, God responds with Saul. God has shifted gears to accommodate the people's decision, but the negative context of 8:7-9 still holds, reinforced by the fact that Samuel does not comment on the LORD's command. Can this young man who does not even know who Samuel is and who must borrow money from his servant compare to Moses?

9:18–10:16. Samuel privately anoints Saul. The meeting between Samuel and Saul sets the tone for their relationship. Saul is unaware of the significance of what is happening and Samuel tells him more than he wants to know without actually explaining much. Samuel honors the young man but also orders him around. Saul passively accepts both attitudes. The anointing takes place without witnesses. Samuel, in spite of his strong doubts of chap. 8, anoints Saul as *nagid* to defeat Israel's enemies, and even kisses the chosen one.

Saul does not respond at all to Samuel's speech in chap. 10. Verse 9 tells us that all the signs Samuel promised were fulfilled that day, but only the third is described. Saul receives the Spirit of the LORD in the company of charismatic prophets, unusual behavior on the part of the dutiful Saul, which surprises the people. Saul's unexpected and unnerving adventures excite no comment from him; he simply goes home. His silence may stem from disbelief or confusion; in any case, "whatever he sees fit to do" (v. 7) is nothing.

10:17-27a. God publicly chooses Saul. It is important here, as in chap. 12, to note that God acts but does not speak. Samuel continues to control events by summoning the people to Mizpah, apparently for the purpose of selecting a king by lot. He quotes God in v. 18, but v. 19 is reported as Samuel's words. Here he informs the people that they have rejected God, something God told Samuel in 8:7-8, but neither then nor later told him to tell the people. God has not said a negative word on kingship since, but Samuel is not convinced. He divides the people into clans without telling them why, but sounding as if they are to be punished.

Since this practice usually reveals transgressors (cf. Josh 7:14-15), Saul's hiding makes sense, but it means that he is passive even when being proclaimed king. He also does not seem to trust Samuel, although since Samuel has gone out of his way to be sudden and mysterious all along his caution is understandable. The lots eliminate the people until Saul is reached—God acting to reveal the chosen one to the people after Samuel's stalling. Even though Samuel obviously has doubts about this whole enterprise, he presents Saul in an entirely favorable light as God's chosen but cannot bring himself to call him either "designate" or "king."

The people, relieved by this positive outcome after Samuel's ominous opening statement and procedure, dutifully cheer God's chosen king whom they do not know. Samuel's explanation of the rights and duties of the king must include the fact that Saul will not be like kings of other nations but will be under the theocracy as represented by Samuel, which may explain why some *worthless fellows* (v. 27; cf. 2:12) grumble when all had cheered him previously. As was the case in the anointing episode, Saul simply goes home without commenting.

The People Choose Saul, 10:27b–11:13

The Ammonites provide Saul with the opportunity to show his might in warfare; this is particularly important since military power is all the people seem to really want in a king. They already shouted on his behalf, but only some followed him. The new king frustrates our expectations first by being found placidly farming, and then by responding with surprising strength to the news of the Ammonite threat, which provides his first real action in the narrative.

Saul is possessed by the Spirit (11:7) and shows that despite his earlier passivity he has power and leadership, demonstrating understanding of the theocratic nature of his kingship by calling the people out *after Saul and Samuel* (11:7). He delivers Jabesh-gilead so effectively that his enthusiastic people try to punish those who doubted him in the previous chapter, but Saul again shows his mettle by stopping the lynch party and crediting God with the victory.

Samuel Accepts the Situation, 11:14–12:25

Samuel begins to accept the situation in 11:14, referring to Saul's rule as *kingship*. However, v. 15 says that *Saul and all the Israelites*—but not Samuel—rejoice. While Samuel may feel that the chosen king has been vindicated, he still cannot celebrate. Like Moses and Joshua, Samuel has a farewell address, but unlike them he does not then depart the scene. Note that although God will support the old judge in v. 18 with *thunder and rain*, at no point is the speech presented as the words of anyone but Samuel. Here his previously unvoiced feeling of personal rejection comes to the fore (in 8:7 God identified this as the cause of Samuel's initial displeasure with the people's request).

Samuel, the man who has spent literally his whole life in service to God and Israel, has the normal human need for reassurance. He repeats the familiar idea that success depends on faithfulness, but now he adds *if both you and your king who reigns over you will follow the LORD your God* (12:14), reminding the people that they can be punished for the sins of their leaders (as they were with the Elides).

Samuel again says that the request for a king was wrong and the people, alarmed by the unseasonal thunderstorm Samuel calls on the LORD to send, agree and ask for his intercession as they have before (7:8). The storm shows God's support for Samuel and his belief that God is the true king, but God has long since responded to the people's request. Samuel, having gotten them to admit for the first time that they were wrong (and, perhaps, mollified by the fact that they still need him), reassures them of God's faithfulness and his own continued help. Saul is not even mentioned by name after 11:15, underscoring the continuing importance of Samuel in the new regime.

The kingship has been established. The people asked for it, but it is God and not they who choose Saul. They cheer him as God's chosen in 10:24 but accept him themselves in chap. 11. Samuel is slow to accept the change, trying to talk the people out of it at every turn, but his quarrel is clearly with the request and not with Saul himself. Their relationship is complex. Samuel dominates and Saul allows it, but while at times Samuel seems proud of the man he anointed, chap. 12 shows his deep unease with what Saul represents. Here we see Samuel not as a mindless automaton conveying messages from God to people, but rather as a powerful yet vulnerable human being. He has more trouble than God does in dealing with his feelings of rejection; individual emotions and ego always play a great role in affairs of religion and state.

Samuel and Saul: the Rejecting Mentor and the Abandoned Protege, 13:1–15:35

Saul's story has been about the unexpected rise of the lowly. Now it will become a story about the fall of the great. As Saul first was chosen by God, then accepted by the people, and finally by Samuel, he first will be rebuked by Samuel, then the people, and finally by God.

Saul Is Rebuked by Samuel, 13:1-15

This section is introduced by the formula that will begin the account of every king of Israel and Judah in 1–2 Kings. The corruption of the first verse in the Hebrew text—and its absence in the SEPTUAGINT—makes Saul's length of reign difficult to determine (Acts 13:21 gives the standard figure of forty years). The accepted date for the beginning of his reign is 1020 BCE. Saul sees his task as mainly military, and so at once begins to muster the Israelites against the Philistines, although Jonathan (not identified as Saul's son until 13:16, distancing Saul from his exploits) wins the first victory.

The Israelites respond to their king's call; all is ready except that Samuel is not present. Saul is torn between two priorities: Samuel clearly said that he would come to offer the sacrifices within a week (10:8), and as a theocratic king Saul is bound by Samuel's word. The already demoralized and outnumbered troops are leaving, however, and a king chosen primarily for military purposes cannot let the situation degenerate any further. Saul chooses to offer the sacrifices himself; Samuel appears as soon as this prerogative has been taken. Offering no explanation and paying no attention to Saul's defense, Samuel warns Saul in v. 14 that God "will choose a man after his own heart" (author trans.; the verb form may indicate future action the speaker believes to be assured) to rule Israel, although the writer says nothing about God's rejecting Saul until 15:10. Since Samuel, although obedient, was so reluctant to accept the kingship, it is certainly possible that his absence was at least subconsciously intentional to set Saul up for failure.

Saul Is Rebuked by the People, 13:16–14:52

This section contains an Israelite victory, but its purpose is to show the further degeneration of Saul's leadership.

13:16–14:23. Jonathan achieves victory over the Philistines. The Philistines, stalemated in chap. 7, are still a threatening and well-armed presence in Israel. Jonathan and his armor-bearer scout out the enemy garrison while Saul stays in the camp, unaware that anything is going on. The fact that he is accompanied by a descendant of the ineffective Elides (Eli's great-grandson, Phinehas's grandson) adds an ominous note.

14:24-52. Saul's vow leads to an unsatisfactory conclusion. Saul's vow reminds readers of the oaths in Judg 11:30-31 and 17:2, each of which accidentally endangered the speaker's child. Saul's instinct for failure is nowhere better shown than here, where he inadvertently jeopardizes his son who is also Israel's foremost warrior. The lots that brought him public acclaim (10:20-24) now bring disaster as he, torn as in chap. 13 between the practically and theologically correct, sentences Jonathan to death. The problem is not that God wants Jonathan dead but that Saul's rashness has put him in the untenable situation of either breaking the vow in which he invoked God's name or killing his son.

The people see the victory as proof that God was with Jonathan (and not with Saul?). They flocked to Saul after his first victory but refuse to follow him now, favoring a greater warrior. Unwilling to cross the people (who originally initiated the kingship and whose favor is more important now that Samuel's is lost), Saul lets his son be redeemed at the cost of his vow. While Jonathan will always trust and be faithful to his father, dying by his side in battle, this scene prepares us for problems between them. Already unnerved by the divine silence that let him know his command had been broken (vv. 37-9), Saul breaks off the war. His later victories are only summarized, ensuring that his confusion at Michmash makes the strongest impression on us.

Saul Is Rejected by the LORD, 15:1-35

15:1-9. Saul takes prisoners and booty in the battle. In spite of 13:13-15, Samuel recognizes that Saul is still chosen by the LORD and continues to deal with him on that basis. He presents his credentials, pointing out that Saul owes his throne to God as he orders him to carry out a holy war against Amalek. He is also careful to give Saul his status as king; Samuel has not previously addressed Saul by his title. *Saul and the people* (v. 9), however, save Agag and the best of Amalek's herds, destroying only the things for which they have no use rather than consecrating all that was the enemy's to the LORD. As in 13:8-9 and 14:45, Saul is shown as being easily led by the will of the people when practicality and religious duties clash.

15:10-35. Samuel delivers the LORD's rejection of Saul. Saul has not disobeyed one of Samuel's orders as in 13:9, or gone back on his own vow as in 14:45; he has, instead, disregarded a direct word from the LORD. Samuel again shows his complexity (not to mention human orneriness) by crying out to God against the rejection of the king he never wanted in the first place and attacked in 13:13-15. Samuel is, nonetheless, as faithful in carrying out the distasteful task of rejection as he was in carrying out the distasteful task of anointing. Like Eli, Saul is blind to his situation in his pride (v. 12), in his contention that he has in fact fulfilled his task (vv. 13, 20), and most of all in his refusal to take responsibility for what the people he rules have done (vv. 15, 21). His statement that the animals are for sacrifice does not help. The claim is suspicious since v. 9 says the animals were saved for their value; and in any case Saul's orders have never included making sacrifice. His references in vv. 15 and 30 to *the LORD your God* show his lack of understanding of his own role.

Samuel's words in vv. 22-23 are an excellent example of prophetic religion (cf. Amos 5:21-24; Isa 1:11-17). They convince Saul of his sin, but while Saul the person can be forgiven, Saul the king who has failed so completely to grasp the nature of his theocratic task cannot continue to be entrusted with it. From this rejection there is no turning back. The deuteronomistic emphasis on punishment for unfaithfulness means that God's regretful rejection of it shows divine consistency rather than fickleness (v. 29). But while Samuel has had to reject the king he still has affection for the person (cf. 16:1) and concern for the nation that they lead together, and so before the people Samuel is willing to present a united front.

It is hard not to sympathize with Saul, who has the unenviable task of being a king over a people who had never had one. God, Samuel, and the people make clear that they see the king as a military leader, and Saul is gifted in that practical area. But there is more to being king than that, and it is in the theological demands of the kingship that Saul fails. As one who is "little in his own eyes" (15:17), he is always anxious to please (9:5; 11:13; 13:12; 14:45; 15:13), but this means he cannot stand up even to the people he is supposed to lead (13:8; 14:45; 15:15). The man who did not succeed in the first task we saw him undertake has neither the faithfulness nor the depth for this one.

It is also hard not to sympathize with Samuel, whose years of faithful judgeship end so abruptly but who still finds himself drawn to the man he cannot help but regard as a supplanter. The rejection seems to be a private affair between the

LORD, Samuel, and Saul. The people do not know of it and those who are loyal to Saul (who will be king until he dies) are never seen as purposefully going against God's will. Only Saul and Samuel know that he is no longer God's chosen leader.

Samuel and David: the Old Judge and the Young Shepherd, 16:1-23

This short section is given equal weight with the four that have preceded it because it is so important. Chapter 16 introduces us to the major human character of 1–2 Samuel, who is also the most glamorous hero of the Bible. David's coming has been prefigured: he is the *man after [the LORD's] own heart* of 13:14, the *neighbor* of 15:28, the real anointed king of 2:10. He is more complex than any preceding character, and he will find both greater success and greater failure. Like the story of Saul, David's story begins as a rags-to-riches tale. Perhaps he, too, will suffer a reversal.

David's introduction in many ways resembles the anointing of Saul. Both rise in tandem with the previous leader's loss. The future king's appearance is appealing; so far Saul and David are the only two characters in 1 Samuel to be described physically. God reveals the chosen one to the anointing agent, who in both cases is Samuel. Both anointings take place secretly with little explanation offered. Both Saul and David receive *the spirit of the LORD* (10:6; 16:13) on the day of anointing, but neither comments in any way on what has happened to him.

One difference is important: Saul, however inadvertently, seeks Samuel out, but Samuel purposefully travels to find David. God chose Saul to make the best of a bad situation, since the people were insistent on forming a monarchy, but God's hand is in no way forced in the choosing of David. It will be years before a new king is actually needed, giving time for the selection and molding of the man after God's own heart.

Verses 6-7 show, as we have already suspected, that Samuel does not always perceive God's intentions accurately. As usual, Samuel plays his cards close to the vest, not telling anyone (including David) what is going on; perhaps he feels that Saul's knowledge of his destiny led him to take too much initiative. At the moment that David receives the spirit, Saul loses it. Saul's credentials for the kingship were that Samuel said God had chosen him and his own possession of the spirit. After losing Samuel and spirit, Saul still has the overwhelming task of leading the nation but now he knows that he is alone and no longer qualified. Saul's behavior in the ensuing chapters resembles manic depression, but that is a modern diagnosis. To the narrator, the absence of divine guidance is sufficient cause for Saul's madness.

Saul went home after his anointing; David leaves. Whether or not he suspects that Saul's torment is connected to his own strange experience, he ministers to him. Even more than with Samuel and Saul, we find the leader who is losing status drawn to the one who is gaining it, while the supplanter is bound to the one whose place he is to take. The carefully drawn similarities between Saul and David force us to wonder if the new anointed one will make the mistakes of the old.

Saul and David: the King and His General, 17:1–19:17

David's meteoric rise to power begins in this section. Saul is seen as a frustrated, almost impotent leader, while David's youthful energy and undeniable charm capture everyone's heart—including Saul's. But his very success sows the seeds of disaster as the love-hate relationship with Saul is established.

Israel versus the Philistines under Saul's leadership, 17:1-58

17:1-11 The Israelites fear Goliath. Chapter 14 ended with a stalemate between Israel and the Philistines because of Saul's weakness (14:45-46). Chapter 17 opens with a stalemate because of Goliath's strength. He is a better physical specimen even than Saul and he is well prepared for battle. Goliath's armor and weapons (a Philistine strength, as noted in 13:19-22) are amazing. He is confident, while Saul and his men are afraid and unable to respond.

17:12-23. David journeys to Saul. Verse 12 recalls chap. 16, literally describing David's father as *an Ephrathite of Bethlehem in Judah.* David, both shepherd and musical therapist, is still presented as his father's errand boy. The stories of Samuel and Saul also began with a journey commissioned by a parent that took them to the national leader and resulted in glory (1:24-28; 9:1-15). Verses 20-23 show David's attention to detail and his eagerness to see the action. Saul was slow to respond to his anointing; we wonder how this divinely chosen king anointed so like Saul will react to Goliath's repeated challenge.

17:24-40. David volunteers to fight. Saul will not meet Goliath himself but simply offers a prize for his death. David's character is captured in the first words attributed to him (v. 26). His first priority is personal reward and his second is the honor of God and people. His charm works on everyone except Eliab, who knows him better than anyone else and may also feel the frustration of losing the unexplained competition of the previous chapter. In spite of the necessity of ending the stalemate, Saul responds with concern when David volunteers. David's later reputation as a poet (and probably for exaggeration) is seen in vv. 34-37. His eloquent words are enough to convince the pliable Saul. Saul does his best to prepare David, but his armor only comically hampers the young man. David will meet the enemy on David's own terms, not Saul's.

17:41-58. David is victorious. The contrast between the armored Goliath and the lad with five smooth stones is an easy one to make, but David's choice of weapon in fighting one so much bigger reflects shrewdness more than naivete. He could not afford to get close to the long-armed Philistine. The more important contrast is between Saul and David. Saul met his first enemy with a huge army behind him (11:8). Now he is behind the lines while a younger man fights (cf. 14:1-15). Saul appears to put his trust in armor; David faces the enemy armed with his trust in the LORD. Goliath, stunned by a blow to his one unprotected area, subsequently is killed by his own sword. It is his good fortune that the expression "Achilles' heel" is more popular than "Goliath's forehead."

The head of Goliath could not be taken to Jerusalem until much later (v. 54; cf. 2 Sam. 5:6-7), yet v. 57 describes its immediate disposition. Saul's questioning David's identity is a sign of the increasing mental degeneration described in 16:14-23. Since David has seen this before, he is not surprised. The meeting between Samuel and Saul encapsulated their relationship (9:18–10:8); the stories of Saul's and David's also encapsulate theirs. Saul will often forget who David is and treat him as a stranger, but the greatly gifted David will respond with gentleness.

Saul Fears David's Success, 18:1–19:17

Saul's jealousy of David after his victory makes more sense when we remember that the people have consistently understood *king* as one who will *go out before us and fight our battles* (8:19). He is also aware of what no one else but Samuel knows: the God who chose him has rejected him for another (15:28). The king who was so solicitous of David before he fought Goliath ends up trying to kill him himself after watching David effortlessly win over the people and even Saul's own family, suspecting that he may be the new anointed one.

18:1-9. David is popular. Jonathan and David form a friendship upon their first meeting that will drastically affect the outcomes of their lives, and Saul's. It is significant that we are told twice how Jonathan loves David but never how David feels (cf., however, the moving tribute from David upon learning of Jonathan's death, 2 Sam 1:19-27, esp. vv. 25b-26). The man whose first words asked about the possibility of advancement might have reasons for cultivating the king's son that have nothing to do with friendship. Jonathan gives his friend what he needs to be a successful soldier, and a success he is. The people's impudent cry in 18:7 would grate on any king's ears. One with Saul's problems could not help but be upset.

18:10-16. Saul tries to kill David I: the spear. Similar to 16:14, the *evil spirit from God* that *rushed upon Saul* (v. 10) reflects the Israelite belief that God is behind all that happens (cf. 2 Sam 24:1). The loss of the spirit is torment enough for Saul. The attempted murder is narrated matter-of-factly, perhaps reflecting how common such events were around the fragile king. It is not David but Saul who is afraid afterwards. Saul sends him away, but this only contributes to David's glory as he fulfills Israel's concept of king more than ever.

18:17-30. Saul tries to kill David II: the marriage. Saul offers Merab to David as a snare so the people will see how Saul loves their hero, but will not suspect him of complicity in his death. He does not keep his word, but when MICHAL genuinely loves David the trap is set again. Saul is clever; since most men will resist circumcision by sword, he is sure that one out of a hundred Philistines so attacked will manage to kill David, but the scheme backfires. David, like any hero, fulfills the absurd task set by the king and wins the hand of his daughter.

The offer of Merab had been private; this is a more public affair and Saul cannot back out of it, so the marriage takes place. The Bible nowhere records what Saul does with the requested marriage present. As with Jonathan, we are told twice of Michal's love for David but not of his feelings for her. Saul, who intended

David's death, is now forced to make him part of the family. David's success increases.

19:1-17. Saul tries to kill David III: the spear. This attack is almost identical to the one in chap. 18, but in this context it is more serious because two of Saul's children are involved against him. First Jonathan intercedes for David with his father, who is now serious enough to declare publically his murderous intentions. Saul swears in God's name not to harm David, but (as with the vow of 14:24) does not keep his word, pursuing David after missing him with the spear. Jonathan failed to save David through words, but Michal will save him through action. She initiates David's flight and the following coverup. David, who has grown used to Saul's rages, does not consider his situation dangerous. Michal may know that their marriage was a subtle plot against David, alerting her to the fact that her father's murderous intentions do not always express themselves in recognizable ways. David flees and Michal lies for him, although she tells her father that David forced her to help (v. 17).

David and Saul: the Fugitive and His King, 19:18–26:25

In this section Saul is obsessed with killing David while David is forced by Saul to assemble a power base of his own. Saul is now sure that David is God's new chosen—and he is absolutely right—but his sickness prevents him from seeing that the admittedly ambitious David never threatens him. While David engages in some questionable behavior, the narrator is careful to show that David is, in fact, innocent of wrongdoing towards Saul.

One of the worst aspects of Saul's condition is that at times he remembers that he loves David only to find himself trying to kill him again. As Saul degenerates, David slowly changes from a powerless but opportunistic man to a powerful and responsible one as he makes positive relationships. Saul, who has already lost Samuel and the LORD, becomes less responsible and royal as he makes negative ones. This is shown especially in their relationships with God who, behind the scenes as always, supports David through the prophetic word and subtle action on his behalf, rather than through dramatic miracles.

David Flees from Saul, 19:18–21:15

19:18-24. Samuel and David. This is only the second meeting we are told of between Samuel and David but (as in the first) no real interaction between them is presented. Here we see God sending the spirit not upon a chosen leader or messenger but upon those who mean ill to the chosen one. Its purpose is not to illuminate but to prevent, the only time in the Bible in which this is so. In 15:35 we are told that Samuel and Saul never met again. Here they do, but since Saul is possessed by the spirit (which Samuel described in 10:6 as becoming a different person) they do not meet in any real sense of the word. Ironically, the first time Saul fell into prophetic frenzy (10:10-12) was a sign of his being chosen. Here, it is a sign of his rejection.

20:1-42. Jonathan and David. David, on the run from Saul, seeks help not from his family but from Saul's. Perhaps Eliab in 17:28-30 reflects David's family's views about him. Michal had to persuade David to go; now he wants to see how serious things really are. Jonathan believes he averted the danger in 19:6, but to reassure David he devises an elaborate plan to protect and yet help him learn the extent of his danger. Verses 13-17 show Jonathan's absolute loyalty to his friend and his belief that it is David and not he who will someday have power. His rueful statement that the LORD *has been with my father* (v. 13) may reflect his understanding that the loss of the LORD lies behind Saul's madness, yet he still claims Saul as father. The covenant of faithfulness between the friends gives Jonathan no advantage, since David is fleeing for his life. It is Jonathan, who might expect to be king, who gives all—including that expectation. Again, we are told of his love for David but not David's for him. Verse 14 asks David for *the faithful love of the* LORD, but Jonathan is the one who displays it.

Saul's surprise at David's absence reflects his continuing mental degeneration. Either he does not remember his murderous attack, or he expects David to ignore it (as he has before). Saul is angered by his son's taking another's part. Such behavior is shameful and so he responds to his opponent (as in many cultures) by insulting his mother (v. 30). The fact that he is speaking of his own wife underscores his loss of perspective. Although he does not know of the covenant of vv. 13-17, Saul speaks the truth: Jonathan's kingdom will never be established because of *the son of Jesse* (v. 31) whom Saul cannot bear to name. He attacks his son as he has twice already attacked David, since to Saul both are rebels. Jonathan tries to warn David according to the plan, but they are both in such despair that it is abandoned as the friends say farewell.

21:1-9. Ahimelech and David. After days of hiding in a field David needs food, so he manufactures a mission from Saul to deceive the priest into thinking his presence is legitimate. He is not concerned about holy bread, which is intended as a priestly portion (cf. Lev 24:5-9). Survival is his only priority. His departing on such an important mission so unprepared must confuse Ahimelech, but the king's son-in-law cannot be questioned. The presence of one of Saul's men, especially an Edomite (historically an enemy; cf. Num 20:14-21), alarms David and so he asks for a weapon. With the sword that won him the glory that enraged Saul, the fugitive takes off alone.

21:10-15. David and Achish. This account of seeking help from the enemy underscores David's desperation and ingenuity, as well as offering a note of levity in these tense chapters. Taking Goliath's sword into Philistine Gath would not be wise; perhaps David hid it when Achish's men approached. The Philistines consider him the king of Israel because he rather than Saul has led the fight against them. Their suspicion of David forces him to defend himself with wit instead of sword. Using the common ancient belief that spirits causing mental disorder can move from their host to others (cf. Mark 5:1-13), David elaborately feigns madness while on the run from a mad king. Achish's sarcastic response leads the Philistines to free the man who has killed (and circumcised) so many of them. In the words of S. Thomas Niccolls, "[David] may have been anointed with holy oil, but he often walked in slippery places. This king was not above a clownish pratfall or two" (1981, 279).

David Establishes a Base and Saul Pursues Him, 22:1–23:18

22:1-5. David and his followers. David has been a fugitive since 19:18, but once he finds a safe place near his home of Bethlehem people flock to him—not to aid him but to be aided. Some are in danger because of their relationship to him and some are in need for other reasons, but they all see David even now as one who can help them in their troubles. David proves worthy of their trust. He takes pains to insure the safety of his parents, who have roots in Moab (Ruth 1:4; 4:13-17).

Gad's warning indicates that, as David protects others, the LORD is with him as he moves into more secure Judean territory. Aside from Gad, no recognized prophetic figures deliver God's word to David in 1 Samuel (not even Samuel!). Instead, the word will come to David from some less official but no less genuine sources.

22:6-23. Saul and Ahimelech. David is aided by priest and prophet, but Saul kills the LORD's ministers. Verses 6-10 show Saul in a regal setting as he formally announces that he suspects everyone of conspiring against him and, more surprisingly, lays the blame on Jonathan rather than on *the son of Jesse*. The son who was almost killed by his father in the first encounter we witnessed between them has never held that incident against him, trusting him and being understanding even of his madness. It is Saul who has no love for Jonathan. *Doeg*, whose name was so briefly dropped in 21:7, is the only one to respond: if there is a conspiracy, Ahimelech is involved. The Edomite tells the truth. While chap. 21 did not describe the priest's inquiring of the LORD for David, Ahimelech will agree that he did (v. 15).

Saul at once sends for Ahimelech, whom we discover now to be Eli's great-grandson. The fact that Ahimelech is accompanied by *all his father's house* (v. 11) reminds us of the doom placed on this family in 2:31-33, warning us that this encounter will not turn out well. Ahimelech speaks boldly on David's behalf, not telling Saul of David's pretense except to say he himself *has known nothing of this* (v. 15). Nonetheless Saul gives the death sentence, carrying out against God's priests the holy war he did not accomplish against Amalek (cf. v. 19 to 15:3). His own battlehardened soldiers refuse the order. Only Doeg, who is not an Israelite, is willing to slaughter the anointed priests. One survives (cf. 2:33). David admits his culpability in endangering Abiathar's family and takes his responsibility to the escaped priest seriously (cf. 2 Sam 8:17; Solomon in 1 Kgs 2:26). This represents a change for David, who has previously looked to others to solve his problems. Saul's attempt to wipe out David's "conspiracy" has only added to David's strength: he now has his own priest while Saul has murdered his.

23:1-14. The LORD and David. Although we found in the previous section that David had inquired of the LORD through Ahimelech before, here we have the first recorded encounter between them. This is the first time we have heard God speak directly to anyone but Samuel. Keilah is in southwestern Judah, not far from David's original base of Adullam but now in Philistine hands. David's men are fearful but David, trusting in the LORD as in 17:37, rescues the city. When Saul (wrongly believing that God has betrayed David and having no prophet or priest to tell him otherwise) attacks, David inquires of the LORD again. Keilah is not loyal to David but the LORD is, and so in spite of his greater numbers Saul does not capture David.

23:15-18. David and Jonathan. Here the friends meet for the last time, again to swear their loyalty. Jonathan is the first person to say explicitly that David will be king. On one level, this emphasizes Jonathan's loyalty and understanding of God's actions. Jonathan, who never acts in his own self-interest, is perhaps the only man in 1–2 Samuel who can be called "good." On another level, this statement on the lips of Saul's heir gives David's kingship some legitimation. Just as Saul has lost the prophets and priests, he has lost any relationship with his son; Jonathan will stay by him loyally but he knows his father is not only willfully wrong but doomed as well.

Encounters in the Wilderness, 23:19–26:25

Now there are two opposing armed groups in the wilderness. David's ultimate loyalty to what Saul represents as well as David's ultimate difference from him are both revealed in their encounters.

23:19-29. Saul and David. As the people of Keilah showed (23:12), Saul still commands loyalty among the people. Saul, however, sees the Ziphites' loyalty to the anointed king as *compassion* (v. 21) on him as if he were the underdog. His blessing in the LORD's name, while sincere on his part, is ironic to us since we know the LORD is with David. David really is the underdog and is close to capture when Saul is diverted by a Philistine raid (showing how Saul's obsession is distracting the army from its anti-Philistine purpose). Certainly the Philistines have no thought of saving David. His unexpected deliverance must be read in the light of the LORD's being with him in 23:14.

24:1-22. David and Saul. In the previous episode Saul had the strength; here the balance of power will shift to David even though Saul's elite troops outnumber David's men five to one. Seeing Saul's sudden vulnerability, David's men urge him to act. They cite a saying from the LORD not previously recorded—*I will give your enemy into your hand, and you shall do to him as it seems good to you* (v. 4)—although David said something much like it in 17:46-47 and God spoke a similar phrase to him in 23:4. Both of these statements referred to Philistines, but David's men generalize them to include Israelite enemies.

More significantly, we find here an echo of Samuel as he anointed Saul in 10:7; the words are different, but in each case the action is left up to God's chosen. Saul did nothing; will David do too much? No; Saul *is* in David's hands, but he attacks only the hem of Saul's garment. There is no reason to think David knows of the in-

cident of 15:27, but just as Saul's wild tearing of Samuel's hem led the judge to announce that the kingdom will go to a neighbor, David's cutting of Saul's hem shows
the self-control of which that "neighbor" is capable—a quality Saul never had.

Since David can hardly help but think that he may be king someday, he may
want to set an example of respect rather than violence towards kings in general, but
he also takes Saul's status as *the LORD's anointed* (v. 10) seriously—more seriously
than Saul took the similar status of the priests of Nob. That massacre has made
David (but not Saul) more aware of the results of his actions.

With great emotion, David tells Saul that he is innocent of treason, but he also
promises to leave the situation in God's hands. Saul repeatedly took more on himself than God had given him (cf. chaps. 13, 15), but David is the "man after God's
own heart" who will let the LORD act. Both men are moved, calling each other
father and *son*, another example of the troubled father-son relationships in this book.

Saul adds his voice to Jonathan's (23:17) in proclaiming David's coming kingdom—again, a useful point for David's supporters to make against those who remain loyal to Saul's house after his death. They briefly reach an understanding but
v. 22 shows that David, who trusted Saul after several attempts on his life, will trust
him no longer.

25:1-44. David and Abigail. Now, when even Saul has admitted that David
should succeed him, the last righteous leader of Israel dies. The narrator does not
give the expected summary of Samuel's life, perhaps because that appears in 7:13-
17. In the meantime David provides for those who are loyal to him, proving again
that he is capable of self-control.

It is not unusual for the poor to appeal to a rich man on a feast day, and David
is still a fugitive with many mouths to feed. His request of NABAL for *whatever
you have at hand* (v. 8) echoes his similarly desperate plea to Ahimelech in 21:3.
Moreover, Nabal's shepherds know that he has performed a real service for them
(vv. 14-17), and he offers to do the same for the shearers. Unfortunately, Nabal is
a fool (which is the Heb. meaning of his name; although it may represent the
narrator's judgment rather than an actual name, it alerts us as to what to expect
from him). Nabal belittles the hero of Israel as an otherwise unknown escaped slave.
David does not rant at the response but simply orders his men to prepare for action.
His restraint in chap. 24 was in recognition of Saul's status, but he is still quick to
avenge himself on others.

The clever Abigail instantly understands the danger her husband is risking and
acts to save the household by responding to David's request. She treats the wilderness ruffian with incredible respect, not hesitating to sacrifice her husband's
reputation to save his life. Or is it David she wants to save? Like Jonathan in 23:16-
17, Abigail seems to know more about him than is apparent. She understands that
he (unlike Saul) is fighting the LORD's battles. Abigail also is the third person to
tell David that he will rule Israel (like Jonathan and Saul, she is not a recognized
spokesperson of the LORD's). Her purpose is not to mollify him but to advise: the

ruler God is sure to establish needs an unblemished reputation, and so for his own sake he must trust the LORD to handle the situation. This is the third time we have seen someone warned on the basis of their own interest (cf. 2:34-35; 8:11-18).

For the first time such a warning will be effective, since David instantly understands that Abigail's intervention is from God. Again we are reminded of the Ahimelech story: when Saul was crossed he responded with a massacre. In spite of his guilt after that and his later efforts to behave more responsibly, David would have done the same now without prophetic Abigail to prevent it. Her words are confirmed by Nabal's death by God's hand rather than David's; this chosen one allows the LORD to act on his behalf, and the LORD does. Like Hannah (1:26-28), with no revelation David sees God's hand in what could seem an ordinary event. Earlier, David won a wife from an unwilling father; now he wins one from a foolish husband (to Abigail's apparent delight; note her "hurrying" in v. 42). He also marries into nearby Jezreel, consolidating his power there as well as in Carmel. But Saul, who reneged on his promise to marry Merab to David (18:19), now takes his other daughter Michal away.

26:1-25. David and Saul. The first verse repeats 23:19 and the rest of the story is similar to chap. 24. This emphasizes that the betraying Ziphites, David's vengeful men (as represented by Abishai), and the emotional Saul have not changed since their last encounters, but David has. He is not almost captured (cf. 23:26), nor does he encounter Saul by chance (cf. 24:3). Instead, he is in control. The confusion and guilt of chap. 24 are gone. The man who referred to Saul as *father* in their previous meeting (24:11) now infiltrates the enemy camp with only one companion, as Saul's real son once did (14:6-15), but now the enemy is Saul himself. David once used a sword against its owner (17:51), but he will not let Saul's spear be turned against him even by Abishai. From Abigail he has gained a greater faith in God's action on his behalf, understanding that Saul's destiny is God's business, and he is now willing to let God settle matters between Saul and himself.

David's speech in vv. 18-20 is not the emotional plea of 24:8-15, but a rational explanation that he cannot rectify the situation. Since he knows not God but a man (Saul himself) is behind Saul's obsessive pursuit, his only recourse is to leave the Promised Land. This decision does not come easily: in Gen 4:16 the guilty Cain goes "away from the presence of the LORD" and now the innocent David fears his exile from home will also be exile from God. He briefly hopes that Saul will not let it come to that but realizes that he cannot trust Saul's repentance; Saul will hurt him again if he has the chance. God is the real target of his final speech (vv. 23-24) as David hopes the LORD will continue to be with him even in enemy country. The two men, shouting from opposite hilltops, part forever. Saul's last word to him is a blessing, but they both know there can be no peace between them. The powerless fugitive and powerful king have traded places as even Saul sees David as a righteous man who will and should rule God's people.

David and Saul Separately against Their Enemies, 27:1–31:13

David's Fear of Saul Leads Him to the Philistines, 27:1–28:2

David knows that Saul's obsession means he must leave Israel or eventually die there because he has ruled out the possibility of anyone's harming Saul on his behalf. He does not change his Israelite allegiance even as a Philistine vassal, using his base at Ziklag to attack Israel's enemies and destroying them totally (as Saul did not with his enemy in 15:8). For his part, Achish appreciates a good fighting force and has no problem with using one that the enemy has rejected. David, who was honest with Saul but still had to leave Israel, cheerfully lies to the Philistine king about the objects of his attack. The opening paragraph of chap. 28 makes us wonder how long David can be a loyal Israelite in Gath; we see him rising as quickly in the Philistine ranks as he did in the Israelite's, seeming to agree to fight against Israel. He tells Achish *you shall know what your servant can do* (v. 2). Is this an expression of faithfulness to him or a warning that Achish does not know all now?

Saul's Fear of the Philistines Leads Him to the Medium, 28:3-25

Samuel's death notice is repeated here to emphasize Saul's isolation. Saul has killed his priests and driven David away, and the one who once spoke God's word to him is gone as well. This story is not intended to vilify or honor Saul: the weaknesses and bad judgment that cost him God's favor are evident, but so is the horror of his God-rejected situation. Neither Saul nor God is defended by the narrator for their behavior towards one another. The results of the faithlessness of the one and silence of the other are simply presented.

Saul has had his moments of trying to be a faithful king, as when he enforces the law against mediums (Lev 19:31), but in his fear when he cannot contact the LORD through any legal means he seeks out a medium against his own law. His degeneration is complete. The woman is a genuine necromancer. Unable to recognize the living Saul, she knows the dead Samuel when she sees him. This story provides a rare glimpse of early Yahwistic eschatology. The Bible has little to say about life after death; the focus is always on living as God's people in this world rather than the next.

The pathos of v. 15 is almost unbearable. While Saul's refusal to rule theocratically, his unwillingness to accept responsibility for his people, and his actions have brought him to this moment, we cannot help but feel the pain of the man who still tries desperately to reach the LORD years after there has been any word. He asks for Samuel because Samuel was the only link he ever had to God, although he cannot hope that the judge who rejected him when he was alive will have any good word for him now. Samuel confirms Saul's suspicions about David's destiny but promises Saul only total failure. He who became king to rescue Israel from the Philistines will lose army, heirs, and life to them. The fearful medium, more compassionate than Samuel, is energized by Saul's misery; forgetting her own danger she ministers to him handsomely. The night before his death, Saul is treated like a king.

The Philistine Fear of David Leads Them to Reject Him, 29:1-11

The Philistines encamp at APHEK, as they did before the disaster of 4:1-11. That reminder of the ineffective Elides, added to the picture of Saul in total collapse, makes the image of David in the company of Israel's enemies more bleak. Are there no faithful leaders for Israel?

Achish continues to trust David but the other Philistines cannot forget how he has made them suffer in the past and refuse to fight beside him now. David, meanwhile, is playing a dangerous game. Not wanting to risk Achish's trust, he protests being sent from the battle. When he says that he wants to *fight against the enemies of my lord the king* (v. 8), he is heard in one way by Achish and another by the reader. We are reassured by the knowledge that Saul is the only one David has ever referred to as *my lord the king* (cf. 26:19), and Saul's enemies are the Philistines. Achish's commanders are right. The oddly sympathetic Philistine's statement that David is *blameless in my sight as an angel of God* (v. 9) is strange coming from a pagan enemy but reinforces the concern for David's innocence that has dominated the last few chapters.

David's absence from this battle must be seen as evidence of God working behind the scenes on his behalf. Israel could forgive David's sojourn with the Philistines when Saul drove him away, but if he appeared even briefly on the wrong side in the battle in which Saul was killed, suspicion as to his true loyalties would have prevented acceptance as king.

David Is Victorious over the Amalekites, 30:1-31

David has survived the danger inherent in his Philistine vassalship only to be immediately confronted by another: Ziklag is destroyed and its civilian population taken by an enemy unknown to him. This costs him the support of his men as well. For a moment he seems as lost as he was in chap. 21. We know the additional alarming detail that the enemy are Amalekites, the same people against whom Saul fought so disastrously in chap. 15. Since David has a priest, he has the legal access to God that Saul does not, and so he (and we) are rapidly assured of his victory. Seemingly through luck David finds one who can take him to the enemy, but we know that David is not lucky but blessed by God's care. David finds the unsuspecting Amalekites and fights his first major military engagement since he was Saul's general in chaps. 18 and 19. He is no longer under Saul, but his success on the field has not changed. Although the LORD is not mentioned in the account of the battle, David understands that he has won because God is with him (v. 23). He generously shares the spoil with all his men and wisely shares it with the elders of Judah, perhaps reassuring them that in spite of his Philistine vassalship he is still a loyal Israelite at heart. David has become more responsible in his behavior towards others and more sure of the LORD's presence with him, but he is still David. His last words in 1 Samuel, like his first (17:26), look for his own advancement.

Saul Is Defeated by the Philistines, 31:1-13

While David defeats his enemies without Saul, Saul is defeated without David. The Israelites, again suffering for their leader's failures (cf. 4:10-11) as per Samuel's warning of 12:14-15, are routed by the Philistines. Saul fights a brave last stand over the bodies of Jonathan and his other sons until he is badly wounded (probably fatally) by archers; apparently the enemy did not dare get close to the king. Abimelech, the would-be king of Israel in the Book of Judges, in a similar situation successfully ordered his armor-bearer to kill him (Judg 9:54), but Saul's will not obey his command. His last order may show an awareness of what the Philistines did to Samson when they captured him (Judg 16:21-27). Since he is the king, such treatment would dishonor the nation. It is this rather than pain and death that he fears, since he entered the battle knowing that he would die (28:19).

Saul's suicide is presented not as an act of despair but of bravery; he saves the nation from shame. The Bible never calls suicide a sin. Like Saul, other biblical suicides are presented as people whose bad choices led to failure in their lives (Samson in Judg 16:28-30, Ahithophel in 2 Sam 17:23, Zimri in 1 Kgs 16:18, and Judas in Matt 27:3-5), but it is how they lived rather than how they died that is seen negatively.

The Philistines mutilate Saul, as he had known they would, but they do not get the last word. The men of JABESH-GILEAD, the city he rescued years ago on what may have been the greatest day of his life (chap. 11), when the LORD and the people and Samuel were all with him, travel at great risk into the territory of their victorious enemy to take the bodies of their king and deliverer and his sons home. Saul was a troubled man and a troubled king, but our last glimpse of him is of a mighty warrior who dies with honor and, even after death, inspires great loyalty.

Introduction to 2 Samuel

An Outline

Second Samuel is the second part of the Book of Samuel, originally one volume but divided into two because of length. The sources, date, and themes of the work are discussed in the introduction to 1 Samuel.

Critics have isolated a number of sources behind 1–2 Samuel. Two of them deserve special attention: the Court History or SUCCESSION NARRATIVE (chaps. 9–20; 1 Kgs 1–2) and the appendix (chaps. 21–24; see Miller 1990, 198–99). Chapters 9–20 is generally considered to be a separate source because its focus moves from DAVID the glorious king to David the troubled man, and its intimate picture of David's domestic and court life raises the possibility it comes from an eyewitness (see Cate 1990, 859). Its vivid characterization, portrayal of family conflict, and themes are reminiscent of the J source of the Torah, which is dated to this period as well (see Gregory 1990, 850–51, and Brueggemann 1968, 156–81). It must be noted, however, that interest in David's personal life begins well before the Succession Narrative, and it can be successfully argued that the concern of chaps. 9–20 is more with David's character and its effect on Israel than with who will be king after him (Flanagan 1972, Perdue 1984).

The appendix, on the other hand, is difficult to date in both setting and composition. It contains lists, stories, and songs that belong to various periods of David's life but were not included in the body of 2 Samuel. They are placed at the end of the book immediately before his death, which is recorded in 1 Kgs 1–2.

The appendix and Court History do represent different traditions (as does the rest of the material in Samuel), but this commentary will focus on the way the editors wove them into the fabric of their work, rather than seeing them as undigested blocks of material.

First Samuel described how the faithlessness of the house of ELI resulted in loss to the PHILISTINES. SAMUEL, the last judge of Israel, was the immediate answer to this crisis. A God-guided leader, he achieved a stalemate with the Philistines, but the people ended the prevailing tribal confederacy by asking the aging Samuel for a king to bring them military victory.

Through a controversial and complicated process the nation became a theocratic monarchy under Samuel and King SAUL. Saul, a strong warrior but weak man, ultimately failed. His deterioration parallels the rise of his loved and hated general and son-in-law, David, ending with Saul's death in battle against the Philistines.

Second Samuel is the story of David, a dark and gifted man, and his relationships with God and God's people. Through the presentation of his complex character and experiences it continues to deal with the themes raised in 1 Samuel, including the necessity of God-guided leadership, the way the nation pays for its leaders' failings, the complexity and unpredictability of human nature, and, most of all, the relationships between individuals and between individuals and God. As in 1 Samuel, God takes a backstage role in choosing, advising, and speaking through prophetic figures. Nonetheless, even though the human characters seem to dominate the action, it is God's judgment that ultimately determines the outcome.

For Further Study

In the *Mercer Dictionary of the Bible*: ABNER; ABSALOM; CHRONOLOGY; DAVID; KINGSHIP; MICHAL; MEPHIBOSHETH; PHILISTINES; SAMUEL; SAMUEL, BOOKS OF FIRST AND SECOND; SAUL; SUCCESSION NARRATIVE; WOMEN IN THE OT.

In other sources: W. Brueggemann, "David and His Theologian," *CBQ* 30 (1968): 156–81; J. W. Flanagan, "Court History or Succession Document?" *JBL* 91 (1972): 172–81; L. G. Perdue, "'Is There Anyone Left of the House of Saul . . . ?' Ambiguity and the Characterization of David in the Succession Narrative," *JSOT* 30 (1984): 67–84.

Commentary

David and Saul's House: The Difficult Transition, 1:1–5:5

First Samuel ended on a note of national defeat and solemn mourning. Second Samuel begins at that point but does not stress the crisis Israel faces or the loss of SAUL and JONATHAN. Although the elegy in chap. 1 is poignant, the focus is on the victorious and gracious figure who sings it. The people are not without gifted leadership, and this section will show how the nation recovers from Saul's loss with a stronger, wiser, and generally more able king to unify and lead them.

David Mourns the Deaths of Saul and Jonathan, 1:1-27

We begin this chapter of ironies with David, renowned warrior of Israel, sitting in his Philistine city unaware that the PHILISTINES have killed the king of Israel and his son Jonathan—men who were not only his comrades in arms but also his in-laws. The news of the deaths of those who were once closest to David is brought by an enemy whose people he was defeating while Saul was being defeated. This Amalekite, seeking to ingratiate himself with the victor, tells a different story of Saul's death from the one found in 1 Sam 31. He denies Saul the final burst of strength and courage that saved him from a dishonorable death, taking credit for that death himself. Obviously the messenger expects David to reward Saul's killer, but David is capable of avenging the man who repeatedly tried to kill him and finally drove him into exile. The first information passed from one character to another in 2 Samuel is a self-serving half-truth, but the narrator does not alert the reader. Only by comparing this story to the previous one does the reader find the truth. Even more careful reading will be required as the text unfolds. David, who has earlier shown reluctance to harm *the LORD's anointed* (1 Sam 26:9-16), has many reasons for executing the Amalekite: genuine grief at the deaths of his king and friend, need to distance himself from any involvement in those deaths, and concern for the sanctity of *the LORD's anointed* since he himself enjoys that status (cf. 1 Sam 16).

Although David from his very first words in 1 Samuel has always had an eye to his own advancement (1 Sam 17:26), he refuses the *crown . . . and armlet* (v. 10) the Amalekite took from Saul's body to give him. Instead, he and his people mourn for Saul, Jonathan, and Israel.

The beautiful lament of vv. 17-27 closes the complex relationships David had with the dead men. Saul was his king and Jonathan his closest friend, but Saul's inability to live up to the rigorous demands of Israel's theocratic kingship, coupled with the suspicion and desire that always accompany power, ended the relationship between Saul and David. While David and Jonathan remained loyal to each other, Jonathan's faithfulness to his father separated them as well. It says much for David's character that he wants the people to remember the unstable and violent man who cost him so much (and who stood between him and the throne he had to hope God intended for him) only as a brave warrior who was generous in victory. His lament for Jonathan is more personal, stressing the loyalty Jonathan displayed towards both father and friend. In v. 26 David expresses for the first time his love for the man who was consistently his advocate against his own royal hopes, showing in his language the depth of his emotion and the importance this friendship had for him. *How the mighty have fallen!* (vv. 19, 27) is at the beginning and end of the lament. This phrase is a major motif of 1–2 Samuel: ELI, SAMUEL, and SAUL, the previous leaders of Israel, lost power in various ways. David is on the brink of his glory. Will he also fall from its heights?

David is an opportunistic man; it can hardly be supposed that he has not instantly realized that the deaths of Saul and Jonathan largely clear his way to the throne (in fact, he will begin to act on that assumption as soon as he finishes singing), but that does not diminish the real sorrow he feels at the loss of these men who were so much to him and to Israel. Realizing that he may well benefit from their tragedy could only increase his pain.

David Becomes King over Judah, 2:1-7

In chap. 1 God was referred to distantly (1:12, 14, 16), but now through David's inquiring *of the LORD* (v. 1) God becomes the director of the action. David as the "man after God's own heart" (1 Sam 13:14) allows God to choose who is to rule rather than grasping for himself the trappings of kingship offered by the Amalekite. He has, however, done all he can to assure that the elders of his home territory of Judah will be favorably disposed to him (1 Sam 30:26-31). He chooses HEBRON, the place where ABRAHAM first gained title to part of the Promised Land (Gen 23:1-20), as the place to begin his stronghold there. The Judeans quickly anoint David as their king and the Philistines do not intervene. Probably Achish, who is unaware of how David used him (1 Sam 27:8-13) but thinks of him as a loyal vassal (1 Sam 29:6-10), believes that David will serve the Philistine cause in Judah. David, however, has other ideas. He moves to Hebron with his two wives, both of whom have ties in northern Israel, and sends messengers into the North with the double purpose of thanking those who gave Saul burial and letting them know that he is available to take Saul's place. Note that he asks God whether to move into Judah but apparently looks to Israel on his own.

David Fights for Control over Israel, 2:8–5:5

David easily becomes king of Judah, but he will have a more difficult time establishing control over the rest of Saul's kingdom. The monarchy was formed by twelve tribes, each of which had a history of independent leadership. They were united under Saul and Samuel, but Judah feels no need to continue that union. Israel gives its loyalty to Saul's family; Judah chooses to follow the strongest warrior.

2:8-17. Abner establishes Ishbaal as king of Israel. ABNER is Saul's uncle and the commander of his army. The wording of v. 8 (as well as 3:6-11) indicates that Abner is not so much supporting Ishbaal's (also called ISHBOSHETH) claim as using it to consolidate his own power. Opposing Abner is the leader of David's army, his nephew JOAB, who with his brothers Abishai and Asahel are among David's greatest warriors (8:16; 23:18, 24). When the opponents meet an attempt is made to settle their differences by twelve simultaneous single combats. Like the single combat all of the participants in this one must remember, that between David and Goliath (1 Sam 17), the result is dramatic but settles nothing. David's men win the ensuing battle.

2:18-32. Abner kills Joab's brother. Abner does not want to kill Asahel (they may well have fought together against the Philistines under Saul) and tries to push him away with the blunt end of his spear, but even this blow is fatal. Abner is able to persuade Joab not to let what is already a civil war degenerate into a feud, and both sides return home. Even though the leadership of the nation is at stake, the conflict (like many others in 1–2 Samuel) is very much a family affair.

3:1-21. Abner makes a deal with David. David's house is growing stronger and larger but there is conflict in Saul's. Verse 7 is Ishbaal's only line; it shows him to be frustrated but powerless in Abner's hands. Taking a woman understood to belong to the head of the house or kingdom is tantamount to taking that man's place (cf. Gen 35:22, 49:4); the just-mentioned AMNON, ABSALOM, and ADONIJAH will enact variations of this motif with David (13:1-14; 16:20-22; 1 Kgs 2:13-25). *Rizpah* (v. 7) is chattel here, but in 21:10-14 she is a strong character.

Abner, angry with Ishbaal and seeing David's strength, offers to make him king in the north. Now David shows a new and ultimately disastrous trait. He trusted and respected his first two wives, MICHAL and ABIGAIL, but as he moves closer to greater power he learns from the power broker ABNER to treat women differently. He requires the man who has taken Saul's concubine to give him another of Saul's women: his daughter Michal, David's first wife. Saul gave her to David as a trap although she loved him (1 Sam 18:20-29), but she saved David's life (1 Sam 19:11-17). Now without consulting her he breaks up her home, needing the connection to Saul's house to make him acceptable to the northerners who are loyal to it (notice his initial identification of her in v. 13). *Paltiel* (v. 15), the only man who has ever cared for Michal at all, is forcibly separated from her. Abner energetically prepares the north for David, cheerfully spouting Davidic claims of God's blessing that he as Saul's uncle and general must have fought against for years.

3:22-39. Joab kills Abner. In this story the characters mask their motives with dialogue but the narrative silences are more eloquent still. It introduces us to the complex relationship between David and Joab, foreshadows almost every other murder in the book, and shows the reader how difficult determining the truth of David's life will be. A close reading of the text indicates that the traitorous Abner may be the most straightforward character. The unexpected mention in v. 30 of Abishai as accomplice shows that there are at least two versions of the murder. Why is Abner killed? The narrator discounts Joab's spoken concerns about David's security and offers vengeance for Asahel as the reason for Abner's death. But this seems unreasonable; Joab gave up that cause in 2:27-28, and Abner must believe that the feud is over since he is unsuspicious of Joab.

This leads to a second possibility, that Joab kills to protect himself. Abner is commander of Ishbaal's armies just as Joab is of David's, and no king needs two commanders-in-chief. What will happen to Abner when Ishbaal's armies become David's? While David and Abner twice discuss what David is getting from Abner, it becomes increasingly obvious that no reward for Abner is ever mentioned. Shrewd Abner would never sell out Ishbaal for vengeance alone, no matter how angry he was. Probably Abner's pay is Joab's job; David will offer it to the commander of another rival Israelite army in 19:13, and Joab will kill that general because of it (20:9-10). Or is Abner's death more to David's advantage than Joab's? Once the north has been brought into line—and Abner has already done that—will David be safe with this powerful man who has already betrayed one king? Does Joab kill to benefit David against David's own wishes (as with Absalom in 18:9-15)—a third possibility? Or, fourthly, does he do David's dirty work at David's orders (as with Uriah in 11:14-21)?

The text raises all of these questions. David seems aware of the service Joab has performed, even if only after the fact. He curses Joab extravagantly but it is mere talk; Joab remains his right-hand man. Like his ostentatious mourning, it is designed to calm suspicion of his complicity in Abner's death.

It is a mark of the narrator's skill that the story can be read in any of these ways. The characters keep their own counsel, and the narrator leaves it to the reader to decide where the truth lies. As 2 Samuel progresses, finding the truth will be even more difficult and more vital. The third option above (Joab kills on his own to protect David) seems best; in 7:9 God will tell David I *have cut off all your enemies from before you*, an odd statement if David had in fact had one killed. This shows how human selfishness, greed, misplaced loyalty, and hatred (in this case Joab's) can be used to further God's ends without God creating or endorsing them (cf. the discussion of Assyria in Isa 10:5-19 or the roles played by those who betray, convict, and execute Jesus).

4:1–5:5. Ishbaal is killed; David becomes king over Israel. Abner's murder leaves Ishbaal and his army in disarray; the accidental maiming of MEPHIBOSHETH reflects their panic. It is not surprising, then, that two soldiers resolve the situation by killing Ishbaal, whom they believe cannot hold the kingdom, to win favor with the one they believe can. David, now receiving two messengers who mistakenly believe they will be rewarded for killing a Saulide, again avenges the death of the one who opposed him (cf. 1:1-16). This, along with David's reaction to Abner's death, convinces the Israelite elders that they can support him without reneging on their earlier loyalty. Like Abner in 3:18 (but presumably with more sincerity), they say that the promises God made to Saul in 1 Sam 10:1 are fulfilled in David. The elders thus join Jonathan, David's own men, Saul, and Abigail in giving David a prophetic word that he has not yet received directly himself (cf. 1 Sam 23:17; 24:4, 20; 25:30). The civil war ends with David anointed as king of all of Saul's kingdom.

In this section four people who stood between David and a throne have been killed. David's avoidance of bloodguilt has been a concern ever since 1 Sam 24, when he first had the chance to harm Saul and refused. Nabal (1 Sam 25), Saul, Abner, and Ishbaal all blocked him in some way—Jonathan, as Saul's son, did so as well—but David seems to have followed Abigail's advice and allowed God to remove his enemies (1 Sam 25:26-31). The narrator makes clear that there was suspicion about David's role in these deaths but that his behavior convinced the people of his innocence. However, it is undeniable that David has become Israel's king through treachery, even if the treachery is not his. He has been more active in the pursuit of his destiny, fighting a war to become Israel's king; we are beginning to wonder how much more he will do.

David Alone: Consolidating Power with Ease, 5:6–9:13

This section is the culmination of David's career. With a fought-for kingdom and a new capital, David himself formally receives the promise of God's eternal support of his house. He is victorious on the field; even his potential enemies are under his control.

David Takes Jerusalem and Defeats His Enemies, 5:6-25

The account of how Jerusalem, the city that plays such a pivotal part in the rest of the Bible, comes into Israelite hands is surprisingly brief. Once David becomes king of Israel, he moves to establish a central capital in a region not already connected with either Israel or Judah. The Jebusites taunt David with their belief that their stronghold cannot fall—a tradition that will show up again in Isa 29:5-8 and 31:4-5—but he turns their taunt on them. Through warfare the city named "City of Peace" becomes the City of David.

Verse 10 tells the reader that *the LORD was with him*; v. 12 points out that David understands his greatness is due to God's concern for Israel and not for his (i.e., David's) glory. Strangely, David's response to the perceived care of the LORD is to take more women, reminding us of his taking of Michal in 3:13-16. David may be rewarding himself, or he may merely be trying to make his bloodline even more secure. He also establishes a diplomatic tie with Tyre and defeats the Philistines, who were not concerned with his kingship in Judah but erupt in fury at his taking of Israel as well (finally realizing that he is a rival power).

David Makes Jerusalem His Capital, 6:1-23

6:1-15. The Ark comes into the city. David's first concern is to bring into Jerusalem the most sacred object known to the Hebrews: the ARK of the Covenant, understood to manifest God's presence and power (see Bailey 1990, 63–64). The Ark led the people through wandering and war during the periods of the wilderness and tribal confederacy (cf. 1 Sam 4:1–7:2). By honoring the Ark David acknowledges to God and the people his dependence on *the LORD of hosts* (v. 2). He also shows Israel that in spite of the major changes of the last few decades—the controversial move from the confederacy to the monarchy, the transition from one royal house to another, and the acquisition of a foreign city as the capital—the old traditions are still respected under the new regime.

UZZAH's death (vv. 6-11) in the midst of the festivities strikes an ominous note. Mortals approach holiness unprepared at their peril not because it is antagonistic, but because raw power is inherently dangerous (see Joines 1990, 383–84). Uzzah's intentions to prevent the Ark from tipping over are good. The statement that *the anger of the LORD was kindled against Uzzah* (v. 7) should not be read as God's punishing him, any more than a death resulting from touching an unshielded electric cable should be interpreted as punishment by electricity. The site of his death is known as *Perez-uzzah*, which means "Bursting Out Against Uzzah" (v. 8; NRSV mg.).

This divine disaster and the divine victory of 5:20 have similar names as a reminder that God's power can be fearsome as well as helpful and that even those blessed by God cannot assume that they are automatically lucky. With the proper precautions, David brings the Ark into the city. Even if he has calculated the political expediency of this move, his generosity and dancing (6:16-19) indicate that it is a personal priority as well.

6:16-23. Michal and David argue. The story of an important day in Jerusalem ends with a note about David's domestic life, a matter that received little attention in 1 Samuel but will occupy us more and more as 2 Samuel unfolds. Michal is called *the daughter of Saul* (vv. 16, 20, 23) instead of "the wife of David," reminding us that she is the only woman able to produce an heir that will unite the rival royal families. She seems eager to pick a fight, perhaps still upset over the dissolution of her marriage to Paltiel (3:15), or perhaps angry at now being only one of David's many wives. Their explosive confrontation covers etiquette, history, and theology. Verse 23 shows that the issue is never resolved, meaning that there will be no heir acceptable to both Saulide and Davidic supporters.

This strong, risk-taking woman is never mentioned again (the NRSV reading of *Merab daughter of Saul* in 21:8 is correct [cf. KJV]; Merab was Michal's sister). The young man who escaped with his life on her advice (see 1 Sam 19:11-17) has become a king who will not put up with her opinions.

The LORD Promises to Establish David's House, 7:1-29

Chapter 7 begins when David is at the pinnacle of his career. He has fulfilled both human and divine expectations of the kingship by taking care of the Philistine threat (1 Sam 8:19-20, 9:16) and has publicly acknowledged God's role by bringing the Ark into the city. Any hopes Saul's house still had have been dashed by 6:20-23.

At this crucial time in David's reign we meet NATHAN, who also appears at two other major junctures in David's life (12:1-15; 1 Kgs 1–2). God now initiates communication through an intermediary. Anonymous prophets (cf. 1 Sam 2:27-36; 10:9-13) and a few named ones (cf. 1 Sam 22:5) earlier have spoken and acted on God's behalf, but Nathan is the first among the prophets of the kingdom who will figure so prominently in the affairs of state (and the families of the kings). Nathan, and the prophets like him that will follow, represents the charismatic leadership that is denied by the hereditary monarchy. That Nathan appears precisely at the moment that the monarchy officially becomes hereditary is significant.

God immediately shifts the meaning of *house* (vv. 4-17) from the kind of ornate structure David wants as a sign of his loyalty to the LORD to the royal dynasty that is a sign of the LORD's loyalty to him. God summarizes the historical relationship between Israel and God; while the movable Ark that manifests the divine power has been housed in various structures in its history (as at Shiloh, 1 Sam 1–4), it has never been confined in a permanent abode and will not be for another generation (vv. 6-7, 13). The gift David wants to give—a *house [for God] to live in* (v. 5)—is turned into a gift David will receive: a covenant promising an everlasting dynasty. The Mosaic covenant was conditional (Exod 19:5-6); the Davidic is not (vv. 15-16).

As was the Mosaic covenant, the Davidic covenant is based on divine rather than human faithfulness (vv. 8-9; cf. Exod 20:1-2), although verses like 5:25 indicate that God is faithful because David obediently allows God to be God. This covenant promises military defeat as punishment for human faithlessness (v. 14), but faithlessness will not lead to rejection as it did with Saul (vv. 15-16). David's house will not always be chosen for blessing and good fortune, but it will always be chosen. David's humble response mixes gratitude and inability to believe such good news; Saul's son-in-law knows better than anyone else alive that those once anointed can be rejected and suffer horribly because of it.

David Defeats His Enemies, 8:1-18

David's status as God's chosen king is reflected by his success. In war he is victorious; in peace he makes allies; and in both he gains goods to dedicate to the LORD. The reasons for his wars are not given because the narrator's purpose is to emphasize David's triumphs rather than the details surrounding them. His treatment of the Moabites, with whom he has a distant kinship and who helped him when he was a fugitive (1 Sam 22:3-4), reminds us of the quick and cruel judgment of which kings are capable. Verse 13 also strikes an odd note; here David *won a name for himself* instead of giving credit to the LORD (cf. 5:12). Verses 15-18 is a list of David's officers; 20:23-26 reflects a later period in his reign. Like a judge, David administers justice. His organization contains old faces (Joab and Abiathar [v. 17 should read "Abiathar son of Ahimelech"; see 1 Sam 22:11-23]) and new ones (Zadok, anticipated in 1 Sam 2:35, and Benaiah). Note that military and priestly duties are shared by one old and one new companion. Nowhere else are David's sons priests; later tradition will say only descendants of AARON could be priests, but earlier it was not thought unusual for the sons of the founder of a sanctuary to serve at it (cf. Judg. 17:5).

David Obtains Custody of Mephibosheth, 9:1-13

As in chap. 1, here we see David acting correctly but with a number of motives, some of which are self-serving. The events of 21:1-14 must have already occurred; David's search for *still anyone left of the house of Saul* (v. 1) implies a disaster to that house, but in the direct line only Ishbosheth has died so far in 2 Samuel. David's request harks back to his friendship with Jonathan: in 1 Sam 20:14-15 Jonathan says to him *if I die, never cut off your faithful love from my house, even if the LORD were to cut off every one of [your] enemies.* Now the LORD has done just that. The emphasis on MEPHIBOSHETH's lameness reminds us of the entangled relationships here, since he was crippled in the panic following Abner's murder in David's capital by David's general (4:4). His response in v. 8 to King

David is reminiscent of David's speech to his enemy King Saul in 1 Sam 24:14-15 (v. 15 is especially noteworthy in view of the next encounter between them in 19:24-30).

Mephibosheth has reason to distrust David, who benefits from bringing him to court by having Saul's last adult male heir where he can see him. The existence of Mica (v. 12) shows that Saul's house has expanded to another generation, giving David cause for concern. Whether loyalty or paranoia is David's major motive is difficult to determine; like most people, he acts from a variety of motives, some of which even he may not know.

Now the promises and blessings of 1 Samuel have been fulfilled. David is the king who does what Saul did not (1 Sam 9:16; 10:1), whose coming was foretold (1 Sam 13:14; 15:28). More business from 1 Samuel has been finished as well: the new priest not of Eli's family has appeared (1 Sam 2:27-36) and the covenant between David and Jonathan has been honored. The troubling relationship between David and the Philistines in 1 Sam 27-30 has also been resolved as David has defeated them. Now God has made him king, delivered him from all enemies, and endorsed his dynasty.

David is at the height of his glory, but there are warning signs: his behavior towards Michal and Mephibosheth shows him directing people's destinies for his own ends, and his taking of women in Jerusalem and killing two-thirds of the Moabites reminds us that a king may gratify all of his desires more easily than an ordinary man can.

David and His Family: Keeping Power with Difficulty, 10:1–20:26

This section, which is the heart of 2 Samuel, explores more fully David's ambiguous aspects as his disruptive family life disrupts Israel as well. In 1 Samuel there were many to assure David of his glorious destiny (23:17; 24:4, 20; 25:28-31), but he is now surrounded by those who rebuke him (Nathan in 12:1-14; his servants in 12:21; the wise woman in 14:13-14; Shimei in 16:5-8; and Joab in 12:27-28 and 19:5-7). The tendency we first noted in 3:12-16 for David to see others (esp. women) as his to dispose of as he wishes leads to a tale of personal deception and national intrigue that takes David from success to disaster, costing him sons, reputation, self-respect, and God's favor. Indeed, David almost loses the kingdom itself twice.

Notice how infrequently anyone in these narratives speaks honestly; they manipulatively distort the truth like the Amalekite of chap. 1 (and the reader must work to find the manipulations). At first David is the deceiver but he becomes the dupe as the ramifications of his betrayals close in on him. As always it is in adversity that he is at his best, displaying more character than he shows in victory.

David and Ammon, 10:1-19

Nahash of Ammon, apparently David's ally, was the brutal king Saul defeated in 1 Sam 11. Verse 2 recalls 9:1 and again we find David offering help in a way that makes his own position stronger, since at least he will solidify his relationship with Ammon, and at most he may learn something useful. Whatever David's motives may have been, he clearly has a reputation as a devious man. Joab shows his worth as a tactician and wins the first phase of the war. David, not entering the battle until the second phase, wins a great victory. This may be a retelling of the events of chap. 8 (vv. 6, 15-19 say that David was opposed by some of the same opponents mentioned in the earlier chapter), but even if that is historically so, the editors clearly intend us to read it as a separate battle. The narrative not only points out the pattern of David's questionable generosity, but it also suggests the speed with which a seemingly resolved situation (e.g., the war in chap. 8) can come undone. None of David's success is necessarily permanent.

David, Bathsheba, and Uriah, 11:1-27

11:1-5. David sends for Bathsheba. Verse 1 sets the tone for this passage: kings go to battle, but David stays home. It is a picture of David we have not seen before, the king rising from an afternoon nap while his men fight. Saul first showed himself as a mighty warrior against the Ammonites (1 Sam 11); in the course of this battle David's character will also be revealed. Robert Alter points out that the stories of David taking wives—his love stories—are set in contexts of conflict and death. Circumcising one hundred Philistines allows David to marry Michal (1 Sam 18:20-29), the death of Nabal paves the way for David to marry Abigail (1 Sam 25); and the murder of Uriah leads to Bathsheba's marriage (Alter 1981, 60–61).

David's love and death are connected. From his cool roof (which would be the highest in Jerusalem), David glimpses Bathsheba bathing. Contrary to popular representation, she is not on her roof but must be in an inner courtyard or a room of her own house. In one of the most laconic verses in the Bible David, who has sent Joab to war and sent servants for information, now sends for a woman he knows to be married to a soldier at the front and has sex with her. Uriah is doing David's job; now David will do Uriah's. The king sends at least two people to get (not ask) her; the king has power and the woman with the absent husband has none. Like Susanna, she was observed bathing privately, but unlike Susanna, Bathsheba has no advocate (Sus 1:1-64). Forms of "to send" are used twelve times in this chapter (vv. 1, 3, 4, 5, 6 [three times], 12, 14, 18, 22, 27); each time except v. 5 the sending is done by David or at his will. Bathsheba's only words in 2 Samuel fall like a judgment as she informs David about the one event he has not controlled.

11:6-27. David sends twice to Joab. The plots involving Uriah are entirely David's idea; Bathsheba does not reappear until v. 26. Because of v. 4b there is no way the child can be passed off as Uriah's, and if the issues were not so serious vv. 6-13 would be funny as David uses adolescent innuendo (v. 8), direct pressure (v. 10), and alcohol (v. 13) to try to get Uriah to sleep with his own wife. But the Hittite is more loyal to the wartime code of conduct (cf. 1 Sam 21:4-5) than is Israel's king.

In the last two chapters we have seen David offer help but have not been sure if his motives were honest. Here we cannot misinterpret: David brings Uriah home and offers him food and drink in order to harm him and help himself. He then resorts to greater subtlety and worse betrayal, using faithful Uriah to deliver his own death sentence. He has learned from Saul, who in 1 Sam 18:20-30 tried to have David killed in war. Now David will more successfully use a war to kill someone he sees as a threat. Joab, utterly loyal to David, follows orders even at the cost of additional Israelite men. In his instructions to his messenger he mentions Abimelech, who claimed the kingship but lost the kingdom and his life because of a woman (Judg 9:50-57). The messenger, perhaps sensing the awful appropriateness of those words, does not give David a chance to utter them (although in the LXX he does). David's response in v. 25 is public relations; his musing on the randomness of death in battle could only amuse Joab, but it might reassure some who wonder if Uriah really died by chance. The many messengers involved and the fact that Uriah spent every night with David's servants mean the affair and the paternity of the child are public knowledge; suspicion over Uriah's death would be inevitable.

There is no indication that Bathsheba ever knows the truth about Uriah's death or that her lamentation is not sincere. Her relationship with David has traditionally been seen as a passionate love affair with Bathsheba as a willing if not seductive participant, but it can much more easily be read as the rape of a loyal wife. As we have seen, it is David who sends and plots and arranges murder; v. 27 (again with *David sent*) sounds as if he can hardly wait for the funeral formalities to be observed. While much of David's behavior has been open to doubt since he became king, now he is clearly wrong. Another man who was an obstacle has died conveniently, and there is no confusion as to why. Verse 27 gives us God's first sign of displeasure with his chosen king.

David and the LORD, 12:1-31

The LORD has accepted David's earlier behavior, but now the shepherd boy who learned to let God act on his behalf has become a despot who acts as if he has the right to dispose of people's lives. In keeping with the covenant of chap. 7, David does not lose the kingship but his sin will be punished *with blows inflicted by human beings* (7:14).

12:1-15a. Nathan brings the LORD's indictment to the king. 12:1-15a. God "sends" Nathan to deliver judgment to the one who "sent" others on such sorry errands. His parable involves David's emotions before the king knows what the issues really are. The story is far from an exact allegory of chap. 11, but the theme is there: a powerful man disrupts a powerless man's family by taking and destroying a loved member of it. The lamb in different ways represents both Bathsheba and Uriah. To David's credit, he is enraged at the injustice and pronounces sentence. To his further credit, he does not dispute Nathan's sudden verdict in 7. The one who in 5:12 understood that he had been given much for the sake of Israel now realizes that he has taken more than the gift entitled him to.

David's confession in v. 13 leads to forgiveness, but forgiveness does not mean that the events he set in motion by his public sin can be stopped. In questionable circumstances he once said, *The Lord pay back the one who does wickedly in accordance with his wickedness!* (3:39). The narrative ranging from 12:15 to 20:26 will show this happening as David's older sons' violent passions, like his, lead to rape and murder, costing Israel peace and David the security of the throne, and the lives of four sons (the fourth, Adonijah, does not die until 1 Kgs 2:25).

Only the death of the first is presented as a divine punishment. The rest are the inevitable result of David's behavior; God does not will Amnon's incestuous, violent desires or Absalom's ambitious and patricidal ones. The man who freely committed adultery and murder will pay through the equally free acts of his sons. Like Uriah, many who are innocent will suffer for David's sin, but others will be drawn by their own evil into the context created by David's for even greater catastrophe.

12:15b-25. The births of David and Bathsheba's children. The sentence begins at once. David's fatherly love shows in his genuine mourning in an effort to avert the death of his and Bathsheba's baby; his behavior afterwards shows his pained acceptance. His consolation of Bathsheba (v. 24) is the first evidence of tenderness towards her. The report of God's love for the subsequent child reassures us that he will not also pay for David's crime, although the natural results of David's behavior will still occur. Solomon will not even be mentioned in the rest of 2 Samuel, but in 1 Kgs 1–2 he will succeed to the throne (making it difficult to see 9–20 as a SUCCESSION NARRATIVE).

12:26-31. Joab and David defeat their enemies. We move from these stories of intimate relationships back to the larger world of national policy in which they began. David's disastrous sabbatical from the war ends at Joab's insistence; David cannot afford to lose face any further. The victory is as always a sign of God's presence with Israel, even though the statement is not specifically made here. The treasure and crown of the Ammonite kings (the probable reading of *Milcom* in v. 30) become David's and the Ammonite people are drafted into a labor force. The victorious end of this lengthy war is barely described, however; the focus is on tracing the dissolution begun in David's family.

David and His Children, 13:1–14:33

David's treatment of others creates reactions and further crimes he never intended. The connection noted earlier between David's love and death (see commentary at 11:1-5 above) now displays itself even more destructively in his children. In 1 Samuel we saw strife in father-son relationships with ELI and HOPHNI and PHINEAS, Saul and Jonathan, and Saul and David (who addressed each other with the familial terms "father" and "son"; David even refers to himself as Nabal's "son"). The father-son conflict was also implied with Samuel and his sons (1 Sam 8:1-3). The motif is emphasized more here as one son uses David to achieve incestuous rape, and another tries to kill him only to be killed by his father's men.

13:1-22. Amnon rapes Tamar. Although Amnon is David's eldest, ABSALOM is mentioned first, indicating that he is actually the pivotal character. His *beautiful sister* (v. 1) reminds us that raped Bathsheba was the last woman called "beautiful." Amnon has David's nephew Jonadab as an advisor, a man described as wise (NRSV *crafty*); perhaps his counsel is thought wise at a court where the king takes the wife of one of his men. Jonadab suggests using David's paternal concern for his son to gain access to his daughter. David duly "sends" (recall the importance of "sending" in the Bathsheba story [see commentary at 11:1-5 above]) Tamar to care for her supposedly ill brother (note how often family designations instead of names are used, emphasizing the misuse of these relationships).

Like his father with Uriah (11:13), Amnon uses food to mask betrayal. When his intentions become unmistakable Tamar does not panic but reasons with him, pointing out that a forbidden sexual relationship between them will ruin them both. It doesn't matter. The exact nature of David's taking of Bathsheba is veiled in silence, but there is no doubt that Amnon rapes Tamar. His exaggerated love for her immediately turns to exaggerated loathing. By sending her away he dooms her to an isolated life; there will always be suspicion that she was willing since she was raped in the city (cf. Deut 22:23-24, although that deals with a betrothed virgin).

Our last glimpse of this compassionate and truly wise woman shows her running from Amnon's house in a posture of mourning and abandonment. Out of her large family only Absalom cares for her. While his sons are not named in the text (they probably died young [18:18]), 14:27 says that he names his daughter after his sister who will have no child. David is angry at *all these things* (v. 21; but are "these things" the rape or David's own manipulated role in it?) but does nothing. The kindest interpretation is that he feels he cannot chastise Amnon for giving into the dangerous passions his son must know David himself has gratified, but the text says only that he does not act *because he loved [Amnon]* (v. 21). Clearly he has no such feeling for Tamar.

13:23-39. Absalom kills Amnon. Like David, Amnon uses his power to take a woman to whom he has no right. Like David, Absalom uses his to order a murder. He waits two years to kill his brother, perhaps hoping that David will avenge Tamar. When that hope fails, he uses food to mask betrayal (as did David with Uriah and Amnon with Tamar). Again a son deceives David into sending a victim to him. Although Absalom does not strike the fatal blow himself, everyone understands that he is responsible—in the same way David is responsible for Uriah's death. Jonadab (who does not seem to have warned his friend Amnon of his danger) says the murder is due to Tamar's rape.

Certainly the rape of Tamar fixed Absalom's feelings towards his brother Amnon, but like his father Absalom may be acting from multiple motives. As subsequent events indicate, Amnon's death puts Absalom first in line for the throne (David's second son Chileab may have died young; he is never mentioned after 3:3), a fact which that canny young prince cannot have overlooked. An obstacle to the throne is gone and Absalom flees to his grandfather. We are told that David mourned for his son, but not for which: the rapist or the murderer?

14:1-33. Joab brings Absalom home. Verse 19 indicates that Joab has made earlier efforts to bring Absalom back. Like Nathan (12:1-6), he resorts to a story to engage David's emotions. His coached wise woman is believable and David responds mercifully to her. When she moves the focus to restoring the unnamed Absalom, David, whom she flatters as the one *discerning good and evil* (v. 17), discerns Joab's hand. Joab's motives, like so many in 2 Samuel, are unclear here. Does he think Amnon deserved death? Does he want to restore Absalom out of concern for David?

The relationship between Joab and David is complex. David complains loudly about his violent nephew (cf. 3:39), and Joab alone at court seems totally unimpressed with David's grandeur (cf. 12:28), and yet their partnership is successful for both of them. Joab kills easily to protect himself or David, but he never attempts to seize power for himself; for his part, David obviously puts total trust in Joab's loyalty (11:14-15). Joab, apparently moved, sees the granting of his request as a sign of David's favor, but it seems more likely that David simply cannot fight against his love for his son any longer.

The *wise woman* (v. 2) reminds us of cold Jonadab in 13:3, the only other character described by this word so far in 1-2 Sam (NRSV has *crafty* in 13:3, but the Heb. is the same). There the advice of the wise led to rape and murder; perhaps it is unwise to follow wise counsel. In 14:20 David becomes the third person to be described as having wisdom. The woman means it as a compliment, but like Jonadab, this woman, and the fourth "wise" character in the book (20:16-22), his judgment has led to betrayal and death. The next "wise" character in this story is Solomon (cf. 1 Kgs 2:6, 3:12, etc.); his judgment may be questionable, too.

Like Bathsheba and Tamar, Absalom also is marked by *beauty* (v. 25), suggesting that he may not come to a good end. David is attractive but only his eyes are described by that fatal word (1 Sam 16:12), and it is his beautiful, wandering eyes that begin his troubles (11:2). After five years banished from David's presence, Absalom "sends" (again recall the importance of "sending"; see commentary at 11:1-5 above) twice for Joab, who ignores him. He then strikes at Joab, becoming the only character to cross that fearsome man until another of David's sons has him killed (1 Kgs 2:28-35). This reckless act, reminiscent of David in the wilderness, wins him reconciliation with the king; note that even the narrator does not refer to "the king" as his father.

David's Family Conflict Becomes National, 15:1–19:40

David's treatment of Bathsheba and Uriah created an environment of license and distrust that led to the rape of his daughter, one son's murder, and another's alienation. Absalom is now restored to favor, but his lack of familial address to David indicates that his earlier grievances are not resolved. His subsequent rebellion is the central event of this section, a family conflict that splits the country and splits David himself as his roles of king and father conflict.

15:1-12. Absalom revolts against his father. David's following the wise woman's advice to restore Absalom was a mistake, just as it was a mistake for Amnon to follow wise Jonadab's. There has already been reason to suspect that Absalom may have harbored kingly ambitions (in 13:27 his feast was *like a king's feast*). Now that he is again honored in Jerusalem he adds to his retinue in even more glamorous style than his father did when he became that city's king (cf. 5:13). He is the son most like his father, sharing that larger-than-life quality with the young David whom the people loved more than Saul (1 Sam 18:7, 16); perhaps that is why David cares most for him. David never attacked Saul at all, but Absalom questions David's function as judge. Casting doubts on his ability to fulfill this basic task of leadership is suggesting that he is not capable of being king. David attracted the people, but his son steals their hearts.

The man who waited two years to carry out his plot against his brother waits four to rebel against David, using the LORD in his deception. No motive is given; Absalom feels all the ambition his father did and may have convinced himself that David's inability to respond to Tamar's crisis gives him the right to pursue the kingship. Absalom begins his rebellion in Hebron, where David was first proclaimed king. Perhaps he is taking advantage of his resemblance to his father.

15:13–16:14. David flees before his son. The need for action gets through the paralysis that has gripped David since Tamar's rape, and he becomes again the decisive leader aware of his relationship to God that he was before he became king. His reaction shows the urgency of this crisis: Israel, which was never as loyal to David as the south, has followed Absalom, and by establishing his headquarters in Hebron he has annexed part of Judah as well. David abandons his capital swiftly, leaving only ten women out of all his personal and military retinue in the city he fears Absalom will soon attack. The urgency of the situation is only enhanced by the narrator's report of the many stops along the way, down in the Kidron Valley, up to the top of the Mount of Olives, stopping along the way to conduct urgent affairs.

David's reference to Absalom as *the king* (v. 19) shows his awareness that neither he nor his son is the decisive character in this conflict. He sees it as the fulfillment of 12:11, and as he did before he became king he is allowing God to decide his destiny and Israel's. Perhaps Absalom *is* the king. David has not lost faith in the covenant of chap. 7, but he knows that his behavior merits punishment, and if Absalom defeats him, it will still be his house on the throne. He states more clearly in vv. 25-26 his willingness to let the outcome depend on the LORD, who subtly responds in v. 32. Brueggemann calls David an "emancipated man" because he trusts his destiny to God out of his "enormous faith which puts him at Yahweh's disposal" even if that disposal is not David's desire (Brueggemann 1972, 18).

Although David recognizes the theological issues involved, he has not lost his savvy and realizes that on a purely human level the key factor is AHITHOPHEL's counsel. Ahithophel was one of David's advisors; why he has turned against David is not yet clear (cf. 11:3; 23:34). Even as David prays for Ahithophel's advice to be worthless his prayer is answered by Hushai's appearance, enabling him to put together a plan and a communications network (vv. 33-36). He has found loyalty in his flight, but his last two interviews on the road are not so encouraging. Ziba informs David that Mephibosheth is a traitor. The fact that Ziba brings food for David's train reminds us of how David and his sons have used food as a disguise for betrayal (11:13; 13:6, 24ff.). It is unlikely that Mephibosheth could hope to benefit from Absalom's rebellion, since Absalom spent years creating loyalty to himself, but David does not recognize Ziba's lie and promptly gives him all that he had previously granted to Mephibosheth (cf. 9:7).

David then moves from a disguised enemy to an outright one. Shimei, a Saulide, curses David as a murderer and applauds the rebellion as God's judgment for the deaths in Saul's house. He may be referring to Abner and Ishbaal (3:26-30; 4:5-8), although the events of 21:1-9 are more likely the subject here. Since the narrator has not told that story yet, the accusation is more ambiguous, in keeping with the cloud of general suspicion that has gathered over David. His response to Abishai (who offers similar counsel in 1 Sam 26:8) again shows his willingness to let God be God. David is not passive in this section (e.g., his sending of Hushai). He simply understands the extent to which his actions have made him walk the road from Jerusalem and knows God must decide if he can walk the road back.

16:15–17:23. Absalom and his counselors. Absalom now has more counselors than he needs. Ahithophel gives the first advice, telling David's son to rape David's women, and this is carried out on the spot where David first saw and sent for Bathsheba (see commentary on 3:1-21 above). David evoked God's anger for taking and using Bathsheba and her husband as he desired. The subsequent judgment of 12:11 is fulfilled because David again saw women's lives (his concubines') as his to dispose of to their detriment— they were the only ones of his household that he left in danger (15:16).

Ahithophel's next advice is also practical, brutal, and pleasing to Absalom. Hushai, hoping to buy David time, plays on Absalom's fear of his father and urges caution the young man cannot afford. He also sends David a warning before he knows whose advice Absalom will follow. Ahithophel's counsel is *as if one consulted the oracle of God* (16:23), but God frustrates it in favor of Hushai's. David may not really be *like the angel of God, discerning good and evil* (14:17), but he can discern better than the son who questioned his ability to judge. Ahithophel sees correctly that all is lost and so kills himself.

17:24–18:18. David's army defeats Absalom. The many evidences of support David has received both from God and people make him realize that Absalom has lost. He is not concerned now as a king with a kingdom, but as a father whose son is his beloved enemy. His loyal troops, not David, win the victory, but it is not dwelled on. The narrator's concern at this point is what this war means to David the father. The fleeing Absalom is caught in a tree by *his head* (18:9; not his hair as popularly told) and hangs between heaven and earth, life and death.

His father wills his life, but his father is not there. The soldier who finds him succinctly sums up the convoluted relationships and betrayals in this war. Joab, however, has no inhibitions against killing his cousin. He has many motives to choose from (grudging the burning of his fields in 14:30, unwillingness to leave a dangerous enemy alive), but it seems likely that he and his men kill Absalom because he knows what David cannot face: that his son hates him and will always be a danger to him and to his kingdom. This is borne out by Absalom's slow, careful treachery and his pleasure at Ahithophel's patricidal advice (17:1-4). The fact that Joab apparently had worked on his own to get Absalom home from banishment but then has to be coerced later to bring him into David's presence indicates that having the prince as a neighbor made him reevaluate his character (chap. 14). Perhaps part of the reason he kills Absalom is due to the responsibility he feels for bringing him and David back together.

18:19–19:8a. David receives the news of Absalom's death. David is consistently called *the king* in this section, but his questions to the messengers show him reacting as a father. Telling David of Absalom's death is described in more detail than the death itself. The exuberant Ahimaaz runs to him in spite of Joab's delegating another messenger. David assumes he brings "good news" and he does, but not to the father. Shimei was wrong: God has deemed David worthy of being King, but Absalom must pay the price. The Cushite tries to put the news in its proper context, but David can barely get to privacy before he breaks down. We have seen him grieve for an enemy's death before (1:17-27), but now he is truly broken.

Saul and Jonathan *in life and death were not divided* (1:23); David and Absalom were divided in both. In contrast to the high spirits of Ahimaaz, the soldiers who have saved David's life and kingdom sneak home in victory. Only Joab can make him see the danger of alienating the army, and he does so as bluntly as usual. David, probably not yet aware of Joab's role in Absalom's death, revives enough to greet his men. We sympathize with the bereaved father and admire the man who still loves his child in spite of the worst sort of betrayal, but we cannot help realizing that if he had loved his daughter with a tenth of the feeling he had for any of his sons this day might never have come.

19:8b-40. David and the people. There is disorganization in both Israel and Judah in dealing with the aftermath of the revolt. The title *King David* in v. 11 indicates that the public king and the personal man are again functioning as one, and he immediately begins taking care of his affairs. He makes his first overture to Judah (cf. 1 Sam 30:26-31; 2 Sam 2:1-4), adding a message giving Joab's job to his great-nephew Amasa who had headed Absalom's army (17:25). David can say he is replacing Joab to appease Absalom's followers. Like Abner, Amasa helps David enter a region that followed another king (an ominous comparison for a man taking Joab's job); David is soon restored over Judah.

On his return to Jerusalem David encounters some of those he left on his way out; these meetings indicate the toll events have taken on the king, as well as showing what he will never achieve. Absalom's revolt briefly restored David to the creative, faithful man he had once been; its end leaves him a tired old man beaten in victory. Shimei is first now as he was last before, knowing that his only chance of mercy lies in getting to David while he is rejoicing in his homecoming. As usual, Abishai urges violence, but Shimei's gamble pays off; the king promises not to take his life.

David later regrets his magnanimity; technically he does not violate his oath, but on his deathbed he will tell Solomon to kill Shimei (1 Kgs 2:8-9). This tarnishes the image of the king gracious in victory. Ziba is there as well; perhaps the wily servant knows he too needs to approach David while the king is in a good mood. Before he can speak Mephibosheth appears with proof of his innocence of Ziba's accusations (16:1-4). The narrator carefully never, now or in chap. 16, tells us who is actually telling the truth, but there are sufficient clues in the text to indicate that Jonathan's son is honest (see commentary at 15:13–16:14 above).

It is unfortunate that Mephibosheth comes immediately after Shimei; perhaps David feels that in sparing the latter he has done enough for Saul's house, or maybe the strain of carrying off a celebration based on Absalom's death is more than he can handle for long. In any case, the man who took responsibility for Mephibosheth in chap. 9 now simply divides the property between him and Ziba, not caring which is loyal and which a liar. He and Shimei are among the enmeshed relationships David has built up during his life and can no longer deal with. He seems more like himself with Barzillai (17:27-28), who is unrelated to his previous loves and hates. Barzillai sends Chimham (apparently his son [cf. 1 Kgs 2:7]) with the man whose own heir has just died rebelling against him. Barzillai, an outsider, presents a picture of contented old age surrounded by his family—something David knows he will never know.

David and Israel, 19:41–20:26

19:41–20:3. Sheba leads a second revolt against David. Repairing the division of Absalom's revolt is delayed as Israel and Judah argue over who has the best rights to the king they have both rejected. David, made king independently by north and south, ruled both without melding them into one permanent union (see Miller 1990, 198–99). Now the Israelites are threatened by David's close connection to the south while the Judeans angrily deny that they have benefitted from it. This leads to the revolt of the north led by a member of Saul's tribe (who may have a closer connection with Saul's family; 1 Sam 9:1 traces Saul's descent through one bearing a name similar to Sheba's ancestor).

David's first act on returning home is to clean up one of the most troublesome aspects of the last revolt before dealing with the next one, shutting away his concubines whom his son publicly raped as part of his claim to the throne. At the end of Absalom's story David shows no more concern for these raped women he left in harm's way than he did for the daughter he sent to her rapist at the beginning of it (13:7-21), but he does provide for their care. The rationale is that their experience with David's son makes his resumption of normal relationships with them incestuous, since the OT defines incest as sexual relations not only with blood relatives but with those relatives' partners as well (cf. Lev 18:6-18).

20:4-26. Joab kills Amasa and Sheba. David now orders his new general to take charge of the current trouble. This revolt is dangerous because it is based on loyalty to Saul's family rather than a split in David's. Amasa's unexplained tardiness forces David to resort to the sons of Zeruiah, choosing Abishai rather than Joab whom he has replaced. Nonetheless Joab kills his cousin Amasa. This murder is described in detail (while there are many battles in 1–2 Sam, the narrator always focuses much more on the smaller, more intimate scenes). By this act Joab wins back his old job; David cannot try yet another new general in the middle of a rebellion. He also can never admit that he hates Joab for killing Absalom, since by doing so Joab ended a civil war and saved both David and many troops. When he orders Joab's death as he is dying, he will have to say it is for the murders of Abner and Amasa (1 Kgs 2:5-6). With no further action by David Joab's army traps Sheba, who is betrayed and killed on the advice of the fourth person in this book characterized as "wise" (see commentary on 14:1-33). This ends the North's revolt, but it will rebel successfully against David's house in 1 Kgs 12:16-19. The section closes with another list of officials. Unlike 8:15-18, at this late date no role is given to David or his sons.

Although he has been restored, David has provided another example of the "How the mighty have fallen!" theme he articulated at the book's beginning (1:19, 27)—and for both Saul and David, the "how" is through their own choices. David handles himself well as a soldier and fugitive in 1 Samuel, but the temptations of power distract him from his intended role as the chosen king through whom God could act. This causes great suffering both for individuals and for his kingdom as a whole. Saul, who fails as a leader, is punished by seeing God choose another king and knowing that he will not found a dynasty. David, who fails most in his personal relationships, is punished by seeing those he loves turn against him. This is the penalty God gave, but the narrative shows how little God must do to punish him or anyone else (only 12:1, 24, and 17:14 directly mention God's activity). We are only too eager to do it to ourselves and to each other. It can be argued that David pays a higher price for his failures than Saul does; at least Saul dies with his sons at his side instead of trying to take his throne.

Epilogue. Other Stories about David's Reign, 21:1–24:25

The book ends with an appendix of traditions rooted in different parts of David's reign, shedding light on the material already read while continuing its themes. In four chapters it will retrace 2 Samuel, taking us from the young and glorious king restoring the kingdom after Saul's failure to the old and sinning king endangering God's people after his own. This condensed look at David prepares us for the cynical intrigue of the end of his life in 1 Kgs 1–2.

The appendix takes the form of a CHIASM. Narratives of guilt and expiation in first and sixth place surround stories and lists of David's warriors in second and fifth place. These surround the two central poems in which David summarizes his experience as king under God in third and fourth place.

Israel Endangered by Saul's Guilt, 21:1-14

This story belongs early in David's reign; there are still loose ends left by Saul and the stories of Mephibosheth (chap. 9) and Shimei (16:5-8) have yet to occur. It underscores the basic idea that people pay for the sins of their leaders (1 Sam 12:14-15). Verse 2 refers to Josh 9:3-27, but the story of Saul's slaughtering the Gibeonites is not recorded; the bloody price for it is demanded not by God but by Gibeon. David (again involved with convenient Saulide deaths) easily sends Saul's sons to die for Saul's guilt (cf. Num 35:33), but we have seen that later he will grieve as his own son dies for his (12:15-18).

The horror of the deaths of these innocents is shown through Rizpah, who has already been used in one power play between men (3:7-11); now another disrupts her life more dreadfully. She is as silent in this story as in that one, but she is not passive. Her Antigone-like loyalty to her dead kin moves David to pity. The deaths of the Saulides do not end the famine. David responded to the Gibeonites' vengefulness, but it is not until Rizpah's faithfulness has evoked his compassion that God blesses the land again.

David's Mighty Men, 21:15-22

These stories add to the bare account of the Philistine wars in 5:17-25. Most of 1–2 Samuel stresses David's role, but here we see that Israel has many heroes. David is less the warrior than one who draws out the best in others. New images of him and Abishai are presented as the usually mighty one is rescued and the usually antagonistic one offers aid. Verse 17 gives a possible reason for 11:1. Its absence there makes David's behavior seem even worse, but here it emphasizes the warm relationship between David and his troops. Verse 19 attributes David's first dramatic success to a stranger (1 Sam 17; 1 Chr 20:5 attempts to reconcile the traditions), an assertion made easy to accept by its placement immediately after the story of David's tired dependence on his men. On the other hand, the tradition of 1 Sam 17 is much more developed and integrated into the Davidic material.

The mention of Elhanan again forces us to recognize that the truth of David's life is hard to find. That may be its purpose.

A Psalm of David, 22:1-51

This poem, along with the following poem, constitutes the center of the appendix, showing David understanding his role as God's vessel and not conscientiously but joyfully giving his LORD credit for everything. These poems move the focus away from David in two directions, emphasizing first God as the one empowering David and then David's descendants as the ones inheriting God's promise.

Verses 2-20 and 29-51 of this psalm (essentially Ps 18) are reminiscent of Hannah's song in language (cf. 1 Sam 2:2 and 22:2b-3, 32, 47) and content (the rescue of the needy and the help for the anointed one). David's victories really belong to the mighty and sustaining LORD. But vv. 21-28 strike a jarring note by obliquely reminding us for the first time in the appendix of Bathsheba and Uriah. In all honesty, David *has* been rewarded according to his righteousness (the disasters of chaps. 13-20 are precisely that reward), but how are we to read vv. 22-24? They are not true. Their conventional piety is offensive on David's lips, as the repentant king of 12:13 would agree. Here they are subversive, reminding us that grace gives not only strength and victory but also forgiveness and the ability to continue in relationship with God.

A Psalm of David, 23:1-7

In these *last words* (v. 1) David celebrates God's working through him as the chosen one and rejoices that his house will continue to be used to provide justice to God's people. David's actual last words in the narrative will be largely directed towards revenge rather than justice (1 Kgs 2:5-9); like most of the appendix, the tradition here finds him in a more graceful moment.

David's Mighty Men, 23:8-39

The process of honoring those besides David who led to Israel's victories continues. As in 21:15-22, we find lists of names and a few exploits of warriors, here formed into the orders of *the Three* (v. 8) and *the thirty* (v. 13; the number *thirty-seven* in v. 39 is correct if Joab is added in as commander-in-chief). Credit for their victories, like David's, goes to God.

Verses 13-17 shows the young David in an intimate moment with his men. David's respect and affection for his men as well as his unwillingness to assume that any sacrifice they make for him is only his due shows how he is able to command the loyalty even of heroes and why to the end of his life he will be given loyalty in spite of his failures and reverses. This story, however, also reminds us that David did eventually think of these men's lives as his to dispose of (some of his special troops were among those killed in the plot against Uriah [11:17]), showing why he lost so much loyalty as well. One of those whose loyalty he lost was Ahithophel (15:12). This is finally explained by the mention of Bathsheba's father Eliam (11:3) in v. 34 as Ahithophel's son. Ahithophel turned against the man who raped his granddaughter and killed her husband, giving added irony to 16:20-23 since it is Bathsheba's grandfather who tells David's son to rape his women and this happens precisely where David first saw Bathsheba. Uriah's name, last in the list, brings up this episode for the third time. The king who was one with his men in 13-17 did not stay so.

Israel Endangered by David's Guilt, 24:1-25

This brings us full circle to where the appendix began: the nation pays for the sin of its king, but this time the king is David. Verse 1 says God is the tempter but 1 Chr 21:1 puts Satan in that role. The belief that God is responsible for all that happens, good and evil, is an early one (cf. Exod 4:24). By the Chronicler's time Satan rather than God was understood as the instigator of evil. David's sin in taking a (probably military) census is the one subtly brought up by 23:8-39: his belief that he controls the people's lives and may dispose of them as he will (cf. 1 Sam 8:10-18). But the people are God's, and for the king to act as if he owns them brings judgment on them all (1 Sam 12:14-15).

David repents as he did after Uriah's murder, but again the consequences of his sin must still be borne. He is willing to trust God for the punishment, just as he left the resolution of his son's revolt to the Lord. He is correct to do so, since the plague is halted through divine mercy. David then buys (rather than simply receiving) what will become the site of Solomon's Temple, linking him with an institution that will be important in the rest of the Bible and rooting it in expiation.

The appendix has clarified the material in vv. 1-20. The only person who sins in it is David (Saul's action against the Gibeonites takes place earlier). The roles of the compassionate Rizpah, the mighty and loyal men in David's service, and even the generous Araunah are stressed, while God is given the most credit for all success by David himself, the one who tries at times to take too much. David emerges from the overall narrative of 2 Samuel as an amazing character—not amazingly good or amazingly evil, but fully human. He is less a role model than an accurate picture of the heights and depths of which human nature is capable.

In his novel *God Knows*, Joseph Heller has David say at the end of his life that he has learned that "people are complete, and everybody is capable of everything" (1984, 16). This point is illustrated best in the person of David himself. He is loving and brutal, passive and decisive, generous and grasping, and faithful and betraying, acting both better and worse than we expect. His failures are not ignored or excused in the text, but neither do they wipe out his successes. David is Israel's greatest hero, but he is remembered honestly as a man with strengths and weaknesses who proves that no one has to be perfect to be of use to God and God's people. Perhaps it is as much for his perseverance in spite of his failures before his Lord as for his flamboyant adventures that he exercised such a hold on Israel's imagination. A thousand years after his death, when Jesus rode into Jerusalem the most glorious name the people could think to call him was "Son of David!" (Matt 21:9).

Works Cited

Alter, Robert. 1981. *The Art of Biblical Narrative.*
Bailey, Lloyd R. 1990. "Ark." MDB.
Brueggemann, Walter. 1972. "On Trust and Freedom: A Study of Faith in the Succession Narrative." *Interp* 26:3-1 9.

Cate, Robert L. 1990. "Ishbosheth." MDB.
Eslinger, Lyle. 1983. "Viewpoints and Point of View in 1 Samuel 8-12." *JSOT* 26:61–76.
Flanagan, J. W. 1972. "Court History of Succession Document?" *JBL* 91: 172–81.
Gregory, Russell I. 1990. "Sources of the Pentateuch." MDB.
Heller, Joseph. 1984. *God Knows*.
Joines, Karen Randolph. 1990. "Holiness in the OT." MDB.
Hertzberg, Hans W. 1965. *I and II Samuel, a Commentary*. OTL.
Miller, J. Maxwell. 1990. "David." MDB.
Niccolls, S. Thomas. 1981. "The Comic Vision and the Stories of David." *Encounter* 42:277–83.
Perdue, L. G. 1984. "'Is There Anyone Left of the House of Saul . . . ?' Ambiguity and the Characterization of David in the Succession Narrative." *JSOT* 30: 67–84.

First and Second Kings

Thomas G. Smothers   [MCB 303-22]

Introduction

The Books of Kings—originally one book—conclude the section of the Hebrew Bible known as the Former Prophets (Joshua, Judges, Samuel, Kings). Kings cover the period from the last days of DAVID to the fall of Jerusalem, concluding with a hopeful note about the release of King JEHOIACHIN from prison in Babylon.

Composition

Since the pioneering work of Martin Noth, it has become customary to refer to the Former Prophets as the "Deuteronomistic History" (see DEUTERONOMIST/ DEUTERONOMISTIC HISTORIAN). Noth viewed the Deuteronomistic History as the work of a single author during the exilic age whose purpose was to explain the fall of the Hebrew kingdoms with reference to the cultic and moral ideals of the Book of Deuteronomy (see Noth 1981). Subsequent writers offered modifications of this basic view. Some posited two or three editions of Deuteronomistic History, all exilic (e.g., Smend 1971, 494–509). F. M. Cross argued for two editions of the Deuteronomistic History, one from the time of JOSIAH and the other from the exilic age (1973, 274–89). Later studies have emphasized earlier redactions or editions. Specifically with regard to the Books of Kings, André Lemaire (1986, 221–36) identified four redactions, the first three from the reigns of JEHOSHAPHAT, HEZEKIAH, and Josiah respectively, and the last from the postexilic age, supporting the view of a long historical tradition in ISRAEL and JUDAH.

Sources

The sources utilized by the Deuteronomistic Historian (or, more likely, historians) include popular or traditional narratives, stories about prophets, and administrative archives. Three written sources are named. The *Book of the Acts of Solomon* (1 Kgs 11:41) appears to have been used sparingly; the *Book of the Annals of the Kings of Israel* (1 Kgs 14:19; 15:31; 16:5, 14, 20, 27; 22:39; 2 Kgs 1:18; 10:34; 13:8, 12; 14:15, 28; 15:11, 15, 21, 26, 31) and the *Book of the Annals of the Kings of Judah* (1 Kgs 14:29; 15:7, 23; 22:45; 2 Kgs 8:23; 12:19; 14:18; 15:6, 36; 16:19; 20:20; 21:17, 25; 23:28; 24:5) appear to have been used more extensively. Today readers of 1–2 Kings have access to literary sources from Egypt, Assyria, Babylon, and Syria-Palestine to supplement the historical data in the Books of Kings. The following commentary takes into account such extrabiblical material.

Purpose

The Books of Kings, like the other books of the Deuteronomistic History, serve a theological purpose. Overall, the Deuteronomistic History interprets the tragic history of Israel in the land of Palestine using the central tenets of the Book of Deuteronomy as guiding theological perspectives. To help explain the demise of the Israelite kingdoms and the subsequent exiles, the Books of Kings emphasize these theological concerns: the law of the central sanctuary (Deut 12); IDOLATRY and cultic deviation as COVENANT violation; the *sin of Jeroboam* (2 Kgs 3:3), that is, the establishment of alternate cultic sites and cultic practices to those in Judah and Jerusalem; and the enduring promise of David's dynasty. The role of the prophets in Israelite history is highlighted by showing how events were to be understood on the basis of the prediction-fulfillment scheme.

For Further Study

In the *Mercer Dictionary of the Bible*: CHRONOLOGY; DAVID; DEUTERONOMIST/DEUTERONOMISTIC HISTORIAN; ISRAEL; JERUSALEM; JUDAH; KINGS, BOOKS OF FIRST AND SECOND; SAMUEL; SOLOMON.

In other sources: J. Gray, *I and Kings: A Commentary*, OTL, 2nd rev. ed.; M. Haran, *Temples and Temple Service in Ancient Israel*; T. R. Hobbs, *2 Kings*, WBC; T. Ishida, ed., *Studies in the Period of David and Solomon*; B. O. Long, *1 Kings*, FOTL; R. D. Nelson, *First and Second Kings*, Interp.

Commentary

An Outline

I. Solomon's Succession to the Throne, 1 Kgs 1:1–2:46
   A. The Politics of Succession, 1:1-53
   B. Solomon's Moves to Secure Power, 2:1-46
II. The Reign of Solomon, 3:1–11:43
   A. Solomon's Wisdom and Administration, 3:1–4:34
   B. The Building and Dedication of the Temple, 5:1–9:25
   C. Solomon's Wealth and Wisdom, 9:26–10:29
   D. The Sins of the Kingdom Exposed, 11:1-43

III. Synchronic History of Israel and Judah, 1 Kgs 12:1–2 Kgs 17:41
   A. Jeroboam I of Israel, 12:1–14:20
   B. Early Kings of Judah, 14:21–15:24
   C. Early Kings of Israel, 15:25–16:34
   D. Ahab and Elijah, 16:29–22:40
   E. Jehoshaphat and Ahaziah, 1 Kgs 22:41–2 Kgs 1:18
   F. The Elisha Cycle, 2:1–8:29
   G. From Jehu to the Fall of Samaria, 9:1–17:41
IV. Judah after the Fall of Israel, 18:1–25:30

Solomon's Succession to the Throne, 1 Kgs 1:1–2:46

1 Kings 1–2 forms the conclusion to the what is now generally called the SUC-
CESSION NARRATIVE (also called "The Court History of David"), which begins in
2 Sam 9 (but does not include 2 Sam 21–24). All the sons of David eligible to
succeed to the throne had perished except for ADONIJAH, the son of Haggith, and
SOLOMON, the son of Bathsheba. The conclusion of the narrative relates how Solomon came to the throne.

The Politics of Succession, 1:1-53

The approaching death of King David precipitated the final crisis of his reign.
Who would succeed him on the throne of the empire? The politicians of the court
and the ever-present palace intrigue were given free rein. The chief actors in the
drama were Adonijah on the one side, supported by the priest ABIATHAR and the
military leader JOAB, and the prophet NATHAN and BATHSHEBA on the other side,
supported by the powerful military commander BENAIAH and the priest ZADOK.
Adonijah's strategy depended on the tradition of the succession of the oldest surviving prince, while Nathan's strategy depended on his personal access to David and
on the influence of Bathsheba.

1:1-4. King David's senility. The aging David's ability to inspire trust in his
leadership was put to the final test. Because his circulation was poor and he could
not get warm, a young woman, *Abishag*, from the village of Shunem in the valley
of Jezreel, was brought to the court to minister to the king. The well-meaning strategy was unsuccessful. Although Abishag was *very beautiful* (v. 4), David was unable
to have sexual relations with her. The powerful, decisive ruler who dominated the
narratives of 1–2 Samuel was now viewed as lacking in the necessary vigor and
virility to provide decisive leadership.

1:5-31. Political maneuvering. Adonijah, the oldest surviving son of David,
seems to have taken for granted the ancient Near Eastern practice of primogeniture.
Adonijah *exalted himself*, acting the part of king by assembling a chariot force,
complete with men *to run before him*, and by seeking the aid of two of the most
powerful and influential members of David's cabinet, *Joab* the army commander
and *Abiathar* the priest from Nob. Not included in his retinue, probably because he
declined their participation, were even more powerful elements: *the priest Zadok,
Benaiah*, the commander of David's personal bodyguard, *the prophet Nathan*, and
Shimei and Rei, two of David's mighty men (v. 8). Already the reader is alerted to
the precariousness of Adonijah's position. His fate was sealed when *he did not
invite the prophet Nathan or Benaiah or the warriors or his brother Solomon* to his
sacrifice and banquet (vv. 9-10).

The prophet Nathan countered with his own plan. He suggested to Bathsheba
that she inform David of Adonijah's actions and remind David of his promise to
have her son Solomon succeed him as king, a promise not mentioned in any

previous text. The lives of Bathsheba and Solomon were at stake, and possibly also Nathan's life (v. 21). Immediately after Bathsheba's audience with David, Nathan's presence at court was announced. The prophet recounted fully Adonijah's actions, especially the slight against Zadok, Benaiah, and Solomon, and suggested that events were running outside the king's control. In an attempt at decisive leadership, David confirmed Solomon as his successor. It is a sad picture: the once vigorous, decisive ruler now senile and susceptible to manipulation.

1:32-40. The anointing of Solomon. David gave instructions that Solomon be anointed and enthroned without delay. Solomon rode the royal mule to the spring GIHON at the eastern base of the hill of Jerusalem, where he was anointed. After the ceremony the crowd ascended the hill behind Solomon with loud shouts and music. Solomon thus became coregent with David. The Gihon spring, the main water source for Jerusalem, may have had religious associations, making it an appropriate place for an anointing ceremony (Miller 1990, 331). The site was also a suitable location for the royal procession up into the city, accompanied by the repeated shout *Long live King Solomon* (vv. 34, 39).

1:41-50. Adonijah's panic. Solomon's installation had been accomplished with such dispatch that Adonijah and his guests were still at his banquet at *En-Rogel* (cf. 1:9) when they received the news. The messenger gave an account that could only be from an eyewitness, including David's expression of gratitude to the LORD for allowing him to live to see the kingdom passed safely to his son Solomon (vv. 47-48).

Adonijah's guests fled the banquet in panic, not only because of the *fait accompli* but also because of the overwhelming support for Solomon represented by Zadok, Nathan, and Benaiah, the officer over David's bodyguard and two of its groups, *the Cherethites* (Cretans) and *Pelethites* (Philistines), mercenaries whose only allegiance was to David. Adonijah fled in fear and seized *the horns of the altar* (vv. 50-51; cf. 2:28) thus claiming divine protection at the sanctuary (according to Exod 21:12-14 one innocent of murder could claim sanctuary).

1:51-53. Solomon's response. Adonijah insisted that Solomon swear an oath that he would not slay him. Solomon refused such a guarantee, leaving Adonijah's fate to the course of events. There could be little doubt in Solomon's mind of the threat posed by Adonijah, and later events proved him right. But for the moment, perhaps fearing negative reaction from the populace if he violated Adonijah's claim of sanctuary, Solomon was satisfied with Adonijah's oath of loyalty. At least Solomon could not be accused of precipitate action on a fast-paced day filled with portentous events.

Solomon's Moves to Secure Power, 2:1-46

Although Solomon came to the throne swiftly and with formidable royal and popular support, there remained various groups and dissident persons with the potential to sow discord. David had never enjoyed the support of all the population. Some never forgave him for his perceived treatment of the house of Saul. Others were offended at his moral lapses and his cultic activities undertaken at his own initiative. The first item on Solomon's agenda was to deal with those who could oppose him and to strike fear in the hearts of others.

2:1-9. David's counsel to Solomon. Verses 2-4 are a deuteronomic insert. David's deathbed valedictory reflects deuteronomic concerns: *statutes*, *commandments*, *ordinances*, *testimonies*, *law of Moses*, and the conditional nature of the LORD's promise to perpetuate David's house (cf. Deut 17:14-20). The emphasis upon condition is contrary to the unconditional promises in 2 Sam 7:11-16, where the Davidic covenant is established.

Verses 5-9 contain David's pragmatic advice to Solomon. Personal scores remained to be settled with persons who could also be a threat to Solomon's reign. First was *Joab*, David's nephew and general of the army (see Gregory 1990, 453). David's relationship with Joab was complex. Joab's loyalty was to the person of David alone. David had often complained of his inability to control the sons of his sister Zeruiah, but Joab, Abishai, and Asahel consistently solved David's problems in such a way as to forestall immediate personal criticism of the king. Nevertheless, Joab's murder of two of David's opponents in a time of peace reflected poorly on David. In any case Joab's independence could only be a threat to Solomon, especially in light of Joab's alliance with Adonijah. Then there was *Shimei* of the house of Saul who had placed a curse on David for terminating the house of Saul through bloodshed, a charge David did not deny (v. 8; cf. 2 Sam 16:5-14). David had refused to kill Shimei then and later (2 Sam 19:16-23). But now David advised Solomon to find a way to remove the threat to the kingdom represented by Shimei.

2:10-12. The death of David. This is the first of the formulas used by the Deuteronomistic History editor to conclude the reports of the reigns of kings. However, lacking here is one other typical feature of such formulas: an evaluation of the king's reign.

2:13-25. The death of Adonijah. That Adonijah had not abandoned hope for the kingship is confirmed by his seemingly innocent request of *Bathsheba* to intercede with *Solomon* to grant him permission to marry *Abishag*, David's nurse and member of the harem. When Bathsheba acceded to his wish and made the request known to Solomon, Solomon's response was explosive, for he understood exactly Adonijah's intent. To have access to the king's harem was tantamount to making a claim on the throne. Adonijah was executed by *Benaiah*.

2:26-27. The banishment of Abiathar. During much of David's reign he was served by two priests, ABIATHAR and ZADOK. The potential for discord was always present, but David seemed unable to resolve the issue. When Abiathar supported Adonijah's claim to kingship, Solomon was free to solve the problem of priestly leadership. Abiathar's banishment *to Anathoth* is presented as fulfillment of prophecy concerning *the house of Eli* (v. 27; cf. 1 Sam 2:27-36). References to the fulfillment of prophetic oracles are a characteristic feature of the Books of Kings.

2:28-35. The death of Joab. When Joab heard of Adonijah's execution, he *fled to the tent of the LORD* and claimed sanctuary by seizing *the horns of the altar* (v. 28). At his refusal to leave sanctuary, *Benaiah* was ordered to slay him there for the bloodguilt he had brought to David's house. Benaiah was promoted to general of the army in Joab's place.

2:36-46. The death of Shimei. There remained now only the threat represented by the house of Saul in the person of *Shimei*. Solomon ordered him to reside in Jerusalem in order to keep him under surveillance, and Shimei agreed to the condition. But when two of his servants fled to Gath, Shimei left the city to reclaim them. Solomon now had his legitimate reason to remove Shimei's threat to the stability of his reign, and again Benaiah was sent to carry out the execution. Solomon was now in control of the political situation. The story of the succession was now complete.

The Reign of Solomon, 3:1–11:43

Solomon's Wisdom and Administration, 3:1–4:34

3:1-3. Introduction to Solomon's reign. The account of Solomon's reign began with two characteristic themes: international relations and the emphasis on the Temple. Solomon's treaty with Egypt was formalized by his marriage to *Pharaoh's daughter*, a move that was intended to illustrate his political power and astuteness. And yet, ironically, Solomon's history is concluded with the folly of his marriages to foreign women (see 1 Kgs 11:1-8). Since the Temple was not yet built, Solomon and the people worshiped at *the high places* in the land (v. 2), a matter of grave concern to the Deuteronomistic Historian even at this early date. The reigns of all subsequent kings of Judah up to the time of Josiah were evaluated in light of their relationship to the high places. The high places were local shrines where worship was not under central regulation.

3:4-15. Solomon's prayer for wisdom. Despite the Deuteronomistic Historian's reservations about high places, it was a fact that Solomon had an unforgettable experience at Gibeon, the great HIGH PLACE. In his dream experience Solomon asked of the LORD a receptive mind so that he might discern between good and evil in his governance. In his prayer he acknowledged God's faithfulness to David, he confessed his own inexperience, and he asked for wisdom that only the deity could grant. The LORD not only granted Solomon's request to be given understanding to render right judgments, but also gave him what he had not requested, *long life and riches* (v. 11).

Verse 14 again emphasizes the conditional nature of the promise to David's house characteristic of the Deuteronomist. Solomon became the patron of the wisdom tradition in Israel. Indeed, in the story of his reign, repeated reference is made to his wisdom.

3:16-28. The first test of Solomon's wisdom. This story of the two mothers and their babies, in which all the characters are anonymous, even the king, was utilized to show how all the people came to acknowledge Solomon's divine gift of wisdom. The classic story is a masterpiece of the storyteller's art. All the evidence in the case consisted of the contradictory claims of the two women. How could one determine the mother of the living child? The truth could be ascertained only by a stratagem. The king ordered that the living child be cut in two. The result was as he had hoped: the real mother showed her love by asking that the child be given to the other woman. And so all Israel came to acknowledge that the LORD had given Solomon wisdom to be able to render right decisions.

4:1-28 [MT 4:1-5:8]. Solomon's administration. The location of the account of Solomon's administrative organization of Israel between two passages about his wisdom, 3:4-28 and 4:29-34 (MT 5:9-14), suggests that the Deuteronomistic Historian viewed the organization as an expression of wisdom or sagacity. The account reflects use of official documents. Verses 1-6 list Solomon's cabinet at some point in his reign. The growth in the number of cabinet positions can be determined by a comparison of two lists from David's reign, 2 Sam 8:15-18 and 20:23-26, with this list. Especially significant in Solomon's cabinet was the addition of a bureaucrat who supervised *the officers*.

Solomon divided the kingdom of Israel into twelve districts (vv. 8-19), each under its officer, with all twelve officers under the supervision of *Azariah son of Nathan* (v. 5). The twelve districts sometimes approximated tribal boundaries and sometimes ignored them. Each district had to provide supplies for the court of King Solomon for one month (vv. 22-23, 27-28). The last part of v. 19 should be read "and there was one officer who was in the land," referring to the cabinet official Azariah (v. 5). The text suggests that Judah was not included in the rotation of responsibility to provide for the king (see Kallai 1986, 40–72). Ironically, while Solomon's redistricting is placed literarily in the context of passages highlighting his wisdom, such preferential treatment of Judah and the erasure of some tribal boundaries contributed to the ultimate rebellion of Israel.

Solomon's relationships to the subregions of David's empire continued (vv. 21, 24), whether through occupation or by treaty. The descriptions of Solomon's chariot forces in v. 26 probably should read "four thousand stalls and twelve thousand horsemen" (see 2 Chr 9:25; cf. 1 Kgs 10:26-29).

4:29-34 [MT 5:9-14]. Solomon's wisdom. Wisdom was regarded as a divine gift. The tradition of Solomon's extraordinary wisdom is to be accepted in the light of the long–standing international wisdom traditions to which v. 30 refers. Solomon's wisdom included the collecting of proverbs (the standard wisdom saying), as well as songs, and the making of lists of flora and fauna. Solomon became the patron of wisdom in Israel.

The Building and Dedication of the Temple, 5:1–9:25

Since the account of the building of the Temple and its dedication constitutes the bulk of the history of Solomon's reign, there can be no doubt that the Deuteronomistic Historian viewed this event as the signal act of Solomon's reign. The editorial comment at 9:25—*So he [Solomon] completed the house*—justifies viewing 5:1–9:25 as a literary unit. The account begins with two necessary features: the acquisition of building materials, especially timber, and the organization of the work force.

5:1-12. Solomon's pact with Hiram of Tyre. Solomon continued David's treaty relationship with Hiram (cf. 2 Sam 5:11-12). The phrase *had always been a friend* in v. 1 is treaty terminology. Solomon required timber, which only the mountains of Lebanon could supply. Solomon and Hiram concluded the compact, Hiram agreeing to furnish the timber and Solomon agreeing to make payment with agricultural products. Verse 12 indicates that the business arrangement was viewed in the context of a parity treaty between Solomon and Hiram.

5:13-18 [MT 5:27-32]. The labor force. Solomon raised a work force of 30,000 citizens from Israel (Canaan and Judah are not mentioned) and placed them under the command of Adoniram, the cabinet minister in charge of compulsory labor (4:6). They were to work in Lebanon for one month of every three (vv. 13-14). This treatment of Israelites became a major reason for the later division of the kingdom (11:26-28; 12:1-16). Also, there was a larger work force to quarry and dress stones in the HILL COUNTRY and to transport it to Jerusalem (vv. 15-17). Their nationality is not clear nor are the terms of their employment (unless the work force is the same as that described in 9:20-23), although it is generally held that they were also part of the corvée. The stated number of workers seems very high. An alternative is to understand the word *thousand* to have another of its senses, "unit." Thus there would have been seventy groups or units of carriers and eighty groups of quarrymen overseen by three groups of three hundred (cf. the numbers in 2 Chr 2:17-18).

6:1–7:51. The Temple and its furnishings. The construction of the Temple was begun in the fourth year of Solomon's reign and was completed in seven years. Its main features, floor plan, and furnishings and decorations were typical of contemporary temples in Syria-Palestine. Its dimensions were about ninety feet in length, thirty feet in width, and forty-five feet in height. It was also typical that sanctuaries in the ancient Near East were built according to a perceived heavenly prototype or blueprint (such as given to King Gudea in Sumer, to Moses [Exod 25:9], and to David [2 Chron 28:19]), but nothing of the kind is mentioned here.

The Temple had three main rooms: the entry hall, the central hall, and the inner sanctuary or holy of holies, the repository of the ARK of the covenant and the dimensions of which formed a perfect cube. The Temple was oriented to the east. Constructed along the outside walls on three sides were three floors of chambers. In its floor plan and decorations it would have resembled in many ways the temples in most areas of Syria-Palestine.

Solomon employed Hiram, a craftsman from Tyre, for the exacting and specialized work of casting large items in bronze, such as the two bronze pillars in front of the temple and the bronze sea (7:13-14, 40-44). These bronzes were cast in the alluvial clay east of the Jordan River.

8:1-66. The dedication of the Temple. The service of dedication was begun with the transport of the ark of the covenant, the tent of meeting, and the sacred vessels by solemn procession to the Temple. By this action Solomon intended to demonstrate the continuity of the new era and its new cultic establishment with Israel's formative past. But, as it turned out, the old religion, with its emphasis on a God who was not tied to a place and who could be with the people wherever they went and with its stress on justice for all Israel, fitted poorly the needs of a new dynastic state. The danger, often realized, was that religion would be co-opted by the state to serve its imperial political and economic goals.

It is to be noted that Solomon was the main cultic official on this occasion. He organized and directed the dedication service, he gave the blessings and the prayer, and he consecrated the middle of the Temple court where he offered the sacrifices. In ancient Near Eastern practice the king was by definition the chief priest who delegated to the priesthood the daily cultic responsibilities. If King Saul, a transition figure with no history of kingship in Israel to guide him, could be faulted for challenging priestly prerogatives (as in 1 Sam 13:5-15), Solomon makes clear his intention to be king in every sense.

Solomon addressed the audience (vv. 14-21), recounting the events leading up to the building of the Temple. The passage reflects the concerns of the Deuteronomistic editor, especially in the stress on the *name* of the LORD being resident in the Temple; the name of the LORD dwelled there (cf. v. 27). Thus the God of Israel could not be located in or restricted to any one "place," and therefore could not be limited or manipulated by cultic practices. The tension between these two ideas of the Temple's role is illustrated in the contrast between Solomon's statement in v. 13 and the quotation in v. 16 from 2 Sam 7:5-6. The historian was anxious to negate the idea that the Temple was a guarantee of the LORD's presence among the people (cf. Jer 7).

The prayer of Solomon (vv. 22-53) begins with a recounting of the promises to the house of David. Stress is laid on the Temple as a house of prayer, and Solomon's main request was that prayers offered in this place would receive a favorable hearing in heaven. Seven typical human situations are included to represent the totality of human need (vv. 31-53). This rendition of the prayer is the product of the Deuteronomistic Historian, whose characteristic concerns are reflected throughout: for example, the conditional nature of the promises to David, the "name"-theology, and the idea that calamity is the result of sin.

8:54-66. The conclusion of the dedication service. Solomon blessed the people, asking the LORD to be present with them and ending with an admonition to purity of devotion. There followed the lavish sacrifices appropriate for such an occasion and a feast in which all could participate. The event took place at the time of the traditional Feast of Booths (TABERNACLES) in the autumn.

9:1-9. The second oracle to Solomon. Just as Solomon's reign began with a THEOPHANY (3:3-14), so now at this critical juncture there is a second divine appearance. This theophany is timed well, for it cautions the king, at a time when he might be tempted to overstep his limits, to guard his personal behavior; and it reminds him of the conditional nature of the promises to the house of David. The ORACLE itself reflects the reality of the Babylonian exile and explains ahead of time the loss of Temple and land. Ultimately Solomon failed to heed the admonition in all its terms.

9:10-14. Solomon's financial troubles. After twenty years of extensive building enterprises, Solomon's resources were so diminished that he was forced to engage in a new transaction with King Hiram of Tyre. The building program had been paid for. Now new resources were needed to keep the administration running. This time Solomon had to cede Hiram twenty Israelite towns in consideration of a large amount of cash for current expenses, a deal less than satisfactory to Hiram. The purpose of these verses is opaque unless they intend to presage the future loss of territory because of Solomon's unwise policies.

9:15-25. The account of forced labor. The account of compulsory labor in 5:13-18 seems to relate specifically to the activities relative to the building of the Temple. Here however it is clear that Solomon's nationwide building program required a permanent levy of forced labor, which in turn required a larger group of overseers (v. 23). Verses 20-22 restrict the levy to non-Israelite residents in the land, although 5:13 claimed that Israelite citizens had been pressed into compulsory service. Excavations have recovered considerable evidence of Solomon's building and fortification program.

The *Millo* (v. 15, "filling") refers to the terraced area on the eastern slope of Jerusalem that provided space for small dwellings within the city wall. The area required periodic rebuilding.

The last statement in v. 25 is an editorial addition to indicate that the account of the building of the temple was now complete, bringing an end to the section of narratives that began at 5:1.

Solomon's Wealth and Wisdom, 9:26–10:29

These verses are to be contrasted with 3:1–4:34. Whereas Solomon initially asked for wisdom so that he might render justice for the people, and was promised wealth and reputation in addition, now Solomon employs wisdom for his own enrichment. What began with great promise now begins to founder in excess (see Walsh and Begg 1990, 167).

9:26-28, 10:11-12, 22. Solomon's sea ventures. Surrounding and embedded within the Queen of Sheba story is information about Solomon's overseas ventures. Israel had no maritime tradition. Solomon concluded business agreements with Tyre, a seafaring nation, to engage in trade in the Red Sea area and in the Mediterranean. Solomon financed the building of a fleet and provided Hiram overland access to the Gulf of Aqabah, the eastern arm of the Red Sea, while Hiram provided shipbuilding expertise and trained sailors. In addition Solomon ordered a fleet built to join Hiram's in the Mediterranean trade.

Ophir (9:28) is probably to be located in east Africa (Somalia?; see Van Beek 1962a). *Ships of Tarshish* (10:22) were large, oceangoing ships. (De Vries 1990, 820–21, surveys ships and the place of maritime ventures in the ancient Near East.) It is in the context of such international trade that the visit of the Queen of Sheba is placed.

10:1-10, 13. The queen of Sheba's visit. The kingdom of the Sabeans (Heb. *Sheba*) was located in the southwest corner of Arabia, ideally situated to command the Red Sea trade (see Van Beek 1962b). Although the Queen of Sheba was impressed with Solomon's wisdom and the splendor of the court, her visit was a trade mission (vv. 10, 13). Solomon's successful entry into the Red Sea commerce made such a visit imperative.

The story of the queen's visit serves the historian's purpose of placing Solomon's wisdom in an unfavorable light. Solomon uses the divine gift for personal aggrandizement, and it is the foreign queen who blesses the LORD and who reminds Solomon that his chief duty is to bring justice to all the people (see Walsh and Begg 1990, 167; see also Wiles 1990, 816).

10:14-25. Solomon's wealth. Solomon acquired vast wealth from international trade and from interior taxation (it is possible to read in v. 15 "from the taxes of the traders" [Ugaritic *unt̲*, Akk. *unuššu*]). What is remarkable is that all this wealth was for personal and secular use, none of it for the Temple. Again the historian subtly draws attention to the declining values characterizing Solomon's reign.

10:26-29. Solomon the horse trader. Aspects of these verses are unclear. What is clear is that Solomon was able financially to equip a substantial chariot force and to distribute units to fortress cities in strategic locations. The verses also suggest that Solomon regulated horse and chariot trade between Egypt and northwest Mesopotamia. *Kue* was located in Cilicia. Thus Solomon not only increased his wealth but also was able to secure military intelligence about the forces available to neighboring kingdoms.

The Sins of the Kingdom Exposed, 11:1-43

11:1-13. Solomon's moral failure. The reign that began with such great promise ended miserably. Throughout the account the historian gave hints of incipient trouble for Solomon because of certain policies. In this chapter Solomon is charged specifically with "going after other gods," a particular Deuteronomistic concern. In the LORD's two appearances to Solomon (3:5-14; 9:1-9), the king had been cautioned about the contingent nature of the promises made to the house of David, and particularly about worshiping other gods (9:6-7). Now the historian charged Solomon with allowing his foreign wives to turn away his heart to their gods, with the result that Solomon built shrines for their gods on Israelite soil. Divine judgment was severe: loss of all territory except for the patrimony of Judah. The historian has thus given a moral interpretation to what was also a political and social policy.

11:14-40. Solomon's adversaries. Although the preceding account of Solomon's reign gives little hint of internal or external opposition, this concluding section provides a more realistic picture. The account states that God raised up two adversaries against Solomon, *Hadad the Edomite* (v. 14) and *Rezon . . . [of] . . . Damascus* (vv. 23-24). Hadad had escaped the slaughter carried out by David and Joab (2 Sam 8:13-14) and had been granted sanctuary in Egypt. Rezon had survived David's campaigns against the Aramean army (2 Sam 8:3-6; 10:15-19) and had managed to become king in Damascus. Both kings posed serious threats to Solomon because Edom and Damascus were parts of the empire, although the account offers no indication of their specific actions nor any military response by Solomon.

Of more immediate consequence was the threat posed by *Jeroboam son of Nebat* (12:2), an Ephraimite who had served Solomon as an overseer of forced labor from the house of Joseph during the repair of the Millo. But the story is even more about *the prophet Ahijah* (v. 29), who, like prophets before and after him, was a kingmaker. Ahijah performed a prophetic symbolic act to deliver the oracle of God. He ripped a garment into twelve pieces, gave Jeroboam ten of the pieces, and announced that the LORD was about to rip the kingdom from Solomon's hands. The ten pieces represented the ten northern tribes of Israel, the future kingdom of Israel. Jeroboam was given the same assurance that had been given to Solomon: if he would follow the LORD, he would be given a secure dynasty like David's. When Solomon heard of it, Jeroboam had to flee to Egypt until Solomon's death. This last episode of Solomon's story thus serves as the transition to chaps. 12–14.

11:41-43. Death of Solomon. The Deuteronomistic Historian provides the typical summation to Solomon's reign. The *Book of the Acts of Solomon* (v. 41) was one of several written resources used by the historian, including official registers, memoranda, and archival materials. Solomon was succeeded in Jerusalem by *Rehoboam*, Solomon's son by Naamah of Ammon.

Synchronic History of Israel and Judah, 1 Kgs 12:1–2 Kgs 17:41

From the time of the division of the kingdom of Solomon until the fall of Samaria, the historian correlates the reign of a king of either kingdom with the reign of his counterpart. There were two kingdoms, but from the prophetic point of view, there was still one people of God. (For the evaluation formula, see commentary at 14:21–15:24.)

Jeroboam I of Israel, 12:1–14:20

12:1-25. The division of the kingdom. King David wore three crowns: the crowns of Judah, of Jerusalem, and of Israel. David's relationships with Judah and Israel differed: he had been anointed king over Judah at Hebron (2 Sam 2:4), but he became king over Israel by political agreement, a covenant (2 Sam 5:1-3). Now REHOBOAM, Solomon's successor, seeks Israel's acceptance in the same way. For David and Solomon, the service of the northern tribes had been disproportionately difficult. The elders of Judah, wise enough to understand the rightness of Israel's complaint that Israel had been neglected, advised Rehoboam to change the policy. But Rehoboam, following the insulting and obscene advice of his younger advisors, permanently alienated the northern tribes. Verse 16 includes a familiar dismissal formula (cf. 2 Sam 20:1): *What share do we have . . . ? . . . To your tents. . . . Look now to your own house.*

The cry *To your tents, O Israel!* may signal also an intention to return to the values of the distant past. But in v. 15 the historian pointed out that these events occurred according to the will of the LORD as fulfillment of Ahijah's prophecy to Jeroboam (11:29-31).

Jeroboam, who had sought asylum in Egypt, returned to Israel and was proclaimed king of Israel. To underscore that the division of the kingdom was in accord with the divine will, Shemaiah, a prophet from Judah, delivered an oracle to Rehoboam to desist from war (vv. 22-24). Jeroboam fortified two key sites, SHECHEM in the hill country and PENUEL in Transjordan, to discourage an immediate attack from Judah.

12:26-33. Jeroboam's cultic policy. For political reasons JEROBOAM I instituted cultic changes as alternatives to the Jerusalem cult: alternative sanctuaries at DAN and BETHEL, new symbols (golden bulls), encouragement of high places, a new priesthood not restricted to the Levites, and a new cultic calendar (see Bailey 1990b, 440).

The Deuteronomistic Historian condemned Jeroboam for all these changes, and in the Deuteronomistic History these became the *sin . . . of Jeroboam* (13:34; 2 Kgs 3:3; cf. 1 Kgs 15:34; 16:2, 19; etc.) according to which all the succeeding kings of Israel were judged. (See the recurring phrase *He [or king's name] did what was evil in the sight of the LORD, walking in the way of Jeroboam and in the sin that he caused* Israel to commit [15:34] throughout the narratives of the northern kings.)

It is unlikely that Jeroboam intended the golden bulls to be worshiped as idols. The conservative population of the north would have deposed him summarily. Rather, like the ark and cherubim, the bulls were to be visible symbols of the LORD's invisible presence (see Bailey 1990a, 127). However, the historian's criticism was validated by future events when Israelites did in fact worship the golden bulls as deities.

13:1-34. Jeroboam's intransigence. Jeroboam was condemned, not for his moral failure, but for his cultic innovations. In vv. 1-5 *a man of God* from Judah prophesied the eventual profanation of the cult places by a descendant of David. The chapter concludes with Jeroboam completely undeterred, confirming his policy of appointing non-Levitic priests and placing them at the high places. For the historian the fall of Israel was now determined.

Imbedded in the chapter is the story of the two prophets (vv. 11-32). (Note that both are unnamed, but are distinguished by the designations *the man of God* [from Judah] and *the prophet* [from Israel].) Much is involved in the story: differing political commitments, differing views of the divine will, and differing prophetic traditions. *The man of God* from Judah was faithful in his proclamation of the oracle but was disqualified for his moral failure in terms of the circumstances of his mission.

The prophet from the north lied, but he faithfully proclaimed the other prophet's disobedience. The ability of the people to determine the true prophet remained problematic throughout the remaining history of the kingdoms. In the end no one criterion could be used to determine who was a true prophet from the LORD (see also, e.g., 1 Kgs 22).

14:1-20. The end of Jeroboam's reign. The end of Jeroboam's reign was prophesied by the same prophet who prophesied his rise, AHIJAH of Shiloh. Classical prophecy arose at the same time as the monarchy in Israel and provided a corrective voice from the LORD with regard to royal policy. It is thus important to the historian to emphasize throughout the story of the kingship the crucial role of prophecy in national history, including the making and deposing of kings. Ahijah had informed Jeroboam that the longevity of his dynasty would depend on his faithfulness to the commandments of the LORD (11:38). But Jeroboam's cultic policies doomed him and all the men of his house (vv. 10-16). The immediate death of Jeroboam's infant son ABIJAH was confirmation of the initiation of the judgment, although the historian suggests that Abijah was mercifully spared the sight of the dynasty's eventual ruin (vv. 12-13).

Early Kings of Judah, 14:21–15:24

From this point the historian provides evaluations of the reigns of the kings of Israel and Judah. The formula of evaluation typically offers the following data: (1) the name of the king, the length of the reign, synchronism with the reign of the king of the other kingdom, identification of the capital, and, for the kings of Judah, the naming of their mothers; (2) evaluations of the reigns in terms of cultic activity; and (3) accounts of the kings' deaths, references to other written sources, and the name of each successor.

14:21-31. The reign of Rehoboam. Apart from the treatment of REHOBOAM's disastrous decision related in 12:1-15, the historian highlighted three aspects of his reign. First, all Judah was condemned for cultic sins: worship at high places, use of cultic symbols and images of the Canaanite cult, and sacred prostitution. Second, mention is made of SHISHAK's invasion of the land because it resulted in the loss of the golden shields, which had a cultic use. Third, there is a brief reference to continual warfare with the north despite the prophetic restriction of 12:22-24. Also, twice it is mentioned that Rehoboam's mother was a princess of Ammon (vv. 21, 31), as though to suggest that the reader should expect nothing better from Rehoboam.

15:1-8. The reign of Abijam. Rehoboam's son and successor was Abijam (ABIJAH in 1 Chr 3:10; 2 Chr 13:1ff.), whose name means "my father is Yam," the Canaanite god of the sea. Abijam ruled but three years, but was judged a failure because he followed Rehoboam's example.

15:9-24. Good King Asa. Asa was the first of the reforming kings of Judah, receiving a qualified approval from the historian. His only listed blemish was his failure to remove the high places, a matter of particular importance in every period for the Deuteronomistic Historian. Asa went so far as to remove the queen mother from her office because of her devotion to the goddess ASHERAH. The *queen mother* was the mother of the ruling king and a very important person in the court (in this case of course it was Asa's own mother Maacah [v. 13]): compare, for example, Bathsheba after the death of David (1 Kings 2:13-25).

Asa's cultic reform may have been a part of his plan to inspire a united nationalism in the face of the threat from Baasha, the king of Israel who provocatively fortified Ramah on the border between the kingdoms. So serious was this threat that Asa made a treaty with Aram to break its prior treaty with Israel, and thus come to Judah's aid. This dependence on foreign alliances for national defense was a harbinger for the future, a policy that evoked almost universal condemnation from Israel's prophets. Subsequently Asa imposed compulsory labor for the fortification of Geba and Mizpah, perhaps only for the duration of the crisis.

Early Kings of Israel, 15:25–16:34

15:25-26, 31. Reign of Nadab. NADAB, son of Jeroboam I, reigned only two years and received failing marks from the historian.

15:27-30, 32-34; 16:1-7. Reign of Baasha. Baasha assassinated Nadab while the king was on a military campaign. Before this event Baasha's status is unknown. Baasha's first act as king was to kill all the sons of the house of Jeroboam. This was interpreted by the Deuteronomistic Historian as a fulfillment of Ahijah's prophecy: *I will cut off from Jeroboam every male* (14:10-11). This act of conspiracy and assassination was to be replayed several times in Israel's history, to the detriment of the nation's stability. The prophet Jehu credited Baasha's rise to the will of the LORD to terminate Jeroboam's dynasty, but concluded that because Baasha replicated the sin of Jeroboam, his house also would be terminated (16:1-4).

16:8-14. The reign of Elah. Elah's reign was ended in its second year by the conspiracy of Zimri, one of his military commanders. Zimri destroyed the house of Baasha, again in accordance with the prophetic word (16:1-4). However, the troops of Israel, still at the siege of Gibbethon initiated by Baasha, refused Zimri support and named Omri, the army commander, as king. Zimri's claim to the throne lasted only seven days. The army besieged the capital TIRZAH and Zimri committed suicide.

16:21-28. The reign of Omri. Omri's success against Zimri did not win him universal support. The Israelite population was divided for several years over who should succeed Elah. Omri's forces finally won, and despite the brevity of his kingship there began one of the most remarkable reigns among all the kings of Israel and Judah.

Omri was an able administrator. He moved the capital from the pesthole Tirzah to the virgin site of SAMARIA, thus geographically orienting the insular nation to participate fully in international relations. His dynasty lasted for a generation (forty years), and he so impressed Assyrian officials that they referred to Israel as the house of Omri (*Bit-Humri*) long after his time. Omri's defeat of Moab is recorded on the MESHA STELE (see Pritchard 1955, 320–21). The Deuteronomistic Historian's interest in Omri is virtually limited to his failure to break out of Jeroboam's mold. The historian seems vexed that such a capable ruler should be so foolish and ascribes more evil to him than to any previous ruler. Omri was succeeded by his son Ahab.

Ahab and Elijah, 16:29–22:40

The careers of AHAB and ELIJAH are so interwoven they had to be narrated together. It seems that for the Deuteronomistic Historian Ahab was the prototype of the bad king, since more space is devoted to his reign than to any other king of north or south since the division of the kingdom. Nowhere else can one see more clearly the diametrically opposite agendas of kings and prophets. The reason is clearly summarized in 16:29-34. Omri concluded a political marriage for his son with JEZEBEL, daughter of the king of Sidon, a strong-willed and evangelistic devotee of BAAL Melqart. In the historian's view, this sin exceeded even that of Jeroboam I. (Elijah's career must be understood in the light of the religious threat from Phoenicia, particularly in the struggle to determine which deity was the giver of the rains.)

17:1-24. Elijah's preparation for conflict. Elijah appears without preamble in v. 1, determined to challenge the very heart of the Baal cult: he proclaimed a drought. Baal was venerated as the giver of rain, and thus of life itself. True to the prophetic word, a drought came upon the land for three years, long enough to precipitate an agricultural crisis and to cause an embarrassing theological problem for worshipers of Baal.

The concept of the prophetic word spoken on behalf of the LORD is a major motif of these narratives. But to announce the drought was only part of Elijah's task. Ultimately he had to announce Yahweh's gift of the rain. The three events recounted in chap. 17 prepare Elijah for that crucial announcement.

Two miracle stories narrate Elijah's provisioning by the LORD in the midst of drought (17:3-7, 8-16). The God of Israel, not Baal, is presented as the sustainer of life.

In the second story, Elijah entered ZAREPHATH of Sidon, Baal's domain, where the LORD's sovereignty is affirmed in the matter of the meal and the cruse of oil. The victory of Israel's God is already presaged.

In the third story (17:17-24) the power of the God of Israel to give life to the deceased in Baal's territory is affirmed; the power of the word of the LORD is vindicated in the mouth of a non-Israelite woman (17:24).

18:1-46. The contest on Mount Carmel. Prepared and strengthened, Elijah was sent by the LORD to meet Ahab and to announce that the LORD would *send rain on the earth* (v. 1). Jezebel was already *killing off the prophets of the LORD* (v. 4). Their murder may have been interpreted as the immediate cause of the drought. Obadiah, Ahab's chamberlain, who had kept alive a hundred of the prophets, was sent by Elijah to summon Ahab.

The contest on Mount Carmel was more than a contest of wills between Elijah and Ahab, or between Elijah and Baal's prophets. It was a contest of power between the God of Israel and BAAL. The issue was, which deity actually was giver of rain and thus of life itself? At stake was the faith commitment of the people of Israel; their indecision or vacillation placed the nation's future in jeopardy.

Baal's prophets performed a rain dance (*they limped about the altar*, i.e., performed a knee-bending dance, v. 26), loudly imploring Baal to answer, while they made ritual incisions on their bodies (v. 28). This example of imitative magic produced on the skin parallel rows of incisions resembling the furrows of a plowed field ready to receive the rain, while the dripping blood was thought to cause the rain to fall. Elijah bravely ridiculed their futile efforts (v. 27).

By contrast, after preparing the altar of sacrifice, Elijah calmly prayed to the LORD to answer with fire. When the fire fell and consumed both the offering and the altar (v. 38), the people acknowledged that the LORD was God. It was a great victory, but this powerful vindication of the prophetic word produced no lasting repentance. As the rain began to fall, in exhilaration Elijah ran before Ahab back to Jezreel, apparently in the belief that Ahab was converted.

19:1-21. Elijah at Mountt Horeb. Elijah's euphoria vanished when he discovered that it was Jezebel, not Ahab, with whom he had to deal. When she threatened his life, Elijah fled in haste. Note the piling up of verbs in v. 3: *afraid, got up, fled, came, left.* Elijah deserved censure, but the LORD graciously gave him rest and food for the journey.

Elijah was headed for Mount Horeb, the site where the LORD met Moses in a theophany of fire and thunder and gave him the commandments (there called SINAI). Perhaps Elijah expected the LORD to repeat that ancient event and thus redeem the situation. Instead, Elijah was confronted by the LORD for his cowardice. The LORD accepted no excuses. But the LORD met Elijah's expectations in a totally unexpected way, not by a traditional theophany with convulsions of nature, but in "a sound of quiet stillness" (v. 12; cf. ERV and ASV mg.; NRSV, *a sound of sheer silence*).

Elijah was being taught that the LORD was master, not just of the past, but of the future. Elijah sought the comfort of the past, but he learned that it is the future that conveys meaning (Baly 1976, 86–90). Instead of accepting Elijah's resignation of his office, the LORD gave Elijah new tasks, for example, to *anoint Hazael as king over Aram* (Syria; v. 15). HAZAEL of ARAM would be a source of great suffering for Israel. Furthermore, Elijah was to anoint JEHU as king of Israel. Jehu would terminate Omri's dynasty. Finally, Elijah was to anoint ELISHA as his prophet successor (v. 16). But Elijah was to accomplish only the last task.

20:1-22:40. Ahab's final days. The three episodes in these chapters highlight the increasing conflict between Ahab and the prophets. While Ahab's bravery and political acumen are evident—even on occasion enjoying the LORD's support—his bad decisions and moral failure are credited with hastening his end.

First Kings 20:1-43 narrate two campaigns in Ahab's ongoing struggles with Aram. When Samaria was besieged by the Arameans, Ahab showed exemplary bravery. An unnamed prophet promised victory from the LORD so that Ahab would recognize the supremacy of the LORD, and Israel won an astonishing victory. The next spring a refurbished Aramean army again attacked, and again a prophet delivered a proof oracle promising victory. Again Israel was victorious. But the victories were tarnished by Ahab's decision to spare BEN-HADAD's life and to make a treaty with him (20:31-34). Another prophet denounced this decision and predicted Ahab's death. The victorious king went home *resentful and sullen* (20:42-43).

The episode of Naboth and his vineyard is related in 21:1-29. The vineyard lay adjacent to Ahab's winter palace at Jezreel. Ahab made what appears, on the surface, to be a fair offer of purchase, but Naboth refused to sell because the property was "the inheritance of my fathers" (21:3 RSV). According to legal tradition, family property was not to be alienated permanently. The principle involved was that the land belonged to the LORD; the landholder was steward, not owner (Lev 25:23-24). Persons could not enrich themselves at the LORD's expense by selling the patrimony for monetary gain. Ahab grew sullen because Naboth was legally correct. However, Jezebel arranged a false charge to be brought against Naboth. He was executed by stoning. This judicial murder, the "shedding of innocent blood," brought immediate condemnation from Elijah. Ahab's demise is again predicted, together with editorializing by the Deuteronomistic Historian (vv. 22-26). The story functions as an explanation for Ahab's untimely demise.

The story of Naboth's vineyard calls to mind the parable of Nathan before King David (2 Sam 12). Just as David stood condemned for his moral failures as an Israelite, a son of the covenant despite his being king, so also Ahab stood condemned. Kings were subject to the *divine* claim; while they had the *power* to ignore the claims of morality and covenant, they did not have the *right* to do so. It was Elijah's task to say so and to hold the king accountable for personal misdeeds. Just as David could not commit adultery and then try to cover up the act with murder, so also Ahab and Jezebel could not confiscate the property of a citizen of Jezreel by arranging for the citizen's conviction and execution on false charges. Israel's prophets were not engaged only or primarily in a power struggle with the kings. Their struggle was for the cause of public and private righteousness.

The third episode, 22:1-40, provides the account of Ahab's final battle with Aram, this time with the collaboration of JEHOSHAPHAT of Judah. At the center is another confrontation with a prophet, MICAIAH SON OF IMLAH, who predicted that Ahab would not survive the battle. Ahab died as a result of a chance shot by an Aramean bowman.

This long story of Micaiah and King Ahab is of great value in understanding the struggle between kings and prophets. It offers insights on how prophets came to receive their messages from God, on how such messages were to be heard by the community and its leaders, and on how individual prophets managed to survive when they were out of favor with the political authorities.

While the narrative cannot be dated precisely, it probably belonged to the collection of Elijah and Elisha traditions that the Deuteronomistic Historian had available and incorporated into the Deuteronomistic History. It is thus considerably older than the late-seventh century and probably gives us reliable information on the standing of prophets at least a century earlier.

Prophets received messages through singing (see 2 Kgs 3:15) and dancing (1 Kgs 18), but they also received messages through visions like those of Micaiah—of *all Israel scattered on the mountains, like sheep that have no shepherd* (1 Kgs 22:17) or of the LORD on the throne debating with the heavenly host about Ahab and his misdeeds (1 Kgs 22:19-22). These visions, however, had to be interpreted by prophets, and the interpretations were presented along with the reports of the visions, intepretations and reports that of course could be and at times were falsified (see v. 23).

Micaiah was hated by Ahab, we are told, because he prophesied nothing favorable for Ahab (22:8); his was largely a negative witness. The hundreds of prophets who told the king exactly what he wanted to hear are clearly considered in this story to be less reliable than the one who gave a different message. But Micaiah is also ready to have his message tested by the historical outcome. If Ahab returns from battle unharmed, then the LORD has not spoken through Micaiah (v. 28), and Micaiah the prophet is a false prophet.

But there is a deeper test, suggested by the visions of Micaiah. Prophets are those who have been in the heavenly presence, have heard words and seen plans of events to be played out on earth. Jeremiah (23:22) speaks of God's "council" (Heb. *sôd*) for the prophets; Amos (3:7) affirms that *God does nothing, without revealing his secret* [or "counsel," Heb. *sôd*] *to his servants the prophets*. Yet, such visions require interpretation, human efforts to understand the divine will and state it plainly.

When prophets give such interpretation, they expose themselves to danger. Micaiah can only acquiesce, stay in prison on lean rations, and await results. Like Jeremiah, he can finally only insist, "in truth the LORD sent me to you" (Jer 26:15).

The three episodes in chaps. 20–22 stress the power of the prophetic word to determine national outcomes. (For a discussion of the extent to which prophetic opposition to the house of Omri was religious opposition to Baal of Tyre, see Hayes and Miller, 1977 403–405.)

The treatment of Ahab's reign in these chapters gives only a hint of his positive contributions. Ahab rebuilt Jericho (16:34) and fortified several cities (22:39). He was famed for his "ivory palace" (22:39) and other building projects at Samaria. The Black Obelisk of Shalmaneser III attests to Ahab's participation in the battle of Qarqar in 853 in a coalition of kings against Assyria (Pritchard 1955, 278–79).

Jehoshaphat and Ahaziah, 22:41–2 Kgs 1:18

22:41-50. Jehoshaphat's reign. The reign of JEHOSHAPHAT of Judah is evaluated in terms similar to Asa's evaluation. He is given qualified approval by the historian. What distinguished his reign was his political accommodation with Israel for common political purposes. This arrangement may hint that Jehoshaphat became a tributary to Ahab, for Ahab's daughter Athaliah was married to JEHORAM, Jehoshaphat's son. Jehoshaphat's later independence is suggested by his refusal to let Ahaziah, Ahab's successor, participate in his planned Red Sea maritime ventures (vv. 47-49).

1 Kgs 22:51–2 Kgs 1:18. Ahaziah's Reign. Ahab's successor AHAZIAH, received the typical negative evaluation from the Deuteronomistic Historian. His reign was apparently without consequence except to provide a setting for another wonder story about Elijah. An injury led Ahaziah to send messengers to the god BAAL-ZEBUB at Ekron, one of the Philistine cities (2 Kgs 1:2). *Baal-zebub*, "lord of the flies," is a deliberate distortion of Baal-zebul, "prince Baal" or "lord prince." Ahaziah's act of bypassing Yahweh to secure an oracle brought Elijah onto the scene, dressed in distinctive prophetic garb. Again the power of Yahweh through the prophetic word is determinative, and again by fire as in 1 Kgs 18 (2 Kgs 1:12).

The Elisha Cycle, 2:1–8:29

The Elisha cycle of narratives (with its completion in 13:14-21) was designed to demonstrate the power of the prophetic word and office as over against royal power. Elisha's power covered all areas, from the alleviation of personal tragedy to war policy. In a series of ten stories, most of them reminiscent of high points in Elijah's career, the historian demonstrated the centrality of the prophetic office for Israelite life. The careers of the kings of Judah and Israel were fitted into the cycle where appropriate.

2:1-25. Elisha, Elijah's successor. As commanded by the LORD (1 Kgs 19:16), Elijah designated Elisha as his successor. Elijah's prophetic commission and power were transmitted through the bestowal of his mantle (1 Kgs 19:19). Elisha had slaughtered the oxen with which he had been plowing and prepared a feast for the people, as though to indicate his entry upon a new vocation (1 Kgs 19:21). Then when Elisha saw Elijah taken up in the whirlwind, he cried out, *The chariots of Israel and its horsemen!* (v. 12). By this cryptic phrase he perhaps suggested the central role of the prophet in Israel's life—more important than even the nation's armies.

The first test of Elisha's power confirmed the successful transfer of the prophetic office: he struck the waters of the Jordan and they parted (v. 14), just as Elijah had done (v. 8).

Guilds or associations of prophets (see v. 13: *company of prophets*; Heb. "sons of the prophets") are prominent in the Elisha cycle, as also in the Samuel stories. These were prophetic schools featuring a communal existence. When the prophets of Jericho observed Elisha's power, they placed themselves under his direction (2:15) and were sent by him on occasion to perform prophetic tasks (e.g., 9:1-10).

3:1-27. The war in Moab. Since before the time of Omri, Moab had been a vassal state to Israel. But after the death of Ahab, King Mesha of Moab saw his chance for independence and withheld the annual tribute. This account illustrates the continuing hostility between prophets and kings, although Elisha did predict victory for Israel and Judah. But the victory was not total, and Mesha ultimately succeeded in his revolt.

The events of the time are reflected in Mesha's inscription (see Pritchard 1955, 320–21, and MESHA STELE), discovered in 1868 at Dhiban. Mesha recounted the history of Moab's servitude to Israel during the reigns of Omri and Ahab, along with Mesha's successful revolt. The inscription describes Mesha's annexation of Israelite territory in the Transjordan and some of his building projects.

4:1-8:15. Stories about Elisha. The historian's preoccupation with the power of the prophetic word and with the indispensability of the prophetic office for the life of the nation is illustrated here in a series of ten stories. These stories feature prophetic activity both within and outside Israel. The prophetic power knew no national boundaries.

In the first two stories (4:1-7, 8-37) some of Elijah's feats are replayed, only this time on Israelite soil, as though to provide final confirmation of Elisha's succession to Elijah's office.

As in the first two stories, the third and fourth stories (4:38-41, 42-44) emphasize the prophet's power in the contexts of famine, want, and death.

In the fifth story (5:1-27), the emphasis is placed on the LORD's supremacy over Aram's god RIMMON. This theme is illustrated specifically in the matter of the prophet's power to provide healing for an Aramean, *that he may learn that there is a prophet in Israel* (5:8). The story also tells, perhaps not incidentally, of the faith of a captured child, serving in the household of the warrior NAAMAN. The child believes confidently in the power of Israel's God to heal even the foreign master for whom she labors.

The sixth story, about the axhead (6:1-7), illustrates the prophet's concern for the care of his own prophetic community.

In the seventh story (6:8-23) Elisha's indispensability in time of war is highlighted. Through clairvoyance Elisha provided the means of victory so that Aramean raids into Israel were stopped temporarily. The prophet could accomplish what the king and his army could not.

The eighth story (6:24–7:20) replays the theme of the prophet's role in military victory using the schema of prophecy-fulfillment. Everything happened exactly as the prophet had predicted, followed by the death of the captain who had doubted his prediction.

The ninth story (8:1-6) is a continuation of the second story (4:8-37). The widow, whose son Elisha had restored to life, left for Philistia when famine came.

During her absence her house and property had been taken by others. But the king, impressed by Elisha's great deeds for this widow, had her property restored.

The final story in the Elisha collection (8:7-15) again illustrates the prophet's power of life and death and his capacity to act in international politics. In this episode Elisha carried out the LORD's directive to Elijah to designate Hazael to be king of Aram (see 1 Kgs 19:15).

In all these narratives, the historian demonstrates that it is the prophet, the spokesman of the word of the LORD, whose acts and words are decisive, not the king's.

8:16-29. Jehoram and Ahaziah. In the last days of Elisha's ministry, JEHORAM succeeded Jehoshaphat to the throne of Judah; he in turn was succeeded by Ahaziah (or JEHOAHAZ). Neither king accomplished anything of note. Jehoram's reign was highlighted by successful revolts by Edom and Libnah. Ahaziah allied himself with Joram (also called JEHORAM) of Israel to fight the Arameans. Both Jehoram and Ahaziah are portrayed more as faithful members of the house of Omri than as kings of Judah, for in fact Jehoram was married to Athaliah, Omri's granddaughter, and she was Ahaziah's mother. The Deuteronomistic Historian condemned their reigns because they *walked in the way of the kings of Israel* (8:18; cf. 8:27).

From Jehu to the Fall of Samaria, 9:1–17:41

This section of 2 Kings provides a synchronic history of Israel and Judah from the establishment of Jehu's dynasty to the fall of Samaria, 842/1–722.

9:1–10:36. The reign of Jehu. JEHU's violent rise to power is presented as divine judgment on the house of OMRI. Elisha sent one of the prophets to anoint Jehu, a military commander, thus fulfilling the LORD's final commission to Elijah (1 Kgs 19:16). Also, no fewer than six times does the historian interpret Jehu's actions as the fulfillment of prophecy in accord with the word of the LORD (9:6, 26, 36-37; 10:10, 17, 30). Although Jehu's actions against Omri's house and against the Baal cult receive divine approval, he is still condemned for failing to turn away from *the sins of Jeroboam* (10:30-31).

After Jehu's anointing, the part of the army under his command acclaimed him king. He swiftly set out for Jezreel before the wounded king Joram (JEHORAM) could receive news of the conspiracy (9:14-16). In the confrontation of Joram and Jehu, which ironically took place on the property of NABOTH, Jehu slew the king (9:21-26) and moved immediately to slay Ahaziah (JEHOAHAZ) of Judah who had allied himself with Israel in the war against Aram (9:27-28). When Jehu entered JEZREEL, JEZEBEL tauntingly called him Zimri (9:30-31; cf. 1 Kgs 16:8-20), the murderer of Jehu's master. Jezebel was cast from the presentation window of the palace. However, her death did not mean the end of the cult of the Tyrian Baal in Israel.

Although Jehu was in command of Jezreel, the site of the winter palace, he was not yet accepted as king by the leadership of the capital city, Samaria. Tauntingly, Jehu invited the leaders to place one of Joram's sons on the throne and to let the issue be settled on the field of battle. Out of fear, the officials declined. Jehu then sent another letter with ambiguous terms: send the "heads" of the royal house to Jezreel. The officials had to decide whether to interpret "heads" literally or symbolically as "leaders." Either way they were forced into complicity with the conspiracy. They severed the heads of seventy of the men of the royal family and sent them to Jezreel (10:1-11).

With the support of religiously conservative and politically disaffected groups represented by Jehonadab the son of Rechab (cf. Jer 35), Jehu inaugurated his campaign against the cult of Baal. With cunning Jehu gathered the worshipers of Baal into the temple built by Ahab and slaughtered them, turning the sacred precincts of the *temple of Baal* into a latrine (10:18-27).

The effects of Jehu's policies lasted many years. Contact with Phoenicia was severed. Cooperation with Judah was ended. Aram was soon free to devastate a weakened and isolated Israel (10:32-33). And the rise of Assyrian power under SHALMANESER III (858–824) was a harbinger of cruel days to come. Jehu found it necessary to become tributary to Shalmaneser in 841. Jehu is portrayed on the Black Obelisk of Shalmeneser bowing in obeisance and offering tribute (see Pritchard 1955, 280).

Finally, it must be said that Jehu's religious "reform" was not permanent. Real reform had to consist of something more than the slaughter of people and the trashing of temples. (For a review of Jehu's reign and policies, see Hayes and Miller 1977, 408–14.)

11:1–12:21. Joash of Judah. The reign of JOASH is treated at considerable length for two reasons: the death of Athaliah and the renovation of the temple.

When Athaliah learned of the death of her son King Ahaziah, she moved to eliminate all the royal family because they threatened her policy of alliance with Israel. But prince Joash was hidden away until he could be proclaimed king. On the day of his coronation, Athaliah, daughter of Ahab and protector of the Baal cult in Judah, was slain, and the temple of Baal was destroyed. Thus ended the dominance of the house of Omri over the royal house of Judah. The narrator gives details of the saving of Joash from Athaliah's slaughter, the careful planning of the priest JEHOIADA, and the collaboration of portions of the temple guard. It may be that a deliberate contrast is drawn between the bloody revolution of Jehu in the north and the almost bloodless coup in Jerusalem.

With the end of the Baal cult in Jerusalem, attention was turned to the neglected temple of the LORD. Despite initial inaction due to priestly reluctance, the temple was repaired after a system of payment was agreed upon that preserved priestly income. However, the historian's approval of Joash's repair program is tempered by the notice in 12:17-18 that Joash gave up all the treasures of the temple and palace to avert an invasion by Aram. The success of his reign is further muted by the announcement of his assassination (12:20-21; see Long 1991, 145–62).

13:1–14:29. Israel and Judah under Aramean domination. These chapters are to
be seen as a literary unit because of the theme of the LORD's mercy shown to an
apostate Israel (13:4-5, 23; 14:26-27; see Long 1991, 163–64).

Damascus continued to dominate Israel and Judah militarily. The army of
JEHOAHAZ of Israel was so reduced that it could offer no resistance to DAMASCUS
(13:7). But the LORD had mercy and raised up a deliverer (note the pattern in 13:1-5
reminiscent of the pattern in the Book of Judges). The historian seems to point to
JEROBOAM II as the deliverer (14:23-29). It is also possible to see the Assyrian king
Adad-nirari III (809–782) as a kind of deliverer because of his success against
Damascus during these years (Pritchard 1955, 281–82).

Jehoahaz was succeeded by Jehoash (JOASH) as king of Israel. The death of
Elisha occurred during his reign. The prophet's death represented the passing of an
era, a fact recognized by Jehoash. No longer would the royal court be able to draw
on Elisha's military intelligence. Because of the king's lack of confidence, he was
able to achieve only limited success against Damascus.

AMAZIAH succeeded Joash as king in Judah. His reign was marked by a
disastrous war with Israel after his suggestion of an alliance with Jehoash was inso-
lently rejected (14:8-14). The wall of Jerusalem suffered damage and the temple and
palace treasures were taken away to Samaria. In the face of an untiring Aramean
foe, this was no time for such confusion. No doubt nationalistic discontent with
Amaziah's lack of success figured prominently in his assassination (14:19).

JEROBOAM II (787–747) succeeded Joash as king of Israel. The prosperity of his
reign was made possible largely because the Assyrian king Adad-nirari III had
weakened Damascus. Jeroboam restored the northern border of Israel and gained
territory east of the Jordan River. His reign was marked by stability and renewed
prosperity, although its social inequities energized the prophets of the day.

15:1-38. Israel in decline. This chapter may be read as a literary unit. The
reigns of five unacceptable Israelite kings are enclosed by the reigns of two good
Judean kings (for a full discussion of the structure, see Long 1991, 170–72). The
purpose of the literary unit seems to be to highlight the turmoil and decline of the
kingdom of Israel, while the kingdom of Judah enjoyed relative stability. However,
AZARIAH (UZZIAH) was struck with leprosy, making him ritually unclean. He had to
live outside the capital. Azariah's son Jotham acted as regent (v. 5) and during
Jotham's regency the LORD sent REZIN of Aram and PEKAH of Israel against him,
indicating hard times for Judah as a result of the advance of Assyrian power.

These waning years (ca. 750–730) were turbulent for Israel. Four of the five
kings of Israel during this period were assassinated. Confusion and senseless
violence reigned. With ZECHARIAH's death (v. 10), the dynasty of Jehu was
terminated, having lasted four generations, as the LORD had promised (v. 12).

The main reason for Israel's unease was the growing power of Assyria, with
Assyria's designs on Syria-Palestine. Assyrian power reached its zenith in the reign
of TIGLATH-PILESER III (745–727). In 738 MENAHEM of Israel was forced to pay

tribute to Assyria and to enter into vassalage in order to retain his throne (15:19-20). In 734–732 Tiglath-pileser directed devastating raids against northern Israel, deporting some of the population to Assyria, because of Pekah's alliance with Rezin of Aram to force Judah to join their rebellion against Assyria (15:29, 37; 16:5; Isa 9:1 [MT 8:23]). Pekah's failed policy resulted in his assassination by Hoshea (15:30; for a full treatment of Tiglath-pileser's policy, see Hayes and Miller 1977, 418–20). Israel was approaching its final hour.

16:1-20. Ahaz of Judah. The reign of AHAZ is presented as a low point in Judean history. He is portrayed by the historian as weak and indecisive, an evaluation that is strengthened by the account of Isaiah's failed attempt to inspire courage and faith in Ahaz (Isa 7).

When Rezin of Aram and Pekah of Israel besieged Jerusalem to try to force Ahaz to join their rebellion against Assyria, Ahaz appealed to Tiglath-pileser of Assyria for protection, paid him tribute and became his vassal. The Assyrian complied by devastating northern Israel (15:29) and by putting an end to the kingdom of Aram (16:9).

Although it is unlikely that Assyria normally required vassals to adopt Assyrian religion, Ahaz is presented as going out of his way to welcome the cult of Assyria. He built an altar, probably of Assyrian design, to replace the bronze altar at the Jerusalem temple. He denigrated the LORD's altar by using it for divination (v. 15). He also dismantled other cultic objects *because of the king of Assyria* (v. 18). Ahaz is condemned by the historian as an apostate king who *walked in the way of the kings of Israel* (v. 3).

17:1-41. The end of the kingdom of Israel. HOSHEA was the last of the kings of Israel. He assassinated Pekah in order to come to the throne (15:30), perhaps because of Pekah's ill-advised attempt to throw off the Assyrian yoke. Yet Hoshea in his turn rebelled against Assyria, withholding annual tribute and seeking an alliance with Egypt (17:4). SHALMANESER V (727–722) put Hoshea in prison and besieged Samaria for three years. Shalmaneser V died in the course of the campaign, and his successor SARGON II captured the city. Sargon reported deporting 27,290 Israelites to Assyrian provinces (Pritchard 1955, 284-85).

Verses 7-20 contain the historian's theological interpretation of the fall of Israel. In a historical survey he painted a word-picture of thoroughgoing Israelite apostasy. Despite calls to repent sent by prophets (17:13), Israel pursued every sin that the Deuteronomistic Historian abominated, especially the "sins of Jeroboam" the son of Nebat (17:21-23). In 17:29 there is a forecast of Judah's fate for the same sins.

Verses 24-33 describe the theologically horrific sequel to the fall of Samaria. In accord with Assyrian policy, the conqueror deported Israelites to various places in Assyrian provinces and brought to Israel deportees from other conquered nations. With them the foreigners brought their own deities whom they worshiped alongside the God of Israel.

In 17:34b-41 there is a second theological treatment by the historian deploring the Israelite population's acceptance of the new reality. Again using historical recollection, the historian recounted the LORD's command to Israel not to worship other gods. However, even at the time of the writing of the history, the remaining Israelites continued their centuries-long habit of idolatry.

Judah after the Fall of Israel, 18:1–25:30

The Deuteronomistic Historian provided a lengthy theological interpretation for the fall of the kingdom of Israel (chap. 17). After inserting in 17:19 a literary transition to Judah's life alone, the historian details the last century and a half of Judah's political life. The historian wrote amid the ruin of the Judean state. The history is an explanation of the catastrophe. A mixed picture is presented: alternating reigns of good and bad kings (apostate Ahaz, reforming Hezekiah, apostate Manasseh, reforming Josiah), with the last few years of Judah's life taking place in an atmosphere of confusion in the face of the new foreign foe, Babylonia.

18:1–20:21. Reign of Hezekiah. The reign of HEZEKIAH was for the historian a bright spot in Judean history despite the loss in warfare and the ensuing suffering for the population. Hezekiah is presented as a religious reformer, a king who intended to restore the territory of the kingdom of David, and as one who was unafraid to challenge the power of Assyria.

The historian's laudatory summary of Hezekiah's reign is presented in 18:1-12. In accord with 18:13 Hezekiah's reign began in 715. His policies were opposite those of his father Ahaz. Oddly, only one verse (18:4) summarizes Hezekiah's religious reforms, although the account of the removal of the high places is confirmed by the statement in 18:22 attributed to the Rabshakeh, a high Assyrian official. The removal of the high places and the resulting restriction of worship to Jerusalem were of paramount importance to the Deuteronomistic Historian. Hezekiah was the first king to accomplish this. While Hezekiah's personal religious feelings were an important factor in the reform, the political aspects must not be overlooked. His plan to restore the lost territories of David's kingdom included the development of heightened religious and nationalistic feelings. Centralization of worship could help produce unity. In the fuller account in Chronicles (2 Chr 29:1–31:21) Hezekiah appealed to Israelites in the former kingdom of Israel to celebrate PASSOVER in Jerusalem, even arranging for the Passover to be celebrated in the second month as was the custom in Israel (for a full discussion of the political factors in the reform, see Hayes and Miller 1977, 442–44). In 18:7-8 Hezekiah's rebellion against Assyria and his campaign in Philistia are noted with obvious approval.

It suited the historian's theological purpose to have the fall of Samaria occur during Hezekiah's reign (18:9-12), even though he preserves the tradition that his reign actually began in 715 (18:13). It may simply have been his purpose to contrast the hapless Hoshea's failure to preserve Samaria with Hezekiah's success in preserving Jerusalem from destruction.

A brief, but incomplete, summary of Hezekiah's revolt and the Assyrian campaigns of 701 is provided in 18:13-16. Soon after the successful Assyrian campaigns against Philistia during the ASHDOD rebellion (714–711), Hezekiah successfully campaigned against the weakened Philistine cities. Padi, king of Ekron, was delivered to Hezekiah (see Pritchard 1955, 287). When SENNACHERIB became king of Assyria in 705, he had to devote himself to military campaigns close to home. But in 701 he began a comprehensive campaign against Phoenicia, Philistia, and Judea. Sennacherib's account of his actions against Hezekiah (Pritchard 1955, 287–88) generally agree with 2 Kgs 18:13-16. Hezekiah had to pay tribute, but the city of Jerusalem was not surrendered, nor does Sennacherib claim to have taken it.

Second Kings 18:17–19:37 appear to contain two parallel accounts of the Jerusalem siege (18:17–19:9a, 36-37; 19:9b-35), each having the same format but with different particulars and different endings. Some have thought that these parallel sections describe a later situation, perhaps ca. 690, because Tirhakah (19:9a) became king in Egypt at that time (see Bright 1981, 298–309). However, recent research has indicated that prince Tirhakah was old enough to be a military leader in 701 (Hayes and Miller 1977, 450). Thus, it may be that the parallel accounts provide in their own ways the larger story of the siege of Jerusalem in 701.

The first account in 18:17–19:9a, 36-37 includes the Rabshakeh's devastating speech, delivered in Hebrew, to the city's leaders. Hezekiah went into mourning and consulted ISAIAH, who predicted Assyrian failure. At the word of the approach of Tirhakah and the Egyptian army, Sennacherib returned to Assyria and Jerusalem was spared. The second account in 19:9b-35 gives a briefer account of the Rabshakeh's speech, includes Hezekiah's prayer, Isaiah's taunt song against Assyria, and concludes with the account of the decimation of the Assyrian army by the angel of the LORD. Parallel but differing accounts of the same event are not uncommon in the Bible. The historian apparently included both accounts, respecting his sources, in order to present a fuller picture (cf. Long 1991, 201).

In the context of the events of 705–701, Hezekiah fell ill and was told by Isaiah that he would not recover. However, Hezekiah, the Deuteronomistic Historian's paragon of virtue, prayed to the LORD and the prophetic word was reversed. Fifteen years were added to his life. It is important to note the conjunction of Hezekiah's healing and the promise of the deliverance of Jerusalem from the Assyrian attack. Whereas Ahaz had refused to ask a sign from the LORD (Isa 7:12), Hezekiah's faith in the LORD prompted him to initiate the request for a confirming sign.

Second Kings 20:12-19 give an account of MERODACH-BALADAN's embassy to Jerusalem in 703. In that year the Babylonian ruler had temporarily regained his throne while Assyria was occupied elsewhere. He sought to enlist Hezekiah in his struggle against Assyria. Hezekiah showed his openness to the suggestion by showing the envoys all his treasures that could be contributed to the revolt effort. Isaiah was horrified by this breach of security and by Hezekiah's willingness to depend on foreign alliances for protection. The prophetic pronouncement in 20:16-18 is a chilling forecast of future reality.

The mention of the new water system built by Hezekiah in Jerusalem in preparation for the expected Assyrian attack receives confirmation in the SILOAM INSCRIPTION (see Pritchard 1955, 321). The inscription describes the circumstances of the digging of the tunnel to reroute the water from the GIHON Spring to the collecting pool of Siloam on the southern point of the hill of Ophel.

21:1-26. Manasseh and Amon. For the Deuteronomistic History historian the long reign of MANASSEH was a period of unparalleled disaster for Judah. The historian's concerns are with Manasseh's religious and social failures. There is silence about the political and international factors that must have played a role in Manasseh's policies. Manasseh revoked the reforms of Hezekiah, rebuilt the high places, thus decentralizing the cult, integrated foreign worship into the Jerusalem cult, sacrificed his son, and practiced divination (vv. 3-7). The reference to the shedding of *innocent blood* in v. 16 may apply either to child sacrifice or to judicial murder (execution of people for crimes not punishable by death).

The account of Manasseh's reign in 2 Chr 33 differs markedly from the Deuteronomistic Historian's view. According to 2 Chr 33, after Manasseh's apostasy he was taken by the Assyrians to Babylon where he prayed and repented (2 Chr 33:12-13; see the much later Prayer of Manasseh in the Apocrypha. After he returned to Jerusalem he revoked his apostate actions, with the exception of leaving the high places in place (2 Chr 33:14-17; for a positive view of Manasseh's reign, see Ahlström 1993, 730–39).

Conversely, the Deuteronomistic Historian was single-minded in his condemnation of Manasseh. In vv. 10-14 he reported the messages of anonymous prophets who announced that the fall of Judah was inevitable because of Manasseh. The fate of Samaria would be the fate of Judah. Exile awaited.

Manasseh's son Amon ruled only two years and is judged to have followed his father's policies (v. 21). He was assassinated by members of the court for reasons not clear (v. 23; for the possibilities, see Hayes and Miller 1977, 456). Whatever plans the murderers had in mind, they were negated by the decisive action of *the people of the land* (v. 24), who installed JOSIAH, another descendant of David, on the throne. The exact identity and function of "the people of the land" is disputed. Some view them as a powerful aristocratic group interested in stability for business reasons. Others view them as the mass of the simple people, abused and downtrodden, who rose up in time of crisis to make their will known (for the views and literature, see Hayes and Miller 1977, 456–58).

22:1-23:30. The reign of Josiah. The years of Josiah's reign (640–609) were years of promise. Assyria, pressed on all sides, was in rapid decline. Egypt was stirring, but its power to intervene effectively in international affairs was not yet demonstrated. Judah had some peaceful years, and Josiah made the most of them.

Like Hezekiah, Josiah formulated an integrated religious and political program to restore the glory of David's kingdom in Palestine.

The Deuteronomistic Historian's account of Josiah's reign focuses on just one year, 621. The only other year mentioned was 609, the year of Josiah's death at Megiddo (23:29-30). In 621, while the temple was being renovated (cf. 2 Kgs 12:8-16), a book of the law was discovered (23:8). When it was read to Josiah, he reacted with consternation because the provisions of the lawbook were not in force and had not been followed by his ancestors. When the prophet HULDAH was consulted, she predicted that because the stipulations of the lawbook had been ignored for so long, Jerusalem was doomed (22:15-20; cf. 21:12-15). Yet because Josiah's heart was right, Huldah predicted that he would not have to see the calamity the LORD would bring against the kingdom (22:20).

Nevertheless, Josiah prepared to place in force the provisions of the lawbook relating to cultic matters. He assembled the people and all levels of leadership and made a formal covenant to institute the laws (23:1-3).

The account of Josiah's cultic reform is found in 23:4-24. The historian emphasized the relationship of the book of the law found in the temple to Josiah's reform (in contrast to the Chronicler, who dated the beginning of Josiah's reform to 628, thereby making the book of the law unrelated to the reform).

The lawbook was Deuteronomy or some earlier version of it, because Josiah's reform actions followed closely the distinctive concerns of that book. It is not necessary to view the book as having been written in Josiah's time. Centralization of the cult was first advocated by Hezekiah. Other Judean kings had put down foreign cults and heterodox indigenous cults. But Josiah's reform movement was the perfect realization of Deuteronomy's cultic program. (For the identification of the lawbook with Deuteronomy and literature on the topic, see Hayes and Miller 1977, 461–463.)

Josiah's purpose was to restore a pure Yahwism according to the Deuteronomic model, with all worship centered at Jerusalem. Every vestige of Canaanite cult practices had to be eliminated, including deposing the idolatrous priests at the high places and removal of the cult prostitutes. The priests who served Yahweh at the high places were brought to Jerusalem for supervision. Even the observance of Passover was restricted to Jerusalem in accordance with Deut 16:1-8. However, Josiah's religious program was of a piece with his political aspirations. Because of Assyrian weakness, he moved to reassert the leadership of the house of David over the former kingdom of Israel, first by desecrating the altar at BETHEL built by JEROBOAM I, and then by moving into Philistine territory, and later by opposing Pharaoh Neco (NECHO) at MEGIDDO.

Josiah received the Deuteronomistic Historian's highest praise. He was without peer in all Judean history (23:25).

Second Kgs 23:26-27 are an addition from the last editors of the Deuteronomistic History. Events proved that even the pious reign of Josiah could not avert
disaster.

23:31–24:7. Jehoahaz and Jehoiakim. The remaining years of the kingdom of
Judah were chaotic, with a succession of rulers who were helpless in the face of the
superior forces of Egypt and Babylon. The *people of the land* (cf. the discussion at
21:1-26, above) had chosen JEHOAHAZ to succeed his illustrious father Josiah
(23:30), even though (or because?) he did not follow Josiah's policies. Pharaoh
Neco deposed him because he was the popular choice, in favor of another of
Josiah's sons, JEHOIAKIM. Jehoiakim laid heavy taxes on *the people of the land* in
order to pay tribute to Egypt (23:35).

As a result of the impressive victory of Nebuchadnezzar (also spelled "Neba-
chadnezzar") of Babylon over the Egyptians in 605 at CARCHEMISH, Syria-Palestine
now lay under Babylonian suzerainty. Accordingly, Jehoiakim became Nebuchadnezzar's vassal in 604. In 601 Babylon and Egypt fought a bloody, indecisive battle
on the Egyptian border, and Nebuchadnezzar had to return to Babylon to refit his
army. Jehoiakim seized the chance to throw off the Babylonian yoke. But bands of
area soldiers, loyal to Babylon, attacked Judah and frustrated Jehoiakim's plans.
Jehoiakim died a failure.

24:8–25:7. Jehoiachin and Zedekiah. JEHOIACHIN succeeded his father Jehoiakim, but he ruled only three months. In 598 Nebuchadnezzar focused attention on
rebellious Jerusalem. On March 16, 597, Jerusalem surrendered. Jehoiachin was
deported to Babylon, and another son of Josiah, ZEDEKIAH, was appointed by the
Babylonians as king in Jerusalem. The city, though not destroyed, was despoiled.
The royal family was deported along with government officials and craftsmen.

Jerusalem under Zedekiah was a hotbed of party strife. There were a pro-
Egyptian party, a nationalistic independence party, a pro-Babylonian party, and probably more. Zedekiah finally declared his independence from Babylon. The Babylonian army returned, and in 587/6 destroyed Jerusalem. Zedekiah tried to escape,
but he was caught, his sons were executed before his eyes, and then he was blinded
and taken to Babylon.

25:8-21. Details of the destruction of Jerusalem. These verses detail the destruction of Jerusalem and the profanation of the temple. The walls of the city were
destroyed, a customary practice to halt future rebellion. Larger numbers of people
were exiled to Babylon after key officials had been executed at RIBLAH in Aram
where Nebuchadnezzar was stationed.

25:22-26. Gedaliah the governor. GEDALIAH was a member of the famous house
of Shaphan. For three generations this house had produced distinguished leaders for
the government of Judah. Gedaliah himself had served with the title "Over the
House" (chamberlain) in a previous administration (cf. Jer 40:5). His administrative
expertise and the friendship of the family of Shaphan for the prophet Jeremiah made
Gedaliah acceptable to the Babylonians for the post of governor. His policy was to

inspire political peace so that the remaining population could recover. But several Judean miliary officers who had escaped the Babylonians killed Gedaliah (v. 25), resulting in a further deportation of Judeans in 582. Much of the population fled to Egypt, taking Jeremiah with them (cf. Jer 40–44 for a fuller account of these events).

25:27-30. Release of Jehoiachin. The Deuteronomistic Historian's work concludes with a modest note of hope. In 560 the Babylonians released Jehoiachin from prison, but they did not allow him to return to Judah. However, a son of David still lived, and who knew what the future might hold? Clay tablets mentioning the ration allotments for Jehoiachin, along with that of captives from Phoenicia, Egypt, and Greece, have been recovered (Pritchard 1955, 308).

Works Cited

Ahlström, Gösta. 1993. *The History of Ancient Palestine from the Palaeolithic Period to Alexander's Conquest.* JSOTsup 146.
Bailey, Lloyd R. 1990a. "Golden Calf," MDB. 1990b. "Jeroboam I," MDB.
Baly, Denis. 1976. *God and History in the Old Testament.*
Bright, John. 1981. *A History of Israel.* Third ed.
Cross, F. M. 1973. *Canaanite Myth and Hebrew Epic.*
De Vries, Lamoine. 1990. "Ship," MDB.
Gregory, Russell I. 1990. "Joab," MDB.
Hayes, John H., and J. Maxwell Miller, eds. 1977. *Israelite and Judean History.*
Kallai, Zechariah. 1986. *Historical Geography of the Bible.*
Lemaire, André. 1986. "Vers L'histoire de la Rédaction des Livres des Rois," ZAW 98:221–36.
Long, B. O. 1991. *2 Kings.* FOTL.
Miller, J. Maxwell. 1990. "Gihon," MDB.
Noth, Martin. 1981. *The Deuteronomistic History.* JSOTsup 15.
Pritchard, J. B. 1955. *Ancient Near Eastern Texts* (ANET). Second ed.
Smend, R. 1971. "Das Gesetz und die Völker," in *Probleme biblischer Theologie*, ed. H. W. Wolff.
Van Beek, Gus W. 1962a. "Ophir," IDB. 1962b. "Sabeans," IDB.
Walsh, Jerome T., and Christopher T. Begg. 1990. "1–2 Kings," NJBC.
Wiles, John Keating. 1990. "Sheba, Queen of." MDB.

First and Second Chronicles

Claude F. Mariotinni [MCB 323-72]

Introduction

The Books of 1–2 Chronicles were originally one book in the Hebrew Bible. The division of Chronicles into two books was made by the translators of the LXX in the second century BCE. The Hebrew title of the book is *dibrê hayyāmîm*, an expression meaning "the events of the days." In the LXX the book is called *Paraleipomena*, "things omitted." This title was interpreted to mean that Chronicles includes supplemental material omitted by the other historical books, mainly Samuel and Kings. The English title "Chronicles" goes back to the Vulgate; Jerome called the book "a chronicle of the whole divine history."

Position in the Canon

In the Hebrew Bible Chronicles belongs to the third division of the Hebrew CANON called the *Kethubim* or the Writings. This division is also called *Hagiographa* or Holy Writings. Chronicles is the last book in the Hebrew Bible, appearing after Ezra–Nehemiah which are also considered to be one book. In English Bibles, Chronicles is part of the historical books of the OT; it appears after 1–2 Kings and before Ezra and Nehemiah.

Content

The Books of 1–2 Chronicles may be divided into five sections.

1. First Chronicles 1–9 introduces the history of ISRAEL from ADAM to SAUL. This history is presented in the form of lists and genealogies. Some of the genealogies, however, mention the names of people who lived many years after DAVID, even the names of people living in postexilic JUDAH.

2. First Chronicles 10–29 presents the history of David's kingdom, including the preparation he made for the building of the Temple and the organization of the Levites.

3. Second Chronicles 1–9 focuses on the history of SOLOMON's kingdom. The central point of the history of Solomon's reign is the building of the Temple.

4. Second Chronicles 10:1–36:21 centers on the history of the kingdom of Judah. The history of the kings of the Northern Kingdom is largely ignored by the author of Chronicles.

5. Second Chronicles 36:22-23 is an appendix that introduces the opening section of CYRUS's decree providing for the rebuilding of the Temple in Jerusalem (see Ezra 1:1-3).

Authorship

Until recently most commentators affirmed that Chronicles and Ezra–Nehemiah formed a single work known as the Chronicler's History (Noth 1987). Several reasons were given to affirm this view: (a) The decree of Cyrus at the end of 2 Chronicles (36:22-23) appears at the beginning of Ezra (1:1-3). According to this view, the history presented in Ezra begins where 2 Chronicles ended. (b) Both Chronicles and Ezra–Nehemiah emphasize the Temple, the cult, and the work of the Levites and priests. (c) The use of genealogies and statistical records in Chronicles and Ezra– Nehemiah. (d) The similar language and common vocabulary present in Chronicles and Ezra–Nehemiah.

This view for the unity of Chronicles and Ezra– Nehemiah has been challenged recently by several authors. Japhet (1968, 330–71), although acknowledging the similarity of language, has emphasized the linguistic differences between Chronicles and Ezra–Nehemiah. A similar suggestion was made by Williamson (1982, 7). He said that an analysis of the language and style of Chronicles and Ezra–Nehemiah indicates "differences of usage between the two bodies of writing." Braun (1979, 63) has demonstrated that the emphasis on retribution and on the Davidic monarchy present in Chronicles are absent in Ezra–Nehemiah. This commentary assumes that Chronicles is a work separate from Ezra–Nehemiah. The author is unknown and will be identified as "the Chronicler." For convenience the term CHR will be used throughout the commentary to indicate the final redactor of the book. "Chronicles" will be used to refer to the two books as a unit. To refer to specific biblical passages, the abbreviations 1 Chr and 2 Chr will be used.

Date

It is difficult to determine a precise date for the composition of Chronicles. However, there are indications in Chronicles that point to the end of the fifth century or the beginning of the fourth century BCE. In 1 Chr 3:19-24 the genealogy of David is extended to the sixth generation after ZERUBBABEL. Since Zerubbabel can be dated to 520 BCE (cf. Hag 1:1), the sixth generation must be dated after 400 BCE. Hence, the final composition of the book should be dated between 400 and 350 BCE.

Theology

When the CHR wrote his theological interpretation of the history of Israel, the nation had no king. The people of Israel were trying to reestablish their identity and their religious life following the return from EXILE. The purpose of Chronicles is to provide a positive view of the past and a hope for the future. A central theme that emphasizes the CHR's message is the centrality of the Temple and worship in the life of the nation. Since the Temple was at the center of the life of the postexilic community, worship served to provide continuity with the traditions of the past and a sense of identity for those who had returned from exile.

Another theme developed by the CHR is the centrality of the Davidic monarchy. David served as the model of leadership for the new Israel. In his attempt to idealize David, the CHR omits from the story of David many events that tend to tarnish David's image. He omits the story of David's adultery with BATHSHEBA, his order to JOAB to have URIAH killed, and NATHAN's rebuke of David (2 Sam 11–12). He omits the narrative detailing ABSALOM's revolt against David (2 Sam 13–19), the rebellion of the Northern tribes under the leadership of Sheba (2 Sam 20), David's willingness to sacrifice part of Saul's family at the request of the Gibeonites (2 Sam 21:1-14), and several others. The emphasis of the CHR is David's preparation for the building of the Temple. Yahweh had chosen David and his house to lead Israel, to bless the people, and to build the Temple. David acquired the temple site, organized the temple service, and made preparations for the building of the Temple. SOLOMON also receives unconditional approval of the CHR. Solomon was designated by Yahweh to build the Temple (1 Chr 28:10; 29:1).

Another theme in Chronicles is the doctrine of RETRIBUTION. The CHR believed that the hope of Israel was dependent upon the obedience of the leaders and the people to Yahweh. The CHR correlates blessing with obedience and punishment with disobedience. When the king and the people obey the laws of Yahweh, Yahweh will bless them (1 Chr 28:8). When a leader is unfaithful he will be punished (1 Chr 10:13-14).

For Further Study

In the *Mercer Dictionary of the Bible*: CHRONICLES, FIRST AND SECOND; CHRONOLO-GY; DEUTERONOMIST/DEUTERONOMISTIC HISTORIAN.

In other sources: P. R. Ackroyd, *I and II Chronicles, Ezra, Nehemiah*, TBC; R. Braun, *1 Chronicles*, WBC; E. L. Curtis and A. A. Madsen, *A Critical and Exegetical Commentary on the Books of Chronicles*, ICC; S. J. De Vries, *1 and 2 Chronicles*, FOTL; R. B. Dillard, *2 Chronicles*, WBC; S. Japhet, *I and II Chronicles*, OTL; R. W. Klein, "Chronicles, Book of 1–2," AncBD; J. M. Myers, *I Chronicles* and *II Chronicles*, AncB; H. G. M. Williamson, *1 and 2 Chronicles*, NCB.

Commentary

An Outline

First Chronicles

Genealogies, 1:1–9:44

The purpose of the genealogies in 1 Chr 1–9 is to trace the history of the people ISRAEL from its beginning with ADAM and to serve as an introduction to the work of the CHR. The authenticity of this section has been questioned by several scholars. Noth (1987), for instance, credits only a small portion of these genealogies to the CHR. Although it is clear that several additions by different hands were included into these genealogies, the final composition is the work of the CHR.

Genealogy of the Patriarchs, 1:1-54

The patriarchal genealogies are divided into two sections, each separated by the events of the FLOOD. The first section (vv. 1-23) introduces the genealogies of the ten patriarchs who lived before the flood. The second section (vv. 24-54) introduces the genealogy of ten patriarchs who lived after the flood. The list includes the genealogies of ISHMAEL (vv. 28-31) the children of ABRAHAM by *Keturah* (vv. 32-33), and the children of ESAU (vv. 34-54). The sources of these genealogies are found in Gen 5, Num 26, and Exod 6.

1:1-4. Genealogy of Adam. The genealogy of *Adam* introduces the ten patriarchs who lived before the flood. The list also includes the sons of NOAH.

1:5-27. Genealogy of the sons of Noah. The genealogy of the sons of Noah is introduced in the reverse order from that generally found in the biblical material (see v. 4). The genealogy of JAPHETH (vv. 5-7) is given first, followed by the genealogy of *Ham* (vv. 8-16), and followed by the genealogy of SHEM (vv. 17-27). The genealogy of Shem includes the names of ten patriarchs, from the period immediately after the flood until the time of *Abraham* (vv. 24-27).

1:28-34. Genealogy of Abraham. After a brief introduction of the sons of Noah, the writer introduces the family of *Abraham*, deviating from the sources in Genesis and bypassing the genealogies of HARAN and NAHOR (Gen 11:27-29). The genealogies of the sons of Abraham are arranged according to the names of their mothers. The CHR begins with the descendants of *Ishmael*, the son of HAGAR (vv. 29-31), the Egyptian slave given as a wife to Abraham by SARAH. Then there follow the names of the sons of *Keturah* (vv. 32-33), the wife Abraham took after the death of Sarah, and then the names of Sarah's descendants (v. 34).

1:35-54. Genealogy of Esau. The genealogy of *Esau* is divided into three sections: the descendants of Esau (vv. 35-42), the *kings . . . of Edom* (vv. 43-50) and *the clans of Edom* (vv. 51-54). The five sons of Esau are introduced in v. 35; however, only the descendants of *the sons of Eliphaz* (v. 36) and of *the sons of Reuel* (v. 37) are given. *Seir* (v. 38) was the name of a mountain in Edom, south of the DEAD SEA. According to Deut 2:12, 22, the Horites were the original inhabitants of the area but they were displaced by the sons of Esau. The descendants of Seir (Gen 36:20-30) were assimilated by sons of Esau (Gen 36:8). The list of the Edomite kings (vv. 43-54) predates the establishment of kingship in Israel.

Genealogy of Judah, 2:1-55

2:1-2. The sons of Israel. After introducing the Ishmaelites and the Edomites, the writer abandons them in order to concentrate on *the sons of Israel* (Jacob). The order of the twelve sons of Israel follows the list found in Gen 35:23-26 and Exod 1:1-4 with one difference. In 1 Chronicles Dan has been moved from the ninth position to the seventh (2:2), perhaps to emphasize that Dan was adopted by RACHEL before the birth of JOSEPH and BENJAMIN. The grouping of sons into twelve follows a biblical pattern: the twelve sons of Ishmael (1:29), the twelve rulers of Edom (1:51-54), and the twelve sons of Nahor (Gen 22:20-24). The sons of Israel are enumerated according to their mothers: the sons of LEAH included REUBEN, SIMEON, LEVI, JUDAH, ISSACHAR, and ZEBULUN; the sons of Rachel include Dan (adopted before the births of Joseph and Benjamin), Joseph, and Benjamin; the sons of Bilhah include Dan and NAPHTALI; and the sons of Zilpah include GAD and ASHER.

2:3-4. The sons of Judah. Since the CHR desires to emphasize the theocratic role of David's dynasty in the life of Israel, he begins the genealogies of the sons of Jacob with the genealogy of Judah. The preeminence of the tribe of Judah in the genealogy of Jacob differs from the sources from which the information was taken (Gen 46:8-25; Num 26:5). The reference to the three sons of Judah born of a Canaanite woman may indicate the Canaanite background of the clans of Judah and the marginal relationship Judah had with the other tribes of Israel at the beginning of the confederacy (Deut 33:7). The name of Yahweh (*the LORD*) appears here for the first time in Chronicles. Yahweh appears as the one exacting vengeance for the wickedness of *Er*.

2:5-8. Genealogy of Perez and Zerah. The author accentuates the genealogy of *Perez* because he was one of the forefathers of David (Ruth 4:18). The list of *the sons of Zerah* is original to the CHR. *Achar's* name appears as Achan in Josh 7.

2:9-41. Genealogy of Hezron. *Hezron* was the father of three sons: *Jerahmeel, Ram, and Chelubai* (v. 9). Chelubai appears as CALEB in 2:18. The genealogy of *Ram* (vv. 10-17) is presented first because he was a forefather of David. David is mentioned as being the seventh son of Jesse (v. 15, although in 2 Sam 16:10 he is listed as the eighth). The names of David's sisters do not appear in 1 Samuel. Among the sons of *Caleb* (vv. 18-24) is *Hur*, whose grandson *Bezalel* (v. 20) was selected to build the TABERNACLE in the days of Moses (Exod 31:2; 35:30). This reference to Bezalel serves to associate the tribe of Judah with the building of the tabernacle and its involvement in the cultic life of Israel. Caleb, the son of Hezron, should not be associated with Caleb, the son of Jephunneh, the Kenizzite. Caleb the Kenizzite was a member of a foreign clan that was incorporated into the tribe of Judah (4:15). The descendants of *Jerahmeel* (vv. 25-33) lived in the NEGEB, south of Beer-sheba (1 Sam 27:10). The Jerahmeelites probably were a non-Israelite tribe that was assimilated into the tribe of Judah. The CHR is the only one who identifies the Jerahmeelites as a clan of Judah. The second genealogy of *Caleb* (vv. 42-50a) is an addition to Caleb's genealogy listed above. The descendants of Caleb through *Hur* (vv. 50b-55) became the founders of several well-known Judean cities.

Genealogy of David, 3:1-24

3:1-9. The sons of David. The genealogy of DAVID is divided into two sections. The first section (3:1-4a), which also appears in 2 Sam 3:1-5, gives the names of the six sons of David born while he was reigning over JUDAH in HEBRON. *Daniel*, the son of ABIGAIL (v. 3) appears as Chileab in 2 Sam 3:3. According to 1 Chr 29:27 and 1 Kgs 2:11, the reign of David in Hebron was only seven years. The second section (3:4b-9) gives the names of the thirteen sons born after David moved to JERUSALEM, four of them by *Bath-shua*, the daughter of *Ammiel. Bath-shua* is a variation of the name BATHSHEBA. This list appears also in 2 Sam 5:13-16 and 1 Chr 14:3-7. This list of David's sons born in Jerusalem differs from the parallel passage in Samuel. *Eliphelet* (v. 6) and *Nogah* (v. 7) do not appear in Samuel. The repetition of the names *Elishama* (vv. 6, 8) and *Eliphelet* (vv. 6, 8) may indicate that the CHR used more than one list and that the present text is a conflation of duplicate lists. See the commentary on 8:29-40 and 14:3-7 for additional material on the sons of David.

3:10-16. The kings of Judah. The list names all the kings of Judah who reigned after David. Athaliah's name is not included because she was an usurper. *Azariah* (v. 12) appears in 2 Kgs 15:13 and 2 Chr 26:1 as UZZIAH. *Johanan*, the first son of *Josiah* (v. 15) does not appear in 2 Kings. It is possible that he died young. *Shallum* appears in 2 Kings as JEHOAHAZ (see Jer 22:11). Verse 15 mentions one *Zedekiah* as Josiah's son and v. 16 mentions a *Zedekiah* as Jehoiachin's son. Which

Zedekiah became king of Judah is not clear. Second Kings 24:17 declares that the Zedekiah who became king was Jehoiakim's uncle while 2 Chr 36:10 declares that Zedekiah was his brother. However, 1 Chr 3:16 says that the successor of Jehoiachin (or *Jeconiah*) was *Zedekiah his son*. Since no son named Zedekiah appears in the list of Jehoiachin's descendants in 3:17-18, it seems clear that Josiah's son was the last king of Judah.

3:17-24. David's descendants after the Exile. This list introduces the royal line after the EXILE, covering eight generations of Davidides until approximately 400 BCE. *Shenazzar* has been identified with the Sheshbazzar who brought the first group of refugees from Babylon (Ezra 1:8, 11). *Zerubbabel* is presented as the son of *Pedaiah*; however, in Ezra 3:2, 8 and Neh 12:1 he is said to be the son of Shealtiel. Some have explained this discrepancy by saying that because Shealtiel had died childless, Pedaiah, by the laws of Levirate marriage, took the widow of his brother and Zerubbabel was born out of this second marriage.

Genealogy of the Tribe of Judah, 4:1-23

Chapters 4–9 present a list of the various clans and tribes of Israel, distributed according to their geographical areas in relation to JUDAH. Chapter 4 lists the southern tribes, Judah and SIMEON. Chapter 5 the Transjordanian tribes of REUBEN, GAD, and the half tribe of MANASSEH. Chapter 6 lists the tribe of LEVI; chap. 7 presents the northern tribes of ISSACHAR, BENJAMIN, NAPHTALI, the other half of the tribe of Manasseh, EPHRAIM, and ASHER. Chapter 8 lists a second genealogy of Benjamin and chap. 9 lists the inhabitants of JERUSALEM.

In the list of the descendants of *Judah* (v. 1), only *Perez* is Judah's son. *Hezron* was the son of *Perez* (2:5). Since *Hur* was the son of *Caleb* (2:19) and *Shobal* was the son of *Hur* (2:50), scholars have proposed that *Carmi* should be corrected to "Caleb, son of Hezron." Verses 5-8 continue the list begun in 2:24. Jabez's name (v. 9) is a play on a Hebrew word that means pain. His name is a reference to the pains of childbirth suffered by his mother when the child was born. Since popular ideas related the name of a person with the person's future, Jabez cries to God asking to be delivered from future evil (v. 10). OTHNIEL, the son of *Kenaz* (v. 13), was the judge who participated in the conquest of the land (Judg 1:12; 3:9, 11). *Seraiah* is unknown, but his son *Joab* was *the father of Ge-harashim*. The word *father* in v. 14 means either "the founder of" or "the leader of" Ge-harashim. The word means "Valley of the Smiths" or "Valley of the Craftsmen" (Neh 11:35).

Genealogy of the Tribe of Simeon, 4:24-43

From the earliest days of the confederation the tribe of Simeon was associated with and eventually was assimilated by Judah (cf. Josh 19:9). The list mentions five generations of the descendants of Simeon (vv. 24-27) and the towns and villages where his clans lived (vv. 28-33). It also mentions two migrations of the tribe. The first migration in the days of *Hezekiah* (vv. 34-41) displaced the Hamites and the Meunites who lived at *Gedor* (v. 39). The LXX says that the Simeonites invaded

GERAR, a place located south of CANAAN (Gen 20:1). The other migration, at an unknown time, displaced the Amalekites who lived in the hill country of Seir. The statement in v. 31b may indicate that Simeon ceased to exist as an independent tribe during the reign of David. This may explain why the tribe of Simeon is not listed in the blessing of Moses in Deut 33.

Genealogies of the Transjordanian Tribes, 5:1-26

5:1-10. Reuben. REUBEN lost the right of the firstborn because he defiled the bed of his father by having sexual relations with Bilhah, Jacob's concubine (Gen 35:22; 49:4). The right of the firstborn, a double portion of the father's inheritance, was passed to JOSEPH, who received two portions of the promised land through his sons EPHRAIM and MANASSEH. Although the CHR recognizes Joseph's right of firstborn, he ascribes high honor to Judah because from him came an important Israelite leader. This statement demonstrates the writer's messianic faith in the Davidic dynasty. *Tilgath-pilneser* (vv. 6, 26) is a variant of TIGLATH-PILESER, the Assyrian king who took part of the population of the Northern Kingdom, including several Reubenite clans, into exile (2 Kgs 15:29).

5:11-17. Gad. The CHR begins the genealogy of the tribe of GAD by providing geographical information describing the places where they were settled. Detailed information about the land occupied by the tribe of Gad is found in Josh 13:24-28. Gilead is south of *Bashan*, the land north of the Jabbok River. The genealogy of Gad differs from the list found in Gen 46:16 and Num 26:15-17. The text is not clear concerning the relationship among the descendants of Gad. It seems that the genealogical list of Gad contains at least two unconnected genealogies, one beginning with *Joel* (vv. 12-13) and the other with *Abihail* (v. 14). It is possible that *Ahi* (v. 15) heads a third list; however, the text is not clear. The LXX does not consider *Shaphat* (v. 12) as a personal name and translates it "scribe," adding the title to *Janai*. Braun (1986, 69) proposes "Janai judged in Bashan." The list was composed in the eighth century, during the reign of JEROBOAM II (ca. 750 BCE). The mention of *Jotham* presupposes a co-regency with his father UZZIAH.

5:18-22. Wars of the Transjordanian tribes. It is not clear from the text whether this war of the eastern tribes against their neighbors is distinct from the one in which Reuben fought alone (v. 10). *The Hagrites* are listed as one of the enemies of Israel (Ps 83:6), although David had Hagrite soldiers in his army (1 Chr 11:38; 27:30). *Jetur* and *Naphish* (v. 19) were descendants of Ishmael (Gen 25:15). According to the CHR, the Transjordanian tribes were valiant warriors; known for their prowess in combat, they were men ready for war. The number of fighting men seems excessive, although the census of Num 1 and Num 26 may indicate that such a large army is a possibility. The immense booty may be an embellishment in order to emphasize the importance of the victory and the magnitude of the divine favor.

5:23-26. The half-tribe of Manasseh. *The half-tribe of Manasseh* settled in the fertile plain in the territory east of the Jordan, north of the YARMUK, between BASHAN and Mount Hermon. Of the three eastern tribes, Manasseh was the farthest north. The location of *Baal-hermon* (cf. Judg 3:3) is unknown. *Senir* is identified with Mount Hermon (Deut 3:9). The names of the sons of Manasseh mentioned here are different from the lists mentioned elsewhere in the OT (Num 26:29; Josh 17:2). The leaders of Manasseh were *mighty warriors* (v. 24). This title was applied to a special social class in Israel. They were owners of land who, at times of war, were called to defend it.

The clans of Manasseh were punished for their unfaithfulness to God. They, along with Gad and Reuben, were taken into exile by the Assyrians (1 Kgs 15:29). *Pul* (v. 26) was the name Tiglath-pileser used when he became King of Babylon. The exile of the Transjordanian tribes occurred as the result of the Assyrian invasion at the time of the Syro-Ephraimite war in 734 BCE (2 Kgs 15:19). The names of the cities to which the eastern tribes were deported are identical to the cities to which Israel was deported at the time of the fall of Samaria in 722 BCE (2 Kgs 17:6; 18:11).

Genealogy of the Tribe of Levi, 6:1-81 [MT 5:27–6:66]

6:1-15 [MT 5:27-41]. High priests. *The sons of Levi* (cf. Exod 6:16-23) were the leaders of the three great Levitical families in Israel. The purpose of this list is to trace the genealogy of the high priest through AARON and Eleazar until the EXILE. The number of high priests who served from Eleazar to the building of the Temple was twelve. Since the construction of the Temple was begun 480 years after the Exodus (1 Kgs 6:1), it is possible the writer was presuming on twelve generations of priests from the Exodus to the Solomonic Temple, each generation averaging forty years. This ideal number may indicate that the list is not complete, since ELI and ABIATHAR, who were priests before the monarchy, are not included. Also missing are JEHOIADA (2 Chr 22:11), the high priest who served during the reign of JOASH, and URIAH (2 Kgs 16:10), the high priest who served during the reign of AHAZ. The priest who served in the Temple of Solomon (v. 10) was *Azariah*, the son of *Ahimaaz* and grandson of *Zadok* (1 Kgs 4:2). *Jehozadak*, the eleventh generation of high priests after the construction of the Temple, was the priest at the time of the Exile of Judah. His son Joshua was the first high priest after the return from Babylon (Hag 1:1). The intent of the CHR is to demonstrate the continuity of the priestly line from ZADOK until his own day.

6:16-30 [MT 6:1-15]. Levites. This list introduces the other sons and grandsons of LEVI. These Levites were not part of the priestly family but performed various tasks in the Temple. This list is derived from Num 3:27-29. *Gershom* (6:16 [MT 6:1]) also appears in the OT with the variant spelling Gershon (Exod 6:16). His line is traced for seven generations (vv. 20-21). *Kohath* was the ancestor of Aaron and the one from whom the line of high priests is traced. His son *Amminadab* (v. 22) does not appear in other lists of Kohathites. For this reason scholars have identified Amminadab with Izhar since he appears in all the genealogical lists of Kohath. Among the descendants of Kohath is *Elkanah* (v. 27), the father of SAMUEL. Some versions, following the LXX, add "and Samuel his son" at the end of v. 27 (see NIV).

Since Elkanah and Samuel were from Ephraim (1 Sam 1:1), some scholars believe that the genealogy of Samuel is an addition to the genealogy of Kohath, added to explain the sacerdotal work of Samuel.

6:31-48 [MT 6:16-38]. Levitical musicians. The CHR, emphasizing the special role of music in the Temple and the role David played in the structure of Temple worship, credits David with the organization of the Levitical singers who ministered in the Temple in the CHR's own day. This organization occurred after the Ark of the Covenant was brought to Jerusalem and placed in the TABERNACLE (v. 31; cf. 1 Chr 15). The list mentions the Levitical singers by families. The Kohathites, represented by *Heman*, were in a central place before the tabernacle. The singers from the family of *Gershom*, represented by *Asaph* were on the right side (v. 39). The sons of *Merari*, represented by *Ethan* were on the left (v. 44). In 1 Chr 16 Asaph was the leader, while Heman and Ethan (called *Jeduthun* in 9:16 and 16:41) were in charge of the music in the Temple. These three men appear in 1 Kgs 4:31 as men renowned for their wisdom. Several psalms were ascribed to them: Pss 50, 73–83 are ascribed to Asaph while Ps 88 is ascribed to Heman and Ps 89 to Ethan. In the title of Ps 77, Jeduthun seems to refer to the name of the tune of the psalm.

6:49-53 [MT 6:34-38]. Aaronic priests. While the Levites were in charge of the music in the Temple and had other duties related to the worship in the Temple, the priests were responsible for offering sacrifices upon the altar and for making atonement for the nation. The CHR again lists the genealogy of the high priests, linking the priesthood of Zadok to Aaron.

6:54-81 [MT 6:39-66]. Settlement of the Levites. The list of the Levitical cities follows, with some modifications, the list of cities mentioned in Josh 21:1-42. *The Kohathites* received thirteen cities, nine in Judah and Simeon and four in Benjamin. The omission of Simeon from the CHR's list may be an indication of the early absorption of that tribe into the tribe of Judah. The CHR only lists eleven cities, omitting Juttah (Josh 21:16) and Gibeon (Josh 21:17). The other Kohathites who were not priests received ten cities in Ephraim, Dan and Manasseh, although the CHR only mentions eight cities and does not include the tribe of Dan. The *Gershonites* received thirteen towns in Issachar, in Asher, in Naphtali, and in Transjordan in the territory of the half-tribe of Manasseh. The *Merarites* received twelve cities in Zebulun, in Reuben, and in Gad (Josh 21:40), although the CHR only mentions the names of ten of the cities. Since the Levites were dispersed among the tribes, these forty-eight cities were allotted to the Levites as their portion of the land, rather than a regular geographical allotment.

Genealogies of the Northern Tribes, 7:1-40

The CHR ends his listing of the genealogies of the tribes of Israel by introducing the tribes of the north. He omits from his list the genealogies of Zebulun (Gen 46:14) and Dan (Gen 46:23).

7:1-5. Issachar. The genealogy of ISSACHAR follows Gen 46:13 and Num 26:23-25 with minor variations in spelling the names. Tola's descendants, each designated as a *mighty warrior*, numbered 22,600. They were numbered in the census taken by David, probably the one mentioned in 2 Sam 24 and 1 Chr 21. *Uzzi*, Tola's first-born, was also the ancestor of several leaders of the clan of Issachar. His descendants numbered 36,000. The total number of fighting men available for war from the tribe of Issachar was 87,000. This number does not represent the total of the two groups. The number may include other families not counted in the genealogy of the sons of Issachar since only the genealogies of the firstborn are provided.

7:6-12. Benjamin. The genealogy of Benjamin in the OT is a vexing problem (Mariottini 1992a). In Gen 46:21 Benjamin is said to have ten sons; Num 26:38-41 lists five; our passage lists three; and 1 Chr 8:1-2 lists five sons. Of the three sons of Benjamin mentioned here, *Bela* appears in all four genealogies, *Becher* appears only in Genesis, and *Jediael* appears only here. The genealogy of Bela appears in three places: in Num 26:39-40 he has two sons, in 1 Chr 7:7 he has five, and in 1 Chr 8:3-4 he has nine sons. None of the five sons mentioned in 1 Chr 7:7 appears in the other genealogies. Verse 12 is truncated. *Shuppim* and *Huppim* are the grandsons of Bela, if Ir is to be identified with *Iri* (v. 7). However, they have been identified with Muppim and Huppim (Gen 46:21) and with Shephupham and Hupham (Num 26:38), two sons of Benjamin. *Shuppim* and *Huppim* also appear in 1 Chr 7:15 as descendants of Manasseh. Shephupham (Shephuphan) appears in 1 Chr 8:4 as a son of Bela. These differences indicate that the CHR might have used different traditions in the reconstruction of the genealogy of Benjamin. It is also possible that vv. 6-13 might include a fragment of the genealogy of Dan since Hushim appears as Dan's son in Gen 46:23.

7:13. Naphtali. This genealogy follows, with minor variations, the genealogies of NAPHTALI found in Gen 46:24 and Num 26:48-49. BILHAH was the mother of Dan and Naphtali.

7:14-19. Manasseh. The list of the descendants of MANASSEH is fragmented and at places corrupt, and thus, difficult to interpret. According to Num 26:29 and Josh 17:1-2, Manasseh was the father of Machir, Machir the father of Gilead, and Gilead the father of Asriel. Apparently, *Asriel* entered in v. 14 by dittography. The reference to an *Aramean concubine* (v. 14) of Manasseh is evidence of the important relationship that existed between Manasseh and the Arameans.

The descendants of *Machir* formed the half-tribe of Manasseh that settled in Transjordan (Num 32:39-40). Most scholars believe that the mention of *Huppim* and *Shuppim* in v. 15 is an addition and should be deleted. They appear in Gen 46:21 as sons of Benjamin. The NIV reinterprets the text to declare that Machir "took a wife from among the Huppites and the Shuppites." The NRSV translation of v. 15 declares that *Zelophehad* was the *second* sister of Machir. But according to Num 26:3 and Josh 17:3 he was the grandson of Gilead and the great-grandson of Machir. The word *second* in v. 15 may indicate that ZELOPHEHAD is being listed as the second son of Machir, or perhaps of Manasseh. The Hebrew text as it stands is corrupt and omits the names of the first son and of the father.

7:20-29. Ephraim. This genealogy traces the line of EPHRAIM, the second son of JOSEPH, to *Joshua*, the son of *Nun* (v. 27). The genealogy differs from the list found in Num 26:35-36. The genealogy is composed of two distinct lists (vv. 20-21, 25-27), each containing the name of ten sons, separated by a narrative detailing the death of *Ezer* and *Elead* at the hands of *the people of Gath*. Gath has been associated with Gittaim (2 Sam 4:3) rather than with the Philistine city of Gath.

The conflict between the Ephraimites and the Canaanites has caused much discussion since, according to the Book of Genesis, Ephraim was born and died in Egypt. It is doubtful that the men of Gath came to Egypt to raid the cattle of the sons of Ephraim. It is possible that some of the Israelites continued to have contact with Canaan while they lived in Egypt. It is more probable, however, that this statement may reflect the fact that some groups in Canaan, who later became associated with the Israelite confederacy, may have never been part of the group living in Egypt (Japhet 1979, 205–18).

7:30-40. Asher. The genealogy of *Asher* is based in part on Gen 46:17 and Num 26:44-46. The CHR introduces the line of *Beriah* through his sons *Heber* and *Malchiel*. The source for this genealogical information is unknown and it appears only here. The number of men enrolled for service in war is 26,000. This number is small in comparison to enrollments in previous censuses and it may reflect the decline of the tribe at a later time in ISRAEL. The mention of Asher's daughter *Serah* in all three lists is unusual and may indicate an important position Serah had among the clans of Asher (Mariottini 1992b).

Genealogy of Benjamin, 8:1-40

8:1-28. Descendants of Benjamin. This is the second genealogy of Benjamin in Chronicles. For some of the problems associated with the four genealogies of Benjamin in the OT, see the commentary at 7:6-12 above. Of the five sons of Benjamin listed here, only *Bela* appears in all four genealogies. *Ashbel* fails to appear in 1 Chr 7:6-12 while *Aharah*, *Nohah* and *Rapha* appear only here. The difficulty in harmonizing the four genealogies is an indication that different lists were used by the CHR. Of the sons of *Bela* (vv. 3-5) listed here, the names differ from the other list found in 1 Chr 7:7. *Gera* and *Naaman* appear as children of Benjamin in Gen 46:21 and *Shephuphan* appears as a son of Benjamin in Num 26:38. *Gera* (v. 3) was probably the father of EHUD (Judg 3:15), one of the judges of Israel. If this is true, then *Abihud* should be translated "the father of Ehud" (v. 3 NRSV mg.). The descendants of Benjamin are grouped by place of residence: *Geba* (v. 6), *Moab* (vv. 8-10), *Ono* and *Lod* (vv. 11-12), *Aijalon* and *Gath* (v. 13), *Jerusalem* (v. 28) and Gibeon (v. 29). JERUSALEM, the most important city of Benjamin (Josh 18:28, but cf. Josh 15:63), became the religious center of the nation. The purpose of the second genealogy of Benjamin is to introduce the genealogy of SAUL, who would become the first king in Israel.

8:29-40. Genealogy of Saul. The genealogy of Saul is introduced by mention of *Jeiel* who *lived in Gibeon*, another important city in Benjamin. The relationship of Jeiel to any of the descendants of Benjamin listed above (8:1-28) is obscure. According to the CHR, *Ner* was *the father of Kish* and Kish the father of *Saul* (v. 33). However, in 1 Sam 14:50-51 Ner appears as Saul's uncle. Some Greek manuscripts add the name of Ner after *Baal* in v. 30 (cf. NIV), which is missing in the Hebrew text (cf. NRSV). The reading in the LXX agrees with 9:36 where Ner appears as the brother of Kish. In 1 Sam 14:51 Kish and Ner are listed as the sons of Abiel.

Baal, the son of *Jeiel*, has the same name as the Canaanite god of fertility. The name of the Canaanite deity also appears in the name of Saul's son, *Esh-baal*, "man of Baal" (8:33; 9:39), although the deuteronomistic writer changed his name to Ishbosheth, "man of shame" (2 Sam 2:8; 4:1) and Ishvi, "man of Yahweh" (1 Sam 14:49). *Merib-baal* ("let Baal contend"), a grandson of Saul and the son of JONATHAN, also appears in the OT as MEPHIBOSHETH (2 Sam 4:4).

Genealogy of the Citizens of Jerusalem, 9:1-34

The source for the information concerning the people who returned from EXILE is Neh 11:3-19. The various groups who returned from exile are divided into four groups: the lay people, the priests, the Levites, and those who served in the Temple.

9:1-9. Political leaders. The first part of v. 1 is a concluding statement to the genealogies of the tribes of Israel in chaps. 2–8. *The Book of the Kings of Israel* (cf. 2 Chr 20:34) should not be identified with the Books of 1–2 Kings. The nature of this source mentioned by the CHR is debatable. It is possible that the CHR had access to official royal archives and census lists in reconstructing the genealogies of the tribes of Israel. The reason for the exile of the people to Babylon was *their unfaithfulness* to Yahweh. To the CHR the unfaithfulness of the people was their worship of idols and their pollution of the house of Yahweh (2 Chr 36:14).

The CHR departs from his source in Nehemiah in order to mention that some people from *Ephraim and Manasseh* also settled *in Jerusalem*. Since only people from Benjamin and Judah are listed, it is possible that the CHR is attempting to declare that the two tribes represent *all Israel* and that *all Israel* (v. 1) returned from exile and settled in Jerusalem. Three clans of Judah and four of Benjamin are listed. The numbers for each tribe, 690 for Judah and 1760 for Benjamin, differ from Neh 11:6 and 11:12-14. However, Nehemiah only lists the number of the descendants of Perez and omits the descendants of Zerah. For this reason the numbers in Chronicles cannot be compared with the numbers in Nehemiah since we do not know how the numbers were calculated. The names of the descendants of Judah and Benjamin listed in Chronicles differ considerably from the names in Nehemiah. Since the source for the two lists is unknown, it is impossible to reconcile the differences.

9:10-13. Priests. The six priestly families mentioned here appear with minor variations in Neh 11:10-14. AZARIAH appears in Nehemiah as Seraiah. Nehemiah's list seems to be more comprehensive since it contains several additional names. The number of priests in Chronicles is 1,760; it differs from Nehemiah's 1,192.

9:14-16. Levites. The list is similar to the list in Neh 11:10-17. The Levites are divided into three groups, each according to one of the three great Levitical groups: *Merari, Asaph,* and *Jeduthun.* Merari's name is omitted in Nehemiah. These Levites *lived in Jerusalem* (v. 34) and in Netophah, a nearby village.

9:17-34. Gatekeepers. The function of the gatekeepers was to protect the Temple from trespassers. There were four gatekeepers with 212 subordinates. Nehemiah 11:19 lists only the names of two gatekeepers, Akkub and Talmon, while Ezra 2:42 lists the names of six gatekeepers who returned from EXILE. The CHR identifies the chief gatekeeper as SHALLUM (v. 17); his name is omitted in Neh 11:19. However, Shallum has been identified with Meshullam, a gatekeeper whose name appears with Talmon and Akkub in Neh 12:15. Shallum was stationed at the entrance of the king's gate, the gate through which the king entered the Temple when he came from his palace (Ezek 46:1-3). The levitical descent of the gatekeepers and their identification as *Korahites* (v. 19) emphasizes their importance in the days of the CHR, but according to the CHR, their service follows a pattern that had existed from the days of the sojourn in the desert. This statement intends to declare that, although the exile created a break in the worship experience of the community, the present organization is a continuation of that which existed in the past. The CHR credits the organization of the gatekeepers to David and Samuel (v. 22). Since Samuel died before David became king and since David did not build the Temple, the statement must reflect the priestly influence of Samuel and the involvement of David in the formation of the worship of Israel at the beginning of the monarchy. The Levitical *leaders lived in Jerusalem* (v. 34) because their service was permanent. The other gatekeepers would serve from time to time since twenty-four gatekeepers (26:17-18) had to serve each day for seven days (v. 25).

In addition to being gatekeepers of the Temple, these Levites also had other duties: they were responsible for the treasury of the Temple, to watch over it at night and to open it in the morning (vv. 26-27), for the articles used in the worship service (28), for furniture and utensils used in the Temple, as well as the materials used for the offerings (v. 29). Some Levites were in charge of the preparation of breads and cakes while others were responsible for the music in the Temple. They were free from other duties and lived in the Temple chambers.

Genealogy of Saul, 9:35-44

The genealogy of SAUL and the narrative about his death (10:1-14) serve as a transition to the history of DAVID. The list is repeated here from 8:29-40 with minor differences. Kish and the first king of Israel were descendants of the Benjaminites who lived in Gibeon. The CHR's purpose is to contrast the story of Saul, the unfaithful king, with the fidelity of David, the king chosen by God.

The Reign of David, 10:1–29:30

The first nine chapters of Chronicles has served as an introduction to the history of ISRAEL. The genealogies of the tribes of Israel have also served as an introduction to the kingship of DAVID, the founder of the Davidic dynasty and the central figure of the CHR's work. The last twenty chapters are dedicated to David and his kingdom. Of these, the first twelve chapters reproduce some events and details already narrated in the Books of Samuel. The last eight chapters are original material, detailing David's organization of the Temple service and the Temple personnel.

The Death of Saul, 10:1-14

The life and death of SAUL was a tragic event in the history of Israel. Saul became king over Israel and JUDAH under difficult circumstances. He lived in the shadow of the old traditions, represented by SAMUEL and those who supported the confederation of the tribes. Saul was also confronted with a new political reality, represented by David and his charismatic movement. By omitting the events related to Saul's kingdom and by beginning the story of David with the death of Saul, the CHR is declaring that the end of Saul's kingdom came as divine judgment and that David's kingship was divinely approved and ordained by Yahweh.

The text here reproduces with few changes 1 Sam 31:1-13. The text declares that the PHILISTINES hung Saul's head in the temple of Dagon but omits the fact that they hung his body on the walls of Beth-shan (1 Sam 31:10). The text also fails to mention that the bodies of Saul and his sons were cremated (1 Sam 31:12), perhaps because it was a custom of non-Israelites. The end of Saul's kingdom is ascribed to his unfaithfulness to Yahweh (v. 14), that is, his disobedience (1 Sam 15:22-23), his visit to the medium of ENDOR (1 Sam 28) and his failure to seek Yahweh. Thus, according to the theology of RETRIBUTION developed by the CHR, the disgrace that befell Saul was a result of his unfaithfulness.

The Rise of David, 11:1–12:40

11:1-3. David, king over all Israel. The story of David's reign begins with the gathering of all Israel to anoint him king in HEBRON. The CHR omits the events related to the struggle between David and Saul, the seven-year reign over Judah in Hebron, and the civil war between the house of Saul and David (2 Sam 2–4). David is portrayed as the king elected by God and acclaimed by all the people as the true king of Israel. For this reason, all other details that are not directly related to the formation of the united theocratic kingdom is of little interest to the CHR.

11:4-9. Conquest of Jerusalem. The conquest of JERUSALEM was important to David in his effort to unite all Israel under his leadership. Jerusalem was a Canaanite enclave located between Judah and Benjamin. From a political perspective, its centrality and its neutral character made the city the ideal place for the capital of the kingdom. David subjugated the Jebusites, the original inhabitants of the city, and kept the original name of Jerusalem and ZION. The name Jerusalem appears in the correspondence of Tel-el AMARNA as *Uru-Shalim*, "Foundation of [the god] Shalem." The name Zion was a Canaanite name designating the southeast hill upon which the city was built. The name *Jebus* is related to the original inhabitants of the city. Although it is doubtful that the city was known by the name

JEBUS, Jebus is used four times in the OT to designate the pre-Israelite name of Jerusalem (Josh 18:28; Judg 19:10). According to the CHR, all Israel took part in the conquest of Jerusalem, rather than the men of David only (2 Sam 5:6). JOAB, who later became commander of David's army, had a significant role in the conquest of the city (see 2 Sam. 5:8), although the details of how it was done are not clear. The term *Millo* (v. 8) probably refers to the terraces that supported buildings and other structures built on the steep ridge of the city.

11:10-47. David's men of valor. This list, taken from 2 Sam 23:8-39 with some variations, introduces the legendary men who served in David's army and who dedicated their lives to the service of the king, thus helping him to establish his kingship in Israel. The enumeration of the men of valor is not clear. The MT reads "thirty" (KJV, NRSV mg.) but some manuscripts of the LXX read *three* (NRSV). Another scribal reading (the *Qere*) reads "officers." The three great warriors (v. 12) were *Jashobeam* (v. 11, but see 2 Sam 23:8), *Eleazar* (v. 12) and Shammah (2 Sam 23:11), whose name does not appear in the text of Chronicles. Whether *Abishai* (vv. 20-21) and *Benaiah* (v. 24) should be classified with the group of three or thirty is not clear from the MT. Apparently, Abishai and Benaiah attained leadership positions among the thirty but were not counted among the three. Another possibility is to count Abishai and Benaiah as leaders of a second group of three warriors who risked their lives to bring water from *Bethelem* to David when he was hiding in *Adullam* (vv. 15-19). The names of the thirty warriors (vv. 26-41) are almost identical to the names in 2 Sam 23. The CHR adds sixteen names to the list after *Uriah the Hittite* (v. 41), beginning with *Zabad son of Ahlai*. This may indicate that the number thirty was not a firm number (the total listed in 2 Sam 23:39 is thirty-seven) or that other names were added to the list as the thirty warriors were killed in battle. The presentation of each warrior generally consists, with some variations, of three elements: his name, the name of his father, and the place of birth. The places of birth include locations in both the north and the south. The list also contains two men from Transjordan: an *Ammonite* (v. 39) and a *Moabite* (v. 49).

12:1-7 [MT 12:1-8]. Warriors from Benjamin. Chapter 12 continues the listing of the names of David's warriors. The purpose of this list is to magnify the popularity of David and to emphasize that David had the support of *all of Israel*. The twenty-three warriors from BENJAMIN came to David while he was at *Ziklag* (v. 1; cf. 1 Sam 27:1-7). David, in his attempt to escape from Saul, sought asylum in Gath with Achish, one of the leaders of the Philistines, who gave him the city of Ziklag (2 Sam 27:6), where David remained for sixteen months (Mariottini 1990b). Two of the Benjaminites who fled to David, *Ahiezer* and *Joash*, were from *Gibeah* (v. 3), the city Saul had established as the capital of his kingdom. With the mention of Saul's kinsmen, the CHR emphasizes that David's popularity had reached even the tribe of Saul. *Ishmaiah* is called a leader over *the thirty* (v. 4; see 11:20-21). This is possible because the leadership of this group of warriors probably changed periodically.

12:8-15 [MT 12:9-16]. Warriors from Gath. Eleven men from GAD joined David at the beginning of his struggles with Saul. They came to David before the arrival of the men from Benjamin, at a time when David had taken refuge in the wilderness (1 Sam 22:1). The Gadites were valiant warriors, not experts in the use of the bow and arrow, but adept in the use of the great shield and the spear. They were quick and fierce warriors (v. 8) who had demonstrated their bravery in battle (v. 15).

12:16-18 [MT 17-19]. Warriors from Benjamin and Judah. When other warriors from Benjamin and Judah came seeking David, he was afraid of betrayal (see 1 Sam 23:7-28). He questioned their intention, and *Amasai*, full of the Spirit (lit. "clothed with the Spirit"), responds to David and reassures him. Amasai's speech (v. 18) reflects the concept of prophetic inspiration. Amasai recognizes that God is with David to help him and to bless those who help David. David received them and made them part of his raiding bands.

12:19-22 [MT 12:20-23]. Warriors from Manasseh. The seven warriors from Manasseh were valiant men and expert in war. They came to David before the battle of Gilboa in which the PHILISTINES defeated the army of Israel (1 Sam 29–30). David had gone to join the Philistines in their battle against Saul, but the Philistines did not allow David to join them in their battle against Israel. When David returned to Ziklag he discovered that the Amalekites had sacked the town. The warriors from Manasseh helped David to recover what the Amalekites had taken. The CHR concludes that many more people came to join David's army, until his army became *like an army of God* (v. 22). This Hebrew expression is a superlative and means "an exceedingly great army," great in number and great in the quality of the people who had joined David in his quest for the throne of Israel.

12:23-40 [MT 24-41]. Other supporters of David. This is a list of the people who came to David at Hebron to express their support and to anoint him king over all Israel. All tribes are represented, including the tribe of Levi. The large number of men armed for battle, can be understood in different ways. Myers (1965, 98), following the proposal of Mendenhall (1958, 52–66), believes that the Hebrew word *'eleph*, translated "thousand" in English versions, means part of a tribe or a military unit. Myers translates 12:25: "The sons of Judah who bore shield and spear numbered six units with eight hundred men with military training." If this interpretation is followed, a more realistic view of the number of men prepared for war emerges. On the other hand, if the numbers are taken literally, then more than 340,000 people joined David at Hebron. As for the names of the leaders, only two are mentioned: *Jehoiada*, the leader of the Levites, may have been the father of Benaiah (2 Sam 8:8; 1 Chr 27:5). *Zadok*, a valiant young warrior, was the one who later took the place of ABIATHAR and became high priest under SOLOMON (1 Kgs 2:35). The gathering of Israel for the anointing of David was a time of great celebration and joy. The people had come to Hebron with the purpose and determination to proclaim David king over Israel. They brought provisions for the feast and contributed to the religious ceremonies that were part of David's coronation.

David's Attempt to Move the Ark, 13:1-14

The Ark of the covenant plays an important role in chaps. 13–16. The ARK had a significant place in Israel's cult because it symbolized God's presence among the people. During the days of Samuel, the PHILISTINES had captured the Ark (1 Sam 4:11) and had brought it to the house of Dagon that was located in ASHDOD (1 Sam 5:1-5). After the Philistines returned the Ark, it was kept in the house of Abinadab in *Kiriath-jearim* (v. 6; cf. 1 Sam 7:1). David's desire to bring the Ark to Jerusalem has both a political and a religious motive. With the presence of the Ark in Jerusalem David could make the city the religious center of the nation and at the same time consolidate the tribes around the ark since Yahweh, the God of Israel, was understood to be *enthroned on the cherubim* of the Ark (v. 6). For this reason David consulted with the leaders of the army and the leaders of all Israel. So, David summoned all Israel from *the Shihor of Egypt to the Lebo-Hamath* (v. 5, lit. "the entrance of Hamath"). Although this description of the extent of the land of Israel appears again in the work of the CHR (2 Chr 7:8), the description is highly idealistic, since it reflects the most extensive limits of the land of Israel. The common way for the CHR to describe the boundaries of the land is *from Beer-sheba to Dan* (1 Chr 21:2, but cf. commentary on 21:1-13, below).

The moving of the Ark was carried out with great celebration and joy before Yahweh by David and all Israel. The celebration included dances, the singing of songs, and the playing of musical instruments (v. 8). The death of *Uzzah* (vv. 9-10) marred the celebration and the enterprise ended in failure. The death of Uzzah can be explained by the fact that among the people of Israel the violation of the holy was forbidden. The people neglected the proper ritual and failed to carry the ark in the proper manner. The name *Perez-uzzah* means "the breaking forth upon Uzzah" (see v. 11). The Ark was brought to the house of *Obed-edom the Gittite*, that is, a man from Gath, where it remained for *three months*. Yahweh blessed Obed-edom and his family because of the presence of the Ark in his house. Yahweh also blessed David as a result of his desire to care for the Ark. These blessings are introduced by means of three events in the life of David narrated in chap. 14. If the Obed-edom who kept the Ark is the same individual mentioned in 1 Chr 15:18, 21, then he was granted Levitical status and became a *gatekeeper for the ark* (1 Chr 15:24; cf. commentary on 26:1-19, below).

David's Establishment in Jerusalem, 14:1–16:43

14:1-2. Embassy from Tyre. Before proceeding with the story of the Ark, the CHR introduces three important events in the life of David, although they have little chronological relationship with the ark narrative. By placing these events between David's first and second attempt to bring the Ark to Jerusalem, the CHR is intimating that the blessings David received were the results of his effort to bring the Ark to Jerusalem. The first event is the occasion when Hiram, king of Tyre, sent materials to David to help him build a palace in Jerusalem. Tyre, a Phoenician seaport city north of Israel, was known for its commercial enterprises (cf. 2 Kgs 10:11, 22). The friendship between Tyre and Israel continued even beyond the days of David. Hiram and Solomon developed many joint commercial ventures that benefitted both kings. The CHR underscores once again that Yahweh had blessed David and had exalted his kingdom for the sake of Israel. The gifts that Hiram brought were a sign of the divine blessing that Yahweh bestowed upon David and that Yahweh had confirmed David's kingship.

14:3-7. David's family. The second event is the introduction of David's sons and daughters born in Jerusalem, although only the names of the sons are given. David's large family was another evidence of Yahweh's blessing. This list is taken from 2 Sam 5:13-16 with some differences. It also agrees with the list of David's sons in 1 Chr 3:5-8, although some names are spelled differently (cf. commentary at 3:1-9 above). The CHR says that thirteen sons were born to David in Jerusalem, while the author of 2 Samuel listed eleven. *Elphelet* and *Nogah* are omitted from the list in 2 Samuel. The name *Beeliada* (v. 6) appears both in 2 Sam 16 and 1 Chr 3:8 as Eliada. Beeliada was the original name of David's son. Since the name was compounded with the name of the Canaanite god Baal, it was changed to Eliada, a name compounded with El, the Hebrew word for God.

14:8-17. Victories over the Philistines. The third event, another demonstration of Yahweh's blessing upon David, is the double victory against the PHILISTINES (vv. 8-12, 13-16). After the Philistines heard that David had become *king over all Israel* and had ceased being their loyal vassal, they attacked Israel. They raided the *valley of Rephaim*, located a few miles southwest of Jerusalem. The manner by which David inquired of Yahweh is not clear. Possibly he used the sacred lots, the URIM AND THUMMIM, as Saul had done (1 Sam 14:36-37, 41-42). Yahweh assured David of victory by promising to burst out against the Philistines *like a bursting flood*. The place of victory was called *Baal-perazim*, "Lord of bursting out" (v. 11; cf. NRSV mg.). The word *perazim* is related to the word *perez* in 13:11 (see also 15:13). At the time of the journey of the ark, Yahweh burst out in judgment against Israel. Now he bursts out for salvation on their behalf against their enemy. The Philistines fled in panic abandoning their gods. According to the CHR, David ordered his people to burn the idols. However 2 Sam 5:21 reads: "David and his men carried them away." The difference between the text in Samuel and the text in Chronicles reflects the CHR's effort to present David as obeying the law of Deut 7:25, which commands the burning of the images of the gods of the people of the land.

After their defeat, the Philistines raided Israel again, and again David inquires of Yahweh. By divine command David prepares an ambush against the Philistines. The sound of marching *in the tops of the balsam trees* (v. 15) refers to the movement of the wind on the leaves. This would be a sign for David and his army that Yahweh would lead them into battle and give them victory. David and his men pursue the Philistines from GIBEON to GEZER. Second Samuel 5:25 says that it was from "Geba to Gezer." This change may reflect the reading of Isa 28:21 and the fact that Gibeon was the place of one of Israel's greatest victories (Josh 10). As a result of David's victory against the Philistines, his fame spread throughout the land, another evidence of God's blessing.

15:1-29. Moving the ark. After presenting the blessings Yahweh had bestowed on David because of his faithfulness, the CHR resumes the narrative detailing the relocation of the ark from the house of Obed-edom (13:14) to Jerusalem. The narrative is based on 2 Sam 6:12-19 with several additions by the CHR. In the CHR's narrative the priests and the Levites predominate. This group, together with the commanders of thousands and the elders of Israel, formed a liturgical procession, marked by music, sacrifices, and great celebration.

David prepared a tent to house the Ark, probably fashioned after the tabernacle of Moses, which remained in Gibeon. If David's building of houses for himself in Jerusalem (v. 1) is to be taken literally, then more than three months had passed since the Ark was left in the house of Obed-edom (13:14). Because the first attempt to move the Ark was done improperly (v. 13), David summoned the priests and the Levites and put them in charge of the relocation of the Ark. David commanded that the Levites should carry the Ark because Yahweh had given them charge of the sacred vessels of the Temple (v. 2). The priests in charge of helping transport the ark were ZADOK and ABIATHAR (v. 11). Since the priests have no direct involvement with the events related to the relocation of the Ark, their inclusion here seems secondary. The Levites, who were selected according to their families, are not mentioned in 2 Sam 6, possibly because they did not function as a religious group in the time of David. These were the Levites selected: from the house of *Kohath*, *Uriel* (6:24) with 120 assistants (v. 5); from the house of *Merari, Asaiah* (6:30) with 220 helpers (v. 6); from the house of *Gershon*, Joel (6:21) with 130 attendants (v. 7). Joel does not appear in the list of the family of Gershon, unless he is to be identified with *Joah* in 6:21. Two persons named Joel appear in Chronicles related to the Gershonites (cf. 23:8 and 26:22). Three other Levites from the family of Kohath are listed: *Shemaiah*, from the clan of Elizaphan (Exod 6:22) with 200 assistants (v. 8); *Eliel* from the clan of Hebron (Exod 6:18) with eighty assistants (v. 9); and *Amminadab* from the clan of Uzziel (Exod 6:18) with 112 assistants (v. 10). The total number of assistants helping the Levites was 862. The grouping of the Levites into six classes does not correspond to the usual classification used by the CHR; however, the predominance of the family of Kohath is due to the fact that they were in charge of the objects used in the sanctuary (Num 4:4-15). The priests and Levites were purified according to the proper ritual (Num 8:5-13). The ark was carried by poles inlaid with gold that were introduced into the rings of the ark (Exod 25:12-15).

David also told the leaders of the Levites to select singers to participate in the celebration. The Levites selected three singers: *Heman, Asaph*, and *Ethan*. On other occasions when the Levitical singers are named, Asaph generally appears first (16:5, 41; 2 Chr 5:12; 29:13-14; 35:15 but cf. 1 Chr 6:33-43). Heman, Asaph, and Ethan were selected to play the *bronze cymbals* (v. 19). Other musicians were also selected. They were grouped into three classes, according to their musical instruments. Eight musicians were appointed to play the harp according to *Alamoth* (v. 20) and six to play the lyre according to *Sheminith* (v. 21). *Alamoth* and *Sheminith* probably were musical terms; they appear in the titles of Pss 46 and 6. *Chenaniah, leader of the Levites in music* (v. 22), was in charge of leading the music because he was an expert in this area. *Berechiah* and *Elkanah* (v. 23), as well as *Obed-edom* and *Jehiah* (v. 24) were selected as *gatekeepers for the ark*. Finally, seven priests were selected to *blow trumpets before the ark* (v. 24).

The relocation of the Ark (vv. 25-29) was accomplished with a solemn ceremony that included *the elders of Israel* and the military chiefs (not mentioned in 2 Sam 6). Because David and the Levites had followed the proper procedure in handling the ark, divine favor was obtained and *God helped the Levites* (v. 26). During the march, the Levites offered seven bulls and seven rams as sacrifices. The narrative in 2 Sam 6:13 says that David himself offered the sacrifices. This change reflects the sacrificial practices in the time of the CHR. David and the Levites were dressed with linen vestments. David also wore *a linen ephod* (v. 27), the same kind of garment used by the priests. The joy of the occasion is manifested in the statement that David leaped and danced before the LORD (see 13:8). *Michal*, the daughter of Saul, *despised* David for what she took to be an indiscretion. The CHR omits the reasons for Michal's contempt for David (see 2 Sam 6:20-23). Her identification as a member of the house of Saul may indicate that the CHR is showing the disapproval of the house of Saul for David's concern for the Ark.

16:1-3. End of the ceremony. After the Ark was brought to Jerusalem and placed inside the tent David had prepared for it, sacrifices were made before Yahweh. The narrative follows 2 Sam 6:17-19. David, exercising his priestly functions (although this is attenuated in v. 2; cf. 2 Sam 6:17), offered sacrifices, blessed the people, and gave them provisions.

16:4-6. Organization of the cult. Before declaring that the people returned to their homes (2 Sam 6:19), the CHR inserts a passage into his source, describing David's organization of the ministry of the Levites before the ark in Jerusalem (vv. 4-6) and before the TABERNACLE of MOSES that was left in Gibeon (vv. 37-38; cf. 21:29). Between these two narratives, the CHR inserts a song of thanksgiving (vv. 7-36). The work of the Levites was to minister before the Ark with prayer, music and praise. Asaph was the leader of the group. Under him was Zechariah with eight other Levites (see 15:17-18). They were responsible to play musical instruments and to blow the trumpets before the ark.

16:7-38. A song of thanksgiving. This song of thanksgiving is an anthology of several other psalms:

1 Chr	16:8-22	Psalms	105:1-15
	16:23-33		96:1-13
	16:34-36		106:1, 47-48

Ps 96 has no title in the MT, but according to the LXX Ps 96 was a song of David when the Temple was built after the Exile.

16:39-43. Ministry of the Levites. The ministry of the Levitical singers before the Ark was to be permanent (v. 37). Together with the singers were *Obed-edom* and *Hosah* (cf. 26:10) serving as gatekeepers, and sixty-eight assistants. Their work was to give *thanks to the LORD, for his steadfast love endures for ever* (v. 41; cf. 16:34; Ps 106:1; 107:1; 136:1). *Jeduthun*, the father of *Obed-edom* (v. 38) was one of the chief musicians (vv. 41-42). Presiding over the tabernacle of Moses in Gibeon were Zadok and several other priests. Heman and Jeduthun were in charge of the singers (15:17-22). The reason the tabernacle of Moses was in Gibeon is unknown, but the presence of the ark in Jerusalem means that during the time of David there were two legitimate sanctuaries in Israel, one in Jerusalem housing the ark of Yahweh and the other in Gibeon where the TABERNACLE was located. However, while the Levites were to offer praises and prayer before the ark (16:4), the priests were to offer burnt offerings upon the altar of Yahweh at Gibeon (v. 40). It was to the tabernacle that Solomon came offering sacrifices to God (2 Kgs 3:4; 2 Chr 1:3-6).

God's Promise to David, 17:1-27

This text is one of the most important in the OT. The covenant God established with David made clear that the CHR believed that the Davidic monarch had a role in the redemptive purposes of Yahweh. The text of chap. 17 follows closely 2 Sam 7:1-29 with some modifications that reflect the theological views of the CHR.

17:1-15. Nathan's prophecy. After David had finished building a house for himself and a tent for the ark of God (15:1), he expressed to NATHAN the desire to build a house for God. The word "house" (*bayit*) is used in the text with three different meanings. David's *house* (17:1) was the place he built for himself in Jerusalem. The *house* David desired to build for Yahweh (v. 4) was a temple to lodge the ark of God. The *house* Yahweh would build for David (v. 10b) was a dynasty, the certainty that David's kingdom would be established forever.

Nathan appeared in David's court as a PROPHET and as a political advisor to the king. David appealed to Nathan in order to discover God's will and to receive divine approval. Nathan was favorable to the present project and gave his approval. That night, Yahweh appeared to Nathan in a VISION (v. 15) and overruled the prophet, warning him that David would not build the Temple. Although no reason was given for this prohibition, the CHR will say later that the reason David could not build the Temple was because he was a man of war (22:8; 28:3). The CHR also will describe in detail how David made all the necessary preparations for the building of the Temple (chaps. 21-29). But the idea of a temple was pleasing to God. Yahweh promised that he would establish the house of David (v. 10b) and that a descendant of David would build a house for Yahweh. Although the CHR is intimating that SOLOMON was going to build the Temple (cf. 28:5-7), he is implying the perpetuity of the Davidic dynasty by his fivefold repetition of *forever* (vv. 12, 14 [twice], 23. 27). The messianic import of the CHR's words is that the stability of the Davidic dynasty was related to the presence of Yahweh in the Temple. To the CHR, the cause of Yahweh and the cause of David coincide. While 2 Sam 7:16 speaks of "your house and your kingdom," v. 14 speaks of *my house and . . . my kingdom.* The house of David is now the house of Yahweh and the kingdom of David is now the kingdom of Yahweh.

17:16-27. David's prayer. David's prayer is presented before the ark of God housed in the tent (16:1). The ark symbolized the presence of Yahweh among his people. David gave thanks to Yahweh for his promise, acknowledging that Yahweh had honored him beyond his expectations. He also expressed his confidence that Yahweh would fulfill his promise.

David's Wars, 18:1–20:8

The CHR dedicates chaps. 18–20 to describing David's wars and victories against the enemies of ISRAEL. The CHR's description of David's wars and victories affirmed David as a great military leader. These victories over Israel's neighbors helped David consolidate his kingdom and confirmed God's blessing upon his kingdom (see 18:6b, 13b). The spoils of war became the source of the wealth used for the construction of the Temple. A brief parenthesis in the narrative (18:14-17) provides additional information about David's court personnel.

18:1-2. Philistines and Moabites. The transitional formula *some time afterward* (v. 1) does not provide a chronological framework to date the various battles. The defeat of the PHILISTINES and the subjugation of GATH, one of the five Philistine cities (Josh 13:3), made it possible for 600 men from Gath to serve in David's army (2 Sam 15:18).

The report of Moab's defeat is subdued in the narrative. While 2 Sam 8:2 describes the massacre of two-thirds of the population, the CHR only notes that the Moabites were subjugated and were forced to pay tribute. The omission of the atrocities committed by David is part of the CHR's effort to idealize David.

18:3-11. Arameans. The Arameans formed an alliance of city-states to the north of Israel and posed a great threat to the security of David's kingdom. The conquest of *Zobah* (vv. 3-4), a city north of DAMASCUS, and the subjugation of *Damascus* (vv. 5-6) allowed David to establish garrisons in two strong Aramean states and thus greatly enlarge the borders of his kingdom. The reference to *one thousand chariots* (v. 4) is lacking in 2 Sam 8:4, while the number of horsemen (7,000) has been greatly increased from the reference in the CHR's source (700). Since the Israelites did not use chariots, David and his men incapacitated the horses, allowing only 100 to be used in the formation of an Israelite chariot corps. David brought to Jerusalem the spoils of war, gold, silver, and bronze, and dedicated them to Yahweh to be used in the construction of the Temple. In anticipation of the event, the CHR declares that *Solomon* used the *bronze* for the construction of some of the furniture of the Temple (v. 8).

King Tou of Hamath, who had been at war with *Hadadezer,* was happy that David had defeated his enemy; he sent an embassy to David headed by *his son*

Hadoram. Hadoram carried a large tribute and came to congratulate David on his victory against the Arameans. David also took tribute from five of Israel's neighbors (vv. 9-10). The tribute received from these nations was dedicated to Yahweh to be used in the construction of the Temple (v. 11).

18:12-13. Edomites. The victory of Israel against the *Edomites* is credited to *Abishai* (vv. 12-13). Abishai was David's nephew, the son of Zeruiah, David's sister (2:16). However, 2 Sam 8:13 says that David made a name for himself when he killed the 18,000 Edomites, while the superscription to Ps 60 says that Joab "killed twelve thousand Edomites in the Valley of Salt." This discrepancy may reflect different traditions rather than textual corruption. The repeated assertion that David's victories were given by God (vv. 6, 13) serves to reaffirm God's promise to David that he would subdue his enemies (17:10).

18:14-17. David's officials. The list of the royal administrators is taken from 2 Sam 8:15-18. A second list appears in 2 Sam 20:23-26. *Joab,* David's nephew (2:16), was commander of the regular army. *Jehoshaphat was recorder,* an office that may reflect the function of the herald of Pharaoh. The recorder (Heb. *mazkir*) was the person responsible for the protocol in the ceremonies of the Egyptian palace. *Zadok . . . and Ahimelech . . . were priests.* Since Ahimelech had been killed by Saul and Abiathar was still the priest at the end of David's reign (2 Sam 20:25; 1 Kgs 1:7), the likely reading should have been "Abiathar, the son of Ahimelech" (McCarter 1984, 253–54). *Shavsha was [the] secretary.* He appears as Seraiah in 2 Sam 8:17 and Shisha in 1 Kgs 4:3. Shavsha was a non-Israelite name; it is possible that the different spellings of his name in the Hebrew text may be attempts to convey his name in Hebrew.

Benaiah and Jehoiada (not *Benaiah son of Jehoida,* v. 17) were in charge of the Cherethites and the Pelethites, two groups of mercenary soldiers that formed David's personal army. They were probably part of the foreign population that settled in CANAAN, known as the SEA PEOPLES. The Cherethites have been identified with the Cretans and the Pelethites with the Philistines. David's sons were *the chief officials in the service of the king* (v. 17); 2 Sam 2:18 says that they were priests. The reason for the change was that in the CHR's day, the priests came from the tribe of Levi. Since David's sons were from the tribe of Judah, the affirmation that they served as priests was incompatible with the CHR's view.

19:1–20:3. Ammonites. The story of David's war against the Ammonites and the Arameans is taken from 2 Sam 10. The war against the Ammonites occurred when the delegates David had sent to *Hanun* were humiliated (v. 4; cf. 2 Sam 10:4). Hanun prepares for war against Israel by hiring an army of Arameans. *Mesopotamia* (v. 6) is an area also known as ARAM-NAHARAIM (NIV). According to the CHR, *Maacah* and *Zobah* were paid to participate. Samuel adds Beth-rehob and Tob (2 Sam 10:6). Hanun paid *a thousand talents of silver* (about thirty-seven tons) to hire *thirty-two thousand chariots* (v. 7) and 33,000 foot soldiers (2 Sam 10:6). Confronted with the Ammonites' large army, Joab and his brother Abishai divided

Israel's army into two groups, one to fight against the Arameans in the open country and the other against the Ammonites in their capital city, *Rabbah* (v. 9; cf. 20:1). The Arameans were soundly defeated and the Ammonites retreated back into the fortified city. The Ammonites brought another group of Arameans, commanded by *Shophach the commander of the army of Hadadezer* (v. 16), to reinforce their army. At this point David himself took control of the army (v. 17) to fight against the Arameans. In the battle fought at Helam (2 Sam 10:16) David completely defeated the Aramean army (v. 18) and put them under vassalage. In the final victory, David and his army killed 7,000 charioteers and 40,000 foot soldiers (v. 18); 2 Sam 10:18 says David killed 700 charioteers and 40,000 horsemen. The CHR's numbers probably are inflated in order to magnify David's victory over the enemy.

The narrative of the war against the Ammonites in 20:1-3 is taken from 2 Sam 11–12, with several omissions by the CHR. The CHR, following the pattern of omitting stories that would tend to tarnish the image of David as Israel's ideal king, omits the story of David's adultery with BATHSHEBA, David's request to Joab to have URIAH killed, and NATHAN's rebuke of the king (2 Sam 11–12). The first part of 20:1 comes from 2 Sam 11:1; the second part comes from 2 Sam 12:26.

The CHR then gives the beginning and the end of the account of David's war against the Ammonites. After David's victory he removes *the crown of Milcom from his head* (v. 2) and places it on his own head. KJV, RSV, and NIV translate *Milcom* as "their king" (but see NIV and RSV mg.). Milcom was the name of the Ammonite god who often appears in the OT as MOLECH (1 Kgs 11:5, 7). David also forced the Ammonites to work hard with instruments of iron, probably demolishing the walls of the city.

20:4-8. Philistines. The source of this information is 2 Sam 21:18-22. The CHR mentions three instances of hand to hand combat by David's soldiers against the descendants of the Rephaim, descendants of Rapha, a group of people believed to be *giants*. The NRSV uses the word *giants* to translate "Rephaim" (cf. NIV "Rephaites"). Many of the Philistine soldiers that David and his soldiers killed were descendants of Rapha (cf. 2 Sam. 21:15-22), although only one of them was considered to be a huge man (v. 6).

The first engagement was at GEZER, identified as Gob in 2 Sam 21:18. There *Sibbecai* killed *Sippai*, a descendant of the Rephaim. In the second contest *Elhanan son of Jair killed Lahmi the brother of Goliath* (v. 5). In the third, *Jonathan*, the nephew of David, killed a man *of great size, who had six fingers on each hand, and six toes on each foot* (v. 6; see Barnett 1990, 46–51).

The statement that *Elhanan killed Lahmi the brother of Goliath* seems to be an attempt to resolve the contradiction between 1 Sam 17 in which it is said that David killed Goliath and 2 Sam 21:19 in which it is said that Elhanan killed Goliath. There are two traditions concerning the death of Goliath. The traditional passage, 1 Sam 17:41-49, says that David killed Goliath with stones (2 Sam 17:50) and with a sword (2 Sam 17:51). The second tradition says that Elhanan, a soldier in David's army, killed Goliath (2 Sam 21:19). Some scholars have said that Elhanan was David's given name and that David was his throne name (Bright 1981, 192). It is a fact that many people in the OT have two names (cf. 2 Sam 12:24-25). However, there is no evidence that David was known as Elhanan. Some scholars have said that the accomplishment of Elhanan was attached to David in order to magnify him in the eyes of Israel. Something similar is found in 1 Chr 18:12, where Abishai's victory against the Edomites is credited to David (2 Sam 8:13). The conflict the CHR found between 1 Sam 17 and 2 Sam 21:19 is not easy to solve. The CHR's attempted solution further complicates the matter without providing an adequate solution.

David's Census and God's Punishment, 21:1–22:1

21:1-13. David's Census. Chapter 21 shows that the sin of David in taking a census of Israel was the tragic occasion that caused the selection of a holy place for the location of Yahweh's Temple. The purpose of David's census was primarily for military conscription (vv. 5, 7), although it could also have been used for taxation. In the parallel narrative in 2 Sam 24:1-16, it was God who incited David to number the people. In Chronicles the action is attributed to *Satan* (v. 1). Satan appears in the OT in Job 1–2 where he is one of the sons of God who comes before God to accuse Job. He also appears in Zech 3:1-2 as a member of the heavenly court who accuses Joshua, the high priest. In Job and Zechariah the Hebrew word *satan* appears with a definite article to emphasize his function as the "accuser." He is a being subordinated to the power of God. In 1 Chr 21 *Satan* appears as the personal name of a being who incites an individual to evil. The change made by the CHR may reflect a postexilic theological development of the concept of Satan's work.

Despite Joab's objection, David ordered a census of Israel *from Beer-sheba to Dan* (v. 2). This south-north orientation of Israel is peculiar to the CHR (see 2 Chr 30:5) and contrary to the customary north-south orientation of the OT (cf. 2 Sam 24:2) and may reflect the CHR's view of the importance of the southern kingdom. The number given here, 1,100,000, differs from the 1,300,000 of 2 Sam 24:9. Although different solutions have been offered, it is possible that the discrepancy reflects the fact that the CHR says that Joab did not include Levi and Benjamin in the census.

The displeasure of God in v. 7 is omitted in 2 Sam 24. The CHR says that Yahweh *struck Israel* but this is a reference to the plague, which is not sent until v. 14. The text does not say how David discovered his action was a sin against God. The CHR emphasizes that the census was a sin (v. 3), perhaps to stress that it was a lack of trust in God. David's selection of punishment upon Israel (v. 12) was made after Gad, the seer, offered him three choices of punishment. In 2 Sam 24:11 Gad is called both a PROPHET and seer. The three years of famine here appear as seven in 2 Sam 24:13; however, the LXX agrees with Chronicles and is a preferred reading. The pestilence as the sword of Yahweh is the antithesis to the sword of the enemy.

21:14-30. The LORD's Punishment. The plague was sent by *an angel* of Yahweh (see 2 Kgs 19:35) who acted as the exterminator. With a *drawn sword*, the angel went through Israel, and 70,000 people were killed. Before the angel entered JERUSALEM, Yahweh repented. The repentance of God reflects God's change of attitude towards the punishment. With his sword stretched towards Jerusalem (v. 16), the angel of Yahweh appeared to David *by the threshing floor of Ornan the Jebusite*. Ornan appears in 2 Sam 24:16 as Araunah. The name Araunah seems to be a title, derived from the Hurrian word meaning "lord." The MT in 2 Sam 24:23 calls him a king. The vision of the angel *standing between earth and heaven, [with] a drawn sword stretched out over Jerusalem* (v. 16), caused David to pray, confessing that he alone was guilty. David pleaded that the people be spared from further punishment (v. 17). The angel commanded Gad to tell David to erect an altar on the threshing floor and dedicate it to Yahweh. David approached Ornan and offered to buy the threshing floor. The contract between David and Ornan is similar to the contract between ABRAHAM and Ephron the Hittite for the purchase of the cave of MACHPELAH (Gen 23:1-20). The price of the land, according to 2 Sam 24:24, was only fifty shekels of silver. On the other hand, the price in Chronicles is *six hundred shekels of gold* (v. 25). This discrepancy reflects the CHR's desire to magnify the importance of the site of the future temple, since the amount here is twelve times the amount in Samuel. It is also possible that the difference reflects David's purchase not only of the threshing floor, but of the whole area adjacent to the threshing floor. David built an altar for Yahweh and offered a burnt offering and a peace offering upon it. God demonstrated his acceptance of the sacrifice with two signs: *fire from heaven* (v. 26) and the cessation of the plague (v. 27). The *fire from heaven* (omitted in 2 Sam 24:25) serves the intent of the CHR, which is to underscore the importance of the altar and its divine origin. The THEOPHANY at the threshing floor and the divine approval of David's altar (24:28-25:1) serve to explain why the high place at Gibeon, where the Mosaic sanctuary was located, was abandoned and why the site at Jerusalem was selected as the place where the Temple of God and the altar of sacrifice would be built.

David's Preparations for the Temple, 22:2-19

22:1-5. General preparation. Most of chaps. 22–29 are taken from extracanonical materials, which the CHR relies on for his source of information. After the unusual events at the threshing floor, David understood that God had selected that place for the building of his house. The narrative of 2 Samuel is silent about David's plan to build the Temple. The CHR details the steps David took in preparation for the construction of the Temple. David commanded that *aliens who were residing in the land* be used as *stonecutters* to prepare the stones to be used in the building of the Temple. These *aliens (gerim)* were part of the Canaanite population that had lived among the Israelites (2 Chr 2:16-18). David also provided large quantities of iron, bronze, and cedar. The reason David began to make preparation for the construction of the Temple was that his son Solomon was *young and inexperienced* (v. 5).

22:6-16. Dialogue with Solomon. The CHR expresses the reason David was unable to build the Temple. In 2 Sam 7 no reason was given why David was not allowed to build the Temple. The CHR says David was disqualified because the many wars he conducted with divine approval caused him to shed much blood. His status as *a man of war* (2 Chr 28:3) disqualified him from the task of building God's house. The responsibility of building the Temple fell upon his son Solomon, *a man of peace* (v. 9). This designation plays upon the name of Solomon (a name related to the Heb. word "peace"). David's charge to Solomon (vv. 12-13) is based upon the deuteronomistic view that strict observance of the law was the condition for prosperity (Deut 26:16-19). David then enumerates the materials he has accumulated for the building of the Temple. The amount of gold (100,000 talents or 3,750 tons) and silver (1,000,000 talents or 37,500 tons) is an embellishment that allows the CHR to describe the splendor of Solomon's Temple.

22:17-19. Request for help. David exhorts the leaders of Israel to seek Yahweh and to help Solomon with the construction of the Temple. Their gratitude to God for peace and prosperity would be manifested by the construction of the sanctuary for the housing of the ark of the covenant and the holy vessels of God.

David's Organization of the Temple Personnel, 23:1–27:34

23:1-32. Organization of the Levites. The narrative of the organization of the Levites into guilds is preceded by a brief introduction (vv. 1-2) in which David proclaims before Israel, gathered in a solemn assembly, that Solomon was his chosen successor. The assembly is described in chaps. 28–29.

According to Num 4:3, the Levites came into service at the age of thirty. Later on, the age was lowered to twenty-five (Num 8:24). Because of the greater influence of the Temple in Israelite life and the need for additional personnel for Temple service, the age was lowered again to twenty. The increase in Temple personnel may reflect the needs of the Temple at the end of the monarchy or even of the age of the CHR himself. Twenty was also the age for military service for the men of the tribes of Israel (Num 1). The total number of Levites available for service was 38,000. They were divided into four groups (vv. 4-5): 24,000 Levites were dedicated for the work of the Temple, 6,000 as *officers and judges* (see 2 Chr 19:4-11), 4,000 as *gatekeepers*, and 4,000 as musicians (vv. 4-6). The Levites are listed according to the leaders of the Levitical families: the sons of *Gershon* are listed in vv. 7-11, the sons of *Kohath* in vv. 12-20, and the sons of *Merari* in vv. 21-23. The genealogies of the sons of Levi differ from the genealogy in chap. 6. This may indicate that the CHR was using a list containing the names of the Levitical families of David's time or even his own time. This passage shows the subservient role of the Levites, for they were selected to serve in the Temple under *the descendants of Aaron* (v. 28). *The sons of Moses* and their descendants (v. 15) were also assigned Levitical duties. The duties of the descendants of Aaron were to consecrate the holy things, to burn the sacrifices, and to bless the people. The duties of the Levites were cleaning the Temple, preparing the bread, and assisting in the liturgy. The text describing the Levitical duties (vv. 25-32) may reflect the struggle between priests and Levites in postexilic times, aimed at giving the priests supremacy over the ministry in the Temple (cf. Ezek 44:10-14).

24:1-31. Organization of the Priests. The priests were organized into twenty-four divisions. *Nadab* and *Abihu*, sons of Aaron, had died because of their unfaithfulness (Num 3:4); however, the CHR chose to omit the reason for their death. For this reason only two lines of priests came from Aaron, one from *Eleazar*, represented by *Zadok* and another from *Ithamar*, represented by *Ahimelech*. Since the sons of Eleazar were more numerous than the sons of Ithamar, they were divided into sixteen divisions and the sons of Ithamar into eight divisions, but each with equal standing (v. 5). The divisions were done by lots (v. 5) and the results were recorded by Shemaiah, the son of Nethanel, an unknown Levitical scribe. Most of these names (vv. 7-19) appear in Ezra 2 and Neh 12, since the names of the individuals also became the names of the divisions. Zechariah, the father of John the Baptist, is listed as being from the division of Abijah (Luke 1:5; cf. 1 Chr 24:10). Another group of Levites (vv. 20-31) were divided by lot into several divisions, perhaps twenty-four also, as suggested by v. 31. Since several names in this list do not appear in 23:6-23, it is clear that this list is a revision of the earlier list. The family of Gershon (23:7-11) is missing, probably accidentally omitted by the scribe.

25:1-31. Organization of the musicians. David also divided the Levitical singers into twenty-four divisions. David was helped by *the officers of the army* (v. 1). However, it is possible that David was helped by the leaders of the Levites (see 24:5) who were in charge of the Levites who served in the Temple (Num 8:25). The musicians were grouped around three major Levites: *Asaph*, *Heman*, and *Jeduthun*. Jeduthun is also known as Ethan in 15:17, 19. The ministry of the musicians was considered prophetic. *Heman* is called a *seer* in v. 5. *Asaph* is called a *seer* in 2 Chr 29:30 and *Jeduthun* in 2 Chr 35:15. This suggests that their ministry was accomplished under divine inspiration. The designation of the Temple music as prophetic associates the Temple musicians with the cultic prophets of the OT. The *sons of Asaph* formed four divisions (v. 2); the *sons of Jeduthun*, six (v. 3), and the *sons of Heman*, fourteen (vv. 4-5). Each of the twenty-four divisions had twelve men, for a total of 288 men involved in the music ministry of the Temple (v. 7).

26:1-19. Organization of the gatekeepers. The duty of the gatekeepers was to prevent unauthorized persons from entering the Temple. They were arranged into three divisions. The first division was that of the sons of *Meshelemiah* (vv. 1-3, 9), a descendant of Korah from the family of Levi (Exod 6:16, 18, 21), with a total of eighteen men (v. 9). The second division belonged to the sons of *Obed-edom* (v. 4). The identification of OBED-EDOM in Chronicles is difficult. In 13:13-14 he is a Gittite, one of the PHILISTINES that joined David's army. In 15:18 he is a gatekeeper and in 15:21 he is a musician playing the lyre. In 16:38 he appears as the son of

Jeduthun and is a gatekeeper. In 26:4-8 he appears as a Levite, although the CHR does not present a Levitical genealogy for him. The statement that *God blessed him* (v. 5) is a deliberate effort to identify him with the foreigner who kept the ark (13:14). It seems that because of Obed-edom's willingness to keep the Ark of Yahweh, he and his family were accepted into Levitical service. The division of doorkeepers from the family of Obed-edom was sixty-two. This number differs from 16:38 where the number is sixty-eight. The third division was headed by *Hosah,* a descendant of *Merari* and it had thirteen men. The total number of gatekeepers was ninety-three. This number is less than the number that appears in 9:22 (212), in Neh 7:45 (138), Neh 11:19 (172) and in Ezra 2:42 (139). The difference may be explained by the fact that the need decreased with the passing of time (Braun 1968, 251) or by the fact that it began with a small number but that at a later time it had increased in number.

The assignment of each family was conducted by lot. The east gate was assigned to *Shelemiah* (the *Meshelemiah* of v. 1) and the north gate to his son *Zechariah* (v. 14). The south gate was assigned to the descendants of *Obed-edom* (v. 15) and the west gate was assigned to *Hosah* (v. 16). *Shuppim* (v. 16) should be deleted from the list since his name is irrelevant in the text and should be considered an intrusion. The meaning of the word *parbar* (v. 18 mg.) is unknown. It is generally accepted as a Persian word that the CHR used to refer to an area in the Temple precinct, thus *colonnade.*

26:20-28. Organization of the treasurers. In addition to their duties in the cult, the Levites had other duties. *Jehieli* (or *Jehiel,* cf. 23:8) and his sons (vv. 21-22) were in charge of the treasury of the Temple. This treasury included the money from freewill offerings, sacrifices, tithes, and other things dedicated to God. These Levites were descendants of *Gershon* and his son *Ladan* (or *Libni,* cf. 6:17). The reading of the NRSV, following the MT, suggests that Ahijah was in charge of the treasury of the Temple (v. 2). However, the reading of the LXX provides a better understanding of the passage: "Their fellow Levites were in charge of . . . " (cf. NIV).

Shelomoth and his relatives were in charge of all the treasury accumulated from the spoils of war (v. 21). This portion of the treasury was given by David and his warriors and by some of the great heroes of Israel's past (v. 28). These Levites were Kohathites, from the family of Amram, Moses's father. *Shebuel* (v. 24), a Gershomite, was the chief officer over all the treasuries of the Temple.

26:29-32. Appointment of the administrators. Two Kohathite families (cf. 6:18) were assigned *outside duties.* The family of Izhar was appointed to be *officers and judges* (v. 29). Of the family of Hebron, headed by *Chenaniah and his sons,* 1,700 men were assigned ministry duties to the people west of the Jordan; and 2,700 men, headed by *Jerijah* and his relatives, were assigned duties east of the Jordan, with responsibilities over the tribes of Reuben, Gad, and the half-tribe of Manasseh. It is not clear what these outside assignments entailed. Since the duties included the *work of the LORD* and the *service of the king* (v. 30), it is possible that these Levites were responsible for the administration of the Levitical cities, the collection of religious and state taxes, and the administration of justice. Jazer was one of the Levitical cities (6:81). According to the CHR, these appointments were made *in the fortieth year* of David (v. 31), his last as king.

27:1-34. Military and political leaders. Verse 1 serves as introduction to the whole chapter, although most of the terms describing the leaders apply mostly to vv. 2-15. This summary introduces the leaders of David's army, the tribal leaders, and other officers of the court who served at the pleasure of the king.

27:1-15. Army leaders. David organized his army into twelve divisions, each headed by a chief commander. Every division consisted of 24,000 men who were on active duty for one month each year, after which they were relieved by another division. The total number of men was 288,000. It is possible to interpret these numbers in terms of military units. Since the Hebrew word *'eleph* can also be translated as "military unit," it is possible that David's army consisted of twelve divisions with twenty-four military units in each division. Under this view, the number of men serving the 288 units would be unknown. Most of the names of the twelve commanders appear with some variations in the list of David's mighty men (11:10-47).

27:16-24. Tribal leaders. The naming of twelve leaders over the tribes of Israel may indicate that David was laying the foundation for what became the twelve administrative districts of Solomon (1 Kgs 4:7-19). The listing of the tribes varies from tribal lists in Num 1 and 1 Chr 2. The tribes of GAD and ASHER are omitted from this list. To complete the number of twelve tribes, the CHR includes LEVI and divides the tribe of JOSEPH into East and West MANASSEH and EPHRAIM. The family of Aaron receives a special mention as a distinct group but it is included with the tribe of Levi. The CHR mentions David's census of Israel. The census remained incomplete because of divine displeasure (cf. 21:1-5). The CHR exonerates David from the disastrous consequences of the census by saying that he did not count anyone under twenty years of age because he believed in God's promise to Abraham (Gen 15:1-5) The blame is placed upon Joab because he did not finish numbering the people. *The Annals of King David* (v. 24) detailed the acts of David, and was part of the royal archives.

27:25-31. Administrators of the royal house. This passage portrays David as a large landowner. His estate included agricultural *fields* (v. 26), *vineyards* (v. 27), *olive and sycamore trees* (v. 28) and livestock (vv. 29-30). This list contains the names of twelve administrators who were responsible for the management of David's properties. These properties provided much of the revenue David needed to maintain the expenses of the palace. It is difficult to ascertain if David ever established a system of taxation over JUDAH and ISRAEL. Later on, Solomon imposed heavy taxation upon the nation to help him maintain the extravagances of his court.

27:32-34. Officers of the court. This list consists of several notable men who served the king as his personal advisors. *Jonathan*, David's *counselor*, is listed as his *uncle*. The Hebrew word also means a "relative"; it may refer to David's nephew mentioned in 2 Sam 21:21. *Jonathan* and *Jehiel* served as tutors to David's sons. *Hushai*'s title, *king's friend*, means a close advisor of the king. *Ahithophel* lost his position as counselor because of his part in Absalom's rebellion against David (2 Sam 15:12, 31).

David's Last Days, 28:1–29:30

This section is related to the great assembly mentioned in 23:1. The assembly was called in order to proclaim Solomon the new king and to give instructions about the Temple Solomon was to build for God. David had summoned all the leaders of Israel and, standing before them (28:2), he encouraged them to help Solomon in building the house of God.

28:1-8. David's words to the people. David declared to the people the reason he was unable to build the Temple to house the ark of the covenant (see 22:6-16), the *footstool of God* (v. 2; cf. Pss 99:5; 132:7). Because David was a warrior and a man of war, he had shed much blood. But God was not against the idea of a temple. David said that Yahweh chose Judah to be the leading tribe and from the house of Jesse he chose David himself to be king over Israel. Now he has chosen his son Solomon to continue his work. The reference to Judah and the house of Jesse may be another effort by the CHR to magnify the importance of Judah in the divine plan. Yahweh has chosen Solomon to be the next king and the builder of the Temple. Solomon would enjoy a special father-son relationship with Yahweh because of the pact established with David (2 Sam 7).

28:9-10. David's words to Solomon. According to Braun (1986, 275), David's exhortation to Solomon to *know the God of your father* (v. 9), deals with "conventional covenant terminology which exhorts Solomon to recognize Yahweh as his covenant lord and to conduct himself in accord with his stipulations." Solomon's kingdom would be established forever, provided he obeyed the commandments of Yahweh (vv. 9-10). The same dedication to the commandments of Yahweh is required of the people if they want to continue in the land Yahweh has given to them and if they want to pass this land to future generations (v. 8).

28:11-21. David's plans for the Temple. David gave Solomon the plans he had prepared for the construction of the Temple. The plans for the Temple included details for the *'ulam* or *the vestibule*, for the *hekal* or the sanctuary, and for the *debir*, the holy of holies, where the ark of the covenant was located. *The mercy seat* (v. 11) or propitiatory (*kapporet*) was the cover of the ark. On top of the cover were two cherubim. The reference to *the chariot of the cherubim* (v. 18) appears only here.

The plans also included the design for several rooms in the Temple, information about the ministry of the priests and Levites, and a summary of the gold and silver needed for the vessels to be used in the Temple. The plans David gave to Solomon were written in a document that the CHR says came directly "from the hand of Yahweh" (v. 19, author trans.). This statement indicates that according to the CHR the plans for the Temple were given to David by divine inspiration. According to priestly theology, no one could erect a temple to God without the direct approval from God. David received from Yahweh the plans for the construction of the Temple in the same way Moses received the details for the building of the tabernacle (Exod 25:9-40). The word *plan* (v. 11) in Hebrew is the same word translated "pattern" in Exod 25:40. The exhortation to Solomon (vv. 20-21) appears to be a continuation of the exhortation of v. 10. The order and the manner in which the different classes of Temple workers are presented seems to indicate that this section is a later addition to the text.

29:1-9. David's appeal for offerings. As Moses had done before (Exod 25:1-7; 35:4-9, 20-29), David made an appeal to the leaders of Israel, asking them to help Solomon build the Temple. In vv. 1 and 19, the Temple is called "a palace" (RSV; NIV: "palatial structure"). The Hebrew word was used in postexilic times; it carried the meaning of "palace" or "fortress" (NRSV mg.; cf. Neh 2:8; 7:2). Williamson (1982, 184) suggests that the CHR used the word to declare to his readers "that the kingdom ultimately belongs to God."

In order to move the leaders of Israel to offer generously to the building fund, David spoke of his own generosity. He had given the wealth of his kingdom to help the building of the Temple. In addition, he was giving his personal wealth to God: 3,000 talents (110 tons) of gold and 7,000 talents (260 tons) of silver. The word *segullah*, translated here *a treasure of my own* (v. 3), means personal or private wealth, a special possession (cf. Exod 19:5). Moved by David's generosity, the leaders of Israel "willingly" (vv. 6, 9 NIV) gave with enthusiasm, surpassing David's offering. They gave an abundance of gold, silver, bronze, and iron to be used in the construction of the Temple. The reference to *darics* (v. 7) is anachronistic. The daric refers was a Persian gold coin minted by DARIUS I (522–485 BCE). This reference to the daric is made anachronistically by the CHR as an effort to present an equivalent value to the currency of his day. The numbers are greatly exaggerated. However, the large amount given by David and the leaders and the joyful and willing response of the people clearly indicate that the CHR was expressing the majesty of the Temple, a monument worthy of the God of Israel. *Jehiel the Gershonite* and his sons were in charge of the treasury of the house of the LORD (26:21-22).

29:10-22a. David's prayer of thanksgiving. David, profoundly moved by the generosity of the people, offered to God a prayer of thanksgiving. David exalted God for his grace and glory and for his willingness to bless the people. David acknowledged that as pilgrims and sojourners on this earth, all that he and the people had given to build the Temple they had received from the hands of God. They were simply unmerited receivers of the divine abundance. The only thing David could offer as his own that might please God was *the uprightness of [his] heart* (v. 17). David asked Yahweh to preserve this same disposition in the hearts of the people. He also asked Yahweh to bless Solomon that he might obey the commandments with upright heart and that he might finish the building of the Temple (v. 19). The people blessed Yahweh on that occasion. The next day, with great gladness (v. 22a) all Israel offered a great sacrifice to God.

29:22b-30. Solomon's accession to the throne. Solomon was proclaimed king the first time at the occasion of Adonijah's attempt to seize the throne with the help of the army, an event omitted by the CHR (cf. 1 Kgs 1:32-40; 1 Chr 23:1). The reference to Zadok's being anointed is unusual since he has appeared as a priest in earlier narratives. It is possible that ZADOK was either designated as the sole high priest in Solomon's kingdom or as the successor of ABIATHAR, who had sided with ADONIJAH (1 Kgs 1:5-8). According to the CHR, Solomon had the full support of all Israel, including the support of the political and military leaders who had served under David. The CHR also asserts that Solomon had divine affirmation by saying that Yahweh magnified his reign in the sight of all Israel (cf. 2 Chr 1:1).

David's reign had lasted forty years. The CHR suggests that his seven-year reign in Hebron was over all Israel, although 2 Sam 5:5 says that he reigned seven years and six months over Judah alone. David died of old age, loved by his people, full of honors and riches, clear evidence that Yahweh had richly blessed his reign. The information about David's reign was taken by the CHR from three prophetic annals (v. 29). Although these sources have been identified with the Books of Samuel and Kings, it is also possible that the CHR used additional sources to compose his history of David's reign.

An Outline

Second Chronicles

The Reign of Solomon, 1:1–9:31

The story of SOLOMON as presented by the CHR is inspired by the narratives in 1 Kings. Solomon's reign is marked by the details of the construction of the

Temple. This dominant theme in the Solomonic narrative is the divine fulfillment of the promise made to David and the culmination of David's work. The CHR also focuses on Solomon's wisdom and wealth but these become secondary to the CHR's major theme.

Solomon's Early Reign, 1:1-17

1:1-6. The visit to Gibeon. The establishment of the kingdom in Solomon's hand (cf. 1 Kgs 2:46b) reflects the difficulties Solomon had in winning the struggle against his brother Adonijah (1 Kgs 1:1–2:46). The same expression is used to describe the beginning of the reign of Rehoboam (12:13), Abijah (13:21), Jehoshaphat (17:1), and Jehoram (21:4). The religious focus of the CHR is evident in his declaration that Yahweh was with Solomon.

Because the CHR omits Solomon's struggle with Adonijah, the king's first act becomes his visit to the high place at Gibeon. The narrative in Chronicles differs slightly from that in 1 Kgs 3:4-15. The CHR says that Solomon went to Gibeon with the leaders and officers of Israel (cf. 1 Chr 28:1), while 1 Kings presents the visit to Gibeon as a personal pilgrimage of the new king. The CHR also says that the tent of meeting and the altar of bronze made under the direction of Moses were in Gibeon (1 Chr 16:39-40; 21:29). The Ark was in Jerusalem under the tent David had made when he brought the Ark from Kiriath-jearim (1 Chr 15:1). Solomon offered a large offering upon the bronze altar. The CHR says that Solomon *went up there to the bronze altar*, and offered sacrifices before Yahweh (v. 6). This expression, missing in 1 Kings, affirms that Solomon acted as a priest at this occasion.

1:7-13. The theophany. The THEOPHANY narrative in vv. 7-13 is an abbreviation of 1 Kgs 3:3-15. The CHR does not mention that God appeared to Solomon in a dream, although that may be intimated in v. 7. In the postexilic period dreams had fallen into disrepute because of past abuse (cf. Jer 23:23-28). Instead of power and possessions, Solomon asked for wisdom and knowledge to rule over the people. God granted him what he had asked and in addition promised to bless and prosper him with the wealth and power for which he did not ask.

1:14-18. Solomon's wealth. The accumulation of great wealth by Solomon was seen as the fulfillment of God's promise. Solomon acted as a merchant; he imported chariots from Egypt and horses from Egypt and Kue, a region in southeast Asia Minor identified with Cilicia. Solomon kept some of the horses and chariots and placed them in Jerusalem and in chariot cities he had built for them throughout Israel. Megiddo, Hazor, and Gezer have been identified as Solomon's chariot cities, but this identification has been questioned by some archaeologists. Solomon sold the horses and chariots to the kings of the Hittites and the Aramean kings (1:17 NRSV). Solomon became so rich with his commercial ventures that it was said that gold became as plentiful as the stones in the hills of Israel and the expensive cedar became as abundant as the sycamore tress found in the Shephelah, the low foothills of Judah (cf. 1 Chr 27:28).

The Construction of the Temple, 2:1–5:1

The CHR now begins emphasizing the main event of Solomon's reign, the building of the TEMPLE. So central was the Temple that most of the narrative related to Solomon's reign is given to describing the preparation, the construction, and the dedication of the Temple. The CHR also recounts the feast of dedication and the prayers and sacrifices offered at that occasion.

2:1-18 [MT 1:18–2:17]. Preparations to build the Temple. This chapter deals with Solomon's preparation for the building of the Temple and his dealings with Hiram, king of Tyre.

2:1-10 [MT 1:18–2:9]. Solomon's request to Hiram. Solomon announced his decision to build the Temple of God and his own palace. In Chronicles the building of the palace receives only secondary attention (cf. 2:12; 7:11). The Temple was to be a place for the name of Yahweh (v. 1), a place to burn incense, to make sacrifices, and to celebrate the feasts of God (v. 4). In order to build the Temple Solomon needed people who were skilled workers with metals and fabrics. Thus, Solomon sent a delegation to Tyre requesting assistance from Huram (his name appears as Hiram in Kings and in 1 Chr 14:1).

2:11-16 [MT 2:10-15]. Hiram's response. Hiram answered Solomon's request in writing, although this fact is not mentioned in Kings. His acknowledgement of Yahweh as the God who made heavens and earth is diplomatic language and does not express Hiram's faith in Yahweh. Hiram promised to send a craftsman named Hiram (1 Kgs 7:13, 40, 45) or Huram (4:11). He is also called Huramabi in 2:13 and 4:11. The final element of his name *abi* should be taken as a title, "master" (Dillard 1987, 20), a reading adopted by the NEB, "master Huram" (2:13). This Hiram was the son of a woman from Dan (2:12), although in 2 Kgs 7:14 he is listed as the son of a widow from Naphtali. The timber Solomon needed was to be sent through Joppa (v. 16) where it would be transferred to Jerusalem.

2:17-18 [MT 2:16-17]. The conscription of the workers. Solomon took a census of all the aliens within the kingdom and there were 153,600 available for forced labor (vv. 17-18; cf. 1 Kgs 9:20-23). Solomon assigned 80,000 to be stonecutters, 70,000 to be carriers and laborers, and 3,600 to be overseers over the labor force (v. 2). This figure agrees with 1 Kgs 5:13-18 where, however, the number of overseers is only 3,300. The CHR does not mention that according to 1 Kgs 5:13 Solomon also raised a levy of forced labor from among the Israelites numbering 30,000 men. The CHR emphasizes again in 2 Chr 8:7-10 (cf. 1 Kgs 9:22) that *of the people of Israel Solomon made no slaves* (8:9). However, the evidence that many Israelites were taken into forced labor appears in 1 Kgs 11:28 where Jeroboam was in charge over all the forced labor of the house of Joseph.

3:1-17. Construction of the Temple. The site where the Temple was to be built was the threshing floor of Ornan, where Yahweh had appeared to David at the occasion of the great plague (cf. 1 Chr 21:18–22:1). Ornan appears in 2 Sam 24:16 as Araunah. The site of the Temple is also called Mount Moriah. This name appears in Gen 22:2 to designate the land to which Abraham was instructed to go and offer his son Isaac as a sacrifice. The identification of the site of the Temple with Mount Moriah serves to affirm the election of the place by Yahweh. Solomon began to build the Temple on the second month of the fourth year of his reign. The NIV adds "the second day" but this reading should be considered a dittography and should be omitted. The date is April–May. The year when Solomon began to build is uncertain, since there are several chronologies for the kings of Israel. The CHR omits 1 Kgs 6:1, which places the beginning of the construction 480 years after the exodus from Egypt.

The "foundation of the Temple" (v. 3, against NRSV; cf. NIV) was sixty cubits long and twenty cubits wide. The CHR says that an old standard was used to measure the foundation. Since there were two standards of measurement in use, it is difficult to be precise about the size of the foundation. Its measurement was approximately ninety by thirty feet. The vestibule of the Temple or the *ulam* was overlaid with pure gold (v. 4). The holy place or *hekal* was paneled with cypress and overlaid with gold. The *hekal* was decorated with palm trees, chain designs, and precious stones. The significance of the chain designs is unknown. The beams, doorframes, doors, and walls were all overlaid with gold. The gold came from Parvaim, an unknown place. Cherubim were carved on the walls of the holy place. The most holy place or *debir* was thirty by thirty feet and inlaid with gold. The most holy place was the chamber in the Temple reserved for the high priest who could enter the place only once a year (Lev 16:17). According to v. 14, a veil separated the holy place from the most holy place. This is the only place in the OT where it is said that there was a veil in the Temple. First Kgs 6:31-32 and 7:50 speak of doors separating the two chambers. It is possible that the veil was introduced in the Temple at a later time (cf. Matt 27:51), perhaps influenced by its presence in the Mosaic tabernacle (Exod 26:31-33). Two cherubim made of carved wood and overlaid with gold were in the holy of holies (v. 10). They faced the main hall and their wings touched the walls of the most holy place (vv. 10-13). At the entrance of the Temple (v. 15) there were two freestanding pillars, a feature common in other temples of the ancient Near East. The one in the south entrance of the Temple was called Jachin and the one in the north was called Boaz. The height of the pillars in v. 15 (thirty-five cubits) is different from 1 Kgs 7:15 (eighteen cubits). No satisfactory explanation has been found for this difference. It is possible that the difference is due to an error by the scribe. The pillars were decorated with interwoven chain designs and engraved pomegranates. The function and meaning of these pillars as well as the significance of their names are unknown.

4:1–5:1. The furnishings of the Temple. Solomon commissioned Hiram and the other craftsmen to make the necessary furnishings for the Temple. This section lists several items, the first of which is the altar of bronze (v. 1) where sacrifices were made (1 Kgs 8:64). The molten sea (vv. 2-6) was a basin that held 3,000 baths (17,500 gallons) of water. First Kings 7:26 says that it only held 2,000 baths. The molten sea stood on twelve bulls, divided into four groups of three, each facing a point of the compass. There were also ten smaller basins. The smaller basins were used to wash the animals for sacrifices and the molten sea was used by the priests to wash themselves. The ten gold lampstands (vv. 7-8) were made according to the specifications given by Moses (Exod 25:31-40). The ten tables were used to hold the ten gold lampstands. One hundred basins were made of gold. The purpose of these basins is unknown. They may have been used to collect the blood of the sacrifices or to make the libation offerings (Zech 9:15). There were two courts in the Temple (v. 9). They were indispensable items in the CHR's day. One of them was for the priests and the other for the people. The pots, shovels, and bowls were used to remove ashes or perhaps for the disposing of animal excrement. Solomon used so much bronze that it was not weighed. Verses 19-22 list the remaining furnishings made for use in the Temple. The CHR mentions the tables used for the showbread (Lev 24:5-9) or the bread of the Presence (Exod 25:23-30), although the CHR himself intimates that there was only one table for that purpose (13:11; 29:18).

Dedication of the Temple, 5:2–7:10

5:2-12. The transfer of the Ark. After Solomon had finished building the Temple and its furnishings, he assembled all Israel, the priests, and the Levites and commanded them to bring the Ark of the Covenant to the Temple. The occasion was the feast of the seventh month, the Feast of Tabernacles (Lev 23:33-36). The Levites were in charge of moving the Ark (1 Chr 15:2; cf. 1 Kgs 8:3 where it is said that the priests carried the Ark). They brought the Ark and the tent of meeting to the Temple. First Chr 16:1 says that David had prepared a tent to house the Ark, but the reference here to the tent of meeting (cf. 2 Chr 1:3) seems to indicate that the tent that was at Gibeon had been brought to Jerusalem at some time in the past, although this information is not provided. When the Ark arrived in the Temple, the priests carried it into the most holy place (*debir*) because the Levites were not allowed access into the inner sanctuary (Num 4:17-20). The Ark was placed beneath the cherubim. According to the CHR, the only content of the Ark was the two tables of the law that Moses had received at Sinai (Horeb). In the NT, Heb 9:4 says that the Ark contained a golden urn with manna and Aaron's rod. This information is not found in the OT (cf. Exod 16:33; Num 17:10). After the Ark had been placed in the Temple, the Levites, dressed in special clothing, played their instruments and in unison sang a hymn of thanksgiving to Yahweh. This song (v. 13) is repeated several times in other contexts (Pss 100:5; 106:1; 136:1). This was the same song the Levites sang before the ark as they gave thanks to Yahweh (1 Chr 16:41) and it was the same song sung at the dedication of the new Temple (Ezra 3:10-11).

5:13-14. The glory of Yahweh. In the midst of such solemnity, the glory of Yahweh was manifested. With the presence of the Ark in the inner sanctuary, Yahweh took possession of the house dedicated to his honor.

6:1-2. Solomon's response. The glory of Yahweh had filled the Temple, symbolizing his presence in the sanctuary. Solomon's words reflect the tradition that

Yahweh lived in darkness (Exod 20:21). In the Temple the inner sanctuary was constantly in darkness since the chamber where the Ark resided had no windows.

6:3-11. Solomon addresses the people. In Israel, it was the priest's responsibility to bless the people (Num 6:22-27). Solomon's blessing of Israel is a demonstration of the priestly role the kings at times exercised in the cult. His words to the congregation are a reaffirmation that Yahweh had chosen Jerusalem to manifest his name. *Name* appears fourteen times in this chapter to symbolize the divine presence among the people. Yahweh had also chosen David to be the leader over Israel. Since David was now dead, Solomon was the new leader. The events of that day were the fulfillment of God's promises to David.

6:12-42. Solomon's prayer of dedication. Solomon prayed the dedication prayer kneeling on a bronze platform prepared for this solemn occasion. Kneeling and spreading the hands toward heaven were common gestures associated with prayer. In his prayer Solomon acknowledged that Yahweh was a faithful God who "keeps the covenant and who keeps being faithful" (v. 14, author trans.). Then Solomon made several requests of Yahweh: that Yahweh keep his promise to continue David's dynasty (vv. 16-17); that he hear the supplications of the people made in the Temple (v. 21); that he arbitrate between individuals who seek divine guidance (vv. 22-23); that he forgive Israel whenever they are defeated because of sin (vv. 24-25); and that he hear the prayers of the people in times of drought and other natural disasters (vv. 26-31). Solomon also asked God to hear the prayer of aliens whenever they came to pray in the Temple (vv. 32-33); that he bless the people in times of war (vv. 34-35); and that he forgive the people whenever they sin (vv. 36-39). In 1 Kgs 8:53 Solomon's prayer ends with a reference to the Mosaic covenant. The CHR ends Solomon's prayer with a quotation from Ps 132:8-10. This quotation deals with the ark and God's promise to David. With this substitution, the CHR is clearly emphasizing that the covenant that Yahweh made with Israel culminated with David and his dynasty.

7:1-11. The dedication of the Temple. After Solomon finished his prayer, fire came from heaven and consumed the sacrifice (cf. 1 Chr 21:26). The fire from heaven and the presence of the glory of Yahweh in the Temple serve to legitimate the new sanctuary. Since the THEOPHANY of 7:1-3 appears to repeat the events of 5:13-14, some scholars believe that this passage is an addition to Chronicles and that it is a parallel of the first account (Dillard 1987, 36). When the people saw the glory of Yahweh, they bowed down to the pavement in awe and sang a song of thanksgiving (cf. 5:13). The number of sacrifices offered is very high and would require many days to finish. However, since there were large numbers of people attending the dedication of the Temple, a large quantity of food was needed to feed them, thus making a large number feasible in this context. Hamath and the Brook of Egypt describe the ideal borders of Israel from north to south. According to the CHR (v. 10), the festivities, including the dedication of the Temple and the Festival of Tabernacles (or Booths), lasted twenty-two days, and on the twenty-third day

Solomon sent the people home. However, 1 Kgs 8:65-66 has a different version, in which the festival only lasted seven days. The CHR attempts to explain 1 Kings by saying that both the dedication of the Temple and the celebration of the Festival of Tabernacles lasted three weeks. Verse 11 is a summary statement of Solomon's building activities, since the construction of the Temple took seven years and the construction of Solomon's palace thirteen years (1 Kgs 6:38–7:1).

God's Answer to Solomon, 7:11-22

God's answer to Solomon's prayer came at night, as it had come at Gibeon (1 Kgs 9:1-9). Yahweh had chosen the Temple to be a house of sacrifice (v. 12). He also promised to forgive the sins of the people and heal their land as Solomon had requested, provided the people meet four conditions: they must humble themselves; they must pray; they must seek God's face; and they must turn or repent from their evil ways. In turn, God promised to hear their prayer, forgive their sins, and heal their land. God's answer to Solomon expressed his desire to restore the people. This verse is a clear expression of the CHR's view of immediate retribution. To the CHR reward follows obedience and punishment follows disobedience. To the CHR reward and punishment are not delayed but are dispensed immediately. Yahweh told Solomon that if he obeyed the commandments his dynasty would last but if he disobeyed and worshiped other gods, then the people would go into exile and the exalted house he had built would be destroyed and become an object of ridicule among the nations.

The Glory of Solomon's Reign, 8:1-18

8:1-11. Solomon's political success. The CHR reverses (v. 2) the statement in Kings that Solomon gave twenty cities to Hiram in order to pay his debt (1 Kgs 9:11-13). This reversal may reflect the fact that, since Hiram did not like the cities, he returned them after Solomon paid his debt. The conquest of Hamath-zobah is not mentioned in Kings. Since David conquered Zobah (1 Chr 18:3), the CHR is saying that Solomon's empire included sections of Aramean territory, including Tadmor, the famous caravan city northeast of Damascus (v. 4). The CHR says that Solomon placed the conquered population under forced labor (cf. 1 Kgs 9:20-23). However, the statement in v. 9 that Solomon did not place the people of Israel under forced labor contradicts 1 Kgs 5:13 where it is clearly stated that a levy of forced labor was taken from all Israel (see commentary at 2 Chr 2:17-18). The number of supervisors over the forced labor was 250, which differs from 1 Kgs 9:23 (550 supervisors). The different numbers may reflect a scribal error in Chronicles. The CHR also mentions that Solomon moved the daughter of Pharaoh (cf. 1 Kgs 3:1) from the city of David to the palace he had built for her. Because she was a Gentile and a woman she could not be in contact with the places where the ark had been. This concern reflects the CHR's concern for ritual purity (cf. Lev 15:19-24).

8:12-16. Solomon's religious success. This section is an expansion of 1 Kgs 9:25. It describes the work of Solomon in the presentation of the daily sacrifices, at the weekly sabbath, at the new moon festival, and at the three annual festivals. The role Solomon played in these sacrifices is not clear. The CHR omits the fact that Solomon also offered incense, which was the duty of the sons of Aaron (2 Chr 26:16-21). But by declaring that Solomon offered these sacrifices according to the commandment of Moses, the CHR intimates that Solomon exercised an officiating capacity within the cult. Solomon also appointed the divisions of the priests and the Levites as David had commanded (1 Chr 23–26). The establishment of the sacrifices and the organization of the priests and Levites mark the completion of Solomon's major work, the building of the Temple.

8:17-18. Solomon's commercial success. Solomon's vast commercial enterprise was accomplished in partnership with Hiram, king of Tyre. 1 Kgs 9:26-27 indicates that Solomon's fleet was based at Ezion-geber and Elath (*Eloth* NRSV). With the help of Hiram's expert sailors, Solomon's servants went to Ophir from where they brought much gold. The land of Ophir is unknown (see 1 Chr 29:4). The total amount of gold was reported to be 450 talents (420 talents in 1 Kgs 9:28) or about sixteen tons.

Solomon's Riches, 9:1-31

9:1-12. The visit of the queen of Sheba. This section concludes the CHR's description of Solomon's reign. The narrative of the visit of the queen of Sheba follows 1 Kgs 10:1-13 with the addition of v. 10. Sheba has been identified with the land of the Sabeans in southwest Arabia. The Sabeans were merchants (Isa 60:6; Ezek 27:22) who dealt in frankincense and myrrh (Jer 6:20). To judge from the large gift of spices, gold, and precious stones she brought (v. 1), it is clear that trade was the main reason for her visit. Since Solomon monopolized most of the caravan routes, her spice business was deeply affected. The large gift she offered to Solomon was intended to assure that her trade would have access to the routes controlled by Solomon. According to the CHR, the reason for her visit was Solomon's wisdom and the splendor of his court. When she saw the glory of Solomon's kingdom she praised his God. Her words exalting Yahweh should be understood as the language of diplomacy and not the language of faith. At the end of the visit Solomon granted her request, which is left unmentioned.

9:13-28. Solomon's wealth and fame. The annual revenue received by the court was 666 talents of gold (twenty-five tons), in addition to income from commerce, trade, tolls, and taxation (v. 14). With this gold Solomon made hundreds of decorative shields, which he placed in the House of the Forest of Lebanon, one of the governmental buildings he built in Jerusalem made of wood from Lebanon (1 Kgs 7:2). He also made an ivory throne overlaid with gold (v. 17). Whether the back of the throne "was a calf's head" (cf. 1 Kgs 10:19; so RSV, following the LXX), "had a rounded top" (so NIV following the MT), or *was rounded in the back* is difficult to decide. The CHR avoids the problem of a possible identification of the cow's head with the golden calf of Aaron (Exod 32) and JEROBOAM I (1 Kgs 12:25-33) by saying that the throne had a *footstool* (v. 18).

Most of Solomon's gold was brought in "ships of TARSHISH" (1 Kgs 10:22). The CHR understands Tarshish to be a location (cf Jonah 1:3), perhaps a place in Spain. However, Tarshish should not be understood as a place but rather as a general designation for a seagoing ship or a type of merchant ship used on long voyages (DeVries 1990, 875). Gordon (1962) has proposed that Tarshish designates a distant place. Dillard (1987, 73) has suggested that in the days of the CHR, Tarshish was the equivalent of "going to the ends of the earth." The CHR concludes the narrative of Solomon's reign by summarizing the extent of his wealth (v. 24), his military power (v. 25) and the extent of his reign (v. 26).

9:29-31. Solomon's death. The CHR presents Solomon as a king like David who obeyed the word of God and thus fulfilled the conditions imposed by Yahweh for a successful monarchy (1 Chr 28:5-7). However, the picture that the CHR presents of Solomon is idealized. This idealization of Solomon forces the CHR to eliminate all the negative events that darkened his reign. All of the deeds of Solomon mentioned in 1 Kgs 11:1-39 are omitted by the CHR. The concluding formula for his reign is taken from 1 Kgs 11:41-43. The "Acts of Solomon" mentioned in 1 Kgs 11:41 may refer to court records, similar to the annals of the Assyrian kings. The CHR mentions three additional sources: the writings of Nathan, Ahijah, and Iddo (v. 2). Although many scholars identify these works with the book of Kings, it is possible that they refer to court records available to the CHR.

The History of the Kings of Judah, 10:1–36:21

The remainder of 2 Chronicles deals with the reign of JUDAH and the kings who sat upon the throne of David. The kings of the Northern Kingdom (ISRAEL) are not completely ignored. Some of the northern kings are mentioned, but only when they have some relationship with the kings of Judah. The CHR's emphasis on Judah and the house of David stems from his theological view. This view stresses that royal dignity was given to Judah because of David and because Yahweh had chosen Jerusalem to be his city and the Temple to be his habitation. Some Judean kings receive more attention than others. The amount of attention is directly related to the king's obedience to the word of God. Jehoshaphat, Hezekiah, and Josiah are presented as ideal kings because they were faithful to Yahweh and obedient to his words.

The Reign of Rehoboam, 10:1–12:16

The story of REHOBOAM is lengthy because it is related to the division of the kingdom and its aftermath. Chapter 10 deals with the rebellion of the ten tribes; chap. 11 deals with the events of Rehoboam's reign; and chap. 12 deals with his infidelity and punishment.

10:1-19. The division of the kingdom. After the death of Solomon, Rehoboam was declared king over Judah but needed the approval of the northern tribes to rule over all Israel. So, Rehoboam went to SHECHEM to receive the approval of the ten tribes. There, the elders of Israel, together with Jeroboam, presented their demands to Rehoboam. Jeroboam was the Ephraimite in charge of the forced labor over the house of Joseph (1 Kgs 11:26-28) who had to flee to Egypt to escape Solomon's attempt on his life (1 Kgs 11:40). The elders of the northern tribes requested that Rehoboam lift the forced labor his father Solomon had imposed upon them. Rehoboam asked for three days to consider their request. During this time he took counsel with the elders who had advised his father and they advised him to hear their request: *"If you will be kind to this people and please them, and speak good words to them, they will be your servants forever"* (v. 7). The CHR here changes the words of the elders as found in 1 Kgs 12:7. In Kings the elders ask Rehoboam to be a "servant" to the people and "serve" them. The change reflects the CHR's view that the people of the Northern Kingdom should be subjects to the house of David and not the other way around.

Rehoboam did not accept the advice of the elders who had served under his father. Instead, he took counsel with *the young men who had grown up with him* (v. 8). The expression *young men* may refer to the princes who were members of the royal court (cf. 11:22) or to inexperienced counselors who were not seasoned in the affairs of government. Their advice was to increase the burden Solomon had imposed upon them.

Rehoboam's decision was interpreted by the CHR as *a turn of affairs brought about by God* (v. 15). The division of the kingdom happened to fulfill the words that the prophet Ahijah from Shiloh had spoken concerning the split of the united kingdom after the death of Solomon (1 Kgs 11:29-39). Although the CHR does not give the words of Ahijah, his reference to Ahijah and his prophecy is an indictment of Solomon and an affirmation of the CHR's theology of retribution, that disobedience to the word of God brings immediate punishment. Since the CHR attempted to idealize Solomon, most of the blame for the division of the kingdom is placed upon Rehoboam.

The northern tribes rejected Rehoboam and the house of David by uttering a slogan voiced by Sheba (2 Sam 20:1) when he and several men from Israel rebelled against David. This song of protest had become a slogan for defiance and rebellion against the house of David (cf. 1 Sam 25:10). Rehoboam attempted to restore his control over the northern tribes by sending Hadoram (Adoram, 1 Kgs 12:18; Adoniram, 1 Kgs 4:6), the officer in charge of the forced labor, to deal with the rebellious tribes. The people stoned him and Rehoboam had to flee in his chariot back to Jerusalem. The CHR's statement that *Israel has been in rebellion against the house of David* (v. 19) reflects his view that the true Israel has its home in Jerusalem and its king in David and his descendants.

11:1-4. Shemaiah's prophecy. Rehoboam still had visions of uniting the kingdom again by the power of the army (v. 1). He assembled an army from Judah and from Benjamin to fight against Israel. The size of Rehoboam's army was 180,000 men, a large number that may be exaggerated. However, his army was not as large as the army of Asa with 580,000 men (14:8) or the army of Uzziah with 307,500 men (26:13). Civil war was averted because the prophet Shemaiah intervened and stopped Rehoboam from fighting Jeroboam. He told the king not to fight because the division was from Yahweh. The hostility between north and south was averted temporarily but the animosity continued, for there was continual war between Rehoboam and Jeroboam (cf. 12:5). The CHR believed that *all Israel* lived in Judah and Benjamin (v. 3), as well as in the Northern Kingdom (11:13). To the CHR, the faithful people who lived in the north (cf. 11:13-17) were also part of *all Israel* since they were *kindred* (v. 4).

11:5-12. Rehoboam's fortifications. Rehoboam fortified 15 cities in Judah (the inclusion of Benjamin is to describe the limit of the Southern Kingdom) in order to protect his kingdom from foreign incursions. It is possible that these cities were built before the invasion of Shishak, king of Egypt (cf. 12:2) although some scholars have said that they were built as a result of this invasion. Recent archaeological excavations on these sites have uncovered fortifications that may be dated to the time of Rehoboam. Since these fortified cities were located in the hill country, south and west of Jerusalem, they give evidence that they were built to protect the kingdom against the Philistines in the west and Egypt in the south.

11:13-17. The migration of the Levites. This event has no parallel in 1 Kings. The religious reforms established by Jeroboam (cf. 1 Kgs 12:28-33) were seen as a denial of true Yahwism and prompted the flight of the priests and Levites to Judah (v. 13) and of the faithful people who refused to sacrifice outside of Jerusalem (v. 16). Jeroboam's reforms included several innovations that the faithful Yahwists considered apostasy (v. 15). The high places were the local sanctuaries where sacrifices were made. The satyrs were believed to be demons in the form of goats. The calves were either considered pedestals upon which Yahweh stood or direct representations of Yahweh. In the religion of the Canaanites the calves (or bulls) were symbols of fertility and part of the worship of Baal. The calves were condemned by the prophets because they became objects of worship (cf. Hos 13:2). The faithful Yahwists who migrated to Judah brought peace and security to the nation for three years (v. 17). This means that Rehoboam abandoned Yahweh in the fourth year of his reign (12:1) and that punishment came in the fifth year in the form of the Egyptian invasion.

11:18-23. Rehoboam's family. Rehoboam had a large family. His household consisted of eighteen wives, sixty concubines, twenty-eight sons, and sixty daughters. One of his wives was the daughter of Jerimoth, David's son. Since Jerimoth's name does not appear in any of David's family lists, it is possible he was the son of one of David's many concubines. Another wife was Maacah. Maacah is listed here as the mother of Abijah and the daughter of Absalom, another of David's sons. In 1 Kgs 15:10 she appears as the mother of Asa and thus as the wife of Abijah. In 13:2 she is listed as Micaiah the daughter of Uriel of Gibeah. If Maacah and Micaiah are two different forms of the same name, then the conclusion is that Maacah, the daughter of Absalom, was Rehoboam's wife and Abijah's mother and that Micaiah (or Maacah), the daughter of Uriel, was Abijah's wife and Asa's mother.

Rehoboam's son Abijah was appointed *nagid*, the king designate who would succeed his father upon the throne of Judah. Rehoboam placed his sons throughout Judah and Benjamin and in the fortified cities. This wise move helped Rehoboam to extend his influence over the cities of Judah and at the same time to solidify his kingdom against possible revolt.

12:1-16. Egypt's attack on Jerusalem. The CHRdoes not specify what the sins of Rehoboam and the people of Judah and Benjamin (*all Israel*) were. In 7:19, forsaking Yahweh involves the acceptance and worship of foreign gods. According to 1 Kgs 14:22-24 the people promoted the worship of Asherah and the practice of sacred prostitution. The unfaithfulness of Rehoboam caused the invasion of Shishak, king of Egypt. Shishak (also known as Sheshonq) was the founder of the Twenty-Second Dynasty of Egypt. He ruled from 945–924 BCE. Shishak came with a large army, which included many mercenary soldiers of different ethnic backgrounds. Shishak and his army invaded Judah and, according to an inscription at Karnak detailing the invasion, he conquered more than 150 cities (ANET, 263–64). The prophet Shemaiah came to the king and his nobles in Jerusalem and announced that the invasion of Shishak was in retribution for the king's unfaithfulness. After hearing the pronouncement of the prophet, Rehoboam and the princes repented and the divine anger was subdued. Because Rehoboam and the leaders of Israel had humbled themselves before Yahweh (cf. 7:14), Jerusalem was not destroyed. According to the CHR, the people of Judah would serve Shishak for a period of time in order that they might know the true meaning of serving Yahweh. Shishak took the treasures of the Temple and of the palace. Among the booty were the decorative shields of gold Solomon had made (v. 9).

The concluding statement about Rehoboam's kingship (vv. 13-16) presents a summary of his reign. He began to reign at the age of forty-one and *reigned seventeen years in Jerusalem*. His mother was Naamah, an Ammonite, and he did what was evil in the eyes of Yahweh (cf. 1 Kgs 14:22-24). The CHR ends the narrative about Rehoboam by saying that the remainder of his acts as king were registered in the annals of the prophets Shemaiah and Iddo.

The Reign of Abijah, 13:1–14:1 [MT 13:1-23]

After the death of Rehoboam, his son ABIJAH became king. His name means "My Father is Yahweh." In 1 Kgs 14:31; 15:1, he is called Abijam, "My Father is [the sea god] Yam." Since the CHR was sympathetic with Abijah it is possible that he tried to eliminate the reference to the Canaanite god by giving Abijah a Yahwistic name. His mother's name was Micaiah, the daughter of Uriel (see commentary at 11:20, above).

The narrative about the war between Abijah and Jeroboam is unique to Chronicles; it was taken from an unknown source. The number of troops on both sides cannot be taken as an accurate number. The numbers reflect the census of Israel and Judah taken by Joab (2 Sam 24:9). The purpose is to emphasize the contrast between the two armies and the heroic struggle of Judah to achieve a great victory. Before the fight, Abijah addressed the troops of Israel from a mountain. The location of Mount Zemaraim is unknown. It was located in the hill country of EPHRAIM, probably near the city of the same name (Josh 18:22). The speech was addressed to Jeroboam and *all Israel*. Abijah's pronouncement is typical of speeches found in Chronicles. The CHR develops the speech in order to communicate his theological view to his audience. In the speech Abijah makes two important points: (1) He speaks of the perpetuity of the Davidic COVENANT (1 Chr 17) established with Israel by a covenant of salt (cf. Lev 2:13; Num 18:19). Although the precise meaning of this expression is unknown, the preservative quality of salt makes it "the ideal symbol of the perdurability of a covenant" (Milgrom 1991, 191). Jeroboam and a group of *worthless scoundrels* (v. 7; Heb. "sons of Belial/Beliar"—see 1 Sam 10:27) revolted against Rehoboam and prevailed because he was inexperienced. Williamson (1982, 253) has taken a different approach. He believes the word *defied* (v. 7) should be translated "persuaded." Hence, these *worthless scoundrels* gathered around Rehoboam to persuade him not to listen to the advice of the elders (10:8-11). Abijah appealed to the people of Israel not to resist the kingdom of Yahweh, which was present in the dynasty of David (v. 8). (2) Abijah emphasizes the legitimacy of the Aaronic priesthood and of the Levites. He said Israel followed the sins of Jeroboam when they sacrificed to the golden calves because his religious innovations were an illegitimate cult of Yahweh. Only Judah had remained faithful to God's covenant and only the sons of AARON and the Levites could offer proper sacrifices to God. The expression *do not fight against the LORD* (v. 12) was an appeal to Israel to submit to God and to the house of David. Jeroboam's response was a surprise attack. He divided his army into two groups and attacked Abijah from two sides. Confronted with the superiority of Jeroboam's army, Abijah cried out to Yahweh. The priests invoked the presence of God with the sound of trumpets and as a result Yahweh *defeated Jeroboam and all Israel before Abijah and Judah* (v. 15) because they relied upon Yahweh, the God of their fathers (v. 18). As a result of this victory, Abijah took possession of three northern cities, including BETHEL, the religious center of the Northern Kingdom. But control over Bethel did not last long because before the days of Amos (eighth century BCE) the sanctuary at Bethel was again one of the most important places of worship in Israel (see Amos 7:10-17). Jeroboam did not recover from this defeat. According to the CHR, the Lord smote him and he died (v. 20), but according to 1 Kgs 15:1, 7-8, Jeroboam outlived Abijah. The CHR summarizes Abijah's reign by declaring that Yahweh blessed him with a large family and by saying that the rest of Abijah's acts were registered *in the story of the prophet Iddo* (v. 22).

The Hebrew word *midrash* (v. 22 NAB, NJB; *story* NRSV) appears only here and in 24:27. The word simply means a collection of writings that may or may not have contained some notations. Wagner has suggested that the word may refer to a historical work that was an interpretation of the CHR's source (Wagner 1978, 306). After Abijah's death the land enjoyed rest for ten years (14:1). This statement resembles the formulation found in the book of Judges describing the time of peace during and after the death of a judge.

The Reign of Asa, 14:2–16:14 [MT 14:1–16:14]

The account of Asa's reign is greatly expanded in Chronicles. The CHR dedicates a large portion of his history to the reign of Asa because of the king's effort to bring religious reforms to Judah. Because of his faithfulness to Yahweh Asa enjoyed a prosperous reign. However, the CHR does not gloss over Asa's sin—his reliance on the Aramean army rather than putting his trust in Yahweh (16:7-8).

14:1-8 [MT 14:2-7]. The early years of Asa's reign. During the early part of Asa's reign, the land enjoyed a prolonged time of peace and prosperity. This peaceful period is attributed not to Abijah's victory over Jeroboam (13:13-20) but to Asa's faithfulness to Yahweh (14:2, 6). Asa's reform probably began early in his kingdom. He removed several items associated with Canaanite religious practices. The asherim were cultic poles associated with the cult of ASHERAH, the goddess of fertility. The meaning of the Hebrew word translated *incense altars* (v. 5) is debated. Asa used the time of peace to build new fortifications around the cities of Judah. He also increased his army (cf. v. 8 with 11:1 and 13:3) and equipped it with better weapons. The statement in v. 7, that *the land is still ours* may be a way for the CHR to remind his readers that the land was lost because of disobedience to God.

14:9-15 [MT 14:8-14]. Zerah's invasion. The CHR does not give a reason for Zerah's invasion. Zerah, the Ethiopian or Cushite, has been identified as a Nubian; however this identification has been highly disputed. It is possible that Cushite was "the name of a Palestinian ethnic group" allied with the inhabitants of Gerar (v. 14; cf. De Vries 1989, 299), a city located between Gaza and Beer-sheba. The size of Zerah's army is excessive; in fact, the Hebrew can be understood differently: instead of attacking Asa *with an army of a million men* (v. 9), he attacked "with an army of thousands upon thousands" (NIV mg.). The whole narrative is infused with the terminology of holy war. Yahweh defeats Zerah's army because of Asa's prayer and his reliance upon God. Asa and his army slaughtered the enemy, plundered their cities, and returned from this great victory with the spoils of victory.

15:1-7. The sermon of Azariah. After his victory over Zerah, Asa is met by a prophet of Yahweh. The prophet *Azariah son of Oded* appears only here. His ORACLE is a sermon to Asa and the people (v. 2a) that reflects the preaching ministry of the Levites (von Rad 1966, 271). According to von Rad, the sermon is divided into three sections. The first section, "doctrine," declares that Yahweh would be with Asa and the people as long as they remained faithful to Yahweh (v. 2b). The second section, "application," uses Israel's past history, probably the period of the judges, to show that abandoning Yahweh leads to adversity and national defeat and that loyalty to Yahweh leads to blessing and victory (vv. 3-6). In the third section, "exhortation," Azariah admonishes Asa to continue his work because God will bless him.

15:8-19. Asa's religious reform. Azariah's sermon had its intended effect. Asa continued his reform (vv. 8-15), extending it to the cities he had conquered from Ephraim. There is no reference in Chronicles to Asa's having conquered these cities. As part of the reform, Asa removed the idols worshiped by the people (cf. 1 Kgs 15:12) and repaired the altar of Yahweh. In order to provide religious authority to his reform, Asa called for a solemn assembly in Jerusalem and there gathered Judah and Benjamin together with many immigrants from the Northern Kingdom. The mention in v. 9 of Simeonites living in Jerusalem as resident aliens is puzzling. Simeon was a southern tribe and from the beginning of the monarchy the Simeonites had been assimilated into Judah. It is possible that some Simeonites had to move to Jerusalem because of the military struggle against the Edomites. Asa and the people entered into a covenant in which they made promises to seek Yahweh and be faithful to him. The covenant ceremony was accompanied by great rejoicing (vv. 14-15).

As part of his reform Asa removed his grandmother Maacah (so NIV; cf. commentary at 11:18-23), the queen mother, because of her worship of Asherah. The queen mother had an important role in Israelite society; because of her position, she also had some influence on the religious life of the nation. Asa also destroyed the image of Asherah and brought some free-will gifts to the Temple that he and his father Abijah had accumulated as spoils of war. Asa however was unable to remove the high places from Israel (cf. 1 Kgs 15:14).

16:1-6. Asa's treaty with Aram. The chronological information in v. 1 is related to 15:19. In 15:19 it is said that *there was no more war until the thirty-fifth year of the reign of Asa* (NRSV, REB, and NIV add *more* to clarify the text: "there was no *more* war").

At face value, the CHR's statement is problematic for several reasons. First, it overlooks Asa's wars against Zerah (14:9-15) and against Ephraim (15:8). Second, the CHR's chronological information contradicts several events as narrated in 1 Kgs. In 1 Kgs 15:16 it is said that "there was war between Asa and Baasha all their days." In 1 Kgs 16:8 it is said that after the death of Baasha in the twenty-sixth year of Asa, Elah began to reign over Israel. Williamson (1982, 256–57) accepts Thiele's (1965) view, followed by De Vries (1962, 580–99), that the thirty-fifth and the thirty-sixth year refer, not to Asa's reign but to the division of the monarchy. Dillard (1987, 124), however, rejects Thiele's harmonization for three reasons: it would be the only passage where a dating would be given from the division of the monarchy; because it ignores the clear statement of the text; and because it counters the CHR's theological view that retribution follows immediately after an offense. It is possible the numbers reflect a copyist's error, who misread thirty-five and thirty-six for fifteen and sixteen.

Thus, in the sixteenth year of Asa, confrontation between Asa and Baasha erupted when Baasha built a fortress at Ramah, a city located between the kingdoms of Judah and Israel, about five miles north of Jerusalem.

So intimidated was Asa by the threat posed by Baasha that he took silver and gold to make a treaty with BEN-HADAD, king of Aram, requesting him to break his alliance with Baasha. Ben-hadad accepted Asa's offer. He invaded Israel and conquered several northern cities. Baasha was forced to stop fortifying Ramah and Asa took the materials left behind and used them to build his own fortified cities.

16:7-10. Hanani's rebuke. Asa's decision to rely on Ben-hadad brought a stern rebuke from the prophet Hanani, who condemned Asa for paying tribute to a foreign king rather than relying on God. Hanani reminded Asa that in the past Yahweh gave him victory over his enemies because he had trusted God. Yahweh protects the blameless, those who devote themselves totally to God. Asa spurned the prophet's rebuke and, angry at his words, imprisoned him and the people who protested, probably some of the prophet's supporters.

16:11-14. The end of Asa's reign. The CHR concludes the story of Asa's reign by informing his readers where he found his information. The *Book of the Kings of Judah and Israel* (v. 11) should not be identified with the biblical Book of Kings but rather with one of the many sources used by the CHR. At the end of his reign Asa was struck by a severe foot disease, which the CHR does not identify. The CHR says that even in his illness Asa did not seek Yahweh but trusted the physicians. This statement should not be interpreted as an attack upon doctors. These physicians probably were involved with magic powers or pagan divinities. The CHR emphasizes that Asa trusted the physicians alone and that he did not consult Yahweh. Two years later Asa died. He was buried with much honor in a burial chamber he had prepared for himself. The fire made in his honor should not be understood as cremation but as a memorial to honor the dead king (cf. 21:19).

The Reign of Jehoshaphat, 17:1–20:37

Four chapters of Chronicles are dedicated to the reign of JEHOSHAPHAT. This extensive treatment of the reign of Jehoshaphat is because of his piety and his faithfulness to God. He is praised as a good king whose heart was firm with Yahweh. Most of the information about Jehoshaphat in Chronicles is distinctive to the CHR.

17:1-6. The establishment of Jehoshaphat's kingdom. The CHR stresses that Yahweh blessed Jehoshaphat and established his kingdom because of his faithfulness. Jehoshaphat's heart was firm in the ways of Yahweh. He closed the high places that had become centers of BAAL worship in Judah; he removed the asherim, the wooden poles used in the worship of ASHERAH, the fertility goddess; and he did not go after the Baals. As a result, God established his kingdom, Judah brought tribute, and Jehoshaphat had great riches and honor.

17:7-9. The mission of the priests and Levites. Another sign of Jehoshaphat's piety was that in the third year of his reign he sent five civil servants, eight Levites and two priests to teach the law of Yahweh in the cities of Judah (vv. 7-9). The content of the law of Yahweh is unknown. One possibility is that this Torah was an earlier form of the law of Moses.

17: 10-19. Jehoshaphat's powerful kingdom. Another sign of God's blessing
was that the nations around Judah, recognizing that Jehoshaphat was a powerful
king, made no war against him. The Philistines paid tribute to Jehoshaphat as did
the Arabian seminomadic tribes who brought a large quantity of cattle as a sign of
friendship (vv. 10-11). At the same time Jehoshaphat expanded the defenses of the
kingdom by organizing his army and building fortifications and store cities around
Judah. The large number of soldiers in Jehoshaphat's army, larger than previous
armies, demonstrates, in the CHR's perspective, the great honor Yahweh had
bestowed upon him.

18:1–19:3. Jehoshaphat's alliance with Ahab. In this section, the CHR follows
his source closely, taking his information almost verbatim from 1 Kgs 22. He provides an introduction (18:1-3) and a conclusion (19:1-3) in order to condemn
Jehoshaphat for his alliance with *those who hate the LORD* (v. 2). Jehoshaphat became related to AHAB, king of Israel, by the marriage alliance of his son Jehoram
with Athaliah, the daughter of Ahab and JEZEBEL (on Athaliah's relationship to
Ahab, cf. commentary at 21:1-7). At some indefinite time (v. 2) after this event,
Ahab prepared a great feast for Jehoshaphat to convince him to form an alliance
against Ramoth-gilead. So strong was the CHR against this alliance that he uses a
word found frequently in Deuteronomy (cf. Deut 13:6) to describe seduction into
apostasy (Ackroyd 1973, 144). Verses 4-34 repeat 1 Kgs 22:4-36.

After he was invited to join Ahab against Ramoth-gilead, Jehoshaphat decided
to inquire of Yahweh for divine guidance. Ahab gathered 400 prophets who as one
voice guaranteed victory in battle. Jehoshaphat requests another prophet of Yahweh
(18:6), implying that he was not very sure of the judgment of Ahab's prophets.
While the king's messengers were on their way to bring Micaiah, the son of Imlah,
to provide another oracle, Zedekiah, probably the leader of the prophets, made horns
of iron to validate his conviction that Yahweh would give Ahab total victory against
the Arameans. Micaiah was requested to speak an affirmative word to Ahab, and
when he did the king knew that Micaiah was mocking him. Requested to speak the
truth, Micaiah warns of Israel's defeat. He said that his oracle had come out of a
vision of the heavenly council where he had heard God's decision.

Ahab rejected Micaiah's word, placed him in prison, and went to fight against
the Arameans. Jehoshaphat went to war wearing his royal clothes and Ahab disguised himself in order not to be recognized. The king of Aram came to meet them.
Jehoshaphat cried to Yahweh for help and the Aramean soldiers turned back from
pursuing him. As for Ahab, he was mortally wounded by an archer who "drew his
bow at a venture" (v. 33, RSV).

Ahab died as Micaiah had said and Jehoshaphat returned to Jerusalem only to
be confronted by the prophet Jehu (19:1). Jehu was the son of Hanani, the prophet
who had confronted Asa, Jehoshaphat's father (16:7). Jehu rebuked Jehoshaphat because he had helped the wicked and had loved those who hate Yahweh (19:2). Yet,
because of his previous acts of faithfulness, Jehoshaphat was not punished (19:3).

19:4-11. Jehoshaphat's judicial reform. In order to strengthen his religious reforms Jehoshaphat extended his reform to the system of administration of justice in Judah. Some scholars have denied that this judicial reform took place in the days of Jehoshaphat, but the historicity of the reform has been strongly defended by Albright (1950, 61–82). According to the CHR, the purpose of the reform was to bring the people back to Yahweh (v. 4). Even though the CHR says that the king left his palace in Jerusalem and went throughout the kingdom again, this statement should be understood as a continuation of the teaching mission accomplished by means of his emissaries (17:7). The king went from Beer-sheba in the south to the hill country of Ephraim in the north. This south-north direction for the country represents the CHR's view of the land and departs from the traditional north-south direction.

Jehoshaphat established judges in the fortified cities of Judah to hear the people's cases. He also established a supreme court in Jerusalem comprised of Levites, priests, and the heads of Israelite families (v. 8). The supreme court had civil and religious jurisdiction over the judges of the cities concerning their interpretation of the law. Amariah, the chief priest presided over matters and cases related to God. Zebadiah, the son of Ishmael and the leader of the house of Judah, presided over matters related to the king. The Levites would serve as officials of the court, probably responsible for implementing the decisions of the court. Jehoshaphat exhorts the judges to arbitrate justly, warning them against injustice, partiality, and bribery (v. 7) and reminding them that they themselves stood under the judgment of Yahweh (v. 11).

20:1-30. Jehoshaphat's defeat of Moab and Ammon. This section is distinctive to the CHR; it is not found in Kings. The chronological introduction *after this* (v. 1) does not provide any specific reference to time. The invaders, the Moabites, the Ammonites, and the Meunites, came from the south, from beyond the Dead Sea. According to the NRSV they are coming from Edom. However, this reading follows one Dead Sea manuscript rather than the MT. Following the MT, the text should read "from ARAM," that is, the foreign alliance that was attacking Judah at the instigation of the Arameans.

Without much time to make preparations, Jehoshaphat became afraid and set out to seek divine help. He assembled the people before the new court of the Temple and proclaimed a general fast. This new court (v. 5) may refer to an addition to the Temple constructed in the days of Jehoshaphat. The king prayed a fervent prayer (vv. 6-12). His prayer is reminiscent of Solomon's prayer at the dedication of the Temple (2 Chr 6:24-31, 34-35). Jehoshaphat's prayer affirms God's power to deliver the nation in the present (v. 6) in the same way he delivered the people in the past (v. 7), and then asks God for judgment against the enemies (vv. 8-12).

As the king and the people prayed, the Spirit of Yahweh raised Jehaziel, a Levite from the sons of ASAPH, to respond to Jehoshaphat's prayer. Jehaziel pronounced an oracle of salvation with the formula *fear not* at the beginning and at the end of the oracle (vv. 15-17). Jehaziel announced that Yahweh himself will fight for the people and give them a great victory. The enemy will come *by the ascent* [or Pass] *of Ziz* (v. 16), southwest of Tekoa, a few miles north of Engedi. Jehoshaphat and the assembly of Judah fell down before Yahweh and worshiped as the Levites praised God with a loud voice.

During the march toward the place of victory, Jehoshaphat exhorted the people to believe in God (cf. Isa 7:9) and to believe also in the prophets. The Levites joined the procession singing a hymn of thanksgiving that appears often in the Psalms (106:1; 107:1; 136:1). The intervention of Yahweh was immediate and powerful. Yahweh set an ambush against the invading army and the soldiers killed themselves. So large were the spoils of war it took the people three days to collect them. The place where God gave Judah the victory was called the Valley of Beracah, the "Valley of Blessing." The people returned to Jerusalem with great joy and much celebration. The neighbors of Israel feared Yahweh because they understood that to fight against Israel was to fight against Yahweh.

20:31-37. Jehoshaphat's last days. The CHR ends the story of Jehoshaphat with a summary of his reign. *He was thirty-five years old when he began to reign* and he reigned twenty-five years. He was a faithful king although he was unable to remove all the high places in Judah (but cf. 17:6). The CHR's explanation for this failure was that the people lacked commitment to Yahweh (v. 33).

The rest of his activities *are written in the Annals of Jehu* (v. 34) and in the general history of the kings of Judah and Israel, which here is called *the Book of the Kings of Israel* (cf. 16:11).

The final note mentions Jehoshaphat's joint maritime venture with Ahaziah, king of Israel (but contrast this reference with 1 Kgs 22:48-49). The location of TARSHISH (v. 36) is unknown. Tarshish may be a designation for a distant place (cf. commentary at 9:13-28). The destruction of Jehoshaphat's fleet (v. 37) was a punishment for entering this partnership with the wicked Ahaziah. The oracle of judgment was given by Eliezer, an unknown prophet.

The Reign of Jehoram, 21:1-20

The reign of JEHORAM received only a brief treatment by the CHR. The CHR takes most of his information from 2 Kgs 17–22 but adds additional information to emphasize Jehoram's unfaithfulness.

21:1-7. The murder of Jehoram's brothers. After the death of Jehoshaphat, Jehoram, his *firstborn* (v. 3), succeeded him on the throne of Judah. In general, the king's firstborn son ascended the throne after the death of his father, but the right of succession was not automatically given to the firstborn. Solomon (cf. 3:1-9) and Rehoboam (cf.11:18-22) became kings although they were not firstborn sons. For this reason Jehoshaphat gave gifts of silver and gold to his other sons. The text mentions six sons, although two of them have the same name (v. 2). After Jehoram was established upon the throne he killed his brothers and other persons he considered disloyal or even perhaps pretenders to the throne (v. 4).

Bright (1981, 252) has proposed that Jehoram killed his brothers at the prompting of his wife Athaliah, the daughter of Ahab and Jezebel, because "she felt her own position to be insecure." Athaliah's relationship to Ahab is problematic. She is listed as the daughter of Ahab and Jezebel in 2 Kgs 8:18 and 2 Chr 21:6 and as the daughter of OMRI in 2 Kgs 8:26 and 2 Chr 22:2. NRSV and NIV interpret the Hebrew text to mean that Athaliah was a female descendant of Omri, that is, his granddaughter. Bright contends that since Ahab and Jezebel had been married only about ten years, Athaliah was either Ahab's daughter by a previous marriage or a younger daughter of Omri who was raised by Ahab (Bright 1981, 242).

The CHR notes the consequence of Jehoram's marriage to Athaliah, the daughter of Ahab and Jezebel (v. 6): to follow in the ways of the king of Israel means to promote the cult of Baal and to encourage worship in the high places (see v. 11). The only reason the kingdom was not destroyed was because of the covenant God had made with David promising that a son of his (i.e., a male descendant) would continue to sit upon the throne. The *lamp* (v. 7) represents the permanency of David's dynasty.

21:8-10. The revolt of Edom and Libnah. During Jehoram's reign the Edomites revolted against Judah. Although the CHR says that Jehoram defeated the Edomites (but cf. 2 Kgs 8:21), he was not able to subdue them completely. During his reign Libnah also revolted against Judah. Libnah was located in the lowlands of Judah, southwest of Jerusalem. The rebellion of Edom and Libnah came because of Jehoram's unfaithfulness and as punishment for his sins (v. 10).

21:12-15. "Elijah's" letter to Jehoram. The unfaithfulness of Jehoram prompted the prophet ELIJAH to send a letter to the king pronouncing God's judgment upon him. This letter by Elijah has been the subject of much discussion. Since the synchronism of 2 Kgs 1:17 allows for Elijah to be alive at the beginning of Jehoram's reign, some scholars accept the authenticity of the letter. Other scholars say Elijah was already dead and the letter is a midrash, a composition of the CHR. Others say that it was either a letter from the prophet *Elisha* or a prophecy of an unknown prophet placed in the mouth of the renowned prophet. Since the ministry of Elijah is completely absent from Chronicles and because the content of the letter reflects the CHR's view of immediate retribution, it seems probable that Elijah's letter is the CHR's own composition.

The letter pronounces judgment upon Jehoram for his unfaithfulness and for the murder of his brothers who, in the CHR's view, were better than Jehoram (v. 13). A plague will come upon the people and upon the king's family. The king himself will be afflicted with a serious disease of the bowels (v. 15).

21:16-20. Jehoram's death. The attack by the Philistines and the Arabs is not mentioned in Kings. The Cushites (not Ethiopians, cf. 14:9) were an ethnic group who lived in the southern part of Judah. The invasion is seen as an act of Yahweh in fulfillment of Elijah's prediction. The invaders took away Jehoram's possessions, his sons and his wives. Only Jehoahaz, also known as Ahaziah (cf. 22:1), and Athaliah escaped death at the hands of the invaders. At the end of his life Jehoram became ill with an incurable bowel disease and died in much pain. Three times the CHR emphasizes that Jehoram was not honored in his death (vv. 19-20): the people did not make a fire in his honor (cf. 16:4), he died with no one's regret, and he was not buried in the tomb of the kings. Jehoram came to the throne at the age of thirty-two and reigned in Jerusalem eight years (v. 20).

The Reign of Ahaziah, 22:1-9

The source for this material is 2 Kgs 8:25-29 with some supplemental information provided by the CHR. After the death of Jehoram, Ahaziah, also known as JEHOAHAZ (21:17) was made king. Since Ahaziah was Jehoram's youngest and only surviving son, the inhabitants of Jerusalem proclaimed him king. This unusual act may indicate an emerging crisis that demanded the urgent action of the people. Then, at a later time, Ahaziah was proclaimed king by the whole nation. The MT says that he was forty-two years old when he began to reign (v. 2) but this is incorrect for his father died at the age of forty (21:20). According to 2 Kgs 8:26 he was twenty-two at the time he ascended the throne of Judah. His mother was Athaliah, the daughter of Ahab (MT "Omri": see discussion at 21:1-7). According to the CHR, Athaliah influenced Ahaziah towards the political and religious policies of the house of Ahab *to his ruin* (v. 4). This evaluation of Ahaziah's reign implies that his impious conduct, his evil politics, and his rejection of God were the causes of his having such a brief reign. His death at the hands of Jehu was *ordained of God* (v. 7).

God had commissioned Jehu to destroy the house of Ahab (v. 7; cf. 2 Kgs 9:1-13). When Ahaziah came to visit Jehoram (*Joram*, v. 7) who was recovering in JEZREEL from a wound he had received in his fight against Hazael, king of Aram, Jehu met Ahaziah and the royal entourage and killed them. Ahaziah escaped but was soon captured, brought before Jehu and then put to death. The events related to Ahaziah's death differ from the account in 2 Kgs 9:27-28. In Kings, Ahaziah was wounded in his chariot at the ascent of Gur, near Ibleam, and died in Megiddo. The CHR says he was hiding in Samaria, was captured there, and was brought to Jehu and put to death. The author of Kings also says that his servants brought Ahaziah's body to Jerusalem and buried him in the royal tomb. The CHR says that Jehu and his men buried him in respect for Jehoshaphat's faithfulness to God. These differences may not reflect divergent sources but supplemental information available to the CHR. The death of Ahaziah caused a political vacuum in Judah, since there was no one strong enough to succeed Ahaziah and rule over the nation (v. 9). This final statement prepares the reader for the usurpation of the throne by Athaliah.

The Reign of Athaliah, 22:10-12

Athaliah was not considered a legitimate ruler in the line of David. The CHR omits the traditional succession formula because her reign was regarded as a usurpation of the throne of David. With the lack of a designated heir to the throne after the death of Ahaziah (v. 9), Athaliah attempted to eliminate the remaining members of the royal family. The king's children who were about to be murdered (v. 11) were Ahaziah's sons and Athaliah's grandchildren. Only the infant JOASH escaped the extermination of the royal house. Joash was saved by his aunt Jehoshabeath, who hid him and his nurse in a bedroom of the palace. From there he was taken in the Temple and placed into the care of the high priest. Jehoshabeath's name appears as Jehosheba in 2 Kgs 11:2. She was the daughter of Jehoram (but possibly not of Athaliah) and the sister of Ahaziah. She was also the wife of JEHOIADA, the high priest. Curtis and Madsen (1910, 422) believe her relationship to the high priest was a mere conjecture of the CHR, but there is no reason to doubt this information. Athaliah ruled over Judah six years, the six years Joash spent hiding in the Temple.

The Reign of Joash, 23:1–24:27

23:1-11. The crowning of Joash. The narrative follows 2 Kgs 11:4-12 with some differences that reflect the theological view of the CHR. The crowning of Joash as the legitimate successor to the Davidic throne was done publicly by the assembly with the support of the Levites. In Kings most of these events occurred in secrecy. Instead of making an agreement with the captains of the Carites (2 Kgs 11:4) or Cherethites (1 Sam 30:14; 2 Sam 8:16), the mercenary army established by David, Jehoiada made a covenant with the commander of hundreds to protect the king's son. At the instigation of the military commanders and Jehoiada, the Levites and the leaders of Israelite families came to Jerusalem, and in the Temple made a covenant with Joash and declared him king. Since only the priests and the Levites could enter the Temple, Jehoiada made provisions to exclude from the Temple area those who were not Levites and priests. The Levites were divided into several groups and placed in strategic locations to ensure Joash's safety. Joash then received the crown and the testimony (v. 11 MT: 'ēdût) as the insignias of his office and was anointed by Jehoiada and his sons. The crown was the symbol of his royalty and the testimony was the royal protocol the king received at his ascension to the throne. The Hebrew word 'ēdût may refer to a copy of the covenant Yahweh commanded the king to make (Deut 17:18). The anointing was the pouring of oil on the head of the king to symbolize his ordination as king.

23:12-15. The death of Athaliah. The people and the Levites celebrated the coronation of Joash with the blowing of the trumpets and with musical instruments. When Athaliah saw the people running and praising the new king she came to the house of God. As she arrived there she saw the king standing by his pillar, the designated place the king occupied during worship celebrations. Athaliah tore her clothing as a sign of despair and cried, "Treason! Treason!" (v. 13) but no one answered her voice. Jehoiada ordered the captains of the guard to seize her. She was captured, taken outside the Temple area to the entrance of the Horse Gate, and put to death. The lack of any reference to the length of her reign is an indication that she was never considered a legitimate ruler of Judah.

23:16-21. The enthronement of Joash. As a result of the death of Athaliah, Jehoiada made an attempt at reforming the cult in order to eliminate Baal worship that was probably introduced by Athaliah. He made a covenant with the people and the king promising to remain faithful to God. Then the people destroyed the house of Baal, demolished his images, and tore down the altars dedicated to Baal. They also killed Mattan, the priest of Baal, probably according to the injunction of Deut 13:5-10. Jehoiada put the priests in charge of the Temple according to the organization established by David. He also put the Levites in charge of the security of the Temple. Then the captains of the army, the nobles of Judah, and then people of the land brought Joash from the Temple to the king's house and placed him upon the throne. The CHR mentions the rejoicing of the people over the restoration of the throne of David and the time of peace that followed the death of Athaliah (v. 21).

24:1-3. Evaluation of Joash. This section follows 2 Kgs 11:21-12:3 [MT 12:1-4] with the omission of the synchronism with Jehu and the fact that the high places were not eliminated. Joash began to reign when he was seven years old and reigned in Jerusalem forty years. He is credited with doing what was right in the sight of Yahweh as long as Jehoiada lived. Joash's harem seems to have been limited to two wives given to him by Jehoiada. The mention of sons and daughters is a declaration of God's blessing upon Joash and an affirmation that the threat to the continuation of the dynasty was over.

24:4-14. Joash's Temple restoration. This section follows 2 Kgs 12:4-16 with several additions by the CHR. According to the CHR, the restoration of the Temple was the greatest accomplishment of Joash while Jehoiada was alive. The expression *some time afterward* (v. 4) is only a transition phrase and does not provide a precise chronological reference. However, 2 Kgs 12:6 [MT 12:7] says that by the twenty-third year of Joash the repairs were not yet completed.

Joash commanded the priests and the Levites to receive an annual collection from the people of Judah to repair the Temple, although the Levites did not handle the money (vv. 11-12). The need for reparation arose because Athaliah and her followers had plundered the Temple and used the vessels dedicated to Yahweh in the worship of Baal. The reference to Athaliah's children (v. 7) may be a reference to her followers since 22:10 intimates that she did not have more children.

Joash wanted the work done immediately. But because the Levites did not act fast enough (v. 5), the king summoned Jehoiada to inquire about the delay. The text provides no clear reason for the delay. Dillard (1987, 188) compares the CHR's version with the deuteronomistic historian's version and concludes that Joash had reallocated funds used to pay Temple personnel to be used in the repairs of the Temple (cf. 2 Kgs 12:4 [MT 12:5]). As a form of compromise, Joash commanded that a chest be made to receive the people's offerings (v. 8). According to 2 Kgs 12:9 [MT 12:10] the chest was placed "beside the altar on the right side as one entered the house of the Lord." According to the CHR, the chest was placed *outside the gate of the house of the Lord* (v. 8). The CHR's change reflects the postexilic practice that did not allow the people to enter the Temple area. This offering was similar to the Temple tax decreed by Moses in the wilderness (Exod 30:12-16; 38:25-28). The king's command was executed, a proclamation was made throughout Judah, and the people brought their money until the chest was full. The money was distributed to the people working in the restoration of the Temple and the repairs were finished. The money left over was used to make several utensils to be used in the Temple.

24:15-16. The death of Jehoiada. As long as Jehoiada lived the people were faithful to God and offered sacrifices in the Temple. This statement by the CHR serves to divide the reign of Joash into two periods: his years of faithfulness, which were coeval with the life of Jehoiada, and his years of apostasy, which began with the death of Jehoiada. The death of Jehoiada is not mentioned in Kings. Jehoiada was 130 years old when he died. To the CHR and the people in his days this was an indication that Jehoiada had lived a full and blessed life. He was buried in the city of David, in the royal tomb in recognition for the good done *in Israel, and for God and his house* (v. 16).

24:17-27. Joash's wickedness and assassination. The Deuteronomistic historian had said that "Jehoash [Joash] did what was right in the sight of the Lord all his days" (1 Kgs 12:2 [MT 12:3]). But the CHR presents a different view of Joash after the death of Jehoiada. After the death of Jehoiada, some of the officials of Judah, probably those who had supported Athaliah and who were repressed by Jehoiada, came before Joash and paid homage to him. In turn they received the king's permission to return to their idolatrous practices. The people abandoned the Temple of Yahweh to serve the asherim, the sacred poles used in the cult of Asherah, and to worship idols. This reference to the asherim may be an allusion to 2 Kgs 12:3 [MT 12:4], which notes that the high places were not removed. The wrath of God came upon Judah. Yahweh sent several unnamed prophets to warn them, but the leaders of Judah were unwilling to listen.

Among the prophets sent by Yahweh the CHR mentions Zechariah, the son of Jehoiada. Clothed by the Spirit of God (cf. Judg 6:34), Zechariah warned the people that Yahweh had forsaken them because of their idolatry. With the consent of Joash Zechariah was stoned to death in the court of the house of God. The CHR declares that by killing Zechariah Joash had not remembered the *kindness* (Heb. *hesed*, v. 22) Jehoiada had shown him. *Hesed* carries the idea of loyalty (as in REB) and faithfulness. Jesus refers to this heinous murder of Zechariah in Matt 23:35 and Luke 11:51.

The dying words of Zechariah (v. 22) soon found fulfillment. According to the retribution theology of the CHR, the punishment was not delayed. *At the end of the year* (v. 23), that is, in the spring of the next year, the time when military campaigns took place (cf. 1 Chr 20:1), the king of Aram attacked and defeated Joash. Since the Aramean army was smaller than that of Judah (v. 24), the CHR saw the defeat of the Judean army as a visible demonstration of divine justice. The Arameans killed many Judean officials and took much booty to Damascus. Joash was left badly wounded (v. 25). Two of his servants, an Ammonite and a Moabite, conspired against him and killed him in his bed. According to the CHR, the reason for the conspiracy against Joash was the death of Zechariah (v. 25).

Joash died in disgrace. He was buried in the city of David but not in the royal tomb. To the CHR the manner of his burial was a sign of dishonor and divine displeasure. After his death his son Amaziah succeeded him. The acts of Joash are mentioned in the *Commentary [midrash] on the Book of Kings* (v. 27). On the nature of this commentary, see comments on 13:22, above. The reference that the *midrash* included many oracles against Joash indicates that the *midrash* on the Book of Kings contained prophetic materials interpreting historical events.

The Reign of Amaziah, 25:1-28

25:1-4. The Accession of Amaziah. The CHR introduces AMAZIAH by summarizing his reign over Judah. Amaziah was twenty-five years old when he began to reign and his reign lasted twenty-nine years. However, due to his probable imprisonment by the king of Israel (v. 24), his son Uzziah may have served as acting king during part of his reign (cf. Dillard 1987, 198). He was a good king at the beginning of his reign but the CHR's endorsement of Amaziah is limited (v. 2), perhaps because of his later apostasy. Upon assuming the throne Amaziah consolidated his power by killing those who had murdered his father (v. 3). He spared the children of his father's killers in obedience to the injunction in the law (Deut 24:16), which specified that innocent children should not be punished for the sins of their parents.

25:5-13. War against the Edomites. Amaziah prepares to go to war against the Edomites by taking a census of Judah, similar to the census of Jehoshaphat (2 Chr 17:14-19), conscripting 300,000 men, and organizing them under groups of 1,000 and 100. He also hired 100,000 warriors from Israel to increase and strengthen his army. However, an unnamed prophet intervened and warned Amaziah that reliance upon the men of Israel was unwise because Yahweh was not with Israel. In obedience to the words of the man of God, Amaziah discharged the mercenaries from Israel. This action was very costly because Amaziah had already paid 100 talents of silver for their services. The man of God had assured the king that Yahweh would give him back much more than what he would lose.

As a result of his obedience, Amaziah obtained a great victory against the Edomites. The army of Judah killed thousands of Edomites and took 10,000 captives and cast them from the tops of cliffs to their death. The men of Israel who were dismissed by Amaziah were very angry, probably because they would be excluded from the spoils of Edom. As an act of revenge they attacked several cities of Judah, *killed three thousand people in them, and took much booty* (v. 13).

25:14-16. The apostasy of Amaziah. After the defeat of the Edomites, Amaziah followed a custom popular in the ancient Near East and took the gods of the Edomites as spoils of war and worshiped them. He was confronted by a prophet, probably the same man of God referred to in v. 7. The prophet rebuked the king for worshiping the impotent gods of the Edomites, the same gods who were unable to save their own people. Amaziah was angry at the words of the prophet and threatened him with death. The prophet departed, but warned the king that God had determined to destroy him. The story of Amaziah's apostasy and the prophetic warning serve to explain Amaziah's defeat at Beth-shemesh (vv. 20-24) and his death at the hands of conspirators (vv. 27-28).

25:17-24. Amaziah's defeat at Beth-shemesh. Amaziah's desire to go to war against the Northern Kingdom was a result of his overconfidence after his victory against the Edomites (v. 17). It was also a desire to avenge the raid against Judean cities perpetrated by Israelite mercenaries whom Amaziah had discharged from his army. Amaziah's words to Joash (Jehoash) were an invitation to confrontation. Joash responded by ridiculing Amaziah with a fable that was similar to Jotham's fable in Judg 9:7-15. Joash's fable compared Amaziah to a little bush that dared to challenge the mighty cedar of Lebanon only to be trampled by a wild animal. Joash warned Amaziah by saying that his victory against Edom would not assure him of victory against Israel. Amaziah refused to listen to the words of the king of Israel. The CHR inserts his interpretation of the event by saying that Amaziah's refusal to listen was caused by God's desire to punish Amaziah for his worship of alien gods.

Amaziah and Joash confronted each other in BETH-SHEMESH, a city in the territory of Judah, southwest of Jerusalem. Joash defeated the Judean army, captured Amaziah and brought him back to Jerusalem, and broke down the northern wall, from the Ephraim Gate (Neh 8:16) to the Corner Gate (Jer 31:38), the wall that protected the city against invasions from the north, and took the gold and the silver that were in the Temple. The NRSV adds that Joash also took *Obed-edom* with him (v. 24). This translation, however, does not reflect the text. The family of Obed-edom were gatekeepers and were in charge of the Temple treasury (cf. 1 Chr 26:15). The text says Joash took the silver and the gold and the vessels of the Temple "that had been in the care of Obed-edom" (v. 24 NIV). In addition, Joash took the treasures found in the palace. Amaziah was probably released in exchange for the hostages Joash took to Samaria.

25:25-28. The death of Amaziah. It is not known whether Amaziah was taken to Samaria or how long he became a prisoner of Joash. It is possible that the silver and the gold taken from the Temple, as well as the treasures from the palace and the hostages taken to Samaria, served as a ransom paid to Joash to allow Amaziah to continue as king of Judah. Dillard (1987, 202) suggests that Amaziah was not released until after Joash's death. Amaziah survived Joash by fifteen years. The CHR informs the reader that the events of Amaziah's reign were recorded *in the Book of the Kings of Judah and Israel* (v. 26; but cf. 1 Kgs 14:19). Amaziah's death occurred as the result of a conspiracy planned against him because of his apostasy from Yahweh. Amaziah fled to Lachish, a Judean city located in the Shephelah. The conspirators pursued him and killed him in Lachish. His death fulfilled the words of the prophet concerning Amaziah, that God would destroy him (v. 16). Amaziah was buried with his ancestors. While 2 Kgs 14:20 says that Amaziah was buried *in the city of David* (also v. 28), the MT of v. 28 says he was buried "in a city of Judah" (cf. "the City of Judah," NAB, NIV). This statement by the CHR seems to emphasize that Amaziah's burial in an anonymous tomb in Judah was a punishment for his apostasy (Japhet 1993, 872).

The Reign of Uzziah, 26:1-23

26:1-5. Uzziah's accession to the throne. The name of UZZIAH, king of Judah, is popularly known because of the association of his name with the call of Isaiah to the prophetic ministry (Isa 6:1). His name appears in Chronicles as Uzziah (v. 1) and as Azariah (1 Chr 3:12), although the CHR prefers to use Uzziah, perhaps to distinguish him from the high priest Azariah (26:17). The use of two names for some kings in the OT may reflect the fact that the kings assumed a throne name at the time of their coronation. Uzziah became king at the age of sixteen with the help of the people of Judah. In light of Amaziah's capture by Joash (25:23) and since the CHR twice mentions the accession of Uzziah to the throne of Judah, it is possible that Uzziah ascended to the throne of Judah the first time as a coregent with his father at the time of Amaziah's capture. In light of the conspiracy in Jerusalem against Amaziah (25:27), it is also possible that Amaziah was killed by a conspiracy orchestrated by people in Jerusalem who opposed his return to power. Since there is no evidence that the conspirators intended to place anyone in power, it is also possible that Uzziah was aware of the conspiracy against his father.

Uzziah is presented as a good king who followed in the steps of his father Amaziah. This statement by the CHR is surprising because the author was critical of Amaziah. Since this information is drawn from 2 Kgs 15:3, it is possible that the CHR is restricting his judgment of Uzziah to the early part of his reign as he had done with Amaziah (25:2). The CHR credits Uzziah's piety to Zechariah, who taught him to walk in the fear of Yahweh. Little is known about Zechariah. A prophet named Zechariah appears in the days of Joash, king of Judah (24:20). Another Zechariah is mentioned in Is 8:3 but 2 Chr 26:5 intimates that the Zechariah who instructed Uzziah died before Isaiah became a prophet. The CHR declares that Uzziah was blessed and prospered as long as he remained faithful to God. One of Uzziah's accomplishments was the conquest and restoration of Elath, an important port on the Red Sea that was lost to Judah in the days of Jehoram (21:8-10). The rebuilding of Elath contributed to the great economic prosperity Judah enjoyed in the eighth century BCE.

26:6-8. Uzziah's military campaigns. During his reign, Uzziah enjoyed several military victories. The most important of these was his victory against the Philistines, for it neutralized an old foe and allowed Judah to control the trade routes that passed along the coastal highway. Gath was first conquered by David (1 Chr 18:1) and subsequently lost by Joash (2 Kgs 12:17). Uzziah also conquered Ashdod and Jabneh (Jabneel, Josh 15:11). He built cities in Ashdod and along the borders of other Philistines cities. GATH and ASHDOD were two of the five most important cities dominated by the Philistines (Josh 13:3). Later on in Jewish history, Jabneh came to be known as Jamnia and became an important center of study. Uzziah conquered the Arabs who lived in Gur-baal. This place is unknown; it appears only here in the OT. He also conquered the Meunites. In addition, Uzziah received tribute from the Ammonites, and as a result of these victories, his fame spread to the borders of Egypt. According to the CHR, Uzziah was able to obtain these victories because *God helped him* (v. 7).

26:9-15. Uzziah's achievements. Because of God's help, Judah, under the reign of Uzziah, flourished and became a thriving nation. The CHR lists several areas in which Uzziah was successful and prosperous. He built defensive towers in Jerusalem and outside the city in the wilderness to serve as defense outposts and storage (vv. 9-10a). He dug cisterns to help with his large herds in the Shephelah, the lower hill country located west of Jerusalem, and in the plains. He showed his love for the land by developing agriculture in the fertile lands of Judah, probably the territory around Hebron. He organized and equipped his army to defend the nation and to protect his holdings. A large army, with 307,500 trained soldiers under 2,600 commanders, was equipped with the best and most effective armaments. He also added to his army war machines capable of shooting arrows and throwing large stones. According to the CHR, because Uzziah sought Yahweh (v. 5), Yahweh blessed and prospered him greatly; he became famous and very powerful (v. 15).

26:16-21. Uzziah's sin and punishment. Uzziah's prosperity made him proud and arrogant and led him to his destruction (Prov 16:18; 18:12). His downfall came when he acted treacherously against Yahweh and the Temple. According to the CHR, Uzziah *was false to the LORD his God* (v. 16). The Hebrew word carries the idea of rebellion and unfaithfulness (see NIV). Uzziah sinned against God by entering the Temple and trying to exercise the priestly function by offering a sacrifice upon the altar of incense, an act that was the prerogative of the sons of Aaron (v. 18; cf. Exod 30:7-8). The priests defended the sanctity of the Temple forcibly. Azariah and eighty other priests confronted the king and told him that it was not proper for him to burn incense upon the altar. Uzziah, with the censer in his hand, became very angry. At this moment, the CHR says, Uzziah was struck with leprosy.

The rapidity with which Uzziah was stricken is another way of reaffirming the CHR's theology of immediate retribution. The Hebrew word for "leprosy" does not necessarily mean Hansen's disease. It is a generic term to refer to a variety of skin diseases (cf. Lev 13). This unknown disease made Uzziah unclean and excluded him from the Temple, from the palace, and from contact with other people (Lev 13:45-46). His son Jotham became coregent with his father and was in charge of the affairs of the kingdom (v. 21).

26:22-23. Uzziah's death. Uzziah was a leper until the day he died. After his death he was buried in a field adjacent the tomb of the kings. He could not be buried with his ancestors because he was unclean. After his death Jotham ascended to the throne and became sole regent.

According to the CHR, the record of Uzziah's kingdom was found in a book written by Isaiah the prophet. Many efforts have been made to identify this book with the references to Uzziah in the historical narratives found in the books of Isaiah and Kings. However, it is more probable that the CHR is referring to a different source available to him. But it is very difficult to say whether it was written by Isaiah himself.

The Reign of Jotham, 27:1-9

The CHR offers a summary of Jotham's reign that is richer in details than the parallel narrative in 2 Kgs 15:32-38. Jotham was twenty-five years old when he began to reign and he reigned sixteen years. His mother was Jerushah, daughter of ZADOK. It is possible that the reference to *Zadok* in v. 1 may indicate that Jerushah was a descendant of the Zadok who served as high priest in the days of David and Solomon. According to the CHR, Jotham was a faithful king like his father Uzziah. The CHR also commends Jotham because he did not enter the Temple of Yahweh and did not usurp the work that belonged to the priests. Jotham is portrayed in Chronicles as a faithful and prosperous king. Despite his faithfulness the people did not follow his conduct. The deuteronomistic writer says that the people continued to sacrifice and burn incense on the high places (2 Kgs 15:35).

The CHR stresses Jotham's many building activities and victories over his enemies to emphasize God's blessings. Some of these constructions were a continuation of work initiated by his father. Jotham built the upper gate (the north entrance; cf. 2 Chr 23:20) of the Temple; he fortified Ophel, the walls protecting the city, and built new settlements in the Judean hills. His subjugation of the Ammonites came probably because of their refusal to pay tribute (see 26:8). They were subjugated for three years. During this time they continued paying tribute to Jotham.

The CHR concludes the summary of Jotham's reign declaring that because of his piety he was blessed and prosperous. He was powerful and conquered his enemies because he was firm in the ways of Yahweh. As an attempt to affirm that his reign was devoid of political problems, the CHR omits any reference to the Syro-Ephraimite war (2 Kgs 15:37), although the mention of *all his wars* (v. 7) may be a veiled reference to that conflict. After Jotham's death he was buried with his ancestors in the city of David. Jotham was succeeded on the throne by his son Ahaz.

The Reign of Ahaz, 28:1-27

28:1-4. Ahaz's Iniquity. The CHR is severe in his criticism of AHAZ. He omits any reference to Ahaz's accomplishments as king in order to emphasize his failures and his apostasy. Ahaz was twenty years old when he ascended to the throne of Judah and reigned sixteen years. Unlike David, Ahaz was unfaithful to Yahweh. The CHR compares Ahaz's iniquity to the religious practices of the kings of Israel. The wickedness of Ahaz is vividly illustrated by the CHR: Ahaz made images of BAAL, he made his son pass through the fire, and sacrificed in the high places. Passing one's son through the fire has been associated with child sacrifice, a religious practice connected with the worship of Molech, the Ammonite god. These sacrifices took place *in the valley of the son of Hinnom* (v. 3), a site southwest of Jerusalem. The Hebrew name of this place, Ge-hinnom (HINNOM, VALLEY OF) became associated with GEHENNA or HELL (see Matt 5:22). Child sacrifice was severely criticized by the prophets (Jer 7:30-31) and condemned as an abomination to Yahweh (Lev 18:21; 20:2-5; Deut 12:31).

28:5-7. Ahaz's war against Aram and Israel. The expression *Therefore the Lord his God gave him into the hand of the king of Aram* (v. 5) stresses the CHR's theology of immediate retribution. According to the CHR, the war against Aram and Israel, also known as the Syro-Ephraimite war, was part of the divine judgment on Ahaz because of his sins. The CHR presents the attacks of Aram and Israel as two separate events, although 2 Kgs 16:5-7 and Isa 7:1-6 treat the attacks on Israel as a joint effort by the Syro-Ephraimite forces.

God, through the prophet Isaiah (7:1-17), offered Ahaz an opportunity to save Judah from the agony of war. The king refused to accept the divine sign (Isa 7:12) and because of his lack of faith in Yahweh's power to save, Judah was invaded by the Arameans and Ahaz was soundly defeated. As a result, a number of Judean citizens were deported to Damascus by Rezin, the Aramean king (2 Kgs 16:5) and many more were killed by Pekah, king of Israel.

Zichri, a soldier in the Israelite army also killed Ahaz's son and two of Ahaz's palace officials. The exile and slaughter of Judean citizens are not mentioned in 2 Kings nor Isaiah.

28:8-15. Oded's Oracle. This passage is original with the CHR. Oded was a northern prophet who lived in Samaria. Nothing is known about Oded and his ministry. He should not be identified with the father of the prophet Azariah who prophesied in the days of Asa (2 Chr 15:1). Oded met the army of Israel as they returned with the spoils of war and two hundred thousand captives (v. 8). He acknowledged that Yahweh was punishing Judah for their sins but warned that the army had abused their role as instruments of divine justice by enslaving the people. He requested the soldiers to liberate and repatriate the people of Judah because they were *kindred* to the people of Israel (v. 11). Four tribal leaders from Israel also entreated the army not to add to their sins (vv. 12-13). Oded and the tribal leaders succeeded in convincing the Israelites to allow the Judeans to return to their country. The tribal leaders fed and clothed the captives and returned them to Jericho.

This passage demonstrates the CHR's sympathy for the Northern Kingdom. Even among the sinful people of the North there were faithful people who knew how to act as brothers to the people who lived in Judah. Some of the details of this story, such as the anointing of the wounded with oil, the provision of food and drink, the carrying of the feeble on asses, and the journey to Jericho, have been compared to the parable of the Good Samaritan in Luke 10:29-37 (Spenser 1984, 317–49).

28:16-21. Ahaz's appeal to Assyria. *At that time* (v. 16) refers to the time of the Syro-Ephraimite war. The Edomites and the Philistines took advantage of the political weakness in Judah and raided several Judean cities. The Edomites invaded Judah, conquered Elath (2 Kgs 16:5) and took several people captive while the Philistines raided six cities in the Shephelah and the Negeb. Fearing further invasions, Ahaz requested help from Assyria. He raided (*plundered*) the Temple, the royal coffers, and the houses of palace official to put together the money to pay tribute to Assyria. The plundering of his officials may refer to heavy taxation imposed upon the nobles of Judah.

But because of his unfaithfulness to Yahweh (v. 19), the gifts Ahaz gave to TIGLATH-PILESER III (745–727) were of no help (v. 21; cf. v. 16), for the Assyrian king came against him and made him a vassal (Mariottini 1990, 917–18). Ahaz is called king of Israel (v. 19) because from the perspective of the CHR the Northern Kingdom had ceased to exist. Tiglath-pileser's name appears in v. 20 as *Tilgath-pil-neser*. The variation may reflect a failure to transliterate properly the Assyrian name into Hebrew (see also 1 Chr 5:6).

28:22-27. Ahaz's apostasy. The CHR provides more details of Ahaz's apostasy than his source in 2 Kgs 16:10-18. In his distress Ahaz did not turn to Yahweh but became *yet more faithless* (v. 22). He worshiped the Aramean gods because he believed they had helped the Arameans in their victory against Judah. Since the Arameans had already been conquered by the Assyrians (2 Kgs 16:9-10), it is possible that the CHR is alluding to this fact to point to Ahaz's senselessness in worshiping other gods. Ahaz's apostasy and folly became his ruin and the ruin of Judah. Second Kings 16:17 says that Ahaz removed several objects from the Temple. The CHR adds that he closed the door of the Temple and promoted the worship of other gods *in every corner of Jerusalem* (v. 24) and made high places *in every city of Judah* (v. 25). The CHR does not mention the altar made by Ahaz and placed in the Temple (2 Kgs 16:10). The words of the CHR in v. 27 do not contradict 2 Kgs 16:20. The CHR says that when Ahaz died he was buried in Jerusalem but was not placed in the royal tomb. Kings says that he was buried with his fathers in the city of David. The CHR, however makes a distinction. According to 2 Chr 21:20 and 24:25, Ahaz was buried in the city of David, but, because of his unfaithfulness, not in the royal tomb. It is possible that, like Uzziah, he was buried in the burial field that belonged to David's family (2 Chr 26:23).

The Reign of Hezekiah, 29:1-32:33

The CHR is very fond of HEZEKIAH. He dedicates four chapters to recount the events related to his reign, which makes Hezekiah as important to the CHR as DAVID and SOLOMON. The CHR emphasizes the events in Hezekiah's life that demonstrate his devotion to Yahweh and to the Temple. Hezekiah is portrayed as a reformer who restored the worship of Yahweh in Judah.

29:1-2. The accession of Hezekiah. The CHR presents a very positive image of Hezekiah and his government. Four chapters are dedicated to recapitulate the events related to his reign. The CHR emphasizes Hezekiah's devotion to God and his zeal for the Temple. Special emphasis is given to Hezekiah's cleansing of the Temple and the observance of the passover. The CHR's portrayal of Hezekiah as a reformer who restored the worship of Yahweh and as an individual of profound piety makes him one of the best kings in the history of Israel (v. 2).

29:3-19. The cleansing of the Temple. Hezekiah's first act as king was to reverse the policies of his father, Ahaz, and initiate the cleansing of the Temple. This event occurred in the first month of the first year of his reign (v. 3). Hezekiah assembled the priests and the Levites in the square, east of the Temple entrance, and commanded them to open the doors of the house of God that Ahaz had closed (28:24; but see 2 Kgs 16:10-16). Hezekiah made a public confession of the sins of past generations, similar to the liturgical confessions popular in the postexilic times (v. 9 makes a reference to the Exile of Judah; cf. Dan 9:4-19; Zech 1:1-6). After Hezekiah's declaration of the nation's sins, fourteen Levites, two from each of the seven Levitical families, responded with great enthusiasm to the king's appeal. The priests and Levites sanctified themselves and began the process of removing the impurities of the Temple (v. 16). The Levites took the impurities from the Temple and threw them into the brook of Kidron, as was done in the days of Asa (15:16). The priests cleansed the inner part of the Temple because the Levites were not allowed to enter the most holy place. The process of purification of the Temple and its precincts lasted sixteen days. For eight days they purified the exterior part of the Temple and for eight days they purified the interior section of the Temple (v. 17). When the process of sanctifying the Temple was completed, the priests and the Levites reported to Hezekiah, declaring that the utensils that Ahaz had desecrated were ready to be used again.

29:20-36. The great sacrifice. After the sanctification of the Temple and the removal of the unclean things, Hezekiah and the people prepared to restore the worship of Yahweh. The king and the leaders of Judah made a special sacrifice for the sins of the kingdom, of the sanctuary, and of Judah (v. 21). Sacrifices were made in groups of seven. Seven bulls, rams, and lambs were to be sacrificed as burnt offerings and seven male goats as sin offerings. Hezekiah also made an attempt to include the Northern tribes by commanding that sacrifices be made for all Israel (v. 24).

The sacrifices were accompanied by cultic music. The Levites (v. 25) played the instruments ordered by David (cf. 23:5), and the priests played the trumpets (v. 26). Thus, with musical instruments, the singing of psalms and the worship of the people, sacrifices were offered to Yahweh.

After the burnt offerings were offered for the sins of the nation, Hezekiah exhorted the people to offer sacrifices of praise and thanksgiving. The people responded to the king's exhortation with great enthusiasm and brought their offerings to the Temple. Their gifts were so plentiful the priests could not offer them by themselves, for they were few. The Levites helped the priests with the sacrifices until more priests were ritually cleansed to assume their duties. This incident was used by the CHR to emphasize the ministry of the Levites: *the Levites were more conscientious than the priests in sanctifying themselves* (v. 34). The CHR's praise for the Levites is a veiled criticism of the priests, reflecting the conflict between Levites and priests that existed in the postexilic community.

30:1-12. The invitation to the Passover. Hezekiah, by letter (v. 1) and couriers (vv. 6, 11) invited all Israel to celebrate the Passover. This information is unique in Chronicles, since the deuteronomistic historian does not mention it. The people were unable to celebrate the Passover on the fourteenth day of the first month. It was scheduled for the fourteenth day of the second month and some of the northern tribes were invited to participate. The celebration of the Passover in the second month was celebrated according to the legislation in Num 9:1-14.

Two reasons are given by the CHR for the change of the date (v. 3). One reason was that the priests had not sanctified themselves in sufficient numbers to hold the celebration (see 29:34). The second reason was that because the people had to travel from the north, they were not able to arrive on time for the celebration. Another possibility is that since the northern tribes celebrated the Passover in the second month, Hezekiah attempted to celebrate the feast according to the customs of the northern tribes.

The emissaries of the king went through several of the northern tribes, now part of the Assyrian empire, inviting them to participate in the celebration of the Passover. One of the inducements to the remnant of the northern tribes to come to Jerusalem and celebrate Passover in the Temple was the promise that Yahweh would return the people from exile (v. 9). This promise was based on Solomon's prayer to God (1 Kgs 8:50) and God's answer to Solomon's prayer at the time of the dedication of the Temple, assuring the people of forgiveness and restoration for those who were repentant and would pray in the Temple (2 Chr 7:14-16). The expression "from Beer-sheba to Dan" (v. 5) reflects the CHR's use of the expression to designate the southern and the northern limits of the land that belonged to all Israel (cf. 1 Chr 21:2). Hezekiah's invitation to the northern tribes was met with scorn and indifference (v. 10). Only a few people from Asher, Manasseh, Zebulun

(v. 11) and from Ephraim and Issachar (v. 18) came. The people of Judah responded with enthusiasm, because the hand of God was upon them (v. 10).

30:13-27. The Passover Celebration. The people came to celebrate the Passover (30:1, 2, 5) and the feast of the unleavened bread (30:12-13). Both feasts are celebrated together in Chronicles, as well as in Deut 16:1-8. Some scholars believe that the two feasts were not celebrated together until the days of Josiah. It is possible that the combination of both feasts in Chronicles may reflect the realities of the postexilic community or an effort to equate the reforms of Hezekiah with the reforms of Josiah.

The altars made by Ahaz throughout Judah (28:24) and dedicated to other gods were removed and thrown into the brook of Kidron before the passover lamb was killed (see 29:16). This incident is confirmed by the words of the Assyrian emissary sent to convey a message to the people of Jerusalem (2 Kgs 18:22). The altars for offering incense were also removed (v. 14). The priests and the Levites worked together in the presentation of the sacrifices. Many people from Judah and Israel were unclean when they ate the passover (v. 18). Hezekiah, acting as a mediator, prayed for the people and they were forgiven (vv. 19-20). The people, although unclean, were allowed to participate in the passover because of their devotion to God and the disposition of their hearts.

The celebration of the passover and the festival of unleavened bread reached its climax on the seventh day. Then the people, by unanimous accord and gladness of heart, decided to extend the celebration another seven days. Hezekiah and his leaders provided additional sacrifices for the celebration and this prompted more priests to sanctify themselves (v. 24). The elaborateness of the celebration prompted the CHR to say that no other passover had been celebrated in this manner in Israel since the dedication of the Temple in the days of Solomon (v. 26; see 2 Kgs 23:22-23). At the end of the celebration the priests blessed the people, probably with the priestly benediction mentioned in Num 6:22-27. The NRSV reads: *Then the priests and the Levites stood up and blessed the people* (v. 27). However, the MT read that "the Levitical priests" blessed the people (cf. Deut 18:1). This translation including the Levites in the blessing of the people reflects the reading of several manuscripts and ancient translations. God's acceptance of the priests's prayer indicates the divine approval on the work of Hezekiah.

31:1-19. Hezekiah's religious reforms. The narrative concerning the reforms of Hezekiah is divided into four sections: (1) the destruction of the high places by the people (v. 1); (2) provisions for the support of the Temple ministry (vv. 2-10); (3) the reorganization of the Temple personnel (vv. 11-19); and (4) the evaluation of Hezekiah as king (vv. 20-21).

The destruction of the HIGH PLACES (see 2 Kgs 18:4) was carried out by the people after the celebration of the festival of unleavened bread. According to the CHR, the destruction of the high places was also extended to Ephraim and Manasseh. To provide for the ministry of the Temple (vv. 3-10) the king made a contribution for the burnt offering and exhorted the people to make contributions to support the ministry of the priests and Levites (v. 4) in order that they might devote themselves exclusively to the teaching of the law. The people who responded to the appeal of Hezekiah were those of Judah and those of Israel who lived in the towns of Judah. To the CHR these people formed all Israel. They responded generously to the king's appeal and brought their offerings in abundance. The offerings of the people reflect the laws of the tithe and first fruits used to support the priests and Levites (Num 18:21, 24; Deut 18:1-8).

The reorganization of the priests and Levites (v. 2) was done according to the traditions established by David and Solomon (1 Chr 23:6; 2 Chr 8:14). The priests were responsible to present the sacrifices upon the altar and the Levites were responsible to lead the liturgy of the Temple and for the maintenance and administration of the Temple. Hezekiah also ordered that chambers be built in the Temple to house the offerings dedicated to the priests and Levites (v. 11; cf. Mal 3:10). The collection lasted all summer, from the third to the seventh month, that is, from the beginning of the grain harvest to the time when fruits, grapes, and olives were harvested. Hezekiah appointed some Levites led by Conaniah and his brother Shimei, aided by ten other Levites, to oversee the collection (vv. 12-13). He also appointed Kore to supervise the freewill offerings, the tribute given to support the priests, the Levites, and their families. Kore was assisted by six other Levites who were assigned to work with him outside Jerusalem, in the Levitical cities (vv. 14-15). According to v. 17, the Levites entered their ministry in the Temple at the age of twenty. Two other references provide different information concerning the age at which the Levites entered their ministry: Num 4:3 says that they bagan their service at the age of thirty; Num 8:24 says it was twenty-five. This lowering of the age when the Levites began their ministry may reflect changes in customs or a shortage of Levites in the postexilic community (see commentary at 23:3).

The narrative concludes with an evaluation of Hezekiah's work and faithfulness (vv. 20-21). The CHR says that Hezekiah was deeply committed to the Temple. His evaluation of Hezekiah asserts that his good works came out of his obedience to the law of God. For this reason God prospered him and the work he did. Hezekiah's prosperity was another evidence for the CHR that God blesses and prospers those who are faithful and obedient.

32:1-23. Sennacherib's invasion. This chapter summarizes the events related to the Assyrian invasion under Sennacherib in 701 BCE. The CHR's version is based on materials founded in 2 Kgs 18:13-20:21 and Isa 36-39. In addition, the CHR used other sources that provided supplementary information on Hezekiah and his reign. The invasion of SENNACHERIB, king of Assyria, came after Hezekiah's acts of faithfulness (v. 1). This introduction by the CHR is part of his thesis that God blessed the faithfulness of Hezekiah with a great victory against the mighty Assyrian army. Politically, Hezekiah had made an attempt to declare his independence from Assyria. He broke the alliance that his father had made with Tiglath-pileser III (2 Kgs 16:7) and withheld tribute paid yearly to Assyria. This declaration of independence probably came after the death of SARGON in 705 BCE. With the accession of Sennacherib (705–681 BCE) to the throne of Assyria, Hezekiah made preparations for war. The narrative describing the preparations for war (vv. 2-8) comes from an unknown source, since it is not found in 2 Kings. Sennacherib came against the fortified cities of Judah, believing that he could conquer them for himself (v. 1). This statement by the CHR is in marked contrast with 2 Kgs 18:13 where the deuteronomistic writer says that Sennacherib actually captured them.

The preparation for war against Assyria was accomplished in three stages. The first was the blocking up of the springs that were outside of the city (vv. 3-4). One of the springs that was protected was the Gihon (v. 30), one of the primary sources of water for Jerusalem. The second was the fortification of the walls around the city, the building of an additional wall, and the fortification of the Millo (v. 5a). The Millo were the terraces made of earth and stones built to fortify the walls of Jerusalem. The third was the equipping of the army with improved weapons (vv. 5b-6). Hezekiah also reorganized the army and appointed commanders over the militia. He then brought the people together and exhorted them to trust God and believe that Yahweh would fight for them.

Before invading Jerusalem, Sennacherib sent an embassy with a message for Hezekiah and the people of Judah, probably offering the terms for surrender. According to 2 Kgs 18:17 the embassy was composed of three high officials: the Tartan was the commander of the Assyrian army; the Rabsaris was the chief eunuch, who represented the king of Assyria, and the Rabshakeh, the cupbearer of the king who was the personal attendant of the king. Hezekiah also sent three emissaries to meet the Assyrian embassy: Eliakim was the chief of the palace, Shebna was the secretary of state and Joash was the recorder. These were the highest officials in the Judean court. The dialogue between the Assyrian envoys and the servants of Hezekiah in vv. 10-19 is a condensed version of the narrative in 2 Kgs 18:17-35. The Rabshakeh referred to Hezekiah's destruction of the altars to imply that the invasion was happening because the gods were angry with Hezekiah. The Assyrian envoy also emphasized that the gods of the conquered nations were unable to deliver their people and that Yahweh would be unable to deliver Hezekiah and those who joined him. The dialogue between the envoys of Assyria and the servants of Hezekiah was conducted in the *language of Judah* (v. 18). The language of Judah was Hebrew, also known as the language of Canaan (Isa 19:18). The envoys of Hezekiah requested that they speak in Aramaic, the language spoken by the Assyrians and the language used in diplomacy and commerce. The Assyrians refused and continued to speak in Hebrew *to frighten and terrify* (v. 18) the people (2 Chr 32:18). According to the CHR, the Assyrians blasphemed God because they compared him with the gods of the nations (v. 19).

The mention of the prayers of Hezekiah and Isaiah in v. 20 is a brief reference to the narrative of 2 Kgs 19:1-34. The CHR only mentions the prayer of Hezekiah

(2 Kgs 19:15-19) and the oracle of Isaiah (2 Kgs 19:20-34) describing the deliverance of Jerusalem. Yahweh heard Hezekiah's prayer by destroying the Assyrian army and by causing the return of Sennacherib back to Assyria and eventually his death by his own sons (2 Kgs 19:35-37). The CHR does not mention the considerable tribute of silver and gold Hezekiah paid to avert the destruction of Jerusalem (2 Kgs 18:14-16).

The salvation of Jerusalem from the Assyrian army was God's reward to Hezekiah for his faithfulness. To the CHR the defeat of the Assyrian army was clear evidence that God prospers and blesses those who are faithful to him. Faithfulness to God brought victory, prosperity, and fame to Hezekiah (v. 23).

32:24-31. Hezekiah's illness and prosperity. The narrative of Hezekiah's illness and recovery (vv. 24-26) is a brief summary of 2 Kgs 20:1-11. The CHR omits Isaiah's announcement of Hezekiah's impending death and what the prophet told him he must do to recover (cf. Isa 38:1, 21). Hezekiah recovered because he prayed to God. Yahweh gave him a sign as assurance that he would recover, but Hezekiah's heart continued full of pride. The author of 2 Kgs 20:12-19 (cf. Isa 39:1-8) declares that Hezekiah's pride consisted of the ostentatious display of his wealth and war equipment to the messengers of Merodach-baladan (cf. also Isa 39:1-8). According to 2 Kings, the Babylonian embassy came at the occasion of Hezekiah's sickness. The CHR says that they came because of the astronomical sign given to Hezekiah at the time of his illness, that is, the return of the sun upon Ahaz's dial (2 Kgs 20:10-11). Because of Hezekiah's pride, God declared his wrath upon the nation. But God's wrath would be averted because the king and the people humbled themselves before him. The judgment was postponed but not rescinded. Eventually the nation would go into exile in Babylon (Isa 39:5-8).

The CHR gives another evidence of God's blessing Hezekiah's faithfulness by giving a detailed description of the king's wealth (vv. 27-29). Hezekiah also became involved in the construction of the tunnel that would bring water from GIHON spring, outside of the walls of Jerusalem, into the city. The CHR concludes the narrative by providing a theological interpretation to Hezekiah's illness and the visit of the embassy sent by MERODACH-BALADAN. Their coming was a test of Hezekiah, to help God know what was in Hezekiah's heart and the extent of his commitment (v. 31).

32:32-33. The death of Hezekiah. The notice concerning Hezekiah's death follows the previous pattern used by the CHR. Hezekiah was a faithful king whose deeds were written down by Isaiah the prophet (v. 32). This reference to a work containing Isaiah's visions should not be identified with the canonical book that bears the name of the prophet. The CHR also stresses that Hezekiah was buried in the tomb of the kings. The reference to the "uppermost" (part/section) of the tombs of David's family (v. 33; cf. NEB, REB, NJB) may indicate a second floor of the tomb or may reflect the CHR's desire to honor Hezekiah. The translations in NRSV and NIV seem to suggest that he was buried on the hill where the tomb was located, but not necessarily in the king's tomb.

The Reign of Manasseh, 33:1-20

The CHR divides the reign of MANASSEH into two periods: the first period deals with Manasseh's apostasy (33:1-10); the second period deals with Manasseh's life after his conversion (33:11-20).

33:1-10. Manasseh's apostasy. The narrative of the first period of Manasseh's reign follows 2 Kgs 21:1-16 with a few modifications. The narrative emphasizes Manasseh's worship of other gods and the adoption of alien practices that were contrary to the religious traditions of the nation. Manasseh promoted the cult of Baal and Asherah, rebuilt the high places, fostered the worship of astral deities, the practice of sorcery and divination, the consultation of mediums and those dealing with familiar spirits, and the sacrificing of children in the *Valley of Ben-Hinnom* (v. 6; see HINNOM, VALLEY OF), south of Jerusalem, where the Topheth was. The Topheth was the place where the sacrifice of children was made. The Hebrew word for *valley of* (*gê'*) became associated with the name of the place and became GEHENNA, which in the NT became associated with the place of eternal suffering and destruction (Matt 5:22.29; Mark 9:42-48). The CHR adds that Manasseh introduced the image of an idol, which he set in the Temple, contrary to the command that God had given to David and Solomon (vv. 7-8). The CHR omits the reference to the prophetic criticism of Manasseh's evil practices (2 Kgs 21:10-15), as well as the persecution and murder of those who opposed him (2 Kgs 21:16). In the view of the CHR, Manasseh *misled Judah and the inhabitants of Jerusalem* (v. 9). As a result, the nation's sins became greater than that of the nations that Yahweh had removed from the land.

33:11-20. Manasseh's repentance. The second part of Manasseh's reign covers the period after his repentance. Because of his unfaithfulness, God punished Manasseh. His punishment came when the army commander of the Assyrian king (presumably Asshurbanipal) took Manasseh in chains to Babylon. In his distress Manasseh prayed and humbled himself before God and God returned him to his throne. *The Prayer of Manasseh* is an apocryphal book that professes to contain the prayer Manasseh offered to God at the time of his distress. His humiliation forced Manasseh to recognize that Yahweh was God (v. 13). Manasseh removed the foreign gods and the other items that had been placed in the house of God and commanded Judah to serve Yahweh.

The story of Manasseh's repentance and his religious reforms does not appear in 2 Kings. For this reason many scholars have doubted the authenticity of this story. Some believe that the CHR composed this story describing Manasseh's repentance to explain the theological problem created by the fact that an evil king reigned longer than any of the good kings. According to this view, Manasseh's punishment and repentance are intended to show that his life was not one of irrevocable apostasy. Those who accept the authenticity of the story affirm that Manasseh's repentance was short and that he returned to his evil ways. But this view is contradicted by v. 20 where the CHR's source appears to indicate that

Manasseh was faithful until the end. Others say that Manasseh's repentance was genuine and that his reforms continued as long as he lived and that after his death his son Amon and the people of Judah reestablished the evil practices of Manasseh. The deuteronomistic historian, however, is adamant in his assertion that Manasseh died an evil king and that the destruction of the nation came because of the sins Manasseh committed (2 Kgs 21:10-15; 23:26-27; 24:3; cf. Jer 15:4).

The Reign of Amon, 33:21-25

The CHR's description of Amon's reign parallels the narrative in 2 Kgs 21:19-26 with a major difference. The CHR declares that Amon reverted back to the religious policies of Manasseh and made sacrifices to the images his father had made. But unlike Manasseh, Amon did not humble himself before Yahweh and thus incurred more guilt than his father. Amon was assassinated in his own palace by his servants two years after ascending the throne. The political crisis caused by this palace revolt forced the *people of the land* (v. 25) to act and secure a successor to insure continuity in the house of David. The people of the land were the property owners of Judah who acted together in times of political crisis to safeguard the interests of the nation. Amon's assassins were killed and Josiah, Amon's son, was placed on the throne as the new king of Judah.

The Reign of Josiah, 34:1–35:27

34:1-13. The beginning of Josiah's reform. The CHR has nothing but praise for JOSIAH. Like David, Solomon, and Hezekiah before him, Josiah is presented as a faithful king who obeyed God and *did not turn aside to the right or to the left* (v. 2), but who followed the right path of God's Torah. Josiah came to the throne at the age of eight and on the eighth year of his reign he *began to seek the God of his ancestor David* (v. 3). This turning to God implies a repudiation of the gods Manasseh had assimilated into the worship of Yahweh. It also implies a repudiation of the political yoke Assyria had imposed upon Judah since the days of Hezekiah.

The deuteronomistic writer declares that Josiah's reform began in the eighteenth year of his reign with the discovery of the book of the law. The CHR says that the reform was implemented in stages and that it preceded the discovery of the book of the law. In the twelfth year of his reign, at the age of twenty, Josiah began to remove the high places, the asherim or sacred poles, and the images of false gods. Josiah also burned the bones of the priests who had served on the high places. Josiah made an effort to extend his religious reforms to several of the northern tribes (v. 6) and, according to the CHR, he was successful. In the eighteenth year of his reign Josiah began *to repair the house of the LORD his God* (v. 8), using the money deposited in the Temple. Josiah commissioned three leaders (v. 8) to take the money collected by the Levites from several northern tribes and from Judah and Benjamin to those in charge of the repair of the Temple. The CHR calls the people from the Northern tribes the *remnant of Israel* (v. 9; cf. v. 21). Josiah also put four leaders from the Levites in charge of the work on the Temple. Other Levites who were skilled musicians were in charge of the labor gangs, directing the work. It is possible that the responsibility of these musicians was to mark the rhythm of the work to facilitate the pace of the workers. The CHR emphasizes the active participation of the Levites in the restoration of the worship of Yahweh

34:14-28. The discovery of the book of the law. The account of the discovery of the law book follows the narrative of 2 Kgs 22:8-20, with some changes. The discovery of the book of the law happened while Hilkiah the priest was receiving the money destined for the repair of the Temple. The deuteronomistic historian says that Hilkiah had found "the book of the law" (2 Kgs 22:8), while the CHR is more specific, saying that Hilkiah found *the book of the law of the LORD given through Moses* (v. 14). To the deuteronomistic writer, the book of the law found in the Temple probably was an earlier version of Deuteronomy. The deuteronomic law became the basis for the reforms of Josiah. The words used by the CHR to identify the book found in the Temple imply that he understood the book to be a form of the Pentateuch of today.

Hilkiah gave the book to SHAPHAN, an important government official who served as secretary during the reign of Josiah. Shaphan brought the book to Josiah and read it in the presence of the king. Josiah was highly distressed by the words of the book. He sent a high level delegation that included HILKIAH the priest, Shaphan and his son Ahikam, Asaiah, the personal servant of the king and Abdon, to consult HULDAH the PROPHET concerning the words in the book. (The name of Abdon appears as Achbor in 2 Kgs 22:12, 14.) Huldah was an official royal prophet who was called to validate the words of the book (Morris 1990, 394). Huldah gave an oracle of judgment against Judah, declaring that the curses written in the book would be invoked against the nation because of their sins and disobedience. She also said that Josiah would die in peace because he had heeded the words written in the book and humbled himself before God.

34:29-33. Josiah's reform. The narrative follows 2 Kgs 23:1-3. In the CHR's version of the reform, the Levites were present in the Temple convocation instead of the prophets (2 Kgs 23:2). This may reflect the CHR's own time when the Levites had assumed the function of the cultic prophets. After the delegation returned with the words of Huldah, the king and the leaders of Israel gathered in the Temple with the people. The words of the law book were read once again, this time to the whole congregation. The king stood in his designated place in the Temple (v. 31), probably by one of the two standing pillars (2 Kgs 23:3). The people, assembled in worship, made a covenant to abide by all the stipulations written in the book of the law. The people of Judah and Benjamin pledged to obey the demands of the covenant (v. 32), while the people of the north were required to worship God (v. 33). As part of this covenant Josiah removed all the abominations found in Israel (v. 33). The Deuteronomistic Historian gives detailed information of the measures Josiah took to purge the Temple, the cult, and the nation from pagan influence (2 Kgs 23:1-20). The reforms were also extended to the northern tribes (cf. 2 Kgs 23:15-19). The

CHR says that one of the results of Josiah's reform was the faithfulness of the people to God, which lasted throughout Josiah's reign.

35:1-19. The celebration of the Passover. The Deuteronomistic Historian declares that Josiah commanded the observance of the Passover festival (2 Kgs 23:21-23). The CHR elaborates on the material found in his sources and provides detailed information on the cultic preparations for the celebration of the Passover (see also 1 Esd 1:1-22). The Passover was celebrated on the first month of Nisan, in the eighteenth year of Josiah's reign (v. 19), the same year when the book of the law was found. The preparation for the celebration of the Passover includes the appointment of priests and the separation of the Levites by divisions to carry out their function *according to the word of the LORD by Moses* (v. 6). The Ark was brought back to the Temple. It was probably removed during the repairs of the Temple or hidden during the reign of Manasseh for protection. The Levites play a very important role in the celebration of the Passover. They are set apart to serve God and to assist the people in the sacrifice of the Passover lamb.

Josiah makes a generous contribution for the people (v. 7) to aid the celebration of the Passover, as Hezekiah had done (30:24). The king's officers follow his example and make a contribution for the people, the priests and the Levites (v. 8a). This is followed by the contribution of three Temple officials, including the high priest, who make a contribution for the priests (v. 8b). Hilkiah, Zechariah, and Jehiel are called *nagid* (NRSV *chief officers*, v. 8) of the house of God. This same title is given to the high priest in 1 Chr 9:1; 2 Chr 31:12. Then, six leaders of the Levites make an offering for the Levites (v. 9). The CHR gives a detailed description of the preparation of the sacrifices for the celebration of the Passover (vv. 10-15).

This section again demonstrates the increased religious influence of the Levites. They are the ones who make preparations for the priests (v. 14), for the singers, and for the gatekeepers (v. 15). The CHR emphasizes that Israelites from the north joined in the celebration of the Passover and the festival of unleavened bread. He also speaks of the uniqueness of this event, because no Passover like it had been celebrated in Israel since the days of Samuel (v. 18; cf. 1 Esd 1:20-21).

35:20-27. Josiah's death. The narrative of Josiah's death is based on 2 Kgs 23:29-30. The CHR amplifies his sources and provides additional information about events that led to Josiah's death in the plain of Megiddo. In 609 BCE Neco, king of Egypt, attempted to go to CARCHEMISH to help the remainder of the Assyrian army that was being attacked by the Babylonians. To reach Carchemish, Neco had to cross land that was in Josiah's control. Josiah had successfully taken control of part of the land that had formed the Northern Kingdom and he concluded that a resurgence of Assyrian power, supported by Egyptian, would pose a threat to his autonomy. Josiah therefore attempted to stop Neco from assisting the Assyrians in their struggle with Babylon. Neco assured Josiah that his intentions against him were peaceful and declared that his actions had come as a word from God. To oppose him was to oppose God himself. Neco said to Josiah, *Cease opposing God, who is with me, so that he will not destroy you* (v. 21). Josiah refused to heed the words of Neco and went out to meet him in order to preserve the freedom of his kingdom and his independence from Assyria. In his fateful encounter with Neco, Josiah was mortally wounded and died in Jerusalem.

The death of Josiah caused a crisis of faith and confidence in Judah. The words of God in the mouth of Neco provided the CHR with an argument to explain the death of a faithful king. Josiah was killed because he did not heed the words of God spoken through Neco. Josiah's death was much lamented in Judah. Jeremiah wrote a lament to remember Josiah. This lament has not survived in written form, but Jeremiah makes several allusions to Josiah in his oracles (Jer 22:10, 15, 18). Other laments were written by poets and musicians in Israel, but these have also been lost. The *Laments* mentioned in 35:25 should not be identified with the Book of Lamentations that follows the Book of Jeremiah in English Bibles.

Josiah was buried in the tomb of the kings and all the inhabitants of Judah mourned his death. The CHR evaluates the reign of Josiah very positively by saying that his faithful deeds were performed in accordance to the law of Yahweh (v. 26).

The Reign of Jehoahaz, 36:1-4

With this chapter the CHR brings to a close his history of Judah. He emphasizes the moral and spiritual degeneracy of Judah and above all, its kings, in the last days of the nation. The CHR's source for the reign of Jehoahaz is 2 Kgs 23:30b-34. In the Hebrew Bible the name of JEHOAHAZ appears in an abbreviated form as Joahaz in vv. 2, 4. Jehoahaz was the fourth son of Josiah (cf. 1 Chr 3:15). He was also know as SHALLUM (Jer 22:11-12). It is possible that Shallum was his given name and that Jehoahaz was his throne name, the name he assumed when he became king of Judah.

Jehoahaz was placed on the throne by *the people of the land* (v. 1.; see 33:25). It is possible the other sons of Josiah were bypassed in favor of Jehoahaz because of his anti-Egyptian policies. But after three months on the throne, Jehoahaz was deposed by Neco after Neco's return from Carchemish where he had gone to aid the Assyrian army. Neco also imposed a burdensome tribute upon the people of Judah and deported Jehoahaz to Egypt where he died (cf. 2 Kgs 23:34).

The Reign of Jehoiakim, 36:5-8

Neco appointed Jehoahaz's brother Eliakim to be the new king of Judah, and changed his name to JEHOIAKIM. The act of changing his name demonstrated Neco's superiority over Jehoiakim. Jehoiakim was the second son of Josiah (1 Chr 3:15); he reigned eleven years over Israel. He was a vassal of Egypt for many years; then he became a vassal of Babylon for three years (2 Kgs 24:1). During his reign, Nebuchadnezzar, king of Babylon, attacked Jerusalem and deported some Jews to Babylon (cf. Dan 1:1). Nebuchadnezzar put Jehoiakim in chains and threatened to take him into exile, but he was not deported. Verse 7 indicates that the Babylonian king took the vessels of the Temple to Babylon and placed them in the temple of his gods (NRSV: *in his palace in Babylon*). Jehoiakim was an evil king (cf. Jer 22:13-19; 26:21-24) who abolished many of the reforms of his father and reestablished some of the religious practices Josiah had eliminated. After his death his son Jehoiachin became king in his place.

The Reign of Jehoiachin, 36:9-10

The CHR's narrative concerning JEHOIACHIN's reign is a summary of 2 Kgs 24:8-17. The CHR says that Jehoiachin was eight years old when he began to reign, but 2 Kgs 24:8 says he was eighteen. Since Nebuchadnezzar took Jehoiachin and his wives to Babylon, it is almost certain that he was eighteen rather than eight when he ascended to the throne. Jehoiachin was deported to Babylon. With him were his mother, wives, palace officials, and more than 10,000 people (2 Kgs 24:14), most of them professional people, and others associated with the government and the royal family. Archaeology has provided evidence for the deportation of Jehoiachin. Babylonian documents list the provisions given to Jehoiachin and his family in Babylon.

The Reign of Zedekiah, 36:11-21

36:11-16. The sins of the nation. After the deportation of Jehoiachin, his uncle Mattaniah became king of Judah. Mattaniah was the third son of Josiah (1 Chr 3:15) and when he became king he assumed the name of ZEDEKIAH. Zedekiah became king because Jehoiachin did not have a son old enough to assume the throne. The CHR provides a harsh judgment on Zedekiah. Zedekiah was an evil king who did not heed the words of God spoken by the prophet Jeremiah (v. 12). He was a rebellious king who violated his covenant with Nebuchadnezzar, king of Babylon (cf. Ezek 17:11-15). The CHR also passes judgment on the leaders of the nation. The priests, the nobles, and the people were accused of being unfaithful to God and of having defiled the Temple. The Temple had been polluted and desecrated by their actions. Yahweh had sent his messengers the prophets to admonish the people because God desired to forgive them and spare judgment upon his house. But the people were rebels and did not heed the message of the prophets and mocked them. When God realized that there was no evidence of repentance, he decided to punish his people. This invective by the CHR against Judah (vv. 15-17) is a summary of the religious history of Judah and provides a theological justification for the demise of the two pillars of the theocratic kingdom: the king and the Temple. The religious history of the nation comes to its final days during a crucial time in the history of the ancient Near East. To the CHR the rebellion and apostasy of Judah were the cause for the end of the monarchy, the destruction of the nation, and the deportation of the people.

36:17-21. The exile of Judah. The judgment on Judah came by means of the Chaldeans, who had become the neo-Babylonian empire after the defeat of the Assyrians in 612 BCE. God brought the Babylonians to Jerusalem and they killed without compassion men, women, and children, young and old alike. They also sacked the Temple and the palace and took to Babylon the vessels of the Temple and the treasures found in the palace of the king and in the houses of the nobles. The taking of the vessels of the Temple in the days of Jehoiakim (36:7), in the days of Jehoiachin (36:10) and in the days of Zedekiah (36:18) became the tragic result of the exile of Judah. Without the Temple and *the precious vessels of the house of the LORD* (36:10), the worship of God could not continue. The return of the vessels (Ezra 1:7) marks the beginning of the spiritual and political restoration of the nation. The Babylonians destroyed the wall protecting Jerusalem, burned the Temple, the palace, and the rich houses in Jerusalem. The CHR also says that the Babylonians deported many people, without providing any specific number (see Jer 52:28-30; 2 Kgs 24:14-16). The Exile was a fulfillment of the prophetic word. Jeremiah had prophesied the destruction of Jerusalem and a seventy-year exile of the people (Jer 25:11-12; 27:7; 29:10). Because of the Exile the land would enjoy the sabbath-rest provided by the law (v. 21; see Lev 26:34-35).

Appendix. The Decree of Cyrus, 36:22-23

With this appendix to his history of Israel and Judah, which also appears in Ezra 1:1-4, the CHR announces the beginning of the restoration of Israel. Babylon fell in 539 BCE and this decree was promulgated shortly thereafter. When CYRUS conquered Babylon he began a policy of repatriation of the conquered peoples to their land. Cyrus's decree allowed the return of Israel from exile and the reconstruction of the Temple and of all Jerusalem.

Jeremiah had predicted the time of the captivity. The land had enjoyed its sabbath-rest and now God was about to restore his people to their land by stirring the spirit of the king of Persia to edify the house in Jerusalem. The decree allowed those who were God's people to return under the protection of God and the blessings of the empire to establish a new beginning in the land that was the central element of the nation's existence.

The CHR thus ends his book with an optimistic conclusion, which in his theology reflects the infinite love of God for his people. The gracious God of Israel had forgiven the sinful people and is about to return them to their land, a holy and blessed land.

Works Cited

Ackroyd, Peter R. 1973. *I and II Chronicles, Ezra and Nehemiah.* TBC.

Albright, William F. 1950. "The Judicial Reform of Jehoshaphat," in *Alexander Marx Jubilee Volume,* 61–82.

Barnett, Richard D. 1990. "Six Fingers and Six Toes: Polydactylism in the Ancient World," *BAR* 16/3: 46–51.

Braun, Roddy. 1979. "Chronicles, Ezra, and Nehemiah: Theology and Literary History," VTSup 30:52–64. 1986. *1 Chronicles.* WBC.

Bright, John. 1981. *A History of Israel.* 3rd ed.

Curtis, Edward L., and Albert A. Madsen. 1910. *A Critical and Exegetical Commentary on the Books of Chronicles.* ICC.

DeVries, LaMoine. 1990. "Tarshish," MDB.

DeVries, Simon J. 1962. "Chronology in the OT," IDB. 1989. *1 and 2 Chronicles.* FOTL.

Dillard Raymond B. 1987. *2 Chronicles.* WBC.

Gordon, Cyrus H. 1962. "Tarshish," IDB.

Japhet, Sarah. 1968. "The Supposed Common Authorship of Chronicles and Ezra-Nehemiah Investigated Anew," *VT* 18:330–71. 1979. "Conquest and Settlement in Chronicles," *JBL* 98:205–18. 1993. *I & II Chronicles.* OTL.

Mariottini, Claude F. 1990a. "Tiglath-pileser," MDB. 1990b. "Ziglag," *BI* 16/4: 66–68. 1992a. "Muppim," AncBD. 1992b. "Serah," AncBD.

McCarter, P. Kyle. 1984. *II Samuel.* AncB.

Mendenhall, George E. 1958. "The Census Lists of Numbers 1 and 26," *JBL* 77:52–66.

Milgrom, Jacob. 1991. *Leviticus 1–16.* AncB.

Morris, Wilda W. (Wendy). 1990. "Huldah," MDB.

Myers, Jacob M. 1965. *1 Chronicles.* AncB.

Noth, Martin. 1987. *The Chronicler's History.*

Pritchard, James B, ed. 1955. *Ancient Near Eastern Texts Relating to the Old Testament* (ANET).

von Rad, Gerhard. 1966. "The Levitical Sermons in I and II Chronicles," in *The Problem of the Hexateuch and Other Essays,* 267–80.

Spenser, S. 1984. "2 Chronicles 28:5-15 and the Parable of the Good Samaritan," *WTJ* 46:317–49.

Thiele, E. R. 1965. *The Mysterious Numbers of the Hebrew Kings.*

Wagner, Siegfried. 1978. דָּרַשׁ *dārash*; מִדְרָשׁ *midhrāsh*, *TDOT* 3:293–307.

Williamson, H. G. M. 1982. *1 and 2 Chronicles.* NCB.

Ezra-Nehemiah [MCB 373-94]

David A. Smith

Introduction

The books of Ezra and Nehemiah give a significant theological interpretation of the dangerous and uncertain early postexilic period when Israelites returning from Babylon struggled in spite of external enemies and internal disagreements to reestablish themselves in Judah. Ezra and Nehemiah provide a general picture of the postexilic restoration, but cannot be used to reconstruct the details and sequence of historical events because the materials are arranged for theological, not historical, purposes.

Early Jewish and Christian lists of canonical books treated Ezra and Nehemiah as a single work called Ezra. Origen in the third century referred to them as separate books, 1 Ezra and 2 Ezra. This division was followed by Jerome in the Vulgate and eventually appeared in Hebrew manuscripts and modern language translations where the books are named after their principal characters. At least two other ancient Jewish books bear the name Ezra (Gk., *Esdras*). First Esdras is a Greek work paralleling, with some rearrangements and additional materials, 2 Chr 35–36, all of Ezra, and Neh 7:38–8:12. Second Esdras is a Jewish apocalypse recounting seven visions attributed to Ezra; 2 Esdras has no other relationship to the canonical works. The books of 1 and 2 Esdras are included in the Protestant Apocrypha, but were not always viewed by Catholics as deuterocanonical. Contemporary Catholic Bibles place them among the other deuterocanonical writings.

Authorship, Sources, Purpose and Presuppositions, Date

The ancient Jewish and Christian view that Ezra was the author of Chronicles and Ezra–Nehemiah is still held by a few modern critical scholars. The majority accept common authorship of Chronicles and Ezra–Nehemiah, but not the author's identity with Ezra. They refer to the author as "the Chronicler." Others argue for separate authorship of Chronicles and Ezra–Nehemiah on the basis of differences in language, style, and themes, and find multiple editorial layers in Ezra–Nehemiah. Their analysis cannot be taken lightly, but it still seems probable that Ezra–Nehemiah was compiled by the Chronicler or someone quite like him. In the commentary that follows this author/editor is called "the narrator."

In Chronicles this narrator chose and arranged materials from Samuel–Kings, court records, Temple records, genealogical lists and other official documents to emphasize Israel's God-directed successes in the past. The greatest of these achievements was the establishment of the Temple in Jerusalem as a sacred center in which Yahweh could be worshiped and God's Torah accepted and obeyed. This worship and obedience shaped the people of Israel into the community that Yahweh intended them to be.

In Ezra–Nehemiah the narrator emphasized that the community newly returned to Judah from Babylon had proved themselves to be the true community of faith. The author chose and arranged materials from sources similar to those used in Chronicles, giving special emphasis to two narrative collections, the "Ezra Memoirs" (Ezra 7–10 and Neh 8–10) and the "Nehemiah Memoirs" (Neh 1–7; 12:27-43; 13:4-31; see 2 Macc 2:13), to demonstrate the continuity between the successes of the past and the achievements of the leaders of the restoration: the return from EXILE as a new EXODUS; the rebuilding of the altar and the Temple; restoration of the worship of Yahweh there; rebuilding the walls of Jerusalem; and, most important of all, the acceptance of TORAH as the basis for a renewed COVENANT relationship with Yahweh.

What the narrator and his chief characters attempted and the way they went about it will be clearer for us if we consider three important dimensions of their thought.

(1) Their society was one in which moral and ritual purity separated the *holy* people from the rest of humanity. The standards of purity were clearly stated and widely known.

Israel's relationship with a holy God was maintained by keeping covenant and obeying all of God's commandments. This relationship sustained the divinely intended order of their society and of the cosmos. This sense of the necessity for purity had been heightened to exaggerations in the exilic times of crisis, when any act of impurity could be taken as threatening Israel's existence and even the existence of the world (cf. Douglas 1978, 41–57).

(2) JERUSALEM was for them the sacred center in which rituals celebrated and actualized the divine activity of creation and redemption. By postexilic times Jerusalem was viewed as a place of almost mythical power. Jerusalem clearly symbolized a divinely revealed opening into the realm of the sacred. Jerusalem was the "navel [MT; NRSV, *center*] of the earth" (Ezek 38:12), the highest mountain at the center of the world (Zech 14:10) from which flowed rivers of life-giving water (Zech 14:8 and Ezek 47; Ps 48:1-3), the heavenly city come to earth (Ezek 40:1-4), paradise (Isa 11:6-9; 32:15-20; 51:3), the cornerstone of the new creation (Isa 28:16), and the abode of God (Pss 132:13-14; 46:5).

The walls of the holy city separated this holy place from the profane (Ezek 42:20). The sanctuary in Jerusalem founded the world and dissipated chaos (2 Sam 24:15-25). Its symbols were creative and cosmic: the mountain-like altar built on the "bosom of the earth" (Ezek 43:14, author trans.), the cosmic sea, the bronze pillars, the Holy of Holies where Yahweh was enthroned.

In the midst of the exilic chaos of alien culture and power, Israel's roots still reached deep into the sacred rock of Jerusalem's holy place, "where the break in plane was symbolically assured and hence communication with the other world, the transcendent world, was ritually possible" (Eliade 1961, 45). Jerusalem was "a place that is hierophanic and therefore real, "a supremely 'creational' place" (Eliade 1974, 377). The cosmos was stable because Yahweh dwelled in Zion, and ritual recognition of that sacred presence established Israel's whole world in the midst of chaos. Jerusalem was the source of salvation, justice, and law, which are the realities in history by which mythically understood and celebrated sacred presence sanctifies the world. Jerusalem was the center where *righteousness* reigns so as to establish *peace*. This place, sacred above all others, infused the world with its own character as model and guarantor of present and future paradise because the presence of God there was assurance of divine universality and of human morality.

(3) Not only Jerusalem, but the entire land of ISRAEL was a special place. This land was filled with history. Things that had happened there were remembered and interpreted as having profound theological meaning, meaning that shaped the character of its people and their role in history (Brueggemann 1977, 5). There they had heard and responded to the voice of God, heard sometimes as life-directing Torah, at other times as severe prophetic rebuke, correction, and plaintiff pleas for repentance, and at other times as hopeful promises of restoration and fulfillment. This was a place to which the Messiah would come (Hag 2:23; Zech 6:9-14). This was the place that might even be reshaped by God's renewing grace and power into a paradise like that of Eden (Ezek 47:1-12).

Almost every Israelite leader of the postexilic period would have shared these ideas. Therefore, in their minds, for Israel to have a future, the exiles' return to Palestine and restoration of worship there were essential, and all measures deemed necessary to assure the purity of life lived there were justifiable.

The sources used by the narrator originated at different times, some as early as the late sixth and early fifth centuries BCE and some editorial additions may date from the end of the fourth century BCE or later. The major narrative dates from the early- to mid-fourth century BCE.

For Further Study

In the *Mercer Dictionary of the Bible*: ELECTION; CHRONICLES, FIRST AND SECOND; CYRUS; ESDRAS, FIRST; EZRA; EZRA, BOOK OF; NEHEMIAH; NEHEMIAH, BOOK OF.

In other sources: P. R. Ackroyd, *Exile and Restoration; A Study of Hebrew Thought of the Sixth Century B.C.*, OTL; R. A. Bowman and C. W. Gilkey, "The Book of Ezra and the Book of Nehemiah," IB; D. J. A. Clines, *Ezra, Nehemiah, Esther*, NCB; F. C. Fensham, *The Books of Ezra and Nehemiah*, NICOT; R. W. Klein, "Ezra–Nehemiah, Books of," *AncBD*; J. M. Myers, *Ezra–Nehemiah*, AncB; S. Talmon, "Ezra and Nehemiah (Books and Men),"

IDBsup, and "Ezra and Nehemiah," *The Literary Guide to the Bible*, 357–64; M. A. Throntveit, *Ezra–Nehemiah*; H. G. M. Williamson, *Ezra, Nehemiah*, WBC.

Commentary

An Outline

Ezra

Return to Jerusalem under Sheshbazzar/Zerubbabel: Restoration of the Community of Faith and of Temple Worship, 1:1–6:22

Cyrus's Decree and a New Exodus, 1:1-11

1:1-4. The Cyrus decree. In the first year of his reign over Babylon (538 BCE), CYRUS issued a decree encouraging Jews in Babylon who would to return to Jerusalem to rebuild the Temple and encouraging those who did not want to return to give material support to those who did return. This decree was delivered to Jewish communities throughout Babylon; *throughout all his kingdom* (v. 1) does not require that the proclamation be made to everyone.

The narrator of Ezra–Nehemiah relates this decree to a prophecy of Jeremiah, perhaps Jeremiah's poetical oracle in 51:1–11a, which begins "I am going to stir up a destructive wind against Babylon." The connected prose comment in Jer 51:llb, "the LORD has stirred up the spirit of the kings of the Medes," seems to be a clear reference to Cyrus.

Identification with the prophecy in Jer 29:10 of a seventy-year exile is less likely since it was given in a context of judgment to which the exiles should be resigned. Josephus (*Ant* 11.1-2) suggests that Cyrus was moved by references to himself as God's chosen destroyer of Babylon and liberator of the Jews in Isa 41, 44, and 45. While the Isaiah passages would almost certainly have been in the minds of the narrator and his readers, Cyrus probably had no knowledge of the Isaiah passages. His specific reference to the Jewish god, *the LORD, the God of heaven* (v. 2), indicates a sensitivity to and respect for the religion of the Jews consistent with statements elsewhere about the gods of other peoples. On the Cyrus Cylinder he describes at length the restoration of the gods of many cities and attributes this action to the direction of Marduk, god of Babylon (Pritchard 1955, 315–16). This sensitivity was general and certainly not particularly slanted toward Jewish religion. Cyrus was not a devotee of Yahweh.

Cyrus's motive in these things was political, though doubtless influenced by the positive religious and ethical values of the Zoroastrian religion. He and his successors believed they could win the loyalty of subject peoples by giving them some measure of self-determination and religious autonomy. The Jews, aware of these political motivations, at the same time believed their god had *stirred up the spirit of King Cyrus* (v. 1).

Implicit in this belief is the idea that the LORD is sovereign not only over Israel but over all the nations. That their god's use of Cyrus benefited not only the Jews but all the other peoples over whom Cyrus had authority raises a serious question about the Jews' special relationship to God—the Jewish idea of ELECTION. This question is one with which postexilic Jewish thinkers struggled and one that must be considered in the evaluation of certain actions of both Ezra and Nehemiah. Is Yahweh's universality one of power only, or it is also one of love and grace?

Would the restored postexilic community be an open community in whom "all the families of the earth shall be blessed" (Gen 12:3) and a "light to the nations" (Isa 49:6) or would their insecurity make them into a closed and withdrawn community?

1:5-11. A new exodus. Before the EXILE prophets had repeatedly predicted that God would judge the unfaithfulness of his people by bringing against them powerful kings who would carry them away into exile. Now in contrast Cyrus is proclaimed as God's servant who will use his power and influence to restore the Jews in their homeland. Isaiah declared that in doing this God was doing "a new thing" (cf. Isa 43:19). This new thing was a new EXODUS, but one with interesting parallels to the Exodus from Egypt. In the Exodus from Egypt all the Israelites fled from bondage. Now only those whose spirits were stirred by God returned. The implication of this is, not that God limited the participation by stirring the spirits of only a select few, but rather that only a few responded to God's stirring.

Many Jews were satisfied with life in Babylon where they really enjoyed considerable freedom even before Cyrus, and some Jews were prospering there. In the Exodus from Egypt the Israelites were encouraged to flee to an unknown but fabled land that God had prepared for them. Now the Jews are asked to return to a land known to be war-torn and desolate and probably overrun by alien peoples. Then the Pharaoh was opposed to Israel's leaving and on occasion was confirmed in that opposition by God himself who "hardened Pharaoh's heart" against Israel (see Exod 7:13; 8:15, 19, 32, etc.). Now Cyrus generously encourages and supports a return. Then the fleeing Israelites asked their Egyptian neighbors for jewelry and clothing, and their neighbors, distressed by the plague of the firstborn, let them have what they asked: "And so they plundered the Egyptians" (Exod 12:36). Now the Jews are aided with *gifts* (v. 6) of silver and gold and other goods. In addition, Cyrus returned to the Jews the vessels taken by the Babylonians from the Temple for use in the Temple the Jews were to rebuild. (In the case of other peoples, Cyrus restored the images of their gods to their original places. For the Jews, the return of the sacred vessels carried out the same intention. These holy vessels represented a very concrete objective connection between the past and the future.) Then they left Egypt to establish a community of faith and an independent nation. Now they go to reestablish a community of faith under the sovereignty of Persia.

This comparison with the Exodus intends to do more than merely contrast the past and the present. The narrator of Ezra–Nehemiah uses the Exodus motifs to stress one of his major theological concerns— the continuity between the exilic generation and the whole of the previous history of the Israelite people.

Restoration of the Community of Faith: the List of Families Who First Returned to Jerusalem, 2:1-70

Israel's vision of a new exodus greater than the Exodus from Egypt is given historical reality in a listing of exiles who returned from Babylon. This list, which also appears with some variations in Neh 7:6-73 (and in 1 Esd 5:7-46), was probably compiled from various official records of the time naming the families that settled in Judah in the early years of the restoration and is intended to authenticate their lineages, a concern for cultural purity.

Lists like this, of which there are a good number in Ezra–Nehemiah, are not appealing to the modern reader. They are filled with hard-to-pronounce, strange-looking names that belong to an ancient foreign time and at first glance have little meaning, but there are a number of ways in which this list must have conveyed significant meaning to the Jews who read it in the postexilic age. The list begins by naming twelve leaders (adding Nahamani from the parallel list in Neh 7:7) and the number twelve was always a reminder of the wholeness of the Israelite people (see NUMBERS/NUMEROLOGY).

ZERUBBABEL's name heads the list without further comment. That nothing else is said about him here is surprising, considering his royal Davidic ancestry and the rather grand messianic expectations that the prophets Haggai and Zechariah held for him (Hag 2:20-23; Zech 4:6-7, 9-10; 6:12). Nowhere in Ezra–Nehemiah is there any concern for these things. The narrator is properly wary of royalty in light of the significant failure of the preexilic monarchy. His primary concern with the Davidic dynasty focuses on its contribution to the cult. He is not concerned with the possibility of Zerubbabel's reestablishing kingship in Jerusalem, but with Zerubbabel's helping to reestablish the worship of Yahweh there.

After leaders, extended family groups are designated by their ancestral head or by their ancestral town. Then the list mentions authenticated priests, Levites, and other Temple personnel, ending by mentioning groups of persons who were unable to *prove their families or their descent* (v. 59), among whom were even some descendants of priestly families who were considered unclean and ineligible to serve as priests because they could not trace their genealogies. Only when a chief priest was chosen who could consult URIM AND THUMMIM, the objects used by the chief priest to cast lots, could they be restored to active participation in the priesthood.

These various groups are recorded as totaling 42,360 (v. 64). The same total appears in Neh 7:66 (and in 2 Esd 5:41). In all cases this total exceeds the sum of the numbers given for the various groups, and the numbers given for the various groups in the lists frequently differ. These discrepancies cannot be satisfactorily explained.

The list then adds male and female servants, male and female singers, horses, mules, camels, and donkeys. Extended families or clans of lay people, priests, Levites, and other Temple personnel, servants, singers, horses, mules, camels, and donkeys—such was the company of those who returned from exile and established themselves in their ancestral places in and around Jerusalem. This is to say that the restoration could only be accomplished by the common cooperation of everyone of all stations in the community of faith.

Early Jewish readers would have been deeply moved to find their ancestral family names or towns included here, and would take pride that they had been among those who had been willing to participate in the return and restoration. This list is an honor roll of faith, an honor roll not of the exceptional persons whose praises are in Sirach's "Hymn in Honor of Our Ancestors" (44:1–50:24) which begins, "Let us now sing the praises of famous men." The names listed here are not of "famous men," heroes bigger than life. These are the names of persons of good, devout, common stock, who in the past and now in the restoration formed the essence of the Israelite community of faith. The list also legitimized the settlement of these families in Jerusalem and the surrounding countryside.

Finally, often overlooked in the interpretation of this list is the fact that most Israelite names have meaning expressing parental hopes and expectations for the child—thanksgiving to God for the child's birth, description of the circumstances of the child's birth, description of the child's appearance, or occasionally evaluations by prophets of the circumstances of the people they addressed (cf. Hos 1:4, 6, 9; Isa 7:3, 14; 8:1). Often these names are one-sentence descriptions of God's activity. In the context of God's doing "a new thing" (cf. Isa 43:19) in the return from exile, would not readers of this list have been sensitive to meanings of names such as *Jeshua* (or Joshua; Heb. "Yahweh delivers"), *Shephatiah* (Heb. "Yahweh judges"), *Adonikam* (Heb. "the Lord has risen up"), *Hezekiah* (Heb. "Yahweh has strengthened"), *Jedaiah* (Heb. "Yahweh has known"), and *Hodaviah* (Heb. "give praise to Yahweh").

This list, which began with the naming of twelve leaders of the return and restoration calling to mind the twelve-tribe wholeness of traditional Israel, ends with all Israel settled *in their towns* (v. 70). Obviously the restoration of the community of faith was not complete, but this list of returning exiles already represents the eventual fulfillment of the restoration. The journey from Babylon was filled with danger and difficulty and the restoration of life in a war-devastated and long-abandoned countryside would require long and hard work. The simple statement that the returning exiles *lived in Jerusalem* and *lived in their towns* (v. 70) omits any reference to the difficulties faced by those who returned (cf. Haggai and Zechariah).

In spite of these difficulties families continued to return and gave generously to the work of rebuilding the altar and the Temple and the walls of Jerusalem. These subsequent returns continue the ongoing process by which God, with this kind of faithful response, would reestablish the community of faith.

Restoration of Worship, 3:1–6:22

3:1-6. The restoration of the altar. The restoration of the altar began in *the seventh month*, the month of the New Year's celebration, the Day of Atonement, and the Feast of Booths (Tabernacles), when all the Israelites "gathered as one man to Jerusalem" (v. 1, RSV) to rebuild it. Again the narrative emphasizes the cooperation of rulers, priests, and lay people. They built the altar of natural unworked stones as prescribed in the Law of Moses (Exod 20:25), on the site of the preexilic altar that had been chosen by David on the basis of a revelation from God—continuity with preexilic Israel reaching back to the earliest times.

During the exile, the people who remained in Judah had continued to offer sacrifices on the remains of the preexilic altar (Jer 41:5). Returning leaders, however, considered themselves and their followers to be the true people of God and for them the ruined altar was unclean; worship therefore could not begin for the restored community until the new altar was built. Until it was built they felt threatened by hostile neighbors and without the protection of Yahweh. Building the altar established a center of divine presence around which those who worshiped there had sanctuary (divine protection).

Building the altar also symbolized their claim that the land of which it was the center was their land. Building an altar was a ritual repetition of the creation of the cosmos and of society. Building the altar at New Year's symbolized living in sacred time, the time when God is near and active to create and redeem. At New Year's Yahweh was celebrated as creator in two senses—the creator of heaven and earth in the beginning and the creator of Israel in the Exodus, the covenant of Sinai, and the conquest of Canaan. When the work was finished the whole of preexilic worship was renewed: regular ongoing daily worship, prescribed worship on feast days for the entire community (with the exception of the Day of Atonement, which could not properly be observed until the Temple was rebuilt), and for individuals the opportunity to make freewill offerings. But only those who had returned from exile, who were in true continuity with the past, were legitimate worshipers at this rebuilt altar.

The celebration of the Feast of Booths (TABERNACLES, FESTIVAL OF) was particularly appropriate for the circumstances of the newly resettled exiles. Booths was a festival with intertwined dimensions of meaning. It was a fall harvest festival during which people lived out in the fields in shelters constructed of branches and vines to guard the crops. There was great rejoicing over God's gifts of the fruits of the land. The exiles had not been back in Judah long enough to have planted, tended, and harvested crops, so their first Festival of Booths was a celebration of memory and anticipation.

Considering what they had endured they must have experienced great pleasure in eating and drinking the meager amounts of food and wine available to them. They had been the people who could not sing the songs of Zion in a foreign land (cf. Ps 137:3-4). Of Jerusalem, their enemies had cried, "Raze it, raze it! Down to its foundations!" (Ps 137:7, RSV). They had returned to build it again. Now they must have sung the songs of Zion with great joy. Booths also was a reminder of the postexodus days of wilderness pilgrimage when their ancestors lived in tents, a striking parallel to their own immediate past experience. Finally, Booths was a time of covenant renewal at which the community recommitted itself to the covenant demands of God (cf. the discussion of Neh 8–9, below).

Worship was restored, but in a temple still in ruins, for *the foundation of the temple of the Lord was not yet laid* (v. 6).

3:7-13. Initial work on the Temple. In this account of the rebuilding of the Temple, the narrator subordinates historical and chronological concerns to a theological emphasis on the continuity between the experiences of the returned exiles and those of the preexilic community of faith.

The altar was restored soon after the exiles arrived in Judah in 538 BCE, but under threats from "the peoples of the lands" (3:3, RSV; NRSV, *neighboring peoples*; cf. 4:4-5), no work was done on the Temple, beyond Sheshbazzar's beginning to lay the foundation (5:14-16), until 520 BCE (cf. Hag 1). The narrative in Ezra 3 gives no indication that eighteen years passed before work on the Temple itself began. Chronological gaps like this trouble those who look for a full summary history of the postexilic period. The narrator, however, is concerned with certain major, pivotal events, which he will emphasize and even rearrange in chronological sequence to suit his theological purposes.

Preparation for Temple reconstruction began with the hiring of masons and carpenters and, as in Solomon's time, the arrangement with Sidonians and Tyrenians to bring cedar trees by sea from Lebanon to Joppa. This transport would take considerable time and it was only in the second year after they turned their attention to the building of the Temple that construction actually began (v. 8).

ZERUBBABEL and JESHUA, leaders of the second return from Babylon, led in rebuilding the Temple. Jeshua was the High Priest and Zerubbabel the governor (cf. Hag 1:1; 2:2). They appointed Levites, age twenty or older, to oversee the work. The beginning age of twenty is younger than usual (cf. Num 8:23), apparently a concession to the fact that surprisingly few Levites participated in early returns from Babylon. Under Levitical leadership the work on the foundation of the Temple was soon finished (because they worked hard, but also because much of the foundation of the preexilic Temple remained).

When the foundations were completed, there was a joyous celebration like that which celebrated the construction of "the Temple of Solomon" (2 Chr 5:12-13).

They praised the LORD with instrumental music and singing "according to the directions of David" (2 Chr 29:25-30). The Levites and the priests sang antiphonally, *For he is good, for his steadfast love endures forever toward Israel* (3:11). This verse of praise suggests the type of psalms of praise that would be sung in their entirety on occasions like this (e.g., Pss 100, 106, 107, 118, 136).

The people's response to the dedication was a mixture of loud weeping and shouting for joy. The old priests, Levites, and heads of households who had seen the first Temple wept. Why did they weep? Was it because they remembered the splendor of the former Temple and could not imagine this new structure rivaling that splendor, or did they weep for joy? Apparently they wept out of disappointment.

4:1-5, 24. Opposition to the rebuilding of the Temple. The Temple, however, was still not rebuilt in 520 BCE (cf. Hag 1:4). Haggai blamed this delay on the people's selfishness and lack of religious commitment. The narrator in Ezra blamed it on conflict with peoples who lived roundabout whom he called adversaries. Initially, these people do not seem to have been adversaries, but cooperative neighbors. Their offer to help in the construction of the Temple, and their reason for making this offer—their longstanding worship of Yahweh—was genuine.

Suggestions that they had ulterior motives of political or economic kind are conjectures without any real evidence to support them.

The response of the Jewish leaders did not question their worship of Yahweh or suggest that they also still worshiped the gods from their countries of origin. Their offer was rejected on the expressed grounds that the commission from Cyrus to build the Temple did not include them. Implicitly, the rejection of this offer of help is based on the returning exiles' concept of themselves as the only legitimate remnant of the preexilic community of faith.

Throughout this account of the restoration the narrator repeatedly emphasizes that the true community of faith includes only the returning exiles from the tribes of Levi, Judah, and Benjamin. No mention is made even of Jews from these three tribes who had remained in Judah during the exile. *In Israel* (v. 3) means returning exiles from these three tribes. The list in chap. 2, this rebuff of their neighbors, and the limiting of the community of faith to returning Levites, Judahites, and Benjaminites, however important for maintaining the purity of the community, suggest an emerging exclusivism that would have serious consequences for the future. The returnees' rejection of this offer to help build the Temple turned their neighbors into *adversaries* (v. 1) who took various means to hinder the Temple's construction.

4:6-23. Parenthetical account of later opposition. At this point the sequence of events becomes confusing because the narrator uses accounts of later opposition to the building of the wall of Jerusalem during the reigns of Ahasuerus (Xerxes I, 486–465 BCE) and Artaxerxes I (465–424 BCE) to justify the rather harsh rejection of the offer of help in Temple construction from those he designated as *adversaries* in 4:1. The narrator presents letters sent to ARTAXERXES in opposition to the building of

Jerusalem's walls, and the king's responses, all in Aramaic, the official language of the PERSIAN EMPIRE. From 4:8 through 6:18 the entire narrative is in Aramaic.

Persian officials of the province *Beyond the River* (v. 10, i.e., beyond the Euphrates) wrote to Artaxerxes suggesting that the rebuilding of Jerusalem's walls was an act of rebellion like those of which Jerusalem had been guilty in the past. If the walls were rebuilt, the Jews would withhold taxes from Persia, and Persia would lose the entire province. Paid by and favored by Artaxerxes (the apparent meaning of *we share the salt of the palace*, v. 14) they felt obliged to inform Artaxerxes of this danger and assured him that if he checked *the annals of your ancestors* (v. 15, suggesting chronicles of earlier Assyrian, Babylonian, and Persian kings), he would see that the danger was real. The suggestion that the entire province would be lost is obviously an exaggeration, but the history of rebellion was confirmed by the records. Artaxerxes, therefore, ordered his officials in *Beyond the River* to stop work on the walls. The narrative continues in Aramaic but returns to the building of the Temple.

4:24–6:18. Rebuilding of the Temple continued. In 520 BCE the prophets Haggai and Zechariah strongly encouraged the completion of the work on the Temple, and Zerubbabel and Jeshua began to rebuild. This activity was questioned by the Persian governor Tattenai and his associates who asked the Jews by what authority they were finishing the Temple and for a list of names of those who were doing the work. Unsatisfied with the response, they wrote to Darius to inquire about the legitimacy of the Jewish claim that the work had been authorized by Cyrus. Out of deference to Darius they also asked for a decision from him: *Let the king send us his pleasure in this matter* (5:17).

A search in Persian records verified the Jewish claim. A decree of Cyrus was found *in Ecbatana* (6:2), one of the provincial capitals of Persia, not identical with the decree of 1:2-4, but clearly authorizing the same activity. Darius, therefore, strongly affirmed support of the restoration of worship in Jerusalem, including the use of tax revenues from the province *Beyond the River* (6:6) and whatever else the priests needed for worship. He threatened severe punishment on anyone who altered his decree. His request to the Jewish God to put down all opposition is consistent with the Persian belief that Yahweh had authority over Jerusalem and Judah and with the fact that he, like Cyrus, saw restoration of Jewish life in Judah to be in his own interest.

Tattenai did as Darius ordered and the work on the Temple was completed in 516 BCE, the sixth year of Darius. The success of the endeavor is attributed to the interesting combination of the God of Israel, the Persian rulers Cyrus and Darius (*Artaxerxes* in 6:14 is a scribal addition, perhaps to indicate that Persian kings consistently treated Israel with justice), who commanded the work to be done, HAGGAI and ZECHARIAH who encouraged it, and the Jewish leaders and workers responsible for the actual construction. The divine command could be carried out only with the cooperation of the various human persons involved.

The service of dedication was patterned after that of Solomon (1 Kgs 8; 2 Chr 7:4-7) and the sin offering at the dedication of the restored Temple by Hezekiah (2 Chr 29:24). The sin offering of twelve male goats was made for all the tribes of Israel even though only Levi, Judah, and Benjamin were present. Here again the narrator emphasizes that the returning exiles are the true community of faith. With the Temple dedicated, the priests and the Levites were assigned their ritual responsibilities. This account of the Temple's dedication ends the Aramaic section.

The account of the rebuilding of the Temple intentionally parallels the construction of Solomon's Temple: cedars of Lebanon were imported for lumber; masons and carpenters came from Sidon and Tyre; the work began in the second month; priests and Levites oversaw the work; and the two Temples were dedicated in similar ways. These parallels demonstrate religious continuity between the postexilic community and that of their ancestors. Inevitably the returned exiles saw the smallness of their work compared to the greatness of Solomon's, and those who remembered the first Temple wept.

There is, however, another significant implied comparison. Solomon's Temple was the accomplishment of a nation in the height of its power; this Temple was built under adverse circumstances—in a war-devastated land and over against strong opposition. Its completion in spite of opposition implies that the accomplishment of the returned exiles was greater than that of Solomon; the prophet Haggai could exclaim, "The latter splendor of this house shall be greater than the former" (Hag 2:9). Its completion was the guarantee of greater things.

6:19-22. Celebration of Passover and Unleavened Bread. The first ceremony performed by the newly appointed priests and Levites was PASSOVER. The account of the restoration of worship (Ezra 3:1–6:22) gives special attention to the celebration of important feast days: Tabernacles after the dedication of the altar, Passover after the dedication of the Temple. Ritually pure priests made the Passover offering on behalf of a "pure" Israel composed of those who had returned from exile and those from other backgrounds who *separated themselves from the pollutions of the nations of the land to worship the* LORD (v. 21).

Who these latter persons were is not clear—persons from Judah who had been in exile?, other Jews who lived in and around Jerusalem?, gentile proselytes who converted to Judaism? The circle of the community of faith has become slightly larger but still is exclusive. Any who differed in any way from the perspective of the returning exiles, whether Gentiles or Jews, were ritually polluting outsiders.

Return to Jerusalem under Ezra, 7:1–10:44

Ezra's Identity, Commission, and Response, 7:1-28

Chapter 7 begins the story of Ezra's work, supposedly based on the so-called "Ezra Memoirs."

7:1-6. Ezra's identity. Ezra (Heb. "help") is a shortened form of AZARIAH (Heb. "the LORD [has] helped"). Ezra's genealogy, though incomplete (Seraiah, listed as his father, lived about 150 years before Ezra), traces his ancestry through the high-priestly line back to Aaron. Although not a high priest himself, as a member of the high-priestly family he had the best of priestly credentials.

Ezra is also described as *a scribe skilled in the law of Moses* (v. 6). The word *skilled* originally meant "quick"—one who could write fast—but here and elsewhere defining scribe it refers to the wisdom and expertise of a highly capable official. Ezra was a student and teacher of the written Torah, the first and greatest of a class whose work became increasingly important in the postexilic period. As a skilled interpreter of the Law of Moses (the Pentateuch), he was responsible for acting upon that Law. One could not really know the Law without acting upon it. He *had set his heart to study the law of the LORD, and to do it, and to teach the statutes and ordinances in Israel* (v. 10). Artaxerxes commissioned this priest and scribe, who held the position of *the scribe of the law of the God of Heaven* (7:12), perhaps the title of a Persian official of considerable importance, to go to Jerusalem and administer the Law there.

7:7-10. Summary statement of the return to Jerusalem led by Ezra. This section is a brief introduction to Ezra's journey from Babylon to Jerusalem. The journey is treated in more detail in 8:1-36. See the text units below for commentary on the journey.

7:11-26. Ezra's commission. Ezra's commission by Artaxerxes in an official Aramaic document (vv. 12-26) is probably authentic. It authorized him to travel to Judah to reform Jewish religious and social life. That it has a certain Jewish character can be explained by the possibility that Ezra himself drafted the document. Ezra, on the highest authority, *sent by the king and his seven counselors* (v. 14), was to go to Jerusalem with any of the people of Israel who wished to accompany him, taking with them offerings for the Temple given by the king and his counselors, by the people of Babylon, and by Jews who preferred to remain in Babylon. These gifts were to be used for a major sacrificial offering on their arrival in Jerusalem. Any that remained would be used at the discretion of Ezra and his priestly colleagues as God directed them. Continuing support for the ongoing Temple services could be drawn by Ezra from the treasury of the province *Beyond the River* (v. 21).

Ezra's commission also exempted Temple personnel from Persian taxation. On arrival in Jerusalem Ezra was *to make inquiries about Judah and Jerusalem according to the law of your God, which is in your hand* (v. 14). What does the phrase *which is in your hand* mean? Did Ezra carry a scroll of the entire Pentateuch written in Babylon and now for the first time made available to Jews already in Jerusalem?

Surely the Pentateuch was already known to the Jews there (cf. v. 25). The phrase then would mean the law on which Ezra was an authority—the cultic law that had previously been the concern of the priests. With the help of judges and magistrates whom he would appoint, Ezra was to determine if the restored community understood and followed the ritual requirements and cultic practices through which Yahweh was approached and the proper observance of which maintained society. This commission to enforce the law of God was consistent with Ezra's own wishes as summarized in v. 10, wishes that Ezra may well have made known to the king and that then were incorporated into the royal decree.

7:27-28. Ezra's response. Ezra's response was twofold: first, a prayer of gratitude for the steadfast love of God's grace and then the selection of Israelite leaders to return to Jerusalem with him.

Preparations for and Return to Jerusalem, 8:1-36 (7:7-10)

8:1-14. Continuing restoration of the community of faith: the list of families who accompanied Ezra to Jerusalem. This list, which has similarities to the list in chap. 2, is not a precise census of all who returned with Ezra but is designed to demonstrate the continuity between the nation's past, present, and future. The whole of old Israel (twelve tribes) were participating in this return (descendants of the heads of *twelve* families).

The "new Exodus" was not accomplished all at once. It was an ongoing process and no stigma was attached to those who did not participate in the first return. The crucial point was that those who returned, whenever they did so, made up the ideal community of faith.

8:15-34. Preparations for departure and journey to Jerusalem. Ezra's group returned in *the seventh year of King Artaxerxes* (according to 7:7), which was either 458 BCE if it was Artaxerxes I (Cross 1975, 4–18), or 428 if the seventh year should be amended to read the thirty-seventh year (Bright 1981, 391–402), or 398 if Artaxerxes is Artaxerxes II (Rowley 1965, 137–68).

Related to this question of date are those about the extent to which Ezra and Nehemiah worked together and the relationship between their reform efforts. The narrator, or an editor, associates them with one another only in a covenant renewal ceremony (Neh 8:9) and in celebrating the completion of the city wall (Neh 12:33 and 36). The nature and extent of any other relationships is pure conjecture. Whichever date is considered best, the opening phrase of chap. 7, *after this*, covers a considerable number of years. The narrator clearly does not intend a comprehensive historical account of postexilic events. He emphasizes Ezra's journey as the next important step in the ongoing process of restoration. History is understood in theological rather than chronological terms.

Before departure, Ezra's company gathered by one of the irrigation canals flowing out of the Euphrates. Thirty-eight Levites were recruited there to make this return completely representative of the tribal makeup of the restored community of faith—Judah, Benjamin, and Levi—and to make Ezra's caravan conform to the order of march through the desert in the original Exodus. Ezra proclaimed prayer and fasting for God's protection on the journey. Having refused to ask the king for the protection of soldiers and cavalry, he now made practical plans to protect his wealthy caravan. He chose twelve priests, divided the silver and gold and Temple vessels among them and made them responsible for them throughout the journey.

The journey lasted about four months and must have been very difficult, covering approximately 900 miles at the rate of about nine miles per day.

8:35-36. Gratitude for a safe journey and the beginning of reformation. On arrival at Jerusalem they waited three days, apparently to rest, or perhaps to avoid a formal arrival on the Sabbath. On the fourth day the silver, gold, and vessels were weighed and everything was accounted for. Ezra and his company then sacrificed twelve bulls in gratitude for God's protection on the journey and twelve goats as a sin offering to cleanse them from the ritual defilements inevitable on such a journey.

Again the number *twelve* points to the returning exiles as the heirs and continuity of *all* Israel, all of whom had to be ritually pure.

Before beginning to teach the Law and to encourage reforms on the basis of its teachings, Ezra delivered his credentials and Artaxerxes' orders to Persian officials in the area, and these officials gave their support to the Jewish community.

Ezra's Reform: The Problem of Mixed Marriages, 9:1–10:44

Ezra's handling of the problem of mixed marriages is introduced by the somewhat cryptic phrase *After these things had been done* (9:1). To what *these things* refers is not clear. There is an interval of more than four and one-half months between the events of chap. 8 and those of chaps. 9 and 10 (cf. 7:8-9 and 10:9). Many scholars suppose that the account of Ezra's public reading of the Law (Neh 8) originally belonged between Ezra 8 and 9.

After these things, then, would refer to this reading of the Law and the sense of guilt about mixed marriages that it prompted. However, it is difficult to explain the misplacement of this important event in a narrative that is carefully arranged to emphasize the reading and teaching of the Law as Ezra's greatest accomplishment. It seems preferable to suppose that when Ezra met with the Persian officials of the area he discussed with them the importance of determining who of the many peoples living in the region should be considered authentic Jews and, therefore, subject to the Law as administered by Ezra. If so, the question would have been raised about the legitimacy of Jews who had married non-Jewish women of the area.

Investigations into the matter would then explain the concern expressed by *the officials* (9:1) who brought that problem to Ezra's attention. These officials were probably governors of Jewish administrative districts who may well have been among those Ezra first informed about his commission from the king. They certainly would have been among the first to implement a process by which "true" Jews would be identified. In effect these officials were telling Ezra that he faced a major problem, since among those who had married foreign women were priests and Levites.

During the days of Israel's settlement in Canaan after the Exodus from Egypt, marriages between Israelites and people of certain foreign nations had been prohibited (Exod 34:16; Deut 7:1-4) because they could lead to religious syncretism and apostasy. These no longer historically relevant prohibitions forbidding intermarriage with specific people under specific circumstances were interpreted by Ezra as establishing principles that transcended their historical setting. The restrictive actions taken here and in Nehemiah are not so much a specific, legalistic application of Law as they are religiopolitical actions taken on expedient grounds with general references to the Law to support them. Here, however, the concern is more with ritual purity than with syncretism or apostasy. By marrying foreign wives, even some of those primarily responsible for ritual purity (9:2) had broken the Laws of Holiness that forbade the mixing of unlike things (Lev 19:19), making themselves impure and endangering the purity of the cultus and the community.

Surrounded by threats to their very existence, the returned exiles needed to have a clear understanding of their distinctiveness and how to maintain it. Rituals of purity defined them as the "holy" people of God and distinguished them from the rest of humanity. Indeed, the system of annual feasts and ongoing daily sacrifices was a reminder of the divine order of creation.

The round of rituals maintained a life-sustaining relationship with the sacred. Ritual purity was essential to the preservation of their world as a cosmos—a world of order, being, security, and meaning in which everything has its place. Anomalies like the unclean animals of the dietary laws of Lev 11 and the prohibited mixtures of other foodstuffs disrupted the order of things, subjecting the world to the ravages of chaos, insecurity, nonbeing, and meaninglessness. Mixed marriages, especially those of priests and Levites, would violate the system of order that the returning exiles were seeking to recover by reestablishing Jerusalem and the Temple as a sacred center. As Ezra saw it, much more was at stake here than racial purity. He believed the very existence of the *holy people* to be in jeopardy.

Ezra probably had already learned of these mixed marriages; his reaction, therefore, to this formal accusation was studied and public. In Israelite culture this did not make it any less genuine (cf. the many symbolic acts of earlier prophets, especially Jeremiah and Ezekiel). Ezra's response was extraordinary. He *sat appalled* (9:3), or, better, "horrified."

Dramatically expressing his concern, Ezra acted as though he were grieving over a death (9:3). His public action attracted a crowd to whom his confession to God of all of Israel's past sins and his denunciation of the present evil as a violation of God's steadfast love and of the responsibilities that God had assigned to the returning exiles had the effect of an accusatory sermon. He asked God what the returned exiles should expect from him, having violated their very reason for being in Jerusalem.

10:1-44. The people's reaction to Ezra's prayer. Moved by Ezra's demonstration and prayer, the people wept, and *Shecaniah*, speaking for them, confessed that marriage to foreign women was an act of faithlessness and suggested that a covenant be made with God to send away all wives and children of the mixed marriages. The words he used for *married* (v. 2, Heb. "to cause to dwell") and for *foreign women* (v. 2, Heb. "harlot") suggest that these were not to be considered authentic marriages, so it would be proper to send away these wives and their children.

With Ezra's urging, everyone agreed to Shecaniah's plan. All returned exiles were summoned with threat of serious penalty to come to Jerusalem within three days. Assembled there, they agreed to a plan implementing Shecaniah's covenant. Some time was needed to do so, but investigation by heads of families soon identified those who had married foreign women and *they sent them away with their children* (v. 44).

These are rather disturbing final words. This entire situation is strongly suggestive of exclusivism. Understanding the reasoning behind their actions does not mean that a modern reader must approve of those actions. What they did seems cruel and unjust, subordinating as it does the well-being of persons to ritual concerns. Shecaniah's suggestion that the marriages were not real marriages must have been accepted because there is no reference to the prescribed rules for divorce (Deut 24:1-2; Jer 3:8). This suggestion seems particularly calloused, and Ezra's implied acceptance of it is not admirable. The women and the children involved were real women and children. Where would they go? How would they live? To assume that measures were taken to provide for them goes beyond the evidence, which indicates that the action taken was harsh and cruel.

One factor that may have mitigated the harshness was the provision (v. 14) for the elders and judges of every town to appear with those accused of having married foreign wives as the individual cases were reviewed.

These people saw themselves as the true fulfillment of the Abrahamic covenant (Gen 12:1-3) with its promise of land and descendants. They indeed felt themselves to be the "descendants" now reclaiming "the land," thus enabling God to keep the age-old promise. This intense desire to reclaim the patriarchal promise of land and descendants limited and threatened the possibility that they could be the people through whom God would bless all humankind, the ultimate aim of the promise to Abraham.

Of course, the integrity and purity of the community of faith had to be protected in the dangerous times of postexilic restoration, but the question has to be raised: Was this the only way it could be done? Was this the cost by which Israel would preserve its identity as God's servant people to bring blessing and light to the nations? There must have been a better way.

If this is all that we knew of Ezra's work we would rightly have a low opinion of him. The narrator, however, will later describe Ezra's teaching of the Law as his greatest achievement (see Neh 8).

An Outline

Nehemiah

Nehemiah's Return to Jerusalem: Restoration of the City Wall, 1:1–7:73a

The Book of Nehemiah opens with a first-person account of Nehemiah's distress over the situation of the Jews in Jerusalem. Most, if not all, of the first-person material throughout the book is taken from the so-called "Nehemiah's Memoirs" (see 2 Macc 2:13; cf. commentary on Ezra 7:1, above).

Report from Jerusalem and Nehemiah's Response, 1:1-11

1:1-3. Report from Jerusalem. Nehemiah's name means "the LORD has comforted," which may suggest his family's awareness of God's presence even in exile and some expectation of God's help in the future. Nehemiah was the cupbearer to King ARTAXERXES I (see 2:1) in Susa, the winter capital where the king spent most of his time. As such Nehemiah may have been a eunuch, as some (but by no means all) cupbearers were. There is little other evidence to support the view that he was a eunuch.

He would have been skilled in choosing and serving wine, which he would taste as proof against poison before giving it to the king. Cupbearers were also expected to be congenial, helpful companions to the king. They were often in the king's confidence and were asked for counsel and advice. Nehemiah, therefore, held a position of importance with ready access to the king.

In Artaxerxes' twentieth year Jews from Judah visited Susa. They were brought to Nehemiah by his brother *Hanani* (vv. 1-2). Hanani was either from Judah or, living in Susa, had met the visiting Jews and believed they should meet with Nehemiah. Nehemiah asked them about Jews in Jerusalem, both those who had remained during the exile and those who had returned to Jerusalem from exile. They reported bad news about the devastated condition of the walls of Jerusalem. The impact on Nehemiah suggests that they were not just talking about the Babylonian destruction of the walls, but about some recent event, perhaps that referred to in Ezra 4:23 when Persian officials by order of Artaxerxes I by force stopped the Jews from rebuilding the walls and may even have destroyed what had been rebuilt.

1:4-11. Nehemiah's response. Nehemiah mourned, fasted, and prayed in distress over the conditions in Jerusalem. He felt responsibility to take action to correct the situation. That action would have to be approved and supported by Artaxerxes. Nehemiah was also distressed by the great danger of having to ask the king to overturn his own previous decree. In distress he confessed to the LORD *God of heaven* (v. 5) his sins and those of his people. This corporate sense of sin, the individual's sin affecting the community and the community's sins affecting all of its individuals, is characteristic of nearly all the prominent religious leaders in Israel. They felt a strong sense of identity with their people with whom they shared both responsibility and fate (cf. Isa 6:5). Nehemiah's confession echoes an established liturgical pattern of confession, reflecting his familiarity with Jewish worship. His important position in the court of Artaxerxes had not lessened his dedication to the LORD *God of heaven*. Private prayer is inevitably conditioned by one's experience in public prayer and worship. His prayer addressed an awesome and powerful God who is also characterized by steadfast love and faithfulness. God had punished his people with exile for failure to keep his commandments, but he had also promised to restore them and bring them back to Jerusalem where he had chosen to establish his name; that is, they would live again in Jerusalem in the presence of God. The present conditions in Jerusalem there were an indication that this fellowship of people with the divine presence had not yet been fully achieved.

Nehemiah's first petition was that God might complete the restoration of the holy city and community. His second petition was for his own success in his audience with Artaxerxes to become the instrument through whom God would grant the first petition. Here again is the emphasis on the importance of God and humans working together to accomplish God's purposes. Nehemiah's success would depend upon the cooperation of Artaxerxes and of his fellow Jews. For their cooperation he was dependent upon God.

Nehemiah's Commission from Artaxerxes and His Return to Jerusalem, 2:1-10

2:1-8. Nehemiah's commission. Any expression of Nehemiah's grief might have been misunderstood by Artaxerxes as evidence of plotting against the king since his request required Artaxerxes to revoke his previous decree, or the grief might be resented by Artaxerxes as improper behavior in a companion. Therefore, Nehemiah was careful about the way he made his request.

In this first of many critical encounters Nehemiah displayed considerable diplomatic skills that helped him succeed. In this case his success was achieved (1) by his choice of a New Year's banquet in celebration of the king's birthday or of his inaugural, a time when the king was generous in granting requests; and (2) by his putting the request in terms with which the king would have sympathy: *the city, the place of my ancestors' graves, lies waste* (v. 3). Throughout the Near East ancestral burial places were greatly respected, especially by the upper classes.

Success was also acheived (3) by avoiding any reference to Jerusalem's walls, leaving it to the king to make the connection with his previous decree concerning them, and (4) by his close relationship to the king, indicated by the king's concern when Nehemiah's face finally expresses sadness and by the king's anticipation of his request. *What do you request?* (v. 4) implies willingness to grant the request.

Nehemiah's repeated expressions of anxiety (vv. 2, 3, 4, 7) served both to emphasize his courage and his diplomatic skills and to provide occasion for crediting God for his success: *the gracious hand of my God was upon me* (v. 8).

The interplay between Nehemiah, the king, and God throughout this scene presents again the theme that restoration of the community of faith depended upon the response to God by the Persian rulers and by the leaders in the restoration.

Nehemiah's request was granted. He was given letters guaranteeing safe passage to Judah and authority there (as governor?) to rebuild the Temple. He was also given permission to use timber from the king's forest (perhaps in Lebanon, but probably in Judah, which was more heavily forested in ancient times than now). These timbers would be used for the gates of the Temple fortress that would guard the vulnerable northern approach to the Temple mount, for the gates and towers of the city wall, and for Nehemiah's house (perhaps the restoration of his family's pre-exilic home).

2:9-10. Return to Jerusalem. No details are given about the journey to Jerusalem. The presence with Nehemiah of *officers of the army and cavalry* (v. 9; contrast Ezra's refusal of such protection, Ezra 8:22) guaranteed a peaceful journey. But Sanballat's and Tobiah's displeasure over Nehemiah's mission ominously foreshadowed future problems. As the narrative continues, each accomplishment is paralleled by continuing and increasing opposition.

Rebuilding the Walls,
in Spite of Opposition and Economic Hardship, 2:11–6:19

Nehemiah's "memoirs" unhesitatingly depict him as a man of bold action and quick, clear, and correct decisions. Anticipating trouble, Nehemiah acted swiftly and secretly to begin the work on the walls.

2:11-16. Night inspection of the walls. Three days after arriving in Jerusalem and without revealing his plans for the city to anyone, Nehemiah and a few trusted companions inspected the walls by night. Secrecy was necessary because his opponents Sanballat and Tobiah had allies in the city, and Nehemiah did not want to betray his intention to build the walls until it was clear what that would require. They left the city by a gate overlooking the Tyropoeon Valley on the west side, moved counterclockwise along the base of the walls until they reached a point on the east side overlooking the Kidron Valley where the rubble left by the ruined walls was so extensive that they could not go farther along the base of the wall.

They had to move down to the floor of the valley, and Nehemiah climbed the rubble to inspect the ruins.

How they proceeded from this point is not clear. They could have completed the circuit of the city, but there is no reference to the northern or northwestern parts of the wall. It is possible that during the three days after his arrival Nehemiah had already inspected the northern portion of the wall without anyone's knowing his purpose. Inspection of the eastern wall would have been a much more obvious activity. Nehemiah's secret inspection of the area led him to make the important decision that the rebuilt wall would be on the crest of the ridge. When this decision had been made, the inspectors either continued to finish their counterclockwise circuit of the city or they retraced their steps; probably they retraced their steps.

2:17-20. Nehemiah's presentation of his plans to the Jewish officials. When Nehemiah revealed his plans to the various officials in Jerusalem, he supported them by citing divine and royal approval (v. 18). The officials agreed to build, and Nehemiah described their decision as a commitment to the common good, that is, his success and theirs. Sanballat and Tobiah, joined now by Geshem the Arab, mocked and ridiculed this decision as an act of rebellion against Artaxerxes. These three represented a formidable opposition to Nehemiah's work.

Sanballat was governor of Samaria. He is called the Horonite, a designation of uncertain meaning, perhaps being a contemptuous term used by Nehemiah who never calls Sanballat governor. Sanballat probably was a worshiper of Yahweh (his sons' names are compounds with *yah*, the short form of Yahweh). Perhaps he was a descendant of an Israelite family not carried to exile in 722 BCE Tobiah was either an Ammonite official under Persian authority or an assistant to Sanballat, probably the latter.

Geshem was ruler, under nominal Persian oversight, of considerable territory to the south and east of Judah. Nehemiah dismissed the ridicule and accusations of these formidable opponents by declaring that God would give him and his colleagues success, that they were determined to build, and that Sanballat, Tobiah and Geshem had no authority, political rights or religious rights (the phrase *historic right* [v. 20] is used frequently in association with the system of worship) in Jerusalem.

3:1-21. Work on the walls. Chapter 3 moves around the walls counterclockwise beginning with the Sheep Gate. It lists those who worked on each section of the wall and the various gates and towers included in each section. Although there are some omissions, this description provides valuable archeological and historical information. After the lines of the wall have been described, it becomes clear that Nehemiah's city was smaller than preexilic Jerusalem. It included only the eastern ridge and the Temple area. A considerable area of the preexilic city extending onto the western hill was not included. Moreover, the list of the various groups involved in the work mentions five administrative centers in Judah and their rulers. The location of these administrative centers and the listing of other place names define a province of Judah less than half the size of the preexilic kingdom of Judah. The rulers of these administrative centers were Jews, most of whom came from families who had not been in exile. Nehemiah's caution, expressed in chap. 2, was justified since the administration of the province was in the hands of officials who might have resented the intrusion of those who returned from Babylon. Memory of the earlier unpleasantness over the construction of the Temple might have raised doubts about how they would be allowed to relate to the community returned from exile. Their cooperation on the work on the wall is a credit to Nehemiah's administrative skill and, on this occasion, his openness to such people.

The groups who worked on the wall are further identified by family or profession or place of residence. All classes of the Jewish community were represented in this common task. Nehemiah had persuaded the entire community to participate, strengthening its unity. He motivated good work by assigning each group a part of the wall in which they had a vested interest. They worked on sections opposite their homes or their places of business. With such organization and cooperation the work went rapidly.

4:1-23. Work on the wall in the face of opposition. Sanballat's reaction to the work on the wall reflects a certain desperation and fear that Nehemiah might be successful. He asked his own people ridiculing questions about the work as much to bolster their morale and his own as to intimidate the Jews. His questions suggested that God was not behind the venture, that the Jews were over-optimistic about the possibility of success and that the materials being used were inadequate to build a strong wall. These questions reached the workers on the wall and discouraged them. The wall they were building *was* rough and crude compared to the earlier walls of Jerusalem. Kathleen Kenyon's excavations uncovered part of this wall, which she described as "solidly built . . . but rough" (Kenyon 1967, 111).

Nehemiah's response was an angry prayer. He interpreted these ridiculing comments as directed against God and asked God to punish Sanballat and Tobiah without mercy with the same punishment Israel had earlier received—exile and captivity. This prayer has much in common with the prayer of Hezekiah when Sennacherib threatened Jerusalem (2 Kgs 19:14-19), with the imprecatory Psalms of lament (Pss 35, 58, 59, 69, 109 and 137), and with the bitter prayers of Jeremiah's laments or "confessions" (Jer 17:18; 18:23). Nehemiah's prayer is disturbing, first, because it views God as an avenging power to be used by his people against their enemies and, second, because it reflects an attitude toward enemies that is inconsistent with better Jewish and Christian tradition. In context this view of God and this attitude toward enemies is consistent with those of the times and with the difficult situation in which Nehemiah finds himself. They are understandable, therefore, if not acceptable.

Of course it is to Nehemiah's credit that he asked God to punish his enemies rather than taking vengeance on them himself, although this might be interpreted as expediency since Nehemiah was in no position to take vengeance into his own hands. Perhaps the best thing that can be said about this prayer and others like it is that they are admirably honest. They do not pretend love for enemies when those who pray really hate enemies. Nehemiah revealed his true feelings here, made no attempt to conceal them, and presented them to God.

Something is also revealed about God here who neither carried out Nehemiah's request nor punished him for the bitter spirit with which he made it. Although difficult for all to accept, in that time and later, God is the loving father who listens to the angry ranting and raving of his children and gently but firmly encourages them to "bless those who persecute you; bless and do not curse them" (Rom 12:14) and thus to come to the better way of loving even the enemy.

Nehemiah and the people responded to the opposition of Sanballat and Tobiah by quickly raising the wall to half its height. Prayer and work was a common pattern followed by Nehemiah. Each step of progress, however, was followed by increasing opposition from Sanballat and Tobiah, supported now by Arabs, Ammonites, and Ashdodites. Now they threatened to attack the city, and the Jews responded by prayer and by guarding the city against attack.

Their opponents, though, had made a point. Disheartened workers on the wall feared that Sanballat was right and they would never be able to finish. They even began to sing a little song to that effect. Sanballat continued to threaten the city, and Jews became more and more anxious and discouraged. Repeatedly Jews from outlying villages came and asked their men who were working on the wall to return home. Nehemiah, to display his strength, stood in an exposed place along the wall and called the armed people together. He encouraged them with words like those used in holy battles of old. This perhaps forestalled any immediate attack by Sanballat, and the work on the wall continued, but under different circumstances.

Half of a select group of men personally responsible to Nehemiah worked on the wall; the other half, fully armed, guarded the city, their officers standing to direct them. These men were better armed than any of the others. The other workers were armed as appropriate to the work that they were doing. Since the workers were spread all around the city, everyone was told to listen for a trumpet call and rally to the place from which it came to drive away any attackers. Everyone was to stay in Jerusalem to work by day and guard the city by night. By this arrangement the workers from outlying villages were kept in Jerusalem. Nehemiah and his select men remained dressed and armed day and night. Nehemiah was careful to accept the full responsibility and burden of leadership.

5:1-13. Economic difficulties and their solution. Abruptly a new problem is introduced—Jews crying out against Jews about various levels of economic hardship. They brought their complaints to Nehemiah whose commission from Artaxerxes is now revealed not to be limited to rebuilding the city but to include his appointment as governor (5:14). Three groups presented experiences of the kinds of economic problems everyone was facing. The first group desperately needed food (v. 2). They were probably landless families whose meager wages were not adequate for survival. The second group were surviving only by mortgaging their lands and homes for food (v. 3). The third group had borrowed money to pay the Persian taxes on their fields and vineyards (v. 4). All were at the point of having to sell their children as laborers to other Jews. Some of their daughters had been ravished. Perhaps slave girls were expected to submit to their masters' advances. Three factors had contributed to making the difficult situation of living at the subsistence level now a desperate situation. Apparently the failure of the barley and wheat crops caused a famine (v. 3). Nehemiah's requirement that the builders not leave Jerusalem while the wall was being built left the farms understaffed at the time of harvest. Finally, some wealthy Jews had acted as moneylenders, taking advantage of the situations—*our fields and vineyards now belong to others* (v. 5). Moneylending and the enslaving of children for debts were legal (Exod 21:2-11; 22:25-27; Lev 25; Deut 15:1-18) but were to be controlled in the interest of the poor by regulations that unfortunately were seldom followed.

Legal or not, Nehemiah felt these actions were immoral. Controlling his great anger (*after thinking it over* [v. 7]) he brought public charges against *the nobles and the officials* who were taking interest from their fellow Jews. Again Nehemiah's diplomatic skill is evident. First he pointed out the absurdity of Jews selling Jews into slavery to Jews at the very time when the restored community was buying back Jews who had been sold into Gentile slavery. This was not just a matter of business; it was a violation of the family of faith to wrong their *own people* (v. 7) and their *own kin* (v. 8). Finally, he confessed that his own family and their servants had also been lending money and grain to the needy (v. 10). This behavior gave non-Israelites a misleading and embarrassing image of the Israelite community of faith and their God (v. 9).

In the presence of priests, the nobles and officials took an oath to cancel all debts. Then Nehemiah, in a manner like earlier prophets (cf. Ezek 4:1-5, 17; Jer 19:1-13), symbolically enacted a curse on all who did not keep their promises, including himself. He emptied his robe of all the objects carried in its tucks and folds and said of those who did not keep their promise, *"Thus may they be shaken out and emptied"* (v. 13).

Acts like this were understood to initiate the judgment they represented if right behavior did not continue. It was as if Nehemiah had said, "The judgment is already in effect. Be sure you do not fall under it!" Nehemiah's proposals were carried out.

5:14-19. Nehemiah's integrity as governor. Nehemiah then added a note about his integrity and financial generosity during his term as governor. He accused previous governors of abusing taxation rights for personal gain and the servants of these governors for lording it over the common people. In contrast Nehemiah rightly depicted himself as a God-fearing, dedicated, self-supporting, public servant, who with his servants worked on the wall along with the other people. He claimed no food rations from tax funds, despite the fact that he was regularly responsible for feeding large numbers of officials and visitors. He bore these expenses of office himself. Though the contrast is less dramatic, one is reminded of Jeremiah's contrast of unrighteous Jehoiakim and righteous Josiah (Jer 22:13-17). Nehemiah concludes with a brief prayer that God remember him for his service to his fellow Jews.

6:1-19. Opposition against Nehemiah's person. Work on the wall must have continued during the economic crisis, for it was soon finished except for the gates. Therefore, Sanballat and Geshem, conceding that the wall was there to stay, focused their opposition on Nehemiah's person. Four times they invited him to meet them at a village outside of Jerusalem. He refused to go. They may have had good intentions. The extensive correspondence between Tobiah and prominent nobles of Judah (vv. 17-18), including one who strongly supported Nehemiah's building program (3:6), perhaps indicates that they were hoping for a compromise, but Nehemiah did not trust them. Besides, his view of the returned exiles as *the* people of God made compromise impossible. When Sanballat sent a public letter open to anyone (was it read aloud at various places around the city?) accusing Nehemiah of ambitions that would lead to rebellion against Persia, Nehemiah denied them.

Finally, an agent of Sanballat in Jerusalem, speaking like a prophet, warned Nehemiah that his life was in danger and urged him to flee into the Temple for sanctuary. Thus he hoped to lure Nehemiah into the cultic sin of intruding into the sacred area open only to God and priests. Sanctuary was possible at the altar outside the Temple but only under certain circumstances (Exod 21:12-14), which did not include flight from a foreign enemy. It was most difficult for Nehemiah to evaluate this ruse because prophetic proclamations were always taken seriously and it was never easy to discern a true prophet from a false prophet. Nehemiah did, however, recognize the falseness of this man's prophetic claim and refused to do what he suggested.

Nehemiah's response to these attempts on his person was to ask God to judge those who had attempted to frighten him, a petition reminiscent of his earlier prayer against Sanballat and Tobiah (4:4-5) leaving retribution in the hands of God.

That the wall was finished in fifty-two days in spite of opposition is a credit to Nehemiah's strong leadership. Of course, the old wall was not completely down, the eastern wall was higher on the slope than the previous wall and, therefore, not as long, and the new wall was not of the highest standard. Even so, the wall's completion impressed the people roundabout and caused those leaders who had opposed the work to lose face (6:16).

The List of Families Who First Returned to Jerusalem, 7:1-73a

The information treated in this section is very similar to that in Ezra 2:1-70. Refer to that sefction in the commentary on the Book of Ezra, above.

Covenant Renewal, 7:73b–9:37

The account of a great ceremony of COVENANT renewal in chaps. 8 and 9 interrupts the Nehemiah story. The obvious sequel to chap. 7 is chap. 11. This account of covenant renewal focuses on Ezra's work and is based to a large extent on the

Ezra Memoirs. Nehemiah is mentioned only twice (8:9 and 10:1, probably editorial additions) and plays no prominent role. Historically this event must have taken place much earlier than the time of the wall's completion. Ezra's commission was to establish the "law of the God of heaven" (see Ezra 7, esp. v. 21) in Judah. If he returned in 458 BCE, he would not have waited more than ten years to do so. The narrator placed this covenant renewal account of the establishing of Law here to demonstrate that covenant obedience to the Law was essential for the continuing success of all the other accomplishments of the restored community. For him, Ezra's teaching of the Law was *the* significant achievement of the postexilic age—the climax of the restoration of sanctuary, cultus, and holy city.

Preparation for Covenant Renewal, 7:73b–8:18

This ceremony of covenant renewal based on the Law was Ezra's great achievement, the fulfillment of Artaxerxes' commission to make the Law of God the basis for Jewish life in Judah and the realization of his own sense of God-given vocation. The Law that Ezra brought with him from exile was probably the Pentateuch in more or less final form. Much of it would have been known and would have guided the lives of the earlier returnees, but it is obvious that in this covenant renewal ceremony Ezra gives new place and meaning to the Law. The Law was not just the province of the priestly class but was Torah for all the people. Law, not political authority, was to give direction to the people's lives—the rule of Law rather than the rule of women and men. Faithfulness to God, therefore, is demonstrated by faithfulness to the Law, and obedience to the Law is not slavish legalism but willing response to divine direction.

8:1-8. Reading of the Law. At the request of the people who gathered in a large open square before the Water Gate (areas around gates were often places of public forum), Ezra read from the Law for more than six hours. Accompanied by thirteen men whose purpose is not clear, Ezra stood above the people on a wooden platform and opened the scroll; the people stood up out of respect for the Law. Ezra pronounced a benediction and the people bowed to the ground in the presence of God. Clearly, Ezra here intended to make God present to the people and the people acknowledged that presence by bowing down before divine presence. Worship in Israel always was this kind of acknowledgment of the presence of the sacred, but note here that the sacred presence was not represented by ritual nor did it occur in the Temple. The sacred was present in the reading of the Law and this presence affected all of their lives. The Law was read and explained to *all* the people—men, women and children (all who could hear with understanding [v. 2]). Only with priestly assistance could an Israelite approach God through Temple ritual, but even an understanding child could meet God in obedience to the Law.

8:9-12. A time for joy. As the people heard this formal reading and interpretation of the Law they wept because they had not adequately met its demands. This was an appropriate, but only partial and not the final, response. Ezra and the assisting Levites encouraged them not to mourn on a holy festive day. (The inclusion of

Nehemiah's name here is a scribal insertion; even if Nehemiah and Ezra were contemporaries, it is extremely doubtful that Nehemiah would have taken a leader's role in this ceremony.) They should be joyful. Their response to the God who reveals himself in the Law should include remorse and confession, but should end in *the joy of the LORD* (v. 10) because the Law is also a revelation of God's grace.

The Law (i.e., the Pentateuch) is heavy with rules and regulations, but it is also a declaration of the wonderful story of *Heilsgeschichte* ("salvation history"), those acts of God that every generation relives in worship. The God who requires is the same God who forgives and saves. The requirements of the Law, therefore, can be met gladly with gratitude not because one *has* to obey, but because one freely *wants* to obey. The Law as Ezra apparently viewed it was not legalistically restrictive and punitive. It was rather an expression of divine expectations that a true community of faith would eagerly try to meet. The image of the Law left by the Pauline attacks upon it (see, e.g., Romans and Galatians) is an impression of the Law that is, for the most part, foreign to Ezra—his strict application of it in certain circumstances notwithstanding. Ezra encouraged the people to have a feast and to rejoice at this understanding of the Law, which requires them, among other things, to sit down at the same table with God and celebrate (Lev 3).

8:13-18. The Feast of Tabernacles. During further study of the Law on the following day, the people realized that it was the time for the celebration of *booths* (v. 14, also known as the Feast of Tabernacles; see TABERNACLES, FESTIVAL OF), a celebration at harvest time in joyful gratitude for the produce of the land and a reminder of the deliverance of the Israelites from Egyptian bondage—the greatest divine act in their salvation history. They prepared for and observed this celebration in a manner not equaled since the time of Joshua. As families and as a community they celebrated with *very great rejoicing* (vv. 16-17).

Covenant Renewal, 9:1-37

The day of national mourning and confession described in chap. 9 is clearly an extraordinary event and represents the climax of Ezra's work in establishing the Law in Jerusalem. It follows the reading of the Law and the celebration of Tabernacles as a solemn moment of covenant commitment to God. Limiting it to the sorrow of the people about mixed marriages (Ezra 9–10) makes it far less significant than it must have been. This so-called "great confession" is clearly the awesome confession that preceded the community's recommitment not to a part of, but to the whole of God's will (in this case, the whole of the Law) in the ceremony of covenant renewal.

9:1-3. Fasting and mourning, study and confession. The reading of the Law, the festive holy day and the celebration of Tabernacles together prepared the people of Israel for a ceremony of covenant renewal. On the twenty-fourth day of the month they fasted and gathered in Jerusalem dressed as mourners *in sackcloth, and with earth on their heads* (v. 1). Apparently some of the people of the land were allowed to participate in the celebration of Tabernacles, but now the Israelites *separated themselves from all foreigners* (v. 2) for confession of their sins. The Law's account of salvation history represents God as always faithful, but Israel was often unfaithful and, therefore, guilty under the judgment of the Law. The way to move from guilt to rejoicing obedience to God that the Law intended is the way of confession and repentance. After a long informal study of the Law and a long period of informal individual confession (v. 3), the Levites summoned them to the formal ceremony of covenant renewal.

9:4-37. Ceremony of praise and confession. This ceremony began with a benediction acknowledging the exalted greatness of God (v. 5). Invitation to praise the God whose Law causes them to grieve because they have disobeyed it was appropriate because in the Law itself as a guide for life God has given his people every reason to praise him. Then Ezra (MT lacks *and Ezra said* [v. 6], which NRSV supplies from the LXX) prayed a long prayer of confession. This public sermonic prayer, which juxtaposes the unfaithfulness of Israel and the faithfulness of God, recites the mighty acts of God with echoes of the Psalms of community thanksgiving (cf. Ps 136). In its confession of Israel's repeated sinfulness it echoes the Psalms of community lament (cf. Ps 106). It is also quite like Ps 78, a covenant-renewal Psalm with the purpose of bringing the people to a climactic moment of confession and recommitment to God's covenant.

In ever-changing human circumstances it is necessary for the community of faith regularly to examine God's requirements of them and take the appropriate measures to see that these requirements are met and to recommit themselves in covenant to God whose covenant commitment to them is unbroken. Ezra's new emphasis on the Law inevitably required these acts of covenant renewal.

The recitation of God's mighty acts begins with praise of God as creator, the giver of life worshiped by all of nature and *the host of heaven* (v. 6, the stars?, the heavenly beings?, the heavenly powers?). This is appropriate, for in each event of covenant renewal the community of faith is being recreated. God's choice of Abraham and his promise to give him descendants and land follows. The restoration community, as Abraham's many descendants, now lives on that land as new settlers trying to protect it from all outsiders (vv. 7-8). The Exodus experience is recalled to remind the restoration community of their similar experience in return from exile. The Law given at Sinai was in essence the Mosaic Law taught them by Ezra, which they are covenanting to obey. The recitation of Israel's repeated unfaithfulness that follows is a warning to the restored community to avoid their ancestors' tendency to turn away from God in spite of his good deeds on their behalf and their pledges to be faithful to his covenant demands.

Throughout his recitation of Israel's unfaithfulness, Ezra made special note of God's righteousness (v. 8), readiness to forgive (v. 17), mercy (vv. 17, 27, 28, 31), and covenant faithfulness (vv. 17, 32). Key to the possibility of covenant renewal is the understanding of God as *ready to forgive, gracious and merciful, slow to anger and abounding in steadfast love* (v. 17; cf. 31-32; see also Exod 34:6-7). This is reminiscent of Micah's classic summary of the prophetic faith: "What does the LORD require of you but to do justice, and to love kindness, and to walk humbly with your God?" (Mic 6:8). In renewing covenant the returned exiles must humbly submit themselves to the God who in his own being, actions, and Law embodies the characteristics that he requires of his people. As best they can they are to be like God himself as his representatives. The prayer ends with a petition: *Do not treat lightly all the hardship that has come upon us* (v. 32). Ezra described them as still not fully free. They were no longer exiles in a foreign land, but they suffered under the irony of being subject to Persian masters in their own land.

This account of covenant renewal ends without any reference to the covenant requirements on Israel or to the ceremony by which the people committed themselves to keep them. These requirements had already been presented by Ezra's interpretation of the Law as relevant in constantly changing historical circumstances (cf. the discussion of Ezra 9–10 in this commentary, above). In the reading and interpretation of the Law at the time of covenant renewal, the interpretation of Law is regarded as virtually equal to Law itself (cf. 8:8). This application of the Law to the immediate situation and explanation of it in such a way that those who hear can understand its relevance was Ezra's contribution to the methodology of interpretation.

A Document of Commitment to Certain Specific Reforms, 9:38–10:39

This agreement made under Nehemiah's leadership was used here by the narrator as the conclusion to the Ezra covenant-renewal ceremony. Such an agreement to keep God's Law would be an appropriate conclusion to a ceremony of covenant renewal in which national disobedience of certain requirements of the Law had been repeatedly lamented. However, the limited focus of the commitments of this document and the absence of Ezra's name from the list of those who signed it precludes its being the climax of a covenant renewal based on an extensive reading and study of the Law like the one described in chaps. 8–9.

10:1-27. The list of witnesses. This *firm agreement* (9:38), rather than *covenant*, was signed by distinguished witnesses and each signature was verified by the signer's seal. Nehemiah's name as governor heads the list. The second name, ZEDEKIAH, interestingly, is one of those sentence names of which the LORD is the subject: *The LORD has been righteous.* This is the only use of the name in postexilic times, and although this is probably mere coincidence, Zedekiah's name here states the fundamental basis upon which all such agreements rested—the righteousness of God. The meaning of other names in the list emphasize this coincidence: AZARIAH—"the LORD has helped"; AMARIAH—"the LORD has promised"; ABIJAH—"the LORD is father," to mention only a few. The meanings of these names would not go unnoticed by postexilic readers of this document.

10:28-29. The general commitment to keep God's Law. Everyone, including women and children, pledged themselves *to walk in God's Law . . . and to observe and do all the commandments of the LORD our Lord and his ordinances and his statutes* (v. 29). But this general pledge of observance is significantly modified by the specific pledges that follow.

10:30-39. The specific pledges. To permit no more mixed marriages (v. 30; see the commentary on Ezra 9–10, above) with no reference to prior mixed marriages; to honor the SABBATH by refusing to buy merchandise from the people of the land on the Sabbath or on any holy day (v. 31a); and to observe the sabbatical year by letting the land lie fallow (cf. Lev 25:2-7; Exod 23:11) and by forgiving all debts every seventh year, which goes beyond the Law's requirements for the sabbatical year (v. 31; cf. Deut 15:1-18).

This remarkable agreement goes far beyond the temporary measures of Neh 5. The farmers and the merchants who would be disadvantaged in turn by the fallow law and by the forgiving of debts equally pledged themselves to keep laws that hitherto had never been really observed. This was a grand commitment but, unfortunately, an empty one, for there is no evidence that those who thus pledged themselves ever kept these idealistic social laws.

To pay a tax for the upkeep of the sanctuary (vv. 32-33). Darius had pledged assistance for the maintenance of the Temple and its cultus (cf. Ezra 6:9-10), but we do not know for how long. Apparently depending on this support, Jews did not give their tithes regularly, and many Levites were forced to neglect their Temple responsibilities and maintain themselves by farming (Neh 13:10). Traditionally the tithes were paid in produce, but during the Persian period Jerusalem and Judah began to develop a monetary economy. The one-third-shekel tax reflects that development. The money was for daily and seasonal offerings. Lots were cast to determine by whom the wood for the altar fires would be regularly supplied (v. 34).

To support the Temple personnel with proper offerings (vv. 35-39). The agreements made to maintain the Temple are not based on any specific laws in the Pentateuch, but were considered necessary to support a cultus prescribed by the Law these people were swearing themselves to observe.

While this particular *firm agreement* (see 9:38) is not directly related to Ezra's covenant renewal, it indirectly is the result of his sense of the meaning of the Law and of his method of interpreting the Law. For Ezra, keeping of the Law is the responsibility of everyone, not just kings and Temple personnel, and the Law is kept alive for everyone by necessary reinterpretation, modification, and addition.

The Repopulation of Jerusalem, 11:1–12:26

11:1-2. Arrangements for repopulation. After a long interruption the narrator returns to the account of the repopulation of Jerusalem begun in chap. 7. Political and religious leaders were already living in Jerusalem. What had to be decided was which lay people should live there also. The people themselves determined the procedure for making this choice. Probably using the census list that Nehemiah had found (7:5bff.), they cast lots to bring one family out of ten to live in the city. This left the choice to God, because anytime lots were cast "the decision is the LORD's alone" (Prov 16:33). *To live in the holy city Jerusaelem* (v. 1) was an awesome responsibility but also a great privilege— to live near the Temple where the presence of the Lord was felt (Pss 23, 122, 126, 128, 133). Those chosen by lot, therefore, gladly accepted the decision, in spite of the inconveniences involved in making the move. Some families even volunteered to move to the city, *and the people blessed all those who willingly offered to live in Jerusalem* (v. 2), perhaps to affirm their voluntary decisions as decisions in which God had a part. It was a matter of honor for those families who lived in Jerusalem to have their settlement there noted in the list.

11:3–12:26. Settlement lists. By listing families from Judah and Benjamin, and priests and Levites who settled in Jerusalem and in the nearby countryside, the narrator is identifying those families deemed to be the true and faithful continuity with preexilic Israel. The presence of military terms—*valiant warriors* (11:14), *overseer* (11:9, 14, 22)—indicates that the defense of Jerusalem was an important concern in the distribution of the population. The distribution of the families living outside of Jerusalem indicates the size of the postexilic province of Judah.

The narrator attributes these lists to the *Book of the Annals* (12:23), perhaps the official Temple records— not to be confused with the canonical books of Chronicles, although the Hebrew title of both is identical. These and other lists used by the narrator have been the subject of much speculation by scholars attempting to reconstruct the history of the postexilic period. Their accuracy has been vigorously attacked and vigorously defended. Whatever their accuracy, they are important sources that must be considered in historical reconstructions of the postexilic period. This was not, however, the narrator's reason for citing them. The concern is to show continuity between the past and the present, in this case between the generation of the first return who built the Temple and that of the time of Ezra–Nehemiah. The narrator does so by pointing out the close family relationships that span both periods.

Dedication of the Walls, 12:27-43

These verses are the description of the last of many stages in the restoration of Jerusalem, achievements that the narrator sees as not of equal importance, but closely related to and dependent upon one another: an altar built in a ruined Temple (Ezra 3:1-7); a Temple built in a ruined city (Ezra 3:8–7:22); ruined walls rebuilt to protect the city (Neh 2:11–7:4); and the reading of the Law and covenant renewal (Neh 8 and 9). In a sense each of these achievements had been a meaningful ritual action by which the returned exiles reclaimed the land of promise. They had restored Jerusalem as a fit place to be the center of the sacred presence of Yahweh, and they had recommitted themselves to be the people of the promise.

Now one thing remained—to dedicate the walls. Apart from the participation of Ezra (v. 36) in the dedication of the walls, the ceremony of dedication is quite straightforward. Ezra's inclusion here, like Nehemiah's participation in the covenant-renewal ceremony (8:9), is to make the literary/theological point that the achievements of the two important postexilic leaders were complementary. Their actual participation together remains uncertain and, in the final analysis, whether their careers overlapped or not makes little difference. As the narrative reads, the significant activity of each was carried out independently of the other.

Gathering of the Levites and the Ritual Purification, 12:27-30

Levites were brought into Jerusalem from their outlying villages because the dedication ceremony was to be a joyous one with singing and instrumental music. A solemn ritual of purification preceded the celebration. Priests and Levites would have purified themselves by fasting, cleansing the body, and abstinence from sexual intercourse (cf. Num 8:7, Lev 16:28-31 for typical examples of purification). The people would have washed themselves and their clothes and would have been sprinkled with water by the priest (Exod 19:14). The wall and its gates were also purified, probably by sprinkling with water. This was an important ritual because everything involved in the dedication of the walls, especially the walls themselves, had to be separated from all impure contacts that would have jeopardized the entire enterprise of restoring Jerusalem as a sacred center. Rituals of purity celebrated the divine ordering of creation and helped maintain that order. The walls were more than just a defensive barrier. They were a symbol of sacred space separating Jerusalem from the outside, threatening and dangerous, and chaotic space. They marked Jerusalem as a *cosmos* organized and full of meaning and value, where full being could be realized in the presence of God.

The Ceremonial Procession of Dedication, 12:31-43

The purified participants formed two groups, ascended to the top of the wall and from the same starting point, probably the Valley Gate, moved in joyous celebration to the right and the to left to meet again at the Temple where they offered sacrifices and continued rejoicing. This procession ritually enclosed the city with divine security. The restoration of the altar, the Temple, the city, and the walls was complete. *The joy of Jerusalem was heard far away* (v. 43). The main narrative of the restoration ends with this climactic cry of joy, but there is a postscript.

A Summary Postscript, 12:44–13:3

In two connected passages that interrupt the first-person account from the "Nehemiah Memoirs," the narrator idealistically reflected on the entire period of the restoration. The opening phrase, *on that day* (12:44 and 13:1), should be taken as a general reference, like "at that time." From *the days of Zerubbabel* to *the days of Nehemiah* (v. 47), the returned exiles generously supported the priests and the Levites who, in turn, protected the community from dangers by rituals of purification, and this was all done as it had been done earlier in the days of David and Solomon. The restored community was, indeed, in keeping with its ancestral origins. Furthermore, they apparently continued reading the *book of Moses* regularly (13:1).

Based on a reading from Deut 23:3-6, the source of the reference to BALAAM, they took further steps to separate themselves from those of foreign descent. There is no indication that these foreigners were expelled from the community, only that they were excluded from worship. This is one of the earliest accounts we have of the reading of scripture in worship as a basis for religious and social action, a pattern that becomes common later in the synagogue and the church. Would that it had been for a more worthy end.

The Reforms of Nehemiah's Second Administration, 13:4-31

The remainder of chap. 13 is taken from "Nehemiah's Memoirs." After serving as governor for approximately twelve years, Nehemiah returned to the Persian court. We do not know why nor do we know how long he remained there before he asked permission to return to Jerusalem *(After some time I asked leave of the king and returned to Jerusalem* [vv. 6-7]), where he acted with authority, apparently again as governor.

Trouble with Tobiah Again, 13:4-9

During Nehemiah's absence, Tobiah successfully established good relations with the Jews in Jerusalem. Eliashib, a priest who had charge of the storage chambers of the Temple and who was related to Tobiah, allowed Tobiah to live in one of the rooms in the storage chambers. This Eliashib could have been the high priest of 3:1, 20; 12:22; Ezra 10:6 who was related by marriage to SANBALLAT. If so, this heightens the intrigue, but it is unlikely that a high priest would have also been appointed as keeper of the storage *chambers* (v. 4). The person at fault was probably another Eliashib. Whatever their intentions were—and they may have been honorable—Nehemiah was outraged at both Eliashib and Tobiah. He personally threw Tobiah's belongings out of the storage room, which he considered to have been contaminated by the presence of a non-Jew. The sacred center, whose sanctity was of highest importance, had been defiled and it had to be ritually purified.

Measures Taken to Assure the Support of the Levites, 13:10-14

The people had not supported the Levites as they should have, and the Levites had returned to their villages to support themselves, leaving the Temple with inadequate personnel for conducting services. Nehemiah brought them back to the city. He then appointed four carefully chosen men—men of integrity representative of those to whom the stores were distributed (priests, scribes, Levites, and singers)—to oversee the equitable distribution of the Temple stores. ZADOK the scribe (v. 13), one of those who was appointed, may have been Nehemiah's secretary ZEDEKIAH (10:1). If so, Nehemiah was placing the arrangements under his own supervision. Nehemiah prayed that God would remember him for these *good deeds* (v. 14) done for the Temple.

Actions to Insure Sabbath Observance, 13:15-22

Nehemiah strongly condemned the violation of the SABBATH by business transactions and took action to prevent these dealings. The city gates were locked and
guarded by his own servants throughout the Sabbath. Merchants from the
surrounding area spent the night outside of Jerusalem, creating disturbances and
tempting the people in the city to clandestine transactions. Nehemiah threatened
them with violence if they continued, and they ceased. Nehemiah strengthened the
guard on the gates by appointing Levites to assist in preventing violation of the
Sabbath. He prayed that God might remember this to his favor.

The Problem of Mixed Marriages, 13:23-29

Jewish men had married Philistine, Ammonite, and Moabite women, and their
children were running around Jerusalem speaking foreign languages. Not only did
these marriages, which did not conform to the accepted norm, threaten the
community with the destructive contamination of impurity (cf. commentary, above,
on Ezra 9); they also introduced the disruptive force of miscommunication. A common language is an important factor in the unity and security of a people struggling
to maintain their identity in critical situations. Nehemiah was upset with these men:
he *contended with them and cursed them and beat some of them, and pulled out
their hair* (v. 25). He made them swear not to allow their sons and daughters to engage in mixed marriages, citing Solomon as an example of one who had brought
evil on all Israel by marrying foreign women.

The extent to which this was a problem is indicated by the marriage of the
grandson of the high priest Eliashib to the daughter of Sanballat, Nehemiah's archenemy. It was particularly inappropriate for a high priest or one in line for the high
priesthood to marry a foreigner. Lev 21:14 plainly states: "He [the chief priest] shall
marry a virgin of his own kin." Nehemiah banished this man. There is no indication,
however, that this marriage or any of the other mixed marriages were dissolved or
that their children were sent away. Nehemiah asked God to remember this priest
with judgment for defiling the priesthood.

Closing Summary and Prayer, 13:30-31

Nehemiah sums up his achievements in terms of separation of the community
of faith from all things foreign and making provision for all aspects of Temple worship. He asks God to remember him for good.

The one thing Nehemiah did not ask to be remembered for was the building of
the wall.

Works Cited

Bright, John. 1981. *A History of Israel*. 3rd ed.
Brueggemann, Walter. 1972. *The Land*.
Cross, Frank M. 1975. "A Reconstruction of the Judean Restoration." JBL 94:4–18.

Douglas, Mary. 1978. *Purity and Danger: An Analysis of the Concepts of Pollution and Taboo.*

Eliade, Mircea. 1974. *Patterns in Comparative Religion.* 1961. *The Sacred and the Profane.*

Kenyon, Kathleen. 1967. *Jerusalem: Excavating 3,000 Years of History.*

Pritchard, James B. 1955. *Ancient Near Eastern Texts Relating to the Old Testament* (ANET).

Rowley, H. H. 1965. "The Chronological Order of Ezra and Nehemiah." In *The Servant of the Lord and Other Essays on the O.T.,* 137–68. 2nd ed.

Esther [MCB 395-403]

Kandy M. Queen-Sutherland

Introduction

The Book of Esther is one of the five Megilloth or Festival Scrolls connected with the Jewish festal year. Used as the reading for the festival of PURIM, Esther comes last in the annual festal sequence following Song of Songs (Passover), Ruth (Feast of Weeks), Lamentations (Commemoration of the Destruction of the Temple on 9 Ab), and Qoheleth, i.e., Ecclesiastes (Tabernacles). Set in a Persian context, Esther is an ironic tale of intrigue and suspense that moves from a threat of genocide of the Jews to the slaughter of all their enemies. Central to the turn of events is the legendary Jewish heroine, ESTHER.

The Story

The story of Esther begins and ends with a party. The opening scene describes the Persian king Ahasuerus playing host to extended banquets for his noblemen and the inhabitants of the capital city, Susa. While tipsy with wine, Ahasuerus summons his queen to parade before the revelers. Queen Vashti refuses to appear, setting off a chain of events that culminate with Vashti being banished as queen, the proclamation of an empire-wide injunction that all wives obey their husbands, and a royal search for the next queen begun among the virgins of the land. At this point, Esther and her guardian, MORDECAI, enter the story. Both are Jews, but Esther's heritage is kept secret while Mordecai's is public knowledge. Taken into the harem of virgins, Esther quickly wins the favor of palace officials and, at the given moment, the favor of the king as well. Esther is crowned queen, insuring a comfortable life within the palace while Mordecai establishes himself outside the palace gates. From his vantage point Mordecai overhears the plans of a palace coup, and through Esther informs the King, whose life is saved from the would-be assassins.

Haman, the Agagite and leading antagonist, enters the story next through his promotion by the king to grand vizier. From this lofty position Haman commands obeisance from the people, becoming incensed when Mordecai refuses to bow to him. Haman's desire to rid himself of Mordecai escalates into a pogrom against the Jews. Mordecai seeks the aid of Esther to foil Haman's plans. At the risk of her own life Esther appears unsummoned before the king. Again winning Ahasuerus's favor, Esther hosts a series of seemingly innocent dinner parties that masterfully expose the wicked schemes of Haman. Haman is executed, the enemies of the Jews are destroyed, and Mordecai is elevated to vizier. The story ends with the celebration of Purim, a festival-party established by Queen Esther and Mordecai to remind the generations of Jews to come of the time they were saved from their enemies.

Canonicity: A Struggle to Be Heard

The story of Esther has survived in two primary versions. In the Hebrew Bible (the Christian OT contains the same literature, although with a different arrangement) Esther is comprised of ten chapters and located in the biblical section known as the Writings. The LXX or Greek version of Esther, deriving from the late second or early first century B.C.E., contains six additional passages not found in the MT. English translations of Esther vary, with Roman Catholic Bibles (JB, NAB) integrating the MT and Greek additions, while Protestant Bibles translate the shorter Hebrew version and place the Greek Additions to Esther among the noncanonical works known as the APOCRYPHA.

Paralleling the threat of Jewish extinction in the story, the Book of Esther has itself struggled to survive. A perceived lack of religious fervor in the Hebrew version created debate over the value of the book for centuries. The story is told without any mention of God, without reference to covenant or law, without prayers and without concern for Jewish dietary laws. As heroine of the story, the Jew Esther functions apart from such Jewish traditions, accomplishing her task in a gentile world. Although popular within Judaism, the Book of Esther nevertheless struggled for canonical status. Although finally granted standing within Judaism and the Western church by the fourth-century C.E. and by the eighth century in the Eastern church, no allusions to Esther occur in the NT and few in the writings of the Church Fathers. Although the significance is debatable, Esther is the only OT book not found at Qumran.

The acceptance and interpretation of the Book of Esther have been a constant battle. Martin Luther's condemnation of the book in the sixteenth century has been reflected over and over again as Christian skeptics addressed such concerns as its overt Jewish nationalism and questionable morality. Not the least of concern is the story's heroine, Queen Esther. Male commentators have struggled with a female savior while modern women are uncomfortable with a female who sleeps her way to the Queenship and fails to question the established structures. Such skepticism perhaps reflects more on the reader than the Book of Esther, which must be appreciated on its own terms and in its own environment.

The Birth of a Tradition: Provenance, Date, Genre

The Book of Esther is at home in a Persian environment. From the opening lines delineating the boundaries of the Persian Empire (*India to Ethiopia*, 1:1) to the meting out of punishment by impalement (2:23; 5:14; 7:10), the story is colored with Persian distinctives. The repeated references to the famed Persian postal system lends plausibility to what would otherwise be considered unbelievable acts, a decree *to annihilate all Jews* (3:13) and letters allowing the Jews to defend themselves (8:10-11). That King Ahasuerus, at just the right moment, chanced to be reading from official royal diaries and discovered Mordecai's action on his behalf becomes believable in light of extrabiblical sources confirming such Persian record-keeping.

The Book of Esther claims SUSA as its setting, which places it among the Jews of the eastern Diaspora in the Persian empire. King Ahasuerus is traditionally identified as the historical Persian king Xerxes I. If this is accepted, the dating of his reign from 486 B.C.E. to 465 B.C.E. provides the earliest possible date of the book. What is known of Xerxes' reign from the Greek historian Herodotus (*History of the Persian Wars*) would seem to fit the timetable of Esther; the events of *the third year* (1:3) occurring before Xerxes departed in an expedition against the Greeks (483–479), which would allow for the four-year interval between the deposing of Vashti and the crowning of Esther in the seventh year (Clines 1984, 260–61). Yet this observation must be tempered by the fact that historically Xerxes' queen was neither Vashti nor Esther, but Amestris. The dating of the book, therefore, is not so simple, and a range of dates from the fourth to the second centuries B.C.E. has been proposed. There is no Persian record of the events in question nor proof of Mordecai and Esther as historical personages. Indeed, striking similarities have been noted between the names of the prominent characters in the book and those of ancient Babylonian and Elamite gods: Mordecai~Marduk, Esther~Ishtar, principal Babylonian god and goddess; Haman~Humman, an Elamite god. Although undoubtedly the book is late postexilic, much more cannot be said. Should the book come from the Hellenistic era that emerged in the late fourth century B.C.E., the sympathetic view toward the ruling power reflected in the book would certainly be at odds with other books from this time period. The writings of DANIEL and 1 and 2 MACCABEES reflect a much harsher attitude toward foreign powers. During the Greek period the Jews experienced divisions among themselves as well as hostility toward their oppressors. The Book of Esther seems to address Jews familiar with life lived under foreign rulers. Whether the actual event ever occurred or Mordecai and Esther ever lived is inconsequential to the truth of the story. Any Jew from any era who had experienced what it means to be a minority in the face of a foreign power would identify with the threat of oppression and persecution found in the Book of Esther.

The presentation of Esther is in the genre of a *Diasporanovelle* (LaCocque 1990, 57). Like the JOSEPH story (Gen 37–50), DANIEL, and JUDITH, the Book of Esther is a Jewish novella that struggles with the tensions of being Jewish in a foreign land. Historical accuracy is not at issue, rather the telling of a tale that concentrates on plot and action. Characters are developed only to the extent that they enhance the plot. The interest is in presenting a tension that moves through a series of complications until it is eventually resolved.

From the outset, Esther is presented as political satire. The four main characters are caricatured through one ironic event after another. The all-powerful Persian king Ahasuerus, whose word is immutable (8:8), is characterized as a party-fool who puts down the wine bottle only long enough to issue inane decrees, even giving over an entire people to death without asking their name. Haman, as the force outside the party doors, literally rises from nowhere into the heights of power from where he looks down upon all who must bow before him. Such lofty attainment goes to his head as he becomes single-mindedly bent on ensuring that the faces of Mordecai and the Jews are literally rubbed into the ground. But Haman will be required to bestow the honor he seeks on the one he most despises, and will himself hang from the gallows he constructed for Mordecai.

Mordecai is the Jew. He lives on the outskirts of the action, yet is fully aware of even the most intimate details of the realms of power. He is wise, steadfast and within earshot of the plot. Haman may rise but Mordecai will not bow; and eventually he will attain heights denied even to Haman.

Esther is the beauty, whose sexuality wins the crown. She is virginal, secretly a Jew, obedient to Mordecai, and at the beck and call of the king. All of her qualifications fit her for pampered life in the palace. She is the most unlikely of saviors. Yet she will save her people.

Through these characters a story of excess and threatened violence unfolds. The story of Esther has a political cartoon quality about it, where the reader at times may chuckle, at other times gasp, and in the end recognize truth. Esther shows that life lived under the power of others is risky. One day you are invited to a party; the next day you could be slaughtered. Nothing is impossible. A Jewish maiden can become queen and, when the time arises, emerge a heroine. Such times must be faced with courage and the ability to live by one's wits. In the end all must face the truth that *if you keep silence at such a time as this, relief and deliverance will rise for the Jews from another quarter, but you and your father's family will perish* (4:14).

For Further Study

In the *Mercer Dictionary of the Bible*: APOCRYPHA, MODERN; APOCRYPHAL LITERATURE; ESTHER; ESTHER, ADDITIONS TO; ESTHER, BOOK OF; FEASTS AND FESTIVALS; LOT/LOTS (CASTING OF) IN THE BIBLE; MORDECAI; PERSIAN EMPIRE; PURIM.

In other sources: J. W. H. Bos, *Ruth, Esther, Jonah*; D. J. A. Clines, *Ezra, Nehemiah, Esther*, NCB, and *The Esther Scroll: The Story of the Story*, JSOTSup; M. V. Fox, *Character and Ideology in the Book of Esther*; A. LaCocque, *The Feminine Unconventional: Four Subversive Figures in Israel's Tradition*; S. A. White, "Esther," in *The Women's Bible Commentary*.

Commentary

An Outline

The Disrobing of Queen Vashti, 1:1-22

The Persian Court, 1:1-9

The story of Esther opens in the Persian court of King Ahasuerus. Palace doors are thrown open to admit outside observers into the royal world of wealth and power. The grandeur of the court at SUSA testifies to the richness of the empire. Unencumbered by affairs of state, the merry king displays his majesty and greatness through a series of banquets. One hundred and eighty days—half the king's third year of reign—are given to a royal party for the recognized elite in the realm.

1:5-9. Two other banquets. Not only noblemen and people of status are treated to the delights of the kingdom. Following the six-month feast for the aristocracy, the citizenry of Susa partake of a seven-day feast where the only rule is to drink to your heart's content. Any disgruntled subject is soothed by free-flowing wine from *golden goblets* (v. 7) as the peasantry taste the royal riches.

While the men drink the week away, Queen Vashti entertains the women. In a one-verse statement (v. 9), the queen appears without introduction and no details of the third banquet are provided. The only point of note is the location of the party, King Ahasuerus's palace. The impression is clear. Vashti may serve as hostess, but the party premises belong to the king.

Queen Vashti's Refusal to Appear, 1:10-12

The story's return to the final day of the week-long feast finds the king merry with wine. Having shown off the royal objects, the king wishes to display his royal wife. Seven royal EUNUCHs are dispatched to parade Queen Vashti through the party. Queen Vashti refuses to come. The text offers no reason for her response, prompting speculation as to what is left unsaid. Rabbis of old suggested Vashti's refusal was out of modesty, the implication being that she was to appear naked before the banqueting guests. Others see in her actions the refusal to be treated as a concubine, the women who would appear once the drinking got heavy and the wives sent home. Whatever the reason, it is private and remains with Vashti. The response of the king, like his other actions, is completely visible. No longer *merry with wine* (v. 10), anger consumes him.

The First Royal Decree, 1:13-22

Although successful at giving parties, the king's first command is a public failure. As Ahasuerus turns to his seven wise men for advice, the queen's refusal becomes a matter of national interest. What is the law in a case like this? A response by one named *Memucan* (vv. 14, 16, 21) gives a new twist to the issue, moving from legality to practical concern. By his reasoning the king and queen become representative of all husbands and wives and Vashti's disregard for Ahasuerus's command precedent for wives everywhere. Indeed a veritable uprising among the women of the land is feared. Nothing short of a royal decree can stop the perceived whispering of anarchy already underway. Vashti must be denied what she did not want, to appear before the king. The queen is to be stripped of her royal robes and all women everywhere commanded to show honor to their husbands.

One wife refuses the bidding of her husband. An "if it were my wife . . ." consultation becomes the setting for a group of partying men to ensure it won't happen to them. A scorned king influenced by wine and self-interested counselors sets the famed Persian postal system in motion with an empire-wide decree, firing off letters to every province. Like the royal banquets, the problem and its solution are exaggerated to the point of incredulity, causing one to wonder about this king and his seven wise men.

The Crowning of Esther, 2:1-23

The Gathering of Virgins, 2:1-4

With the party and its aftermath faded to the past, the memory of Vashti and her fate haunt the king. The decree's gain for other men is his loss. Lord of their homes, the king's counselors leave Ahasuerus wifeless. Again at a loss for action, the king's servants propose the solution. A beauty contest of royal proportions will determine the next queen. The men of the land have their wives but the king will have his pick of the virgins. Not surprisingly, the proposal pleases Ahasuerus.

Esther Favored by the King, 2:5-18

2:5-11. Mordecai and Esther appear at court. With the search for the new queen underway, two of the story's main characters are introduced. MORDECAI is first and foremost a Jew. His genealogy is traced to KISH, the father of SAUL, Israel's first king. He is by tradition and heritage a loyal Benjaminite, standing in the line of SHIMEI (see 2 Sam 16:5-14; 1 Kgs 2:36-46). Both his family history and personal experience speak of banishment. The tragedy of King Saul and the loss by those loyal to him are repeated in Mordecai's own story of captivity and exile.

The emphasis on Mordecai's Jewishness is contrasted with the suppression of Esther's. Her Hebrew name, *Hadassah*, gives way quickly to the Persian, *Esther* (v. 7; the name means "star"). A captive orphan, she is cousin and adopted daughter of Mordecai. The real interest in Esther, however, is her appearance. Like the other woman in the story, the banished Vashti, Esther possesses the gift of physical beauty.

The king's edict results in Esther's being taken into the palace. Quickly winning the favor of *Hegai*, the overseer of the women, Esther and her seven appointed maids advance to the head of the harem. Using language established as the ground rules for determining the contest's outcome (v. 4), the maiden pleasing the man who stands between the women and the king foreshadows the coming events. With Esther on the inside, Mordecai begins his vigil of watching and waiting from the outside. Although separated by palace walls, the bond between the two remains as Esther follows the advice of Mordecai in keeping her heredity secret.

2:12-18. Esther wins the King's favor. An assembly-line of beautifying moves the virgins-in-waiting through the king's bedroom to the harem of experienced women. Their year-long preparation for a night with the king results in royal concubinage that may or may not be repeated based on the king's desire. Each woman is thus left waiting for the king to remember her delights.

As Esther's turn approaches, the text recalls her relation to Mordecai and emphasizes that the king's man in charge of the proceedings favors her. In the same manner she heeded Mordecai, Esther now takes Hegai's advice. That she *was admired by all who saw her* (v. 15) prepares her for the role Vashti turned down. The king loves her and makes her his queen. In the king's seventh year a fourth banquet is held. At his best when it comes to parties, Ahasuerus throws a wedding feast for Esther that spills over into favors for the rest of the land.

Mordecai and Esther Show Loyalty to the King, 2:19-23

The story shifts to Mordecai at the king's gate. Whether he is there in an official role or only loitering is unknown. From his vantage point Mordecai overhears a plot against the king and conveys the news to Esther, who reports it to Ahasuerus. The plot is thwarted and recorded in the royal Chronicles. With Esther, the unrevealed Jew, established as queen and Mordecai the Jew in place as the loyal, unrewarded servant of the king, the stage is set for the major scenes of the story.

Haman's Plot to Destroy the Jews, 3:1-15

Haman versus Mordecai, 3:1-6

3:1-2b. The advancement of Haman. The promotion of *Haman . . . the Agagite* (v. 1) is the first independent act of the king apart from banqueting. That all should bow to Haman is the king's third command; men being lord of their own homes the second (1:22), Vashti having refused the first. Like Mordecai, Haman's family tree reaches into the past to recall unsettled animosity between the two lines. Designated *the Agagite,* Haman is the present embodiment of Saul's old enemy, Agag, king of the Amalekites, Israel's archetypical enemy (Exod 17:14-16; Deut 25:17-19). Although victorious in battle, Saul's downfall is chronicled in his conflict with King Agag (1 Sam 15:8-33).

3:2c-6. Mordecai's refusal to bow. That Mordecai refused to bow to Haman needs no explanation for an audience familiar with their respective histories. Saul and Agag's battle started on a national level yet came down to a personal duel. Mordecai and Haman face off in a one-on-one conflict that escalates into Haman's determination to destroy the Jews. Thus Mordecai becomes representative of all Jews in the same way that Ahasuerus and Vashti are used to speak generically of husbands and wives.

The Second Royal Decree, 3:7-15

3:7-11. Enlisting the King. Driven by anger (3:5) Haman begins a systematic plan to vent his wrath on Mordecai and the Jews. *In the first month* of Ahasuerus's *twelfth year* (v. 7) the fateful day for the Jews' destruction is determined by casting the lot (Akkadian "Pur"). With the twelfth month of the year, the month of Adar, singled out as the fated time, Haman seeks to enlist the aid of the king. Like the servants who brought Mordecai's behavior to his attention (3:3-4), Haman raises the Jews as a problem for Ahasuerus. Without identifying his target, Haman speaks in generalities, twisted truths, and innuendo. His characterizations, however, accurately depict Jewish life in the Diaspora. As a people scattered throughout the kingdom, Jews were distinguished by their particular religious laws. What was for the Jews a life accommodating to the tragic consequences of history is painted by Haman as conspiracy and rebellion. No evidence is given of his assertion that they disobey the king's laws. No mention is made of Mordecai. Even Haman is smart enough to know he can't argue for the destruction of a whole people because one Jew failed to bow to him.

Haman's task is to bring the king to action. Should the king fail to respond to the assertions of external threat, Haman sweetens the pot with the promise of financial gain. Where Haman intends to get the rather substantial amount goes unmentioned. Nor does the king question such an offer. By refusing the money and giving his signet ring to Haman, the king removes his own hands from the plan, yet makes possible a pogrom against a people whose name he has yet to hear.

3:12-15. Publishing the news. Once again the famed Persian postal system is put into action as the edict to destroy all the Jews is dispatched throughout the empire. On *the thirteenth day of the twelfth month* (v. 13), the people of the empire are to rise up against the Jews and wipe them from the face of the earth. No one is to be spared—not women or children, old or young—and their belongings will be for plunder. As an unlucky number for Babylonians and Persians, the thirteenth may signal that disaster awaits not only the Jews.

The slating of the day for twelve months away recalls the virgins' twelve months of beautifying before their fate was determined by their night with the king. Although death was not a threat, life in a harem of enforced barrenness was. Twelve months of preparation are thus begun as destroyer and victim are advised of the coming destruction. With the plan set in motion, Haman and the king return to their drinking. That the inhabitants of Susa are perplexed by these doings would seem a small but necessary counter to an otherwise insane affair.

Esther's Decision to Act, 4:1-17

Mordecai Responds to the News, 4:1-3

In contrast to the celebrating king and Haman, the second decree brings Mordecai to his knees. Clothing himself in the dress of grief, Mordecai appears at the king's gate publicly mourning the scheduled massacre. His actions are repeated across the empire as Jews take up the wailing cry of death.

Enlisting the Queen, 4:4-17

4:4. Esther unaware. Mordecai's behavior in the gate gains the attention of Esther's servants and is reported to her. No dialogue or questioning occurs as she dispatches clothes to the unaccepting Mordecai. Ignorant of the approaching disaster, the scene portrays Esther as a queen cloistered from the world whose servants know more than she does.

4:5-9. Esther informed. The refusal of the clothing by Mordecai prompts Esther to investigate the matter further. Dispatching *Hathach* (v. 5), a eunuch in her service, as go-between, Esther inquires of Mordecai the reasoning for his behavior. The text is silent as to how Mordecai knows the details of Haman's conversation with the king. Through Hathach, Mordecai relates his personal experience and thorough knowledge of the situation in the effort to educate Esther. A copy of the decree is sent as well so that she might see for herself the gravity of the situation. All of this is done so that Mordecai might charge Esther to act. She is to take the matter to the king, speaking to him on behalf of her people.

4:10-17. Esther decides to act. Until this point the exchange between Esther and Mordecai has been reported in narrative form only. With Mordecai's challenge of Esther to action, the narrative gives way to speech as the two struggle to a decision. Esther's immediate reaction is to remind Mordecai what everyone else knows. The king alone initiates his audiences. To appear uninvited risks possible death, and Esther, for some unknown reason, has not been summoned for some time.

Esther's fearful hesitation to risk her own life is countered by Mordecai's assertion that inaction will result in certain death for her and her family. The palace is no haven. The fate of the Jews is Esther's fate as well. The idea that deliverance might come from some other source is a vague argument without detail. Should she choose silence, not everything might be lost. This, however, is no out for Esther. Either she acts or dies. Who knows, such a time as this may be her destiny.

Queen Esther rises to the occasion. Her decision made, Esther becomes the controlling character. Now it is Mordecai who will obey her words. The Jews of Susa are to join her in a preparatory fast. Whether for life or death, Esther is committed.

Esther's Plot to Destroy Haman, 5:1–8:2

Ahasuerus and Haman on Esther's Grounds, 5:1-8

5:1-3. The robing of Queen Esther. Unlike Esther's first appearance before the king that followed intensive beautifying, the unsummoned visit reveals the haste necessitated by crisis. Fasting is her preparation and queenly garments her attire as Esther appears at the throne-room entrance. True to their respective characters, Esther wins the king's favor and he extends an exaggerated offer.

5:4-8. Invitations to dinner. Were it not so serious, the situation would be laughable. Esther risks her life. The king offers half his kingdom—all for a couple of dinner invitations! "What do you want Queen Esther?" "Can you and Haman come to dinner tonight?" (vv. 3, 4). The action is swift as Haman is fetched and the two men sit down at Esther's table. The queen knows her king. While drinking, the affable Ahasuerus shows his bent toward excess, even to half his kingdom. A second dinner invitation stalls Esther's response to the king, who promises to grant a petition that he has not yet heard.

Haman's Self-glorification, 5:9-14

Having dined with the king and queen, Haman is full of himself. He basks in his good fortune and lauds himself before his friends and his wife. Life could not get much better except for one constant irritation, Mordecai the Jew. No mention is made of the approaching decree. Rather his audience, like the counselors of Ahasuerus in his conflict with Vashti, suggests a public solution to rid him of this embarrassment. The matter is simple for someone so close to the king. All he must do is order an eighty foot pole erected, tell the king to have Mordecai impaled, and be off to dinner. Like the duped Ahasuerus before him, Haman liked the plan.

The Robing of Mordecai, 6:1-13

The night between Esther's two dinner parties is the turning point for Mordecai and Haman. Beginning with a sleepless night for the king, one coincidence after another is strung together until Mordecai and Haman effectively change places in the story.

Unable to sleep, Ahasuerus demands to be read to from a book that happens to record Mordecai's earlier deed that saved the king's life. At the moment the king becomes concerned about Mordecai's reward, Haman enters the court. Acting according to character the spontaneous king seeks advice for his next move and the deliberate Haman responds. Only the reader is aware of the motives that drive each man. Ahasuerus needs Haman's help in honoring Mordecai while Haman must gain

Ahasuerus's support to dispose of Mordecai. The conversation between the two is hypothetical in nature. Like Haman's unidentified enemy (3:8-11), the king's honoree goes unnamed. Thinking the honor is his, Haman answers with what he most desires: a public display in royal trappings. Expectedly, the king follows Haman's advice, calling upon him to execute the plan. The ironic twist comes as Mordecai is revealed to Haman as the designee. Haman's dream of grandeur becomes a living nightmare as he leads in honoring the man he most despises. Instead of Haman's gallows Mordecai is lifted upon the king's horse and cloaked in royal robes. At the end of the display, Mordecai resumes his vigil at the king's gate and Haman, deflated, returns home disgraced. The same wife and friends who bolstered Haman's arrogance a few hours before now foretell his doom. Haman crumples before the reader's eyes as the text for the first time alludes to an indestructibility of the Jews.

A Deadly Dinner, 6:14–8:2

As the fateful words are spoken, eunuchs arrive to hurry Haman off to the second dinner. A day of eating and drinking passes into another as Ahasuerus once again asks Esther to make known her request. The gaiety of the situation changes rapidly as Esther pleads for her life and the life of her people, who still remain unnamed. Using language that recalls Haman's bribe, Esther describes their plight of being sold to destruction. For once, Ahasuerus is interested in the particulars, asking who stands behind this situation. Esther names the enemy, *this wicked Haman* (7:6). Haman shakes with fear while the angry king paces in the garden. Seeing that his fate lies with Esther, Haman turns to her. The picture of his falling upon the couch where the queen sits is related to the prophetic language spoken earlier by his wife and friends (6:13) concerning his fall before Mordecai. The king's propensity for failing to see the whole of a situation had aided Haman's cause in the past, but now works against him. The misreading of Haman's actions by Ahasuerus, coupled with information from a servant, leads to Haman's death on his own gallows. Thus the order for execution that Haman had sought from the king comes to pass, with Haman instead of Mordecai as the victim.

Esther receives Haman's house and Mordecai the king's signet ring when Mordecai's relationship to Queen Esther is revealed. Established over the house of Haman, Mordecai the Jew is publicly victorious over the enemy, Haman.

The Jews Destroy Their Enemies, 8:3–9:19

Enlisting the King, 8:3-8

Although Haman is dead, his evil plot to destroy the Jews remains in effect. Esther must approach the king again. Her ingratiating words harbor no condemnation of the king nor does he accept responsibility for the situation. He is, however, more than willing to turn matters over to Esther and Mordecai so long as they in no way alter or contradict the earlier edict. The dilemma centers on the immutable word of the king. What is written in his name and sealed with his signet cannot be revoked. True to character, the all-powerful Ahasuerus takes himself out of the picture, leaving the crisis to the ingenuity of Esther and Mordecai.

The Third Royal Decree, 8:9-14

Two months after Haman's decree to slaughter the Jews was sent out, a decree in Mordecai's words bearing the king's stamp is dispatched across the land. On the fated day of destruction all Jews are to rise to their own defense and slay the enemy. Published to Jew and non-Jew alike, the decree gives notice that the Jews will not meet the day as helpless victims. With opposing royal orders set for the same day, to attack and to defend, the question of what will actually happen looms on the horizon.

The Jews Respond to the News, 8:15-17

At the issuance of the third decree a spirit of festivity breaks out in the land. Instead of the sackcloth worn upon hearing of Haman's decree, Mordecai appears in the robes of state consistent with his change of status. The threat of doom is effectively lifted from the Jews' heads as they engage in a spontaneous feast of celebration. For many observers the quandary to side for or against the Jews is decided as they align themselves with the Jews. The stage is set for the thirteenth of Adar, some nine months away.

The Thirteenth of Adar, 9:1-19

When the day finally arrives, the Jews band together to meet the enemy head on. The ensuing battles are recalled with little or no detail, the results more significant in the tradition. The number of enemy slain (the figures total 75,800) is an intriguing element of the passage. Until this point in the story the only known enemy of the Jews is Haman—and he is long since dead. Mordecai replaces him in function, power and prestige. Although there is no physical bowing to Mordecai as was the case with Haman, an image of the mighty of the land falling before him is conveyed. The man earlier sentenced to death now elicits fear in the hearts of rulers. Just as Mordecai triumphed over Haman, the Jews triumph over their enemies. No Jewish blood is shed and the last of the house of Haman is wiped away.

Tradition recalls the occasion as a time of reversal for the Jews. Intended victims gain mastery over the attackers as Jews turn the tables on the enemy. A distinction in the tradition is made between the urban Jews and their experience within Susa proper and the rural Jews of the provinces. Two days are given to the fighting in Susa and only one in the countryside, which explains the difference in the dates of celebration between the two.

Institution of the Festival of Purim, 9:20–10:3

Mordecai's Decree, 9:20-28

Such a momentous occasion must not be forgotten. From his seat in the Persian bureaucracy Mordecai ensures the commemoration of this event by future generations of Jews. The imperial postal system carries Mordecai's letters of instruction throughout the empire, setting forth the fourteenth and fifteenth days of the month of Adar each year as festival days to recall the deliverance from their enemies. The setting aside of the two days for the celebration dispels any potential conflict among differing groups of Jews over which day shall be held in memoriam. The spirit of the celebration is to be one of rejoicing and gladness, the euphoric partying that comes when the threat of disaster is removed. It is a time for giving gifts to each other and of sharing with the poor.

By differing somewhat in detail from the extended account, the capsule retelling of the story in 9:24-25 drives home the providential nature of the event. Only Haman, the one who hatched a plot against the Jews, is addressed by name. In the Hebrew text, Esther appears as the "she" who comes before "the king," again unnamed. Three times in the two verses the Hebrew word for "plot" or "plan" occurs in noun or verbal form (חשׁב, NRSV "plot" and "devised"). But when "she" appears, the king "turns around" (Heb. שׁוב) the evil plans so that they fall upon Haman's own head. The situation brings to mind another victim set right in a foreign court: Joseph saying to his brothers, "you planned (חשׁב) evil against me, God planned (חשׁב) it for good" (Gen. 50:20). God may not be mentioned in Esther, but Jewish tradition brings to mind divine aid in foreign places.

The festival is called PURIM, a festival of "chance." The text connects *pur* with the "lot" that was cast by Haman to determine the day of extermination for the Jews. If a Persian origin for the festival, which included the casting of lots to determine destinies, lies behind the observance, then the festival of Purim takes a Persian feast and makes it distinctively Jewish. By "chance" the Jews were to be destroyed. Then "she" appears before the king and the Jews are saved. The Jewish observance of Purim grows out of the historical experience of dispersion when Jews found themselves scattered throughout a non-Jewish world. In that world they knew the threat of destruction and the joy of victory where "chance" can be overcome by the actions of a "she," an unnamed woman, a young Jewish girl, tradition remembers as Queen Esther.

Esther's Decree, 9:29-32

Although the sending out of a letter by Esther would seem redundant after Mordecai's earlier dispatchment, the text emphasizes the establishment of a festival that is to be a part of the Jewish festal calendar for all generations to come. Stress is put on the written record, thus giving authority to the observance of a festival not established by Jewish Torah. Even more, the woman whose appearance before the king results in the salvation of her people takes her place in tradition as Queen Esther. She may have entered the palace through the king's bedroom, a beauty who found favor in his eyes, but it is as a Queen with the power and authority to speak to generations of Jews that in the final scenes she is portrayed.

The Fame of Mordecai, 10:1-3

Like the Jewish festival he inaugurated, the memory of Mordecai is committed to history. The ending of the story with the exaltation of Mordecai is the final ironic twist in a tale of unexpecteds. Haman, the archenemy, has long since passed from the scene and Mordecai, the Jew, sits at the right hand of the Persian king. Unlike Haman, Mordecai's standing in the court bodes well for Persian and Jew alike, and through the Persian Chronicles and the Jewish legend of Esther, Mordecai, the Jew, passes into history.

Works Cited

Clines, D. J. 1984. *Ezra, Nehemiah, Esther*, NCB.
LaCocque, André. 1990. *The Feminine Unconventional: Four Subversive Figures in Israel's Tradition*.

Mercer Commentary on the Bible
Volume 2. *History of Israel*

Mercer University Press, Macon, Georgia 31210-3960.
Isbn 0-86554-507-3. Catalog and warehouse pick number: MUP/P134.
Text, interior, and cover designs, composition, and layout
    by Edmon L. Rowell, Jr.
Cover illustration (*Esther and Mordecai*) by Andrea Mantegna (1431?–1506).
Camera-ready pages composed on a Gateway 2000
    via dos WordPerfect 5.1 and WordPerfect for Windows 5.1/5.2
    and printed on a LaserMaster 1000.
Text fonts: TimesNewRomanPS 10/12; ATECH Hebrew and Greek.
Display fonts: TimesNewRomanPS bf and bi,
    plus University Roman titles (covers and title page).
Printed and bound by McNaughton & Gunn Inc., Saline, Michigan 48176,
    via offset lithography on 50# Natural Offset and perfectbound into 10-pt.
    c1s stock, with 4-color process illustration and lay-flat lamination.
                                                    [December 1998]

110398ELR